COLLINS
ALBATROSS BOOK OF
VERSE

COLLINS
ALBATROSS BOOK OF
VERSE

ENGLISH AND AMERICAN POETRY
FROM THE THIRTEENTH CENTURY
TO THE PRESENT DAY, EDITED
BY LOUIS UNTERMEYER

Revised and Enlarged

COLLINS, PUBLISHERS
LONDON AND GLASGOW

First published 1933
This edition 1960
Latest reprint 1984

ISBN 0 00 424670 5

© 1960
William Collins Sons and Company, Ltd.

Printed and bound in Great Britain by
William Clowes Limited,
Beccles and London

PREFACE

The reader may well demand an explanation for this compilation. In its first edition it was known as the *Albatross Book of Living Verse,* and the title was altered only because some had mistaken it for a book devoted entirely to contemporary verse. The selections in this volume are living poetry in the sense that they have persisted in spite of changing times and shifting tastes. Thus (even in the section devoted to modern verse) they seem to possess the quality which implies permanence. Furthermore, they contain that vitality which is independent of form and fashion.

It should be said, at the outset, that the compilation does not pretend to include *all* the poetry which is the chief power of English literature. It does, however, aim to present, within the confines of a small volume, such verses as have stirred the imagination of countless readers differing in temperament and traditions, verses whose essential quality is acknowledged by the caught breath and the quickened pulse. Analysis may rationalise the reaction to such poems, but recognition is spontaneous, requiring no knowledge of metres, mannerisms or technical devices. Poetry is a language that tells us, as Edwin Arlington Robinson phrased it, " something that cannot be said. And it seems to me that poetry has two outstanding characteristics. One is that it is, after all, undefinable. The other is that it is eventually unmistakable." Robert Frost extends the implications when he says, " It is absurd to think that the only way to tell if a poem is lasting is to wait and see if it lasts. The right reader of a good poem can tell the moment it strikes him that he has taken an immortal wound— that he will never get over it. That is to say, permanence in poetry, as in love, is perceived instantly. The proof of a poem is not that we have never forgotten it, but that we knew at first sight we never could forget it."

The intent of this book, then, is immediate and intuitive instead of analytic. I have not attempted to draw the line between " experimental " and " traditional," realising that the revolt of one period is often the convention of the next. In general my tests have been Palgrave's: " That a poem shall be worthy of the writer's genius; that colour and originality cannot atone for serious imperfections in clearness, unity or truth; that a few good lines do not make a good poem; that popular estimate is serviceable as a guide-post more than as a compass; above all,

that excellence should be looked for rather in the whole than in
the parts." To these canons I have added one more: that there
should be that combination (as well as communication) of
passion and personality which is, at least for this editor, a touch-
stone for poetry.

As a result, certain " key-poems " stand out—poems which
have provoked movements and given rise to new tendencies—
but no effort has been made to chart schools or define groups.
The arrangement is generally chronological (except for the group
of early ballads) and the separation by centuries has no other
object than to provide convenient divisions. Nor, even in the
brief summaries which introduce the nine sections, have I intended
to limit or define what is meant by poetry. The art is great enough
to include not only the profoundly moving, but the lower-pitched
though scarcely less memorable musics—the crisp epigrams of
Pope and Landor, the colloquial intensities of Coventry Patmore
and Robert Frost, the devout fancifulness of George Herbert,
even the inspired nonsense of Lewis Carroll. It is one editor's
opinion that Milton is no less magnificent and Shakespeare no
less Shakespeare for appearing in their company.

I am, naturally, conscious of my debt as editor to preceding
compilations, especially to Palgrave's *The Golden Treasury* and
Quiller-Couch's *The Oxford Book of English Verse*. But my excuse
for thrusting yet another anthology upon the world is, if I may
pervert the proverb, " other times, other rhymes." It is more
than sixty years since Quiller-Couch revalued Palgrave's collection
(which appeared in 1861, in the middle of the Victorian period)
and even the most admirable gathering invites, actually demands
reappraisal. Each generation claims the right not only to
emphasise the present, but to re-estimate the past. The last forty
years have been especially rich in poetry—in America a renaissance
dates from about 1900—and a new awareness gives us a keener
appreciation of all that has gone before. Modernity no longer
means the pet innovations of the latest decade. The human
spirit finds its mirror in every age; we recognise our contem-
poraries in the Canterbury pilgrims of the fourteenth century.

In an effort to maintain this freshness I have adopted (where
uniform spelling was impossible) a generally modern one. The
living accent draws us rather than an archaism, no matter how
interesting or etymologically significant the latter may be.
However, where it has been necessary to translate an early English
lyric or a selection from Chaucer, I have accompanied the original
text with a modernised version rather than clutter the pages with
a glossary.[1] I have done this believing that the prime object of

[1] Except where specified, the modern versions are by the editor.

poetry is to increase enjoyment rather than to increase a fourteenth-century vocabulary. Chaucer has been " modernised " ever since 1700 when Dryden presented him in the style native to the eighteenth century. Since the gulf between Chaucer's idiom— " quaint " to us but not to fourteenth-century ears—and that of the twentieth-century reader is a wide as well as a treacherous one, a rendering in modern verse provides, at least, a bridge to the poet's meaning.

This is to admit that the collection is not for advanced scholars. It is, primarily, for those who lack either intimacy with the great body of English and American poetry or immediate leisure to pursue the acquaintance. It is, except for the few recent discoveries, a brief vista—a sort of primer-panorama—of the high levels of the last seven hundred years. Naturally, in a survey ranging from the thirteenth to the twentieth century, many poems, especially certain longer and metaphysical verses which are among the glories of English verse, will not be found here, although some of them are listed in the Appendix. In a field so vast and varied, selection is a difficult and often perilous business. For example with Keats, one is inclined to forget editorial restrictions and reprint all eight odes; since the exigencies of space make that impossible, one is tempted to include " Lamia," " Isabella or the Pot of Basil " and " The Eve of St. Agnes " merely because they do not appear in *The Oxford Book of English Verse*. The danger of sedulously avoiding what other anthologists have chosen is likely to prove as great a pitfall as blindly following their lead. In the end one is forced to repeat that a good poem remains a good poem, no matter how often it has been read and reprinted, and that, allowing a certain latitude in judgement, Fame has, on the whole rendered fair verdicts. At the same time, where a choice has been compelled between two poems of equal worth, I have (perhaps arbitrarily) chosen the less familiar.

The texts are as authoritative as can be determined. Here and there, following the precedent of Palgrave and others, I have taken the liberty of excising certain stanzas for the sake of unity. In such cases, the condensations have been indicated either in the title or in the poem itself. Every anthologist must make such experiments and it is hoped that the few shortened selections, such as Pope's " Rape of the Lock " and Smart's " A Song to David," justify themselves.

The confines of this volume have compelled me to omit, though with some regret, all translations from foreign languages, even those which have become classics of their kind. The same limitation has compelled me to omit all blank verse passages from poetic plays, even the most purple patches from the dramas of Marlowe and Shakespeare. If the intent of the volume is not implicit in its contents, it can scarcely be made more explicit by any amount of introduction. It should be noted, however, that although most—if not all—of the great names may be found in these pages, the emphasis throughout is on the poem rather than on the poet.

My thanks are due to the publishers without whose consent the section devoted to recent poetry would have been impossible. This indebtedness is specifically acknowledged to:

THE SOCIETY OF AUTHORS—for *Slow Spring* by Katharine Tynan, reprinted by permission of Miss Pamela Hinkson from *The Collected Poems of Katharine Tynan*, published by Macmillan and Company and as the literary representative of the Trustees of the Estate of the late A. E. Housman, and Jonathan Cape, Ltd., publishers of A. E. Housman's *Collected Poems*—for *Loveliest Of Trees, On Wenlock Edge, Is My Team Ploughing ?, Bredon Hill, When I Was One-and-Twenty*, and *The Chestnut Casts His Flambeaux* by A. E. Housman.

ERNEST BENN LTD.—for *The Lake Isle of Innisfree* and *When you are old* by W. B. Yeats, reprinted by permission of the late W. B. Yeats, author, and Ernest Benn Ltd., publishers.

BURNS OATES AND WASHBOURNE LTD.—for the poems by Alice Meynell.

THE CAMBRIDGE UNIVERSITY PRESS—for the poem by Charles Hamilton Sorley.

JONATHAN CAPE LTD.—for the poems by W. H. Davies and H. D., and for part six of *The Magnetic Mountain* and *The Conflict* from the *Collected Poems* of C. Day Lewis.

CHATTO AND WINDUS LTD., and MRS. OWEN—for the poems by Wilfred Owen, and for *Missing Dates* by William Empsom, and *The Fish* by Elizabeth Bishop.

CONSTABLE AND COMPANY—for the poems by Walter de la Mare, reprinted by permission of the late Walter de la Mare, author, and Constable and Company, publishers.

THE JOHN DAY COMPANY, INC.—for the selections from *High Falcon* by Léonie Adams.

J. M. DENT AND SONS, LTD.—for the poems by G. K. Chesterton, and for the poems *When All My Five and Country Senses See, Especially When The October Wind, After the Funeral, Do Not Go Gentle into that Good Night* by Dylan Thomas.

DOUBLEDAY, DORAN AND COMPANY—for the selections from *Man Possessed*, by William Rose Benét, and from *Poems and Ballads* by Stephen Vincent Benét, copyright, 1918-1931, by Stephen Vincent Benét.

FABER AND FABER, LTD.—for the selection from the poems of T. S. Eliot, in *The Ariel Poems*, and for *The Hollow Men* by T. S. Eliot, and for *Poetry* and *Silence* by Marianne Moore; *Sunday Morning* by Louis MacNeice; *Who's Who, Lay Your Sleeping Head My Love*, and *In Memory of W. B. Yeats* by W. H. Auden; *An Elementary School Classroom in a Slum* and *I Think Continually of Those* by Stephen Spender ; *Swans* by Lawrence Durrell ; *O Tender Under My Right Breast* and *Sonnet To My Mother* by George Barker ; *Colloquy In Black Rock* by Robert Lowell ; *After The Last Bulletins* by Richard Wilbur ; and *The Zulu Girl* by Philip Larkin.

FARRAR AND RINEHART—for the poem by Lizette Woodworth Reese.

HARCOURT, BRACE AND COMPANY—for the selections from *Smoke and Steel, Good-Morning, America*, and *Selected Poems* by Carl Sandburg.

WILLIAM HEINEMANN LTD.—for the selection from *Poems 1914-1926* by Robert Graves, and from *Counter-Attack* by Siegfried Sassoon.

HENRY HOLT AND COMPANY—for the selection from *Cornhuskers* by Carl Sandburg.

DAVID HIGHAM ASSOCIATES, LTD. and MACMILLAN AND CO. LTD.—for *Sir Beelzebub* and *Still Falls the rain* from the *Collected Poems* of Dame Edith Sitwell.

HOUGHTON MIFFLIN COMPANY — The selections from *Selected Poems* by Amy Lowell; *Streets in the Moon* and *New Found Land* by Archibald MacLeish are used by permission of, and by special arrangement with, Houghton Mifflin Company, the authorized publishers.

INGPEN AND GRANT.—for the poems by Edward Thomas.

ALFRED A. KNOPF, INC.—for the selections from *Nets to Catch the Wind* and *Angels and Earthly Creatures* by Elinor Wylie; *Two Gentlemen in Bonds* by John Crowe Ransom; *Harmonium* by Wallace Stevens.

HORACE LIVERIGHT, INC.—for the poems by Ezra Pound, Hart Crane, and for *Age in Prospect* and *Promise of Peace* by Robinson Jeffers.

LONGMANS, GREEN AND COMPANY—for the poems by Robert Frost.

MACMILLAN AND COMPANY—for the selections from *Collected Poems* by Thomas Hardy; from *Enslaved and Other Poems* and *Collected Poems* by John Masefield; the selections from *Later Poems* by W. B. Yeats, reprinted by permission of the late W. B. Yeats, author, and Macmillan and Company, publishers; for poems by Ralph Hodgson and James Stephens, reprinted by permission of Ralph Hodgson and the late James Stephens, authors, and Macmillan and Company, publishers; the selections from *Collected Poems* by Vachel Lindsay, and the poem by Padraic Colum.

THE MACMILLAN COMPANY, NEW YORK—for the selections from *Collected Poems* by Edwin Arlington Robinson, and from *Flame and Shadow* and *Dark of the Moon* by Sara Teasdale.

LINCOLN MACVEAGH : THE DIAL PRESS, INC.—for the selection from *XLI Poems* by E. E. Cummings, copyright, 1925, by E. E. Cummings.

THE MARVELL PRESS, HESSLE, YORKSHIRE—for permission to include *Next Please* by Philip Larkin, reprinted from *The Less Deceived*.

METHUEN AND COMPANY—for selections from *Barrack Room Ballads*, *The Seven Seas*, and *The Five Nations*, reprinted by permission of the late Rudyard Kipling, author, and Methuen and Company Ltd., publishers.

JOHN MURRAY, LTD.—for *The Arrest of Oscar Wilde at the Cadogan Hotel* by John Betjeman from the *Collected Poems* of John Betjeman.

THE OXFORD UNIVERSITY PRESS—for the poems by Robert Bridges and Austin Dobson.

THE POETRY BOOKSHOP—for the selections from the poems of Charlotte Mew; and the poems of Anna Wickham, reprinted by permission of Anna Wickham, author, and The Poetry Bookshop, publishers.

LAURENCE POLLINGER, LTD.—the Executors to the Estate of the late Mrs. Frieda Lawrence, and William Heinemann Ltd.—for *Lightning* by D. H. Lawrence.

RANDOM HOUSE—for *Birthday Sonnet*, from *The Poetry Quartos*, by Elinor Wylie.

ROUTLEDGE AND KEGAN PAUL, LTD—for *Early Spring* and *Neutrality* by Sidney Keyes.

SIEGFRIED SASSOON—for selections from *Picture Show*.

CHARLES SCRIBNER'S SONS—for the selections from *John Deth and other Poems* and *Preludes for Memnon* by Conrad Aiken; *The Black Panther* by John Hall Wheelock; *Poems* by Allen Tate 1928-1931, and the translation of Chaucer's ballade from *The Man Behind the Book* by Henry Van Dyke.

MARTIN SECKER AND WARBURG, LTD.—for the poems by James Elroy Flecker and Edna St. Vincent Millay, and for *Elegy for Jane* by Theodore Roethke and *Neither Here nor There* by W. R. Rodgers.

SIDGWICK AND JACKSON and the Literary Executors—for the selections from *Collected Poems* by Rupert Brooke.

Acknowledgments are also due to John Masefield and to the late Sir William Watson for permission to reprint their poems. Robert Graves, whose permission to reprint his poem is also acknowledged, wishes it to be stated that he only allows it to stand because it appeared in the American edition before he made a rule of not granting permission to any anthologies to include poems of his, because to omit it would have upset the photomechanic printing arrangements, and for no other reason.

Note: The book's division into centuries is, as has been stated, a convenient device rather than a series of sharp demarcations. Thus the authors do not in all instances appear in the century in which they were born, but in the century in which they produced the chief part of their work.

Unless otherwise specified, the poets are those of the British Isles. (A) before the date of birth indicates that the author was born in America.

CONTENTS

EARLY BALLADS
OF UNKNOWN DATE AND AUTHORSHIP

EARLY SONGS
OF UNKNOWN DATE AND AUTHORSHIP

THE FOURTEENTH TO SIXTEENTH CENTURIES

CHAUCER TO THE ELIZABETHANS

THE SEVENTEENTH CENTURY
CAVALIERS, PURITANS, METAPHYSICIANS

THE NINETEENTH CENTURY
FIRST HALF: ROMANCE AND PROPHECY

THE NINETEENTH CENTURY
SECOND HALF: VICTORIANS AND AMERICANS

THE TWENTIETH CENTURY
ROMANTIC REALISM

COLLINS
ALBATROSS BOOK OF
VERSE

EARLY BALLADS

Beginning this volume with the anonymous ballads disturbs, to some extent, the chronological scheme. But this is inevitable. The unknown authors of the metrical narratives, rhymed romances and historical songs flourished between the twelfth and the seventeenth centuries—in *The Canterbury Tales* Chaucer quoted and parodied several ballads which were already old in 1380. Nor is it possible to arrange the ballads themselves in the order of their origin. No one can say for certain when the original of such a " late " ballad as " Sir Patrick Spens " was composed, or that " St. Stephen and King Herod," presumably the oldest, actually antedates " Edward, Edward " in the Danish version.

Nor can any editor speak too assuredly concerning the final authority of his examples. In the advertisement to his *Reliques of Ancient English Poetry*, Percy stressed the difficulties confronting even the most careful students of the old manuscripts. The records—which are the uncertain transcripts of an oral, not a written, literature—" are sometimes extremely incorrect and faulty, being in such instances probably made from defective copies, or the imperfect recitation of illiterate singers; so that a considerable portion of the song or narrative is sometimes omitted and miserable trash or nonsense not unfrequently introduced into pieces of considerable merit."

But, as Allingham maintained, a century or so after Percy, " the ballads owe no little of their merit to the countless riddlings, shiftings, siftings, omissions, and additions of innumerable reciters. The lucky changes hold, the stupid ones fall aside." Researchers may demand all the interpolations and eccentricities in the variants of, say, " The Two Sisters of Binnorie." But the lay reader demands, instead of twenty comparative renderings, one—preferably superlative—version. What to do? Again Allingham gives us the key. The right course, he says in his preface to *The Ballad Book*, is to present one form—the best of the many, according to the editor's judgment and feeling—" in firm black and white, for critics and for readers cultivated and simple. The ballad itself is multiform and even shifting, vapourlike, as one examines it. . . . To make the narrative clear, and bring out forcibly the dramatic points, is what every balladist aimed at; the comparative success with which this is done tests the value of this version—or that—of a story."

No statement could be more explicit, for it is as a story that the ballad was designed. The happy turns of phrase, the flashes of sheer poetry are incidental, almost accidental. First and last, the singer was intent on his tale, whether the narrative happens to be fanciful with faery magic as in " True Thomas "—that wild forerunner of Keats's " La Belle Dame Sans Merci "—or half bantering, half bickering as in the domestic dialogue of " The Old Cloak," or darkly macabre as in " The Wife of Usher's Well " or rudely bucolic as in " Get Up and Bar the Door," or quivering with the tragic suspense of " Lord Randal," or naked with drama and violence as in " The Douglas Tragedy " and

"Edward, Edward," or poignant with the compound of tenderness and irony which distinguishes "The Cherry-Tree Carol."

The spirit, the spontaneous movement, the strong feeling are as fresh to-day as when these rhymed narratives were composed three to five hundred years ago. In an effort to recapture, or rather to maintain, the strength and simplicity which are the very blood of the ballads, I have not only presented what seemed to me the best version of many (sometimes a composite of several), but I have modernised them. That is to say, I have changed the spelling freely and have even, when necessary, translated an archaic term into its modern equivalent. Something is lost to linguistics by this liberty, but it is my hope that something is gained in speed and in that heightened communication which is the very purpose of the old story-poems. For those who wish a wider background there is Scott's *Minstrelsy of the Scottish Border*, in which the poet and adapter have joined hands; while for those who desire a closer study of the originals, as well as the continual and almost countless variations, there is always Francis James Child's far more remarkable work of extended scholarship, *English and Scottish Ballads*.

CHILDE MAURICE

Childe Maurice hunted the Silver Wood,
    He whistled and he sung:
"I think I see the woman yonder
    That I have loved so long."

He called to his little man John,
    "You do not see what I see;
For yonder I see the very first woman
    That ever lovèd me."

"Here is a glove, a glove," he says,
    "Lined all with fur it is;
Bid her to come to Silver Wood
    To speak with Childe Maurice.

"And here is a ring, a ring," he says,
    "A ring of the precious stone:
He prays her come to Silver Wood
    And ask the leave of none."

"Well do I love your errand, master,
    But better I love my life.
Would you have me go to John Steward's castle,
    To tryst away his wife?"

"Do not I give you meat?" he says,
  "Do not I give you fee?
How dare you stop my errand
  When that I bid you flee?"

When the lad came to John Steward's castle,
  He ran right through the gate
Until he came to the high, high hall
  Where the company sat at meat.

"Here is a glove, my lady," said he,
  "Lined all with fur it is;
It says you're to come to Silver Wood
  And speak with Childe Maurice.

"And here is a ring, a ring of gold,
  Set with the precious stone:
It prays you to come to Silver Wood
  And ask the leave of none."

Out then spake the wily nurse,
  A wily woman was she,
"If this be come from Childe Maurice
  It's dearly welcome to me."

"Thou liest, thou liest, thou wily nurse,
  So loud as I hear thee lie!
I brought it to John Steward's lady,
  And I trow thou be not she."

Then up and rose him John Steward,
  And an angry man was he:
"Did I think there was a lord in the world
  My lady loved but me!"

He dressed himself in his lady's gown,
  Her mantle and her hood;
But a little brown sword hung down by his knee,
  And he rode to Silver Wood.

          .   .   .   .   .

Childe Maurice sat in Silver Wood,
  He whistled and he sung,
"I think I see the woman coming
  That I have loved so long."

But then stood up Childe Maurice
    His mother to help from horse:
" O alas, alas! " says Childe Maurice,
    " My mother was never so gross! "

" No wonder, no wonder," John Steward he said,
    " My lady loved thee well,
For the fairest part of my body
    Is blacker than thy heel."

John Steward took the little brown sword
    That hung low down by his knee;
He has cut the head off Childe Maurice
    And the body put on a tree.

And when he came to his lady—
    Looked over the castle-wall—
He threw the head into her lap,
    Saying, " Lady, take the ball! "

Says, " Dost thou know Childe Maurice' head,
    When that thou dost it see?
Now lap it soft, and kiss it oft,
    For thou loved'st him better than me."

But when she looked on Childe Maurice' head,
    She ne'er spake words but three:
" I never bare no child but one,
    And you have slain him, trulye.

" I got him in my mother's bower
    With secret sin and shame;
I brought him up in the good greenwood
    Under the dew and rain."

And she has taken her Childe Maurice
    And kissed him, mouth and chin:
" O better I loved my Childe Maurice
    Than all my royal kin! "

" Woe be to thee! " John Steward he said,
    And a woe, woe man was he;
" For if you had told me he was your son
    He had never been slain by me."

Says, " Wicked be my merry men all,
 I gave meat, drink and cloth!
But could they not have holden me
 When I was in all that wrath? "

THE DOUGLAS TRAGEDY

" Rise up, rise up, Lord Douglas! " she says,
 " And put on your armour so bright;
Let it ne'er be said that a daughter of ours
 Was married to a lord under night.

" Rise up, rise up, my seven bold sons,
 And put on your armour so bright;
And take better care o' your youngest sister,
 For your eldest's away this night! "

Lady Margaret was on a milk-white steed,
 Lord William was on a gray,
A buglet-horn hung down by his side,
 And swiftly they rode away.

Lord William looked over his left shoulder
 To see what he could see,
And there he spied her seven bold brothers,
 Come riding over the lea.

" Light down, light down, Lady Margaret," he said,
 " And hold my steed in your hand,
Until that against your seven bold brothers,
 And your father, I make a stand."

O, there she stood, and bitter she stood,
 And never shed one tear,
Until she saw her brothers fa',
 And her father who loved her so dear.

" O hold your hand, Lord William! " she said,
 " For your strokes are deep and sore;
Though lovers I can get many a one,
 A father I can never get more."

O she's taken off her handkerchief,
   It was o' the holland so fine,
And aye she dressed her father's wounds;
   His blood ran down like wine.

" O choose, O choose, Lady Margaret,
   Will ye go with me, or bide? "
" I'll go, I'll go, Lord William," she said.
   " Ye've left me no other guide."

He lifted her up on her milk-white steed,
   And mounted his dapple-gray,
With his buglet-horn hung down by his side,
   And slowly they rode away.

O they rode on, and on they rode,
   And a' by the light o' the moon,
Until they came to a wan water,
   And there they lighted down.

They lighted down to take a drink
   O' the spring that ran so clear,
But down the stream ran his red heart's blood;
   And she began to fear.

" Hold up, hold up, Lord William," she said,
   " I fear me you are slain!"
" 'Tis but the shadow o' my scarlet cloak
   That shines in the water so plain."

O they rode on, and on they rode,
   And a' by the light o' the moon,
Until they saw his mother's ha',
   And there they lighted down.

" Get up, get up, lady mother," he says,
   " Get up, and let in your son!
Open the door, lady mother," he says,
   " For this night my fair lady I've won!

" Now make my bed, lady mother," he says,
   " O make it wide and deep,
And lay Lady Margaret close at my back,
   And the sounder will I sleep! "

Lord William was dead long ere midnight,
  Lady Margaret long ere day,
And all true lovers that go together
  May they have more luck than they!

Lord William was buried in Mary's Kirk,
  Lady Margaret in Mary's Quire;
And out of her grave grew a bonny red rose,
  And out of the knight's a brier.

TRUE THOMAS

True Thomas lay on Huntlie bank;
  A marvel he did see;
For there he saw a lady bright,
  Come riding down by the Eildon tree.[1]

Her skirt was of the grass-green silk,
  Her mantle of the velvet fine;
On every lock of her horse's mane,
  Hung fifty silver bells and nine.

True Thomas he pulled off his cap,
  And bowed low down on his knee;
" All hail, thou mighty Queen of Heaven!
  For thy peer on earth could never be."

" O no, O no, Thomas," she said,
  " That name does not belong to me;
I'm but the Queen of fair Elfland,
  That hither am come to visit thee.

" Harp and carp, Thomas," she said,
  " Harp and carp along with me;
And if ye dare to kiss my lips
  Sure of your body I will be! "

" Betide me weal, betide me woe,
  That weird shall never daunten me! "
Then he has kissed her on the lips,
  All underneath the Eildon tree.

[1] The Eildon tree was the tree of magic under which the Rhymer delivered his prophecies.

" Now ye must go with me," she said,
    " True Thomas, ye must go with me;
And ye must serve me seven years,
    Through weal or woe as may chance to be."

She's mounted on her milk-white steed,
    She's taken True Thomas up behind;
And aye, whene'er her bridle rang,
    The steed flew swifter than the wind.

O they rode on, and farther on,
    The steed flew swifter than the wind;
Until they reached a desert wide,
    And living land was left behind.

" Light down, light down now, Thomas," she said,
    " And lean your head upon my knee;
Light down, and rest a little space,
    And I will show you marvels three.

" O see ye not yon narrow road,
    So thick beset with thorns and briers?
That is the path of righteousness,
    Though after it but few enquires.

" And see ye not yon broad, broad road,
    That stretches o'er the lily leven?
That is the path of wickedness,
    Though some call it the road to heaven.

" And see ye not yon bonny road,
    That winds about the green hillside?
That is the way to fair Elfland,
    Where you and I this night must bide.

" But, Thomas, ye shall hold your tongue,
    Whatever ye may hear or see;
For if ye speak word in Elfin land,
    Ye'll ne'er win back to your own countree! "

O they rode on, and farther on;
    They waded through rivers above the knee,
And they saw neither sun nor moon,
    But they heard the roaring of a sea.

It was mirk, mirk night; there was no star-light;
    They waded through red blood to the knee;
For all the blood that's shed on earth,
    Runs through the springs o' that countree.

At last they came to a garden green,
    And she pulled an apple from on high—
" Take this for thy wages, True Thomas;
    It will give thee the tongue that can never lie! "

" My tongue is my own," True Thomas he said,
    " A goodly gift ye would give to me!
I neither could to buy or sell
    At fair or tryst where I may be.

" I could neither speak to prince or peer,
    Nor ask of grace from fair ladye."
" Now hold thy peace! " the lady said,
    " For as I say, so must it be."

He has gotten a coat of the even cloth,
    And a pair of shoes of the velvet green;
And till seven years were gone and past,
    True Thomas on earth was never seen.

THE WIFE OF USHER'S WELL

There lived a wife at Usher's Well,
    And a wealthy wife was she;
She had three stout and stalwart sons,
    And sent them o'er the sea.

They had not been a week from her,
    A week but barely one,
When word came to the mother herself,
    That her three sons were gone.

They had not been a week from her,
    A week but barely three,
When word came to the mother herself,
    That her sons she'd never see.

" I wish the wind may never cease,
    Nor fishes in the flood,
Till my three sons come home to me,
    In earthly flesh and blood! "

It fell about the Martinmas,
    When nights are long and dark,
The mother's three sons they all came home
    And their hats were of birch bark.

It neither grew in marsh or trench
    Not yet in any ditch;
But at the gates of Paradise
    That birch grew fair and rich.

" Blow up the fire, my maidens!
    Bring water from the well!
For all my house shall feast this night,
    Since my three sons are well."

And she has made to them a bed,
    She's made it large and wide;
And she's taken her mantle her about,
    Sat down at the bed-side.

Up then crew the red, red cock,
    And up and crew the gray;
The eldest to the youngest said,
    " 'Tis time we were away."

The cock he had not crowed but once,
    And clapped his wings at dawn,
When the youngest to the eldest said,
    " Brother, we must be gone.

" The cock doth crow, the light doth grow,
    The channelling worm doth chide;
If we be missed out of our place,
    A sore pain we must abide."

" Lie still, lie still, but a little wee while,
    Lie still but if we may,
If our mother should miss us when she wakes,
    She will go mad ere day."

" Fare ye well, my mother dear!
   Farewell to barn and byre![1]
And fare ye well, the bonny lass,
   That kindles my mother's fire."

SIR PATRICK SPENS

The king sits in Dumfermline towne
   Drinking the blood-red wine;
" O where will I get a skilful skipper
   To sail this ship of mine? "

Up and spake an elder knight,
   Sat at the king's right knee:
" Sir Patrick Spens is the best sailor
   That ever sailed the sea."

The king has written a broad letter
   And sealed it with his hand.
And sent it to Sir Patrick Spens
   Was walking on the strand.

" To Noroway, to Noroway,
   To Noroway o'er the foam;
The King's own daughter of Noroway,
   'Tis thou must bring her home! "

The first line that Sir Patrick read
   A loud, loud laugh laughed he:
The next line that Sir Patrick read
   The tear blinded his ee.[2]

" Oh who is this has done this deed,
   This ill deed unto me;
To send me out this time o' the year
   To sail upon the sea?

" Make haste, make haste, my merry men all,
   Our good ship sails the morn."
" Oh say not so, my master dear,
   For I fear a deadly storm.

[1] Byre: cattle-house.   [2] Eye.

" I saw the new moon late yestere'en
    With the old moon in her arm;
And if we go to sea, master,
    I fear we'll come to harm."

They had not sailed a league, a league,
    A league, but barely three,
When the sky grew dark, the wind blew loud,
    And angry grew the sea.

The anchor broke, the topmast split,
    'Twas such a deadly storm.
The waves came over the broken ship
    Till all her sides were torn.

O long, long may the ladies sit
    With their fans into their hand,
Or ere they see Sir Patrick Spens
    Come sailing to the strand.

O long, long may the maidens sit
    With their gold combs in their hair,
Before they'll see their own dear loves
    Come home to greet them there.

Half-o'er, half-o'er to Aberdour
    'Tis fifty fathoms deep;
And there lies good Sir Patrick Spens
    With the Scots lords at his feet.

FAIR MARGARET AND SWEET WILLIAM

As it fell out on a long summer's day,
    Two lovers they sat on a hill:
They sat together that long summer's day,
    And could not talk their fill.

" I'm not the man for you, Margaret,
    You're not the wife for me.
Before to-morrow at eight of the clock,
    A rich wedding you shall see."

Fair Margaret sat in her bower-window
    Combing her yellow hair,
She saw Sweet William and his brown bride
    Unto the church draw near.

Then down she laid her ivory comb,
    And up she bound her hair;
She went out from her bower alive,
    But alive nevermore came there.

When day was gone, and night was come,
    And all men fast asleep,
Came in the ghost of Fair Margaret,
    And stood at William's feet.

" How like ye the lady, Sweet William,
    That lies in your arms asleep?
God give you joy of your gay bride-bed,
    And me of my winding-sheet! "

When night was gone and day was come
    And all men waked from sleep,
Sweet William to his lady said,
    " Alas! I have cause to weep.

" I dreamed a dream, my lady,
    A dream that bodes no good;
I dreamed our bower was full of red swine
    And our bride-bed full of blood."

He callèd up his merry men all,
    By one, by two, by three.
Saying, " I'll away to Fair Margaret's bower,
    With the leave of my ladye."

And when he came to Fair Margaret's bower
    He knockèd at the ring;
And who so ready as her seven brothers
    To rise and let him in?

" O, is she in the parlour? " he said,
    " Or is she in the hall?
Or is she in the long chamber
    Amongst her merry maids all? "

" No, she's not in the parlour," they said,
    " Nor she's not in the hall:
But she is in the long chamber,
    Laid out against the wall."

He turnèd up the covering-sheet,
    And looked upon the dead.
" Methinks her lips are pale and wan,
    She has lost her cherry red."

" I would do more for thee, Margaret,
    Than would any of thy kin:
And I will kiss thy pale, cold lips
    Though thy smile I cannot win."

With that bespake the seven brothers,
    Making a piteous moan:
" You may go kiss your jolly brown bride,
    And let our sister alone."

" If I do kiss my jolly brown bride,
    I do but what is right;
For I made no vow to your sister dear,
    By day nor yet by night.

" Deal on, deal on, my merry men all,
    Deal on your cake and wine!
For whatever is dealt at her funeral to-day
    Shall be dealt to-morrow at mine."

Fair Margaret died on the over-night,
    Sweet William died on the morrow.
Fair Margaret died for pure, pure love;
    Sweet William died for sorrow.

Margaret was buried in the lower chancel,
    Sweet William in the higher;
Out of her breast there sprang a rose-tree,
    Out of his breast a brier.

THE TWO SISTERS OF BINNORIE

There were two sisters sat in a bower;
Binnorie, O Binnorie;
There came a knight to be their wooer;
By the bonny mill-dams of Binnorie.

He courted the eldest with gloves and rings,
But he loved the youngest above all things.

The eldest was vexèd to despair,
And much she envied her sister fair.

The eldest said to the youngest one,
" Will ye see our father's ships come in? "

She's taken her by the lily-white hand,
And led her down to the river strand.

The youngest stood upon a stone;
The eldest came and pushed her in.

" O sister, sister, reach your hand,
And you shall be heir of half my land.

" O sister, reach me but your glove
And sweet William shall be all your love."

" Sink on, nor hope for hand or glove!
Sweet William shall surely be my love."

Sometimes she sank, sometimes she swam,
Until she came to the mouth of the dam.

Out then came the miller's son
And saw the fair maid swimming in.

" O father, father, draw your dam!
Here's either a mermaid or a swan."

The miller hasted and drew his dam,
And there he found a drowned womàn.

You could not see her middle small,
Her girdle was so rich withal.

You could not see her yellow hair
For the gold and pearls that clustered there.

And by there came a harper fine
Who harped to nobles when they dine.

And when he looked that lady on,
He sighed and made a heavy moan.

He's made a harp of her breast bone,
Whose sounds would melt a heart of stone.

He's taken three locks of her yellow hair
And with them strung his harp so rare.

He went into her father's hall
To play his harp before them all.

But as he laid it on a stone,
The harp began to play alone.

And soon the harp sang loud and clear,
" Farewell, my father and mother dear.

" Farewell, farewell, my brother Hugh,
Farewell, my William, sweet and true."

And then as plain as plain could be,
    (*Binnorie, O Binnorie*)
" There sits my sister who drownèd me
    By the bonny mill-dams of Binnorie! "

LORD RANDAL

" O where have you been, Lord Randal, my son?
O where have you been, my handsome young man? "—
    " I have been to the wild wood; mother, make my bed soon,
    For I'm weary with hunting, and fain would lie down."

" Who gave you your dinner, Lord Randal, my son?
Who gave you your dinner, my handsome young man? "—
  " I dined with my sweetheart; mother, make my bed soon,
  For I'm weary with hunting, and fain would lie down."

" What had you for dinner, Lord Randal, my son?
What had you for dinner, my handsome young man? "—
  " I had eels boiled in broth; mother, make my bed soon,
  For I'm weary with hunting, and fain would lie down."

" And where are your bloodhounds, Lord Randal, my son?
And where are your bloodhounds, my handsome young man? "—
  " O they swelled and they died; mother, make my bed soon,
  For I'm weary with hunting, and fain would lie down."

" O I fear you are poisoned, Lord Randal, my son!
O I fear you are poisoned, my handsome young man! "—
  " O yes! I am poisoned; mother, make my bed soon,
  For I'm sick at the heart, and I fain would lie down."

GLASGERION

Glasgerion was a harper good,
  He harpèd to the King;
Glasgerion was the best harper
  Who ever played on a string.

He'd harp a fish from the river,
  Or water from a stone;
He'd harp the heart from a maiden's breast
  To love but him alone.

He's taken his harp into his hand;
  He's harpèd and he's sung;
And aye he harpèd to the King
  Who never thought it long.

The King and all his nobles
  Sat drinking at their wine;
The King would have none but his daughter
  To wait on them as they dine.

Glasgerion's taken his harp in hand
    Till he's played them all asleep,
All but the fair young Princess
    Whom love did waking keep.

She said, " Play on, Glasgerion,
    Play on and never cease;
There's never a stroke comes from thy harp
    But it gladdens my heart with peace."

At first he played a slow, grave tune
    And then a gay one flew;
And many's the sigh and the loving word
    That passed between the two.

" Come to my bower, Glasgerion,
    When all men are at rest,
As I am a lady true to my word,
    Thou shalt be a welcome guest."

Home then came Glasgerion;
    A glad man, Lord! was he.
" And come thou hither, Jack, my boy;
    Come hither unto me.

" For the King's daughter," Glasgerion said
    " Hath granted me a boon,
And at her bower I must be
    At the setting of the moon."

" Lie down in your bed, dear master,
    And sleep as long as you may;
I'll keep good watch and waken you
    Three hours before 'tis day."

But up he rose, that worthless lad,
    His master's clothes did don;
A collar he cast about his neck;
    He seemed the gentleman.

And when he came to the lady's bower
    He lightly rattled the pin.
The lady she was true to her word;
    She rose and let him in.

He did not kiss that lady's mouth,
   His love-making was rude;
And much that lady did mistrust
   He was of churlish blood.

Home then came the worthless lad,
   Took off both cloak and shoon,
And cast the collar from his neck—
   He was but a churl's son.

" Wake up, wake up, good master,
   I fear 'tis almost dawn,
Wake up, wake up, the cock has crowed;
   'Tis time that you were gone."

Then quickly rose Glasgerion,
   Put on his cloak and shoon,
And cast a collar about his neck—
   He was a lord's true son.

And when he came to the lady's bower
   He lightly rattled the pin.
The lady was more than true to her word;
   She rose and let him in.

" O whether have you left with me
   Your bracelet or your glove?
Or are you returnèd back again
   To know more of my love? "

Glasgerion swore a full great oath
   By oak and ash and thorn,
" I was never before in your chamber, lady,
   Since the time that I was born."

" O then it was your vile foot-page
   Who hath beguilèd me."
Then she pulled forth a little sharp knife
   That hung down at her knee.

O'er her white feet the red blood ran
   Or ever a hand could stay,
And dead she lay on her bower-floor
   At the dawning of the day.

But home then went Glasgerion,
    A woe man, Lord! was he.
" And come thou hither, Jack, my boy;
    Come hither unto me.

" If I had killed a man to-night,
    Jack, I would tell it thee;
But if I have taken no life to-night,
    Jack, thou hast taken three."

Then he pulled out his bright, brown sword,
    And dried it on his sleeve,
And he smote off that vile lad's head
    And asked for no man's leave.

He set the sword's point to his breast,
    The pommel to a stone.
Through the falseness of that lying lad,
    These three lives were all gone.

BARBARA ALLEN'S CRUELTY

All in the merry month of May,
    When green buds they were swelling,
Young Jemmy Grove on his death-bed lay
    For love of Barbara Allen.

He sent his man unto her then,
    To the town where she was dwelling:
" O haste and come to my master dear,
    If your name be Barbara Allen."

Slowly, slowly she rose up,
    And she came where he was lying:
And when she drew the curtain by,
    Says, " Young man, I think you're dying."

" O it's I am sick, and very, very sick,
    And it's all for Barbara Allen."
" O the better for me you'll never be,
    Tho' your heart's blood were a-spilling!

" O do you not mind, young man," she says,
    " When the red wine you were filling,
That you made the healths go round and round,
    And slighted Barbara Allen? "

He turned his face unto the wall,
  And death with him was dealing:
" Adieu, adieu, my dear friends all;
  Be kind to Barbara Allen."

As she was walking o'er the fields,
  She heard the dead-bell knelling;
And every beat the dead-bell gave,
  Cried, " Woe to Barbara Allen! "

" O mother, mother, make my bed,
  To lay me down in sorrow.
My love has died for me to-day,
  I'll die for him to-morrow."

EDWARD, EDWARD

" Why does your sword so drip with blood,
  Edward, Edward?
Why does your sword so drip with blood,
  And why so sad are ye, O? "
" O I have killed my hawk so good,
  Mother, mother,
O I have killed my hawk so good
  And I have no more but he, O."

" Your hawk's blood was never so red,
  Edward, Edward,
Your hawk's blood was never so red,
  My dear son, I tell thee, O."
" O I have killed my red-roan steed,
  Mother, mother,
O I have killed my red-roan steed,
  That was so fair and free, O."

" Your steed was old and your stable's filled,
  Edward, Edward,
Your steed was old and your stable's filled,
  Now say what may it be, O."
" It was my father that I killed,
  Mother, mother,
It was my father that I killed,
  Alas, and woe is me, O."

" What penance will ye do for that,
    Edward, Edward?
What penance will ye do for that,
    My dear son, now tell me, O? "
" I'll set my feet in yonder boat,
    Mother, mother,
I'll set my feet in yonder boat,
    And I'll fare over the sea, O."

" What will ye do with your towers and hall,
    Edward, Edward?
What will ye do with your towers and hall,
    That are so fair to see, O? "
" I'll let them stand till down they fall,
    Mother, mother,
I'll let them stand till down they fall,
    For here nevermore may I be, O."

" What will ye leave to your babes and your wife,
    Edward, Edward?
What will ye leave to your babes and your wife,
    When ye go over the sea, O? "
" The world's room—let them beg through life,
    Mother, mother,
The world's room—let them beg through life,
    For them nevermore will I see, O."

" And what will ye leave to your own mother dear,
    Edward, Edward?
And what will ye leave to your own mother dear,
    My dear son, now tell me, O? "
" The curse of Hell from me shall ye bear,
    Mother, mother,
The curse of Hell from me shall ye bear:
    Such counsel ye gave to me, O! "

MAY COLVIN

False Sir John a-wooing came,
    To a maid of beauty rare;
May Colvin was the lady's name,
    Her father's only heir.

He wooed her indoors, he wooed her out,
   He wooed her night and day;
Until he got the lady's consent
   To mount and ride away.

" Go fetch me some of your father's gold
   And some of your mother's fee,
And I'll carry you to the far Northland
   And there I'll marry thee."

She's gone to her father's coffers,
   Where all his money lay;
And she's taken the red, and she's left the white,
   And lightly she's tripped away.

She's gone down to her father's stable,
   Where all his steeds did stand;
And she's taken the best and left the worst,
   That was in her father's land.

He rode on, and she rode on,
   They rode a long summer's day,
Until they came to a broad river,
   An arm of a lonesome sea.

" Leap off the steed," says false Sir John;
   " Your bridal bed you see;
For it's seven fair maids I have drownèd here,
   And the eighth one you shall be.

" Cast off, cast off your silks so fine,
   And lay them on a stone,
For they are too fine and costly
   To rot in the salt sea foam."

" O turn about, thou false Sir John,
   And look to the leaf o' the tree;
For it never became a gentleman
   A naked woman to see."

He's turned himself straight round about
   To look to the leaf o' the tree;
She's twined her arms about his waist,
   And thrown him into the sea.

" O hold a grip of me, May Colvin,
  For fear that I should drown;
I'll take you home to your father's gates,
  And safe I'll set you down."

" O safe enough I am, Sir John,
  And safer I will be;
For seven fair maids have you drownèd here,
  The eighth shall not be me.

" O lie you there, thou false Sir John,
  O lie you there," said she,
" For you lie not in a colder bed
  Than the one you intended for me."

So she went on her father's steed,
  As swift as she could away;
And she came home to her father's gates
  At the breaking of the day.

Up then spake the pretty parrot:
  " May Colvin, where have you been?
What has become of false Sir John,
  That wooed you yestere'en? "

" O hold your tongue, my pretty parrot,
  Nor tell no tales on me;
Your cage will be made of the beaten gold
  With spokes of ivory."

Up then spake her father dear,
  In the chamber where he lay:
" What ails you, pretty parrot,
  That you prattle so long ere day? "

" There came a cat to my door, master,
  I thought 'twould have worried me;
And I was calling on May Colvin
  To take the cat from me."

BONNIE GEORGE CAMPBELL

High upon Highlands,
    And low upon Tay,
Bonnie George Campbell
    Rode out on a day;
Saddled and bridled,
    And gallant to see:
Home came his good horse,
    But home came not he.

Out ran his old mother,
    Wild with despair;
Out ran his bonnie bride,
    Tearing her hair.
He rode saddled and bridled,
    With boots to the knee:
Home came his good horse,
    But never came he.

" My meadow lies green,
    And my corn is unshorn,
My barn is unbuilt,
    And my babe is unborn."
He rode saddled and bridled,
    Careless and free:
Safe home came the saddle,
    But never came he.

THE WRAGGLE TAGGLE GIPSIES

Three gipsies stood at the Castle gate,
They sang so high, they sang so low;
The lady sate in her chamber late,
Her heart it melted away as snow.

They sang so sweet, they sang so shrill,
That fast her tears began to flow.
And she laid down her silken gown,
Her golden rings, and all her show.

She's taken off her high-heeled shoes
All made of the Spanish leather, O.
She would in the street with her bare, bare feet
All out in the wind and weather, O.

" O saddle to me my milk-white steed,
And go and fetch my pony, O!
That I may ride and seek my bride,
Who is gone with the wraggle taggle gipsies, O! "

O he rode high, and he rode low,
He rode thro' wood and copses too,
Until he came to an open field,
And there he espied his lady, O!

" What makes you leave your house and land?
Your golden treasures to forgo?
What makes you leave your new-wedded lord,
To follow the wraggle taggle gipsies, O? "

" What care I for my house and my land?
What care I for my treasure, O?
What care I for my new-wedded lord,—
I'm off with the wraggle taggle gipsies, O! "

" Last night you slept on a goose-feather bed,
With the sheet turned down so bravely, O?
But to-night you'll sleep in a cold open field,
Along with the wraggle taggle gipsies, O! "

" What care I for a goose-feather bed,
With the sheet turned down so bravely, O?
For to-night I shall sleep in a cold open field,
Along with the wraggle taggle gipsies, O! "

THE CHERRY-TREE CAROL

Joseph was an old man,
An old man was he
When he wedded Mary
In the land of Galilee.

Joseph and Mary walking
  In the midst of a wood
Saw berries and cherries
  As red as the blood.

O then bespoke Mary,
  So meek and so mild,
" Pray get me one cherry,
  For I am with child."

O then bespoke Joseph,
  So rude and unkind,
" Let him get thee a cherry
  That got thee with child."

O then bespoke the babe
  Within his mother's womb,
" Bow down, thou tall cherry-tree,
  And give my mother some."

Then bowed down the tall cherry-tree
  To his mother's right hand,
And she cried, " See, Joseph,
  I have cherries at command! "

And Mary ate her cherry
  As red as the blood;
Then Mary went on
  With her heavy load.

ST. STEPHEN AND KING HEROD

Saint Stephen was a clerk
  In King Herod's hall,
And served him with bread and cloth
  As every king befall.

Stephen out of kitchen came
  With boar's head on hand,
He saw a star was fair and bright
  Over Bethlehem stand.

He cast adown the boar's head
   And went into the hall;
" I forsake thee, Herod,
   And thy works all.

" I forsake thee, King Herod,
   And thy works all,
There is a child in Bethlehem born
   Is better than we all."

" What aileth thee, Stephen?
   What is thee befall?
Lacketh thee either meat or drink
   In King Herod's hall? "

" Lacketh me neither meat nor drink
   In King Herod's hall;
There is a child in Bethlehem born
   Is better than we all."

" What aileth thee, Stephen?
   Art mad or hast grown wroth?
Lacked thee either gold or fee
   Or any rich cloth? "

" Lacketh me neither gold nor fee
   Nor cloth nor things of greed.
There is a child in Bethlehem born
   Shall help us in our need."

" That is all so true, Stephen,
   All so true, I know,
As if the capon in this dish
   Should come to life and crow."

That word was not so soon said,
   That word in that hall,
The capon crew *Christus natus est*
   Among the lords all.

" Rise up, my true tormentors,
   By two and all by one,
Lead Stephen here out of this town
   And stone him with stone."

They took Stephen
    And stoned him on the way.
And therefore is his even
    On Christ's own day.

THE OLD CLOAK

This winter's weather it waxeth cold,
    And frost doth freeze on every hill,
And Boreas blows his blast so bold,
    That all our cattle may die with chill.
Bell, my wife, who loves no strife,
    She said unto me quietly,
" Rise up, and save cow Crumbock's life.
    Man, put thine old cloak about thee."

HE

O Bell, why dost thou scold and scorn?
    Thou knowest my cloak is very thin:
It is so bare and overworn
    A cricket could not creep therein.
Then I'll no longer borrow nor lend,
    For once I'll new-apparelled be,
To-morrow I'll to town and spend,
    For I'll have a new cloak about me.

SHE

Cow Crumbock is a very good cow,
    She has been always true to the pail,
She has helped us to butter and cheese, I trow,
    And other things she will not fail;
I would be loth to see her pine,
    Good husband, counsel take of me,
It is not for us to go so fine.
    Man, take thine old cloak about thee.

HE

My cloak it was a very good cloak,
    It hath been always true to the wear,
But now it is not worth a groat;
    I have had it four and forty year:
Once it was scarlet and fine of grain,
    'Tis now but a sieve, as you may see,
It will neither hold out wind nor rain;
    And I'll have a new cloak about me.

SHE

It is four and forty years ago
  Since the one of us the other did ken,
And we have had betwixt us two
  Of children either nine or ten;
We have brought them up to women and men:
  In the fear of God I trow they be;
And why wilt thou thyself misken?
  Man, take thine old cloak about thee.

HE

O Bell, my wife, why dost thou flout!
  Now is now, and then was then:
Seek now all the world throughout,
  Thou kenst not clowns from gentlemen.
They are clad in black, green, yellow, or grey,
  So far above their own degree:
Once in my life I'll do as they,
  For I'll have a new cloak about me.

SHE

King Stephen was a worthy peer,
  His breeches cost him but a crown,
He held them sixpence all too dear,
  Therefore he called the tailor " clown".
He was a man of high renown,
  And thou but of a low degree:
It's pride that puts this country down,
  Man, take thine old cloak about thee.

HE

Bell, my wife, she loves not strife,
  Yet she will lead me if she can;
And oft, to live a quiet life,
  I am forced to yield, though I'm good-man.
It's not for man with woman to strive,
  Unless he first give o'er the plea:
As we began, so will we live,
  And I'll take mine old cloak about me.

" GET UP AND BAR THE DOOR "

It fell about the Martinmas time,
   And a gay time it was then,
When our goodwife got puddings to make,
And she's boiled them in the pan.

The wind so cold blew south and north,
   And blew into the floor;
Quoth our goodman to our goodwife,
   " Get up and bar the door."

" My hand is in my household work,
   Goodman, as ye may see;
And it will not be barred for a hundred years,
   If it's to be barred by me! "

They made a pact between them both,
   They made it firm and sure,
That whosoe'er should speak the first,
   Should rise and bar the door.

Then by there came two gentlemen,
   At twelve o'clock at night,
And they could see neither house nor hall,
   Nor coal nor candlelight.

" Now whether is this a rich man's house,
   Or whether is it a poor? "
But never a word would one of them speak,
   For barring of the door.

The guests they ate the white puddings,
   And then they ate the black;
Tho' much the goodwife thought to herself,
   Yet never a word she spake.

Then said one stranger to the other,
   " Here, man, take ye my knife;
Do ye take off the old man's beard,
   And I'll kiss the goodwife."

"There's no hot water to scrape it off,
    And what shall we do then?"
"Then why not use the pudding broth,
    That boils into the pan?"

O up then started our goodman,
    An angry man was he:
"Will ye kiss my wife before my eyes!
    And with pudding broth scald me!"

Then up and started our goodwife,
    Gave three skips on the floor:
"Goodman, you've spoken the foremost word.
    Get up and bar the door!"

KING JOHN AND THE ABBOT OF CANTERBURY [1]

An ancient story I'll tell you anon,
Of a notable prince, that was called King John;
He ruled over England with main and might,
But he did great wrong, and maintained little right.

And I'll tell you a story, a story so merry,
Concerning the Abbot of Canterbury;
How for his housekeeping and high renown,
They rode post to bring him to London town.

A hundred men, as the King heard say,
The Abbot kept in his house every day;
And fifty gold chains, without any doubt,
In velvet coats waited the Abbot about.

"How now, Father Abbot? I hear it of thee,
Thou keepest a far better house than me;
And for thy housekeeping and high renown,
I fear thou work'st treason against my crown."

[1] This, from Percy's *Reliques of Ancient English Poetry*, bears the marks
of much revision on the framework of an old popular ballad. "It
seems," says Percy, "to have been abridged and modernised about the
time of James I from a much older model," but Percy himself took
"considerable liberties" with the stanzas.

" My Liege," quoth the Abbot, " I would it were known,
I am spending nothing but what is my own;
And I trust your grace will not put me in fear,
For spending my own true-gotten gear."

" Yes, yes, Father Abbot, thy fault is high,
And now for the same thou needest must die;
And except thou canst answer me questions three,
Thy head struck off from thy body shall be.

" Now first," quo' the King, " as I sit here,
With my crown of gold on my head so fair,
Among all my liegemen of noble birth,
Thou must tell to one penny what I am worth.

" Secondly, tell me, beyond all doubt,
How quickly I may ride the whole world about;
And at the third question thou must not shrink,
But tell me here truly, what do I think? "

" O, these are deep questions for my shallow wit,
And I cannot answer your Grace as yet;
But if you will give me a fortnight's space,
I'll do my endeavour to answer your Grace."

" Now a fortnight's space to thee will I give,
And that is the longest thou hast to live;
For unless thou answer my questions three,
Thy life and thy lands are forfeit to me."

Away rode the Abbot all sad at this word;
He rode to Cambridge and Oxenford;
But never a doctor there was so wise,
That could by his learning an answer devise.

Then home rode the Abbot, with comfort so cold,
And he met his shepherd, a-going to fold:
" Now good Lord Abbot, you are welcome home;
What news do you bring us from great King John? "

" Sad news, sad news, Shepherd, I must give;
That I have but three days more to live.
I must answer the King his questions three.
Or my head struck off from my body shall be.

" The first is to tell him, as he sits there,
With his crown of gold on his head so fair
Among all his liegemen of noble birth,
To within one penny, what he is worth.

" The second, to tell him, beyond all doubt,
How quickly he may ride this whole world about;
And at question the third, I must not shrink,
But tell him there truly, what does he think? "

" O, cheer up, my lord; did you never hear yet
That a fool may teach a wise man wit?
Lend me your serving-men, horse, and apparel,
And I'll ride to London to answer your quarrel.

" With your pardon, it oft has been told to me
That I'm like your lordship as ever can be:
And if you will but lend me your gown,
There is none shall know us at London town."

" Now horses and serving-men thou shalt have,
With sumptuous raiment gallant and brave;
With crozier, and mitre, and rochet, and cope,
Fit to draw near to our father, the pope."

" Now welcome, Sir Abbot," the King he did say,
" 'Tis well thou'rt come back to keep thy day;
For if thou canst answer my questions three,
Thy life and thy living both saved shall be.

" And first, as thou seest me sitting here,
With my crown of gold on my head so fair,
Among my liegemen of noble birth,
Tell to one penny what I am worth."

" For thirty pence our Saviour was sold
Among the false Jews as I have been told;
And twenty-nine is the worth of thee;
For I think thou art one penny worse than he."

The King, he laughed, and swore by St. Bittle,
" I did not think I was worth so little!
Now secondly tell me, beyond all doubt,
How quickly I may ride this world about."

"You must rise with the sun, and ride with the same
Until the next morning he riseth again;
And then your Grace need never doubt
But in twenty-four hours you'll ride it about."

The King he laughed, and swore by St. Jone,
"I did not think I could do it so soon!
Now from question the third thou must not shrink,
But tell me truly, what do I think?"

"Yea, that I shall do, and make your Grace merry:
You think I'm the Abbot of Canterbury.
But I'm his poor shepherd, as plain you may see,
That am come to beg pardon for him and for me."

The King he laughed, and swore by the mass,
"I'll make thee Lord Abbot this day in his place!"
"Now nay, my Liege, be not in such speed;
For alas! I can neither write nor read."

"Four nobles a week, then I'll give to thee,
For this merry jest thou hast shown to me;
And tell the old Abbot, when thou gettest home,
Thou hast brought a free pardon with thanks from King
   John."

STILL WATERS

Says Tweed to Till,[1]
"What makes you run so still?"
Says Till to Tweed,
"Though you run with speed,
   And I run slow,
For every man that you drown
   I drown two!"

(*c. 1250*)

[1] The Till is a sluggish river in Northumberland, tributary to the Tweed.

EARLY SONGS

The range of early songs of unknown authorship is almost as great in time and in variety as that of the early ballads. Scholars have agreed that the " Cuccu Song " can be dated from the middle of the thirteenth century; the religious and amatory lyrics span the Middle English and Tudor period; while that perfect expression of unaffected fidelity, " There is a lady sweet and kind," has sometimes been assigned to Thomas Ford and certainly was not written before 1600.

Possibly the most engaging, if not the most important of the verses in this section, are the anonymous airs and lyrics generally referred to as Elizabethan. They come chiefly from two sources: (1) the printed miscellanies or anthologies, and (2) the music-sheets and song-books of the period. Apart from the printed volumes there are the rare manuscripts, notably those in the British Museum, the Bodleian Library and the library of Christ Church, Oxford. An examination of the first source alone is sufficient to prove—even without the dramas—the quality of Elizabethan poetry. There is, first of all, that lavish assembly of the time of Henry VIII, issued from the print-shop of Richard Tottel in 1557 under the title *Songs and Sonnets*, and reissued so often that it became popularly known as Tottel's Miscellany. Shakespeare, in *Merry Wives of Windsor*, alludes to it as a contemporary classic. So great was the demand for this anthology that the editor soon received the dubious compliment of imitation. In Elizabeth's reign there followed, in a succession so rapid as to seem rapacious, *A Hundred Sundry Flowers* (1573), *The Paradise of Dainty Devices* (1576), *The Forest of Fancy* (1579), *The Phoenix Nest* (1593), *The Passionate Pilgrim* (1599), falsely attributed to Shakespeare, *England's Helicon* (1600), the best of the Elizabethan collections—actually an anthology of anthologies—and *A Poetical Rhapsody* (1602), the last of them.

Parallel with these miscellanies of poetry *per se*, there were the song-books. Originating with the madrigals imported from Italy, part-songs became a passion in England; if a man could not invent a three-voiced melody, at least he was expected to maintain his part in one. The ear of the Elizabethans must have been sensitively alert, for, though the art was high, it was popular. Scarcely less important were the " airs," as distinguished from the madrigals. It was the " air " that predominated, and the poet matched his skill with the craft of the composer. Slovenly texts were not tolerated; composers employed the best they could find and, when the best was not good enough, called in lyricists of rank to furnish words for their music. Pre-eminent among these books of songs are the composer Byrd's *Psalmes, Sonets and Songs of Sadness* (1588) and his *Songs of Sundry Natures* (1589), the lute-player John Dowland's *First Book of Songs or Airs* (1597), which was followed by three more, and Thomas Campion's *A Book of Airs* (1601). Campion was not only an editor, a scholarly musician, and composer, but a poet of authority. It has been established that he was the author of some of the most delicate Elizabethan lyrics, though no one can say how many of the anonymous contributions to his song-books are from his pen. That Campion's collections soon became the most popular is evidenced by the continued reprintings and the appearance of his *Fourth Book of Airs* as late as 1617 (?). Nor were the lesser editors without merit. Anthologists of the last three hundred years have ransacked Robert Jones's six musical works concluding with *The Muses' Garden for Delights* (1610), as well as Daniel's *Songs for the Lute, Viol and Voice* (1606), Ford's *Music of Sundry Kinds* (1607) and Vautor's *Songs of Divers Airs and Natures* (1619).

Most of the volumes listed in these paragraphs went through several editions and all of them were enriched by a wealth of anonymous lyrics as well as those by recognised poets. The verses either signed by known authors or generally assigned to them will be found chronologically arranged in the section following this one. This division consists of a selection from only the unidentified earlier sources as well as the volumes and manuscripts already mentioned. The verses have been modernised in spelling and punctuation, but no other departures from the texts have been attempted except an occasional condensation and the omission of the " refrains," whose values are musical rather than poetic. The first two archaic songs are presented in two versions: the original, and a translation by the editor.

CUCCU SONG

Sumer is icumen in;
   Lhude sing cuccu!
Groweth sed, and bloweth med,
   And springeth the wude nu.
      Sing cuccu!

Awe bleteth after lomb,
   Lhouth after calve cu;
Bulluc sterteth, bucke verteth,
   Murie sing cuccu!

Cuccu, cuccu, well singes thu, cuccu:
   Ne swike thu naver nu:
Sing cuccu, nu, sing cuccu,
   Sing cuccu, sing cuccu, nu!

(c. 1250)

CUCKOO SONG

Summer is a-coming in,
   Sing a loud " cuckoo! "
The seed grows, the mead blows,
   The wood springs anew.
     Sing, cuckoo!

For her calf lows the cow;
   For her lamb bleats the ewe;
The bull rouses, the buck browses,
   Merrily sing, cuckoo!

Cuckoo, cuckoo, O, sing you well, cuckoo;
   Nor let your song be through:
Sing, cuckoo, now, sing cuckoo;
   Sing cuckoo, sing cuckoo, now!

ALISOUN

Bytuene Mershe ant Averil
   When spray biginneth to spring,
The lutel foul hath hire wyl
   On hyre lud to synge:
Ich libbe in love-longinge
For semlokest of alle thynge,
He may me blisse bringe,
   Icham in hire bandoun.
An hendy hap ichabbe y-hent,
Ichot from hevene it is me sent,
From alle wymmen my love is lent
   Ant lyht on Alisoun.

On heu hire her is fayr ynoh,
   Hire browe broune, hire eye blake;
With lossom chere he on me loh;
   With middel smal ant wel y-make;
Bote he me wolle to hire take
For to buen hire owen make,
Long to lyven ichulle forsake
   Ant feye fallen adoun.

An hendy hap ichabbe y-hent,
Ichot from hevene it is me sent,
From alle wymmen my love is lent
　　Ant lyht on Alisoun.

Nihtes when I wende and wake,
　　For-thi myn wonges waxeth won;
Levedi, al for thine sake
　　Longing is y-lent me on.
In world his non so wyter mon
That al hire bounte telle con;
Hire swyre is whittore than the swon,
　　Ant feyrest may in toune.
An hendy hap ichabbe y-hent,
Ichot from hevene it is me sent,
From alle wymmen my love is lent
　　Ant lyht on Alisoun.

　　　　　　　　　　　　　　(c. 1300)

ALISOUN

From middle March to April
　　When the spray begins to spring
The little birds of the air desire
　　In their own tongue to sing.
While I, I live in longing
For the bliss that she may bring,
The loveliest living thing;
　　To serve her is a boon.
A gracious chance for me was meant;
I know from heaven it was sent
That, from all women, my love was lent
　　And left with Alisoun.

Fair is her hair and soft enough:
　　Her eyes are black, her brow is chaste;
Her voice is light and laughs with love;
　　Slight is her figure, small her waist.
Unless she comes or bids me wait
To take her as my own true mate,
I will not live, but, desperate,
　　I'm like to perish soon.

A gracious chance for me was meant;
I know from heaven it was sent
That, from all women, my love was lent
    And left with Alisoun.

All night long I toss and wake;
    For thee alone my cheeks grow wan.
Lady, it is for thy sweet sake
    My longing rages on.
In all the world the wisest man
Cannot describe her bounty's span;
Her neck is whiter than the swan—
    The fairest maid in town.
A gracious chance for me was meant;
I know from heaven it was sent
That, from all women, my love was lent
    And left with Alisoun.

BY-LOW

By-low, my babe, lie still and sleep;
It grieves me sore to see thee weep.
If thou wert quiet I'd be glad;
Thy mourning makes my sorrow sad.
By-low, my boy, thy mother's joy,
Thy father breeds me great annoy—
    By-low, lie low.

When he began to court my love,
And me with sugared words to move,
His feignings false and flattering cheer
To me that time did not appear.
    But now I see most cruelly
He cares not for my babe nor me—
    By-low, lie low.

Lie still, my darling, sleep awhile,
And when thou wak'st thou'lt sweetly smile;
But smile not as thy father did,
To cozen maids—nay, God forbid!
But yet I fear thou wilt grow near
Thy father's heart and face to bear—
    By-low, lie low.

I cannot choose, but ever will
Be loving to thy father still;
Where'er he stay, where'er he ride
My love with him doth still abide.
In weal or woe, where'er he go,
My heart shall not forsake him; so
    By-low, lie low.

              (*c. 1400*)

THE NIGHTINGALE

The little pretty nightingale
  Among the leaves so green
Would I were with her all the night!
  But ye know not whom I mean!

The nightingale sat on a brier
  Among the thorns so keen
And comforted my heart's desire—
  But ye know not whom I mean.

It did me good on her to look;
  She was all clothed in green.
Away from me her heart she took—
  But ye know not whom I mean.

" Lady," I cried with rueful moan,
  " Mind ye how true I have been.
For I loved none but you alone—
  Yet ye know not whom I mean."

              (*c. 1500*)

A CHRISTMAS CAROL

The other night
I saw a light!
  A star as bright as day!
And ever among
A maiden sung:
  " By-by, baby, lullay."

This virgin clear
Who had no peer
  Unto her son did say,

" I pray thee, son,
Grant me a boon
   To sing by-by, lullay.

" Let child or man,
Whoever can
   Be merry on this day,
And blessings bring——
So I shall sing
   ' By-by, baby, lullay.' "

(*c. 1500*)

WHO IS AT MY WINDOW?

Who is at my window? Who? Who?
Go from my window! Go! Go!
Who calls there, like a strangèr,
Go from my window! Go!

—Lord, I am here, a wretched mortàl,
That for thy mercy doth cry and call
Unto thee, my lord celestiàl,
See who is at thy window, who?—

Remember thy sin, remember thy smart,
And also for thee what was my part,
Remember the spear that pierced my heart,
And in at my door thou shalt go.

I ask no thing of thee therefore,
But love for love, to lay in store.
Give me thy heart; I ask no more,
And in at my door thou shalt go.

Who is at my window? Who?
Go from my window! Go!
Cry no more there, like a strangèr,
But in at my door thou go!

(*c. 1500*)

MOTHER AND MAIDEN

I sing of a maiden
   That is matchless.
King of all kings
   For her son she chose.

He came all so still
   Where his mother was,
As dew in April
   That falleth on the grass.

He came all so still
   To his mother's bower,
As dew in April
   That falleth on the flower.

He came all so still—
   There his mother lay,
As dew in April
   That falleth on the spray.

Mother and maiden
   Was never none but she;
Well may such a lady
   God's mother be.

(c. 1500)

MAD SONG

OR, TOM O' BEDLAM'S SONG

From the hag and hungry goblin
That into rags would rend ye,
   All the spirits that stand
   By the naked man
In the book of moons, defend ye,

That of your five sound senses
You never be forsaken,
   Nor wander from
   Yourselves with Tom
Abroad to beg your bacon.

With a thought I took for Maudlin,
And a cruse of cockle pottage,
   With a thing thus tall,
   Sky bless you all,
I befell into this dotage.

I slept not since the Conquest,
Till then I never wakèd,
   Till the roguish boy
   Of love where I lay
Me found and stript me naked.

The moon's my constant mistress,
And the lonely owl my marrow;
   The flaming drake
   And the night-crow make
Me music to my sorrow.

I know more than Apollo,
For oft, where he lies sleeping,
   I see the stars
   At mortal wars
In the wounded welkin weeping,

The moon embrace her shepherd,
And the queen of love her warrior,
   While the first doth horn
   The star of morn,
And the next the heavenly farrier.

With an host of furious fancies,
Whereof I am commander,
   With a burning spear
   And a horse of air
To the wilderness I wander;

By a knight of ghosts and shadows
I summoned am to tourney
   Ten leagues beyond
   The wide world's end—
Methinks it is no journey.

(c. 1500)

DROUTH

O Western wind, when wilt thou blow
    That the small rain down can rain?
Christ, that my love were in my arms,
    And I in my bed again!

(c. 1500)

HEY NONNY NO

Hey nonny no!
Men are fools that wish to die!
Is't not fine to dance and sing
When the bells of death do ring?
Is't not fine to swim in wine,
And turn upon the toe,
And sing hey nonny no!
When the winds blow and the seas flow?
Hey nonny no!

(before 1600)

LOVE NOT ME FOR COMELY GRACE

Love not me for comely grace,
    For my pleasing eye or face,
Nor for any outward part,
No, nor for a constant heart:
    For these may fail or turn to ill,
        So thou and I shall sever:
Keep, therefore, a true woman's eye,
And love me still but know not why—
    So hast thou the same reason still
        To doat upon me ever!

(c. 1600)

BEAUTY'S SELF

My love in her attire doth show her wit,
    It doth so well become her;
For every season she hath dressings fit,
    For winter, spring and summer.

No beauty she doth miss
    When all her robes are on;
But Beauty's self she is
    When all her robes are gone.

(*c. 1600*)

THERE IS A LADY SWEET AND KIND

There is a lady sweet and kind,
Was never face so pleased my mind.
I did but see her passing by,
And yet I love her till I die.

Her gesture, motion, and her smiles,
Her wit, her voice my heart beguiles,
Beguiles my heart, I know not why,
And yet I love her till I die.

Cupid is wingèd and doth range,
Her country so my love doth change;
But change she earth, or change she sky,
Yet will I love her till I die.

(*c. 1600*)

LOVE, TIME AND MEASURE

When love on time and measure makes his ground,
Time that must end, though love can never die,
'Tis love betwixt a shadow and a sound,
A love not in the heart but in the eye,
A love that ebbs and flows, now up, now down,
A morning's favour, and an evening's frown.

Sweet looks show love, yet they are but as beams;
Fair words seem true, yet they are but as wind;
Eyes shed their tears, yet they are but outward streams;
Sighs paint a shadow in the falsest mind:
Looks, words, tears, sighs, show love, when love they leave;
False hearts can weep, sigh, swear, and yet deceive.

(*c. 1600*)

PHILLADA FLOUTS ME

O what a plague is love!
  How shall I bear it?
She will inconstant prove,
  I greatly fear it.
She so torments my mind
  That my strength faileth,
And wavers with the wind
  As a ship saileth.
Please her the best I may,
She loves still to gainsay;
Alack and well-a-day!
  Phillada flouts me.

At the fair yesterday
  She did pass by me;
She looked another way
  And would not spy me:
I wooed her for to dine,
  But could not get her;
Will had her to the wine—
  He might entreat her.
With Daniel she did dance,
On me she looked askance:
O thrice unhappy chance!
  Phillada flouts me.

Fair maid, be not so coy,
  Do not disdain me!
I am my mother's joy:
  Sweet, entertain me!
She'll give me, when she dies,
  All that is fitting:
Her poultry and her bees,
  And her goose sitting,
A pair of mattress beds,
And a bag full of shreds;
And yet, for all these goods,
  Phillada flouts me.

In the last month of May
   I made her posies;
I heard her often say
   That she loved roses.
Cowslips and gillyflowers
   And the white lily
I brought to deck the bowers
   For my sweet Philly.
But she did all disdain,
And threw them back again;
Therefore 'tis flat and plain
   Phillada flouts me.

Fair maiden, have a care,
   And in time take me;
I can have those as fair
   If you forsake me:
For Doll the dairy-maid
   Laughed at me lately,
And wanton Winifred
   Favours me greatly.
One throws milk on my clothes,
T'other plays with my nose;
What wanting signs are those?
   Phillada flouts me.

I cannot work nor sleep
   At all in season:
Love wounds my heart so deep
   Without all reason.
   I fade and pine away
   In my love's shadow,
Like as a fat beast may,
   Penned in a meadow.
I shall be dead, I fear,
Within this thousand year:
And all for that my dear
   Phillada flouts me.

             (*c. 1600*)

THE MIRACLE

Behold a wonder here!
Love hath received his sight!
Which many hundred years
Hath not beheld the light.

Such beams infusèd be
By Cynthia in his eyes,
At first have made him see
And then have made him wise.

Love now no more will weep
For them that laugh the while!
Nor wake for them that sleep,
Nor sigh for them that smile!

So powerful is the Beauty
That Love doth now behold,
As Love is turned to Duty
That's neither blind nor bold.

Thus Beauty shows her might
To be of double kind;
In giving Love his sight
And striking Folly blind.

(*c. 1600*)

SIC TRANSIT . . .

Ay me, ay me, I sigh to see the scythe afield:
Down goeth the grass, soon wrought to withered hay.
Ay me, alas, ay me, alas, that beauty needs must yield,
And princes pass, as grass doth fade away!

Ay me, ay me, that life cannot have lasting leave,
Nor gold take hold of everlasting joy.
Ay me, alas, ay me, alas, that time hath talents to receive,
And yet no time can make a surer stay.

Ay me, ay me, that no sure staff is given to age,
Nor age can give sure wit that youth will take.
Ay me, alas, ay me, alas, that no counsel wise and sage
Will shun the show that all doth mar and make.

Ay me, ay me, come Time, shear on, and shake the hay!
It is no boot to baulk thy bitter blows.
Ay me, alas, ay me, alas, come Time, take everything away!
For all is thine, be it good or bad, that grows.

(c. 1600)

DISPRAISE OF LOVE

If love be life, I long to die,
   Live they that list for me;
And he that gains the most thereby,
   A fool at least shall be;
But he that feels the sorest fits,
'Scapes with no less than loss of wits.
    Unhappy life they gain
    Which love do entertain!

In day by feignèd looks they live,
   By lying dreams in night,
Each frown a deadly wound doth give,
   Each smile a false delight.
If't hap their lady pleasant seem,
It is for other's love they deem;
    If void she seem of joy,
    Disdain doth make her coy.

Such is the peace that lovers find!
   Such is the life they lead!
Blown here and there with every wind,
   Like flowers in the mead.
Now war, now peace, now war again;
Desire, despair, delight, disdain;
    Though dead, in midst of life;
    In peace, and yet in strife!

(c. 1600)

REST, SAD EYES

Weep you no more, sad fountains;
   What need you flow so fast?
Look how the snowy mountains
   Heaven's sun doth gently waste!
But my sun's heavenly eyes,
   View not your weeping,
   That now lies sleeping
Softly, now softly lies
        Sleeping.

Sleep is a reconciling,
   A rest that peace begets;
Doth not the sun rise smiling
   When fair at even he sets?
Rest you then, rest, sad eyes!
   Melt not in weeping,
   While she lies sleeping,
Softly, now softly lies
        Sleeping.

(c. 1600)

VANITY OF VANITIES

Whether men do laugh or weep,
Whether they do wake or sleep,
Whether they die young or old,
Whether they feel heat or cold;
There is underneath the sun
Nothing in true earnest done.

All our pride is but a jest,
None are worst and none are best;
Grief and joy and hope and fear
Play their pageants everywhere:
Vain opinion all doth sway
And the world is but a play.

Powers above in clouds do sit,
Mocking our poor apish wit,
That so lamely with such state
Their high glory imitate.
No ill can be felt but pain,—
And that happy men disdain.

(*c. 1600*)

LOVE AND HOPE

Love winged my Hopes and taught me how to fly
Far from base earth, but not to mount too high:
    For true pleasure
    Lives in measure,
    Which if men forsake,
Blinded they into folly run and grief for pleasure take.

But my vain Hopes, proud of their new-taught flight,
Enamoured sought to woo the sun's fair light,
    Whose rich brightness
    Moved their lightness
    To aspire so high
That all scorched and consumed with fire now drowned in woe
    they lie.

And none but Love their woeful hap did rue,
For Love did know that their desires were true;
    Though Fate frowned,
    And now drowned
    They in sorrow dwell,
It was the purest light of heaven for whose fair love they fell.

(*c. 1600*)

LOVE WILL FIND OUT THE WAY[1]

Over the mountains
    And over the waves;
Under the fountains
    And under the graves;

[1] This song, said Bishop Percy in his *Reliques of Ancient English Poetry*, is ancient. Nevertheless, it bears evidence of having been extensively " rewritten " by the good Bishop himself.

Under floods that are deepest,
  Which Neptune obey;
Over rocks that are steepest,
  Love will find out the way.

Where there is no place
  For the glow-worm to lie;
Where there is no space
  For receipt of a fly;
Where the midge dares not venture,
  Lest herself fast she lay;
If love come, he will enter,
  And soon find out his way.

You may esteem him
  A child for his might;
Or you may deem him
  A coward for his flight:
But if she, whom love doth honour,
  Be concealed from the day,
Set a thousand guards upon her,
  Love will find out the way.

Some think to lose him,
  By having him confined;
And some do suppose him,
  Poor thing, to be blind;
But if ne'er so close ye wall him,
  Do the best that you may,
Blind love, if so ye call him,
  Will find out his way.

You may train the eagle
  To stoop to your fist;
Or you may inveigle
  The phœnix of the east;
The lioness, ye may move her
  To give o'er her prey;
But you'll ne'er stop a lover:
  He will find out his way.

                                    (*c. 1600*)

THE COMING OF THE KING[1]

Yet if His Majesty, our sovereign lord,
Should of his own accord
Friendly himself invite,
And say, " I'll be your guest to-morrow night,"
How should we stir ourselves, call and command
All hands to work! " Let no man idle stand!

" Set me fine Spanish tables in the hall;
See they be fitted all;
Let there be room to eat
And order taken that there want no meat.
See every sconce and candlestick made bright,
That without tapers they may give a light.

" Look to the presence. Are the carpets spread?
The dais o'er the head?
The cushions in the chairs,
And all the candles lighted on the stairs?
Perfume the chambers, and in any case
Let each man give attendance in his place! "

Thus, if a king were coming, would we do;
And 'twere good reason, too.
For 'tis a duteous thing
To show all honour to an earthly king,
And after all our travail and our cost
So he be pleased, to think no labour lost.

But, at the coming of the King of Heaven,
All's set at six and seven;
We wallow in our sin.
Christ cannot find a chamber in the inn.
We entertain Him always like a stranger,
And, as at first, still lodge Him in the manger.

[1] Some scholars believe these eloquent verses to be part of a longer poem and some suspect the author to be Henry Vaughan (see page 233). But, though they bear his inflection and though the Christ Church manuscript (in which they were discovered) contains other stanzas by Vaughan, it is impossible definitely to declare them his.

THE FOURTEENTH TO SIXTEENTH
CENTURIES

CHAUCER TO THE ELIZABETHANS

Although the dates in this collection are as accurate as can be determined, neither the chronological order nor the general divisions are to be taken too dogmatically. Scholars and editors have agreed on certain classifications, but the poets have a way of escaping categories. A dramatist of Queen Elizabeth's day may be more modern than any playwright of our own, while a sonneteer of this age might well be, in all respects but time, an Elizabethan.

Thus, Chaucer, writing more than five hundred years ago, in a dialect which became the national language, escapes the fourteenth century and is exuberantly alive in any era. His rich inclusiveness, his vivid appreciation, his accurately appraising eye and ear, his unflagging gusto, set him apart from his contemporaries even as they distinguish him from his followers, although one catches something of his unbounded vitality in Byron, in Masefield and, recognisable for all the sea-change, in Whitman. It is almost as dangerous to be strictly categorical with such poets as Thomas Wyatt and Philip Sidney, Walter Raleigh and Edmund Spenser. To place one at the beginning of the Elizabethans and the other at the height of the Renaissance merely because a few years separate them is sheer pedantry.

Nor is category by characterisation trustworthy. To say again that Chaucer was " the father of English poetry " or that Wyatt was the first to employ the Italian sonnet in English verse is to stress the wrong thing. It would sometimes be well if the reader could dismiss all previous associations clustering about long-familiar names. Then he would see—and I confess such a recognition is one of the objects of this book—that Wyatt is something more than a craftsman, that Spenser did not design *The Faerie Queene* merely to torture undergraduates, and that Raleigh wrote other (and far greater) verses than the reasonable if unromantic reply to Christopher Marlowe. The very unfamiliarity would, I suspect, lead the reader to explore further among the lyrics of Lodge and Lyly, and the sonnets, as well as the songs, of Sidney, Spenser and Drayton.

The selections from Chaucer are offered in Skeat's edition of the original as well as in modern translations. For the rest, I have used, as in the preceding sections, the spelling of to-day instead of the changing orthography of the fourteenth to the seventeenth centuries. No modern editor adheres to Shakespeare's spelling, and there seems no more reason to preserve Skelton's or Sidney's.

GEOFFREY CHAUCER

1340 (?) - 1400

PROLOGUE

from " The Canterbury Tales "

Whan that Aprille with his shoures sote
The droghte of Marche hath perced to the rote,
And bathed every veyne in switch licour,
Of which vertu engendred is the flour;
Whan Zephirus eek with his swete breeth
Inspired hath in every holt and heeth
The tendre croppes, and the yonge sonne
Hath in the Ram his halfe cours y-ronne,
And smale fowles maken melodye,
That slepen al the night with open yë,
(So priketh hem nature in hir corages):
Than longen folk to goon on pilgrimages
(And palmers for to seken straunge strondes)
To ferne halwes, couthe in sondry londes;
And specially, from every shires ende
Of Engelond, to Caunterbury they wende,
The holy blisful martir for to seke,
That hem hath holpen, whan that they were seke. . . .

FIVE PILGRIMS

from " The Canterbury Tales "

A KNIGHT

A Knight ther was, and that a worthy man
That fro the tyme that he first bigan
To ryden out, he loved chivalrye,
Trouthe and honour, fredom and curteisye.
Ful worthy was he in his lordes werre,
And therto hadde he riden (no man ferre)
As wel in Christendom as hethenesse,
And ever honoured for his worthinesse. . . .

GEOFFREY CHAUCER

1340 (?) - 1400

PROLOGUE

from " The Canterbury Tales "

When the sweet showers of April follow March,
Piercing its drought down to the roots that parch,
Bathing each vein in such a flow of power
That a new strength's engendered in the flower—
When, with a gentle warmth, the west-wind's breath
Awakes in every wood and barren heath
The tender foliage, when the vernal sun
Has half his course within the Ram to run—
When the small birds are making melodies,
Sleeping all night (they say) with open eyes
(For Nature so within their bosom rages)—
Then people long to go on pilgrimages,
And palmers wander to the strangest strands
For famous shrines, however far the lands.
Especially from every shire's end
Of England's length to Canterbury they wend
Seeking the martyr, holiest and blest
Who helped them, healed their ills, and gave them rest. . . .

(Modern version by L. U.)

FIVE PILGRIMS

from " The Canterbury Tales "

A KNIGHT

A Knight there was, and that a worthy man,
Who, from the moment when he first began
To ride forth, loved the code of chivalry:
Honour and truth, freedom and courtesy.
His lord's war had established him in worth;
He rode—and no man further—ends of earth
In heathen parts as well as Christendom,
Honoured wherever he might go or come. . . .

At mortal batailles hadde he been fiftene,
And foughten for our feith at Tramissene
In listes thryes, and ay slayn his fo.
This ilke worthy knight had been also
Somtyme with the lord of Palatye,
Ageyn another hethen in Turkye:
And evermore he hadde a sovereyn prys.
And though that he were worthy, he was wys,
And of his port as meke as is a mayde.
He never yet no vileinye ne sayde
In al his lyf, un-to no maner wight.
He was a verray parfit gentil knight.

A SQUYER

With him ther was his sone, a yong Squyer,
A lovyere, and a lusty bacheler,
With lokkes crulle, as they were leyd in presse.
Of twenty yeer of age he was, I gesse.
Of his stature he was of evene lengthe,
And wonderly deliver, and greet of strengthe.
And he had been somtyme in chivachye,
In Flaundres, in Artoys, and Picardye,
And born him wel, as of so litel space,
In hope to stonden in his lady grace.
Embrouded was he, as it were a mede
Al ful of fresshe floures, whyte and rede.
Singinge he was, or floytinge, all the day;
He was as fresh as is the month of May.
Short was his goune, with sleves longe and wyde.
Well coude he sitte on hors, and faire ryde.
He coude songes make and wel endyte,
Juste and eek daunce, and wel purtreye and wryte.
So hote he lovede, that by nightertale
He sleep namore than dooth a nightingale.
Curteys he was, lowly, and servisable,
And carf biforn his fader at the table.

A MONK

A Monk ther was, a fair for the maistrye,
An out-rydere, that lovede venerye;
A manly man, to been an abbot able.
Ful many a deyntee hors hadde he in stable:
And, whan he rood, men mighte his brydel here
Ginglen in a whistling wind as clere,

Of mortal battles he had seen fifteen,
And fought hard for our faith at Tramassene
Thrice in the lists, and always slain his foe.
This noble knight was even led to go
To Turkey where he fought most valiantly
Against the heathen hordes for Palaty.
Renowned he was; and, worthy, he was wise—
Prudence, with him, was more than mere disguise;
He was as meek in manner as a maid,
Vileness he shunned, rudeness he never said
In all his life, treating all persons right.
He was a truly perfect, noble knight.

A SQUIRE

With him there was his son, a youthful Squire,
A merry blade, a lover full of fire;
With locks as curled as though laid in a press—
Scarce twenty years of age was he, I guess,
In stature he was of an average length,
Wondrously active, bright, and great in strength.
He proved himself a soldier handsomely
In Flanders, in Artois and Picardy,
Bearing himself so well, in so short space,
Hoping to stand high in his lady's grace.
Embroidered was his clothing, like a mead
Full of fresh flowers, shining white and red.
Singing he was, or fluting, all the day—
He was as fresh as is the month of May.
Short was his gown; his sleeves were long and wide;
Well did he sit his horse, and nimbly ride,
He could make songs, intune them or indite,
Joust, play and dance, and also draw and write.
So well could he repeat love's endless tale,
He slept no more than does the nightingale.
Yet he was humble, courteous and able,
And carved before his father when at table.

A MONK

A Monk there was, a monk of mastery;
Hunting he loved—and that exceedingly;
A manly man, to be an abbot able.
Many a worthy horse was in his stable;
And, when he rode, his bridle all might hear
Jing-jingling in a whistling wind as clear

And eek as loude as dooth the chapel-belle
Ther as this lord was keper of the celle.
The reule of seint Maure or of seint Beneit,
By-cause that it was old and som-del streit,
This ilke monk leet olde thinges pace,
And held after the newe world the space.
He yaf nat of that text a pulled hen,
That seith, that hunters been nat holy men;
Ne that a monk, whan he is cloisterlees,
Is lykned til a fish that is waterlees;
This is to seyn, a monk out of his cloistre.
But thilke text held he not worth an oistre;
And I seyde, his opinioun was good.
What sholde he studie, and make himselven wood,
Upon a book in cloistre alwey to poure,
Or swinken with his handes, and laboure? . . .
Therfore he was a pricasour aright;
Grehoundes he hadde, as swifte as fowel in flight;
Of priking and of hunting for the hare
Was al his lust, for no cost wolde he spare.
I seigh his sleves purfiled at the hond
With grys, and that the fyneste of a lond;
And, for to festne his hood under his chin,
He hadde of gold y-wroght a curious pin:
A love-knotte in the gretter end ther was.
His heed was balled, that shoon as any glas,
And eek his face, as he had been anoint.
He was a lord ful fat and in good point;
His eyen stepe, and rollinge in his heed,
That stemmed as a forneys of a leed;
His botes souple, his hors in greet estat.
Now certeinly he was a fair prelat;
He was nat pale as a for-pyned goost.
A fat swan loved he best of any roost.

A PRIORESSE

Ther was also Nonne, a Prioresse,
That of hir smyling was ful simple and coy:
Hir gretteste ooth was but by sëynt Loy;
And she was cleped madame Eglentyne.
Ful wel she song the service divyne,

And lingering-loud as rings the chapel-bell
Where he himself was keeper of the cell.
The rules of Saint Maurice or Benedict,
Because they were both old and somewhat strict,
This monk passed by, let what was outworn go;
New times demand new customs here below.
He scorned that text not worth a poor, plucked hen
Which says that hunters are not holy men;
Or that a monk, of walls and cloister free,
Is like a fish that's out of water. He—
That is to say a monk out of his cloister—
Considered such a text not worth an oyster.
A good opinion, thought I, and it fits.
What! Should he study till he lose his wits
Poring on books he scarcely understands,
Always at work or labouring with his hands? . . .
Therefore he rode and hunted as he might.
Greyhounds he had, swift as a finch in flight;
Rousing the game and hunting for the hare
Was his delight and no cost would he spare.
His sleeves, I saw, were fitted near the hand
With the grey squirrel's fur, best in the land;
And, to attach the hood beneath his chin,
He had, all wrought in gold, a curious pin:
A love-knot at the larger end there was.
His head was bald and shed the sun like glass,
Likewise his face, as though anointed, shone—
A fine, stout monk, if ever there was one.
His glittering eyes that never seemed to tire
But blazed like copper cauldrons in a fire—
His supple boots, his well-appointed horse—
Here was a prelate! fairness linked with force!
He was not pale or hollow, like a ghost;
He loved a fat swan best of any roast.

A PRIORESS

There also was a nun, a Prioress,
Whose smile was simple, quiet, even coy.
The only oath she swore was, " By Saint Loy! "[1]
And she was known as Sister Eglantine.
Sweetly she sang the services divine,

[1] Saint Loy, or Saint Eligius, was not only the most fashionable but the mildest saint of Chaucer's day. Thus the Prioress, when she swore at all, swore in the best and most genteel tradition.

Entuned in hir nose ful semely;
And Frensh she spak ful faire and fetisly,
After the scole of Stratford atte Bowe,
For Frensh of Paris was to hir unknowe.
At mete wel y-taught was she with-alle;
She leet no morsel from hir lippes falle,
Ne wette hir fingres in hir sauce depe.
Wel coude she carie a morsel, and wel kepe,
That no drope ne fille up-on hir brest.
In curteisye was set ful muche hir lest.
Hir over lippe wyped she so clene,
That in hir coppe was no ferthing sene
Of grece, whan she dronken hadde hir draughte.
Ful semely after hir mete she raughte,
And sikerly she was of greet disport,
And ful plesaunt, and amiable of port,
And peyned hir to countrefete chere
Of court, and been estatlich of manere,
And to ben holden digne of reverence.
But, for to speken of hir conscience,
She was so charitable and so pitous,
She wolde wepe, if that she sawe a mous
Caught in a trappe, if it were deed or bledde.
Of smale houndes had she, that she fedde
With rosted flesh, or milk and wastel-breed,
But sore weep she if oon of hem were deed,
Or if men smoot it with a yerde smerte:
And al was conscience and tendre herte.
Ful semely hir wimpel pinched was;
Hir nose tretys; hir eyen greye as glas;
Hir mouth ful smal, and ther-to softe and reed;
But sikerly she hadde a fair forheed;
It was almost a spanne brood, I trowe;
For, hardily, she was nat undergrowe.
Ful fetis was hir cloke, as I was war.
Of smal coral aboute hir arm she bar
A peire of bedes, gauded al with grene;
And ther-on heng a broche of gold ful shene,
On which ther was first writ a crowned A,
And after, *Amor vincit omnia.*

A WYF OF BATHE

A good Wyf was ther of bisyde Bathe,
But she was som-del deef, and that was scathe.

Intoning through her nose the melody.
Fairly she spoke her French, and skilfully,
After the school of Stratford-at-the-Bow——[1]
Parisian French was not for her to know.
Precise at table and well-bred withal
Her lips would never let a morsel fall;
She never wet her fingers in her sauce,
But carried every titbit without loss
Of even the smallest drop upon her breast.
Manners and good behaviour pleased her best.
She always wiped her upper lip so clean
That not a speck of grease was ever seen
Upon the cup from which she drank. Her food
Was reached for neatly; she was never rude.
Though her demeanour was the very best,
Her mood was amiable, she loved a jest,
She always tried to copy each report
Of how the latest fashion ran at court,
And yet to hold herself with dignity.
But, speaking of her inner nature, she
Was so soft-hearted that she could not see
A mouse caught in a trap, if it had bled.
A few small dogs she had, and these she fed
With roasted meat, or milk and sweetened bread,
And she wept loud if one of them were dead,
Or if a person struck and made them smart—
She was all goodness and a tender heart.
Her wimple draped itself a modest way;
Her nose was straight, her eyes transparent grey,
Her mouth was small, but very soft and red,
Hers was a noble and a fair forehead,
Almost a span in breadth, one realised;
For she was small but scarcely undersized.
Her cloak was well designed, I was aware;
Her arm was graced with corals, and she bare
A string in which the green glass beads were bold,
And from it hung a brilliant brooch of gold
On which there was engraved a large, crowned *A*,
Followed by *Amor vincit omnia.*

A WIFE OF BATH

There was a wife from Bath, a well-appearing
Woman who was (alas!) quite hard of hearing.

[1] A convent near London.

Of clooth-making she hadde swiche an haunt,
She passed hem of Ypres and of Gaunt.
In al the parisshe wyf ne was ther noon
That to th' offring bifore hir sholde goon;
And if ther dide, certeyn, so wrooth was she,
That she was out of alle charitee.
Hir coverchiefs ful fyne were of ground;
I dorste swere they weyeden ten pound
That on a Sonday were upon hir heed.
Hir hosen weren of fyn scarlet reed,
Ful streite y-teyd, and shoos ful moiste and newe,
Bolde was hir face, and fair, and reed of hewe.
She was a worthy womman al hir lyve,
Housbondes at chirche-dore she hadde fyve,
Withouten other companye in youthe;
But therof nedeth nat to speke as nouthe.
And thryes hadde she been at Jerusalem;
She hadde passed many a straunge streem;
At Rome she hadde been, and at Boloigne,
In Galice at seint Jame, and at Coloigne.
She coude muche of wandring by the weye:
Gat-tothed was she, soothly for to seye.
Up-on an amblere esily she sat,
Y-wimpled wel, and on hir heed an hat
As brood as is a bokeler or a targe;
A foot-mantel aboute hir hipes large,
And on hir feet a paire of spores sharpe.
In felawschip wel coude she laughe and carpe.
Of remedyes of love she knew perchaunce,
For she coude of that art the olde daunce.

THE FRERES TALE[1]

Whilom ther was dwellinge in my contree
An erchedeken, a man of heigh degree,

[1] " The Friar's Tale " follows that of the Wife of Bath in *The Canterbury Tales*. Just before the Wife tells her story, the Summoner and the Friar have an argument and each threatens to tell a tale or two about the other. The Friar is the first to draw blood.

She had such skill in making cloth that all
The weaver's guilds of Ypres and Ghent looked small.
In all the parish, not a soul dared offer
A thing to her, or, if they did, they'd suffer—
So loud she railed, so full of wrath was she
That she would lose all sense of charity.
The kerchiefs that she used were finely wound—
I'd take an oath they weighed above ten pound—
Which, of a Sunday, were upon her head.
Her stockings were the finest scarlet-red,
Tightly held up; her shoes were soft and new.
Bold was her face, and fair, and red of hue.
She was a worthy woman all her life;
She'd had five church-door husbands as a wife,
And others in her youth whom she'd allow—
But there's no need to mention such things now.
Thrice had she visited Jerusalem
And she had crossed o'er many a foreign stream.
She'd been at Rome, she'd journeyed to Boulogne,
To Saint James' in Galicia, to Cologne.
She'd gathered much from wandering by the way:
She was gap-toothed and loose-tongued, truth to say.
Upon an ambling mare she easily sat,
Her face half-veiled, and on her head a hat
Broad as a buckler, broader than a shield.
A mantle fell about her, but revealed
Large hips and feet equipped with sharpened spurs.
In company the laugh was always hers.
The remedies for love she knew, perchance—
She knew the art of dancing that old dance!

(Modern version by L.U.)

THE FRIAR'S TALE[1]

Once an archdeacon dwelt within my land—
A man of eminence, and hard of hand

[1] Some facts with regard to the office of both the Friar and the Summoner should be noted. Friars, as opposed to monks, did not live a monastic life, but travelled about the land preaching. Chaucer's Friar was a " limitor " or a friar licensed to beg within a limited district. The Summoner, on the other hand, was an official for the ecclesiastical courts, which were then powerful. These courts handled crimes affecting marriage, morality, church practices and obligations. The Summoner was the agent who notified people to appear.

That boldely dide execucioun
In punisshinge of fornicacioun,
Of wicchecraft, and eek of bauderye,
Of diffamacioun, and avoutrye,
Of chirche-reves, and of testaments,
Of contractes, and of lakke of sacraments,
And eek of many another maner cryme
Which nedeth nat rehercen at this tyme;
Of usure, and of symonye also.
But certes, lechours dide he grettest wo;
They sholde singen, if that they were hent;
And smale tytheres weren foule y-shent.
If any persone wolde up-on hem pleyne,
Ther mighte asterte him no pecunial peyne.
For smale tythes and for smal offringe
He made the peple pitously to singe.
For er the bisshop caughte hem with his hook,
They weren in the erchedeknes book.
Thanne hadde he, thurgh his jurisdiccioun,
Power to doon on hem correccioun.
He hadde a Somnour redy to his hond,
A slyer boy was noon in Engelond;
For subtilly he hadde his espiaille,
That taughte him, wher that him mighte availle.
He coude spare of lechours oon or two,
To techen him to foure and twenty mo.
For thogh this Somnour wood were as an hare,
To tell his harlotrye, I wol nat spare;
For we been out of his correccioun;
They han of us no jurisdiccioun,
Ne never shullen, terme of alle hir lyves. . . .
    This false theef, this Somnour, quod the Frere,
Hadde alwey baudes redy to his hond,
As any hauk to lure in Engelond,
That tolde him al the secree that they knewe;
For hir acqueyntance was nat come of-newe.
They weren hise approwours prively;
He took him-self a greet profit therby;
His maister knew nat alwey what he wan.
With-outen mandement, a lewed man
He coude somne, on peyne of Cristes curs,
And they were gladde for to fille his purs,
And make him grete festes atte nale.
And right as Judas hadde purses smale,

In laying punishment on perpetrators
Of witchcraft, and upon all fornicators,
Defamers, and religious officers,
Bawds and their victims, and adulterers,
Breakers of contracts, those who gave offence
Through wills, or through neglect of sacraments,
And so with perpetrators of many a crime
That we can tell about another time.
With usury he dealt, and simony,
But hardest was his hand on lechery:
He gave it to the lechers till they bleated!
And tithe-defaulters, too, were roughly treated.
Just let some parson name them: once directed,
There was no penalty the man neglected.
For petty unpaid tithe or offering
How piteously he made the people sing!
For ere the bishop caught them with his hook,
This bold archdeacon wrote them in his book,
Then he had power, by right of jurisdiction,
To lay a fine for every dereliction.
He had a summoner close at hand and ready—
No boy in England was so sly and heady;
For secretly he spread his band of spies
Who told him all that he could utilize.
Two lechers he could willingly ignore
If they would tell on four-and-twenty more;
For though he was as crazy as a rabbit,
Yet will I tell of every filthy habit
This summoner had: he cannot make conviction
On us,[1] because he hath no jurisdiction
Over our ways, nor shall have his life long! . . .

    This lying thief, this summoner, said the friar,
Always had bawds, obedient one and all
As any hawk is to the hunter's call,
To tell him what they had of secret news.
They were informers he would slyly use—
Their friendship was not something of the minute.
And thus his labour had great profit in it:
His master knew not always of his winning.
For he would call some foolish man for sinning,
Using no writ, and threaten Christ's own curse;
And they were more than glad to fill his purse,
And feast him at the ale-house well and high.
And just as Judas kept upon the sly
       [1] That is, over the friars.

And was a theef, right swich a theef was he;
His maister hadde but half his duëtee.
He was, if I shall yeven him his laude,
A theef, and eek a Somnour, and a baude.
He hadde eek wenches at his retenue,
That, whether that sir Robert or sir Huwe,
Or Jakke, or Rauf, or who-so that it were,
That lay by hem, they tolde it in his ere;
Thus was the wenche and he of oon assent.
And he wolde fecche a feyned mandement,
And somne hem to the chapitre bothe two,
And pile the man, and lete the wenche go.
Thanne wolde he seye, ' frend, I shal for thy sake
Do stryken hir out of our letters blake;
Thee thar na-more as in this cas travaille;
I am thy freend, ther I thee may availle.'
Certeyn he knew of bryberyes mo
Than possible is to telle in yeres two.
For in this world nis dogge for the bowe,
That can an hurt deer from an hool y-knowe,
Bet than this Somnour knew a sly lechour,
Or an avouter, or a paramour.
And, for that was the fruit of al his rente,
Therfore on it he sette al his entente.

    And so bifel, that ones on a day
This Somnour, ever waiting on his pray,
Rood for to somne a widwe, an old ribybe,
Feyninge a cause, for he wolde brybe.
And happed that he saugh bifore him ryde
A gay yeman, under a forest-syde.
A bowe he bar, and arwes brighte and kene;
He hadde up-on a courtepy of grene;
An hat up-on his heed with frenges blake.
    ' Sir,' quod this Somnour, ' hayl! and wel a-take! '
' Wel-come,' quod he, ' and every good felawe!
Wher rydestow under this grene shawe? '
Seyde this yeman, ' wiltow fer to day? '
    This Somnour him answerde, and seyde, ' nay;
Heer faste by,' quod he, ' is myn entente
To ryden, for to reysen up a rente
That longeth to my lordes duëtee.'
    ' Artow thanne a bailly? ' ' Ye! ' quod he.
He dorste nat, for verray filthe and shame,
Seye that he was a somnour, for the name.

A purse, and was a thief—so he was, too:
His master got not more than half his due.
He was, to praise him fitly and applaud,
A thief, a summoner also, and a bawd!
And in his pay he had some wenches too,
That, were the man Sir Robert or Sir Hugh,
Or Jack or Ralph—whoever it chanced to be
That lay with them, they told him secretly:
The wench and he thus had their understanding.
Then would he bring a bogus writ commanding
Both to the chapter-house immediately,
And skin the man and let the girl go free!
Then he would say: " Friend, since I hold thee dear,
In our black books this wench shall not appear:
So in this case thy suffering shall end;
Where I can serve thee I will be thy friend."
More kinds of robbery this summoner knew
Than I could tell you in a year or two;
For in this world was never a bowman's hound
Knew a hurt deer from one without a wound
Better than this summoner could tell for sure
Lecher, adulterer, or paramour.
And since his knowledge sent his income higher
He gave it all his mind and whole desire.
    So it befell that on a certain day,
This summoner, ever eager for his prey,
Rode out to summon a widow, a poor old crone
He hoped to rob, for cause of guilt was none.
And soon beneath the trees he saw before him
A yeoman on a horse, that gaily bore him;
A bow he had, and arrows bright and keen,
And wore a little jacket all of green,
And hat with fringes black upon his head.
    " Hail, sir, and all good health! " this summoner said.
" Welcome," he cried, " and all good fellows like you!
Where through this greenwood riding?   Whither strike
    you? "
This yeoman answered, " Wilt thou far to-day? "
    This summoner replied and told him, " Nay;
Hard by I go," he said, " where I am bent
To see about the payment of some rent—
A part of that belonging to my lord."
    " Art thou a bailiff then? " " Yea," was his word.
He dared not say, for very filth and shame,
He was a summoner—such was the name!

' *Depardieux*,' quod this yeman, 'dere brother,
Thou art a bailly, and I am another.
I am unknowen as in this contree;
Of thyn aqueyntance I wolde praye thee,
And eek of brotherhede, if that yow leste.
I have gold and silver in my cheste;
If that thee happe to comen in our shyre,
Al shal be thyn, right as thou wolt desyre.'
    ' Grantmercy,' quod this Somnour, ' by my feith! '
Everich in otheres hand his trouthe leith,
For to be sworne bretheren til they deye.
In daliance they ryden forth hir weye.
    This Somnour, which that was as ful of jangles,
As ful of venim been thise wariangles,
And ever enquering up-on every thing,
' Brother,' quod he, ' where is now your dwelling,
Another day if that I sholde yow seche?'
    This yeman him answerde in softe speche,
' Brother,' quod he, ' fer in the north contree,
Wher, as I hope, som-tyme I shal thee see.
Er we departe, I shal thee so wel wisse,
That of myn hous ne shaltow never misse.'
    ' Now, brother,' quod this Somnour, ' I yow preye,
Teche me, whyl that we ryden by the weye,
Sin that ye been a baillif as am I,
Som subtiltee, and tel me feithfully
In myn offyce how I may most winne;
And spareth nat for conscience ne sinne,
But as my brother tel me, how do ye? '
    ' Now, by my trouthe, brother dere,' seyde he,
' As I shal tellen thee a feithful tale,
My wages been ful streite and ful smale.
My lord is hard to me and daungerous,
And myn offyce is ful laborous;
And therfore by extorcions I live.
For sothe, I take al that men wol me yive;
Algate, by sleyghte or by violence,
Fro yeer to yeer I winne al my dispence.
I can no bettre telle feithfully.'
    ' Now, certes,' quod this Somnour, ' so fare I;
I spare nat to taken, god it woot,
But-if it be to hevy or to hoot.
What I may gete in conseil prively,
No maner conscience of that have I;

    " By God's grace," said this yeoman, " dear my
      brother,
" As thou art bailiff, so am I another!
I am a stranger here, and I will pray you
To give me your acquaintance—come, what say you?
Also thy brotherhood if thou be willing.
With gold in sovereign and with silver shilling
My chest is filled, and com'st thou to our shire
All shall be thine, just as thou shalt desire! "
    " *Gra'mercy!* by my faith! " this summoner said.
So each his hand within the other's laid,
Sworn to be brothers till they die, and so
In merry talk upon their way they go.
    This summoner, full of gab and curiosity
As are these butcher-birds of animosity,
Asking of one thing now, now of another—
" Where is your dwelling? " said he. " Tell me, brother,
In case some future day I come a-seeking."
    This yeoman made him answer, softly speaking:
"Brother," he said, "far to the north I fare;
I hope that sometime I shall see thee there.
Before we part, thou shalt have preparation
Will never let thee miss my habitation."
    "Now, brother," said this summoner, "I pray
Teach me, as we are riding on our way,
Since ye too be a bailiff, just like me,
Some cleverness, and tell me truthfully
How shall I make the most from what I do?
And let not sin or conscience hinder you,
But as my brother tell me of your practice."
    " Now, dear my brother, by my truth, the fact is,
As I shall tell a story true in all,
My wages are but limited and small.
My lord is haughty and severe with me,
My work demandeth endless industry,
And by extortions therefore must I live.
I take from men all I can make them give—
Whether by tricks or violence, and so
From year to year I manage as I go—
No truer could I tell were Truth my name."
    " For sure! " this summoner cried. " I do the same.
God knows I take it all—no matter what—
Unless it be too heavy or too hot!
What I can get by shift or sly endeavour
It troubles not my conscience whatsoever:

Nere myn extorcioun, I mighte nat liven,
Ne of swiche japes wol I nat be shriven.
Stomak ne conscience ne knowe I noon;
I shrewe thise shrifte-fadres everichoon.
Wel be we met, by god and by seint Jame!
But, leve brother, tel me than thy name,'
Quod this Somnour; and in this mene whyle,
This yeman gan a litel for to smyle.

'Brother,' quod he, ' wiltow that I thee telle?
I am a feend, my dwelling is in helle.
And here I ryde about my purchasing,
To wite wher men wolde yeve me any thing.
My purchas is th'effect of al my rente.
Loke how thou rydest for the same entente,
To winne good, thou rekkest never how;
Right so fare I, for ryde wolde I now
Un-to the worldes ende for a preye.'

'A,' quod this Somnour, ' *ben'cite*, what sey ye?
I wende ye were a yeman trewely.
Ye han a mannes shap as wel as I;
Han ye figure than determinat
In helle, ther ye been in your estat?'

'Nay, certeinly,' quod he, ' ther have we noon;
But whan us lyketh, we can take us oon,
Or elles make yow seme we ben shape
Som-tyme lyk a man, or lyk an ape;
Or lyk an angel can I ryde or go.
It is no wonder thing thogh it be so;
A lousy jogelour can deceyve thee,
And pardee, yet can I more craft than he.'

'Why,' quod the Somnour, ' ryde ye thanne or goon
In sondry shap, and nat alwey in oon?'

'For we,' quod he, ' wol us swich formes make
As most able is our preyes for to take.'

'What maketh yow to han al this labour?'

'Ful many a cause, leve sir Somnour,'
Seyde this feend, ' but alle thing hath tyme.
The day is short, and it is passed pryme,
And yet ne wan I no-thing in this day.
I wol entende to winnen, if I may,
And nat entende our wittes to declare.
For, brother myn, thy wit is al to bare

But for extortion I were not alive.
Such tricks as these are not for priests to shrive.
Of pity or of conscience I have none:
Father-confessors curse I every one!
By God and by St. James, well met we were!
But, dear my brother," said this summoner,
" Tell me thy name, then."
                                    For a little while
This yeoman smiled the shadow of a smile.
" Brother," he said, " and wilt thou what I tell?
I am a fiend: my dwelling is in hell.
And here I go about my trafficking
To see where men will give me anything.
And what I win this way is all I get.
Look how thou ridest for the same end set:
Something to gain—no thought thou hast of how;
Just so with me—I will go riding now
Right to the world's end, hunting for my prey."
    " Ah! " cried this summoner, " What is this ye say!
In truth, ye seemed a yeoman to my eye.
Ye have as good a man's shape as have I.
Have ye some fixed appearance in addition
In hell, where ye may take your true position? "
    " Nay, certainly," he said, " there have we none;
Yet at our pleasure we can take on one.
Or we can make you think we have a shape:
Now sometimes seem a man, sometimes an ape—
Or like an angel I can ride or go.
This is no wonder, though the thing be so;
A lousy juggler plays his tricks on thee,
And I, by God, know much more craft than he."
    " Why," asked this summoner, " do ye ride or run
In various shapes—not always in the one? "
    " Because," he said, " we seek from day to day
The forms that help us most to take our prey."
    " What is the cause for all this work ye do? "
    " More causes, dear sir summoner, than a few."
Answered this fiend. " But all things have their time.
The day is short, and it is more than prime,[1]
Yet there is nothing I have gained this day.
Now I intend to get it if I may,
And of our secrets shall no further speak.
For, brother mine, thy wit is all too weak

----

[1] Nine o'clock in the morning.

To understonde, al-thogh I tolde hem thee.
But, for thou axest why labouren we;
For, som-tyme, we ben goddes instruments,
And menes to don his comandements,
Whan that him list, up-on his creatures,
In divers art and in divers figures.
With-outen him we have no might, certayn,
If that him list to stonden ther-agayn.
And som-tyme, at our prayere, han we leve
Only the body and nat the soule greve;
Witnesse on Job, whom that we diden wo.
And som-tyme han we might of bothe two,
This is to seyn, of soule and body eke.
And som-tyme be we suffred for to seke
Up-on a man, and doon his soule unreste,
And nat his body, and al is for the beste.
Whan he withstandeth our temptacioun,
It is a cause of his savacioun;
Al-be-it that it was nat our entente
He sholde be sauf, but that we wolde him hente.
And som-tyme be we servant un-to man,
As to the erchebisshop Seint Dunstan
And to the apostles servant eek was I.'
    ' Yet tel me,' quod the Somnour, ' feithfully,
Make ye yow newe bodies thus alway
Of elements? ' The feend answerde, ' nay;
Som-tyme we feyne, and som-tyme we aryse
With dede bodies in ful sondry wyse,
And speke as renably and faire and wel
As to the Phitonissa dide Samuel.
And yet wol som men seye it was nat he;
I do no fors of your divinitee.
But o thing warne I thee, I wol nat jape,
Thou wolt algates wite how we ben shape;
Thou shalt her-afterward, my brother dere,
Com ther thee nedeth nat of me to lere.
For thou shalt by thyn owene experience
Conne in a chayer rede of this sentence
Bet than Virgyle, whyl he was on lyve,
Or Dant also; now lat us ryde blyve.
For I wol holde companye with thee
Til it be so, that thou forsake me.'
    ' Nay,' quod this Somnour, ' that shal nat bityde;
I am a yeman, knowen is ful wyde;

To understand, though I explained to thee.
But, since thou askest why our industry—
Sometimes as instruments in God's own hands
We are the means of doing His commands,
When it shall please Him, on His creatures here.
In various ways and figures we appear;
Surely no power were ours unless He chose us,
At least, if it should please Him to oppose us.
Sometimes, at our petition, we have leave
Only the body, and not the soul to grieve—
As witness Job, to whom we brought such woe.
And sometimes we have power upon the two—
That is to say, the body and the spirit.
And sometimes it is suffered us to ferret
And try the soul and give it great unrest,
But not the body—and all is for the best.
For if the man withstandeth our temptation,
This shall become the cause of his salvation
Though it was not our will indeed to save him,
But rather for the pains of hell to have him.
And sometimes we are servants unto men,
For instance, to St. Dunstan. And again
Unto the apostles was I servant, too."
    Then said this summoner, " Yet tell me true—
Devise ye these new shapes in which ye go
Of elements? " The fiend responded: " No;
Sometimes we feign, and sometimes we will raise
The bodies of the dead in various ways
And through them speak as reasonably and well
As to the Pythoness did Samuel.
Yet there are men who say it was not he!
I have no use for your divinity!
Yet I forewarn thee: thou shalt not be fooled;
Thou hast at all cost longing to be schooled
As to our shapes: hereafter shalt thou be
Where thou shalt have no need to learn of me;
Thine own experience shall fit thee there
To lecture on this matter from a chair
Better than Virgil could before he died
Or Dante. But enough—now let us ride!
For I will still hold company with thee
Until the time that thou abandon me."
    " That," said this summoner, " shall be seen by no
        man.
Both far and wide men know me for a yeoman;

My trouthe wol I holde as in this cas.
For though thou were the devel Sathanas,
My trouthe wol I holde to my brother,
As I am sworn, and ech of us til other
For to be trewe brother in this cas;
And bothe we goon abouten our purchas.
Tak thou thy part, what that men wol thee yive,
And I shall myn; thus may we bothe live.
And if that any of us have more than other,
Lat him be trewe, and parte it with his brother.'
    ' I graunte,' quod the devel, ' by my fey.'
And with that word they ryden forth hir wey.
And right at the entring of the tounes ende,
To which this Somnour shoop him for to wende,
They saugh a cart, that charged was with hey,
Which that a carter droof forth in his wey.
Deep was the wey, for which the carte stood.
The carter smoot, and cryde, as he were wood,
' Hayt, Brok! hayt, Scot! what spare ye for the stones?
The feend,' quod he, ' yow fecche body and bones,
As ferforthly as ever were ye foled!
So muche wo as I have with yow tholed!
The devel have al, bothe hors and cart and hey!'
    This Somnour seyde, ' heer shal we have a pley; '
And neer the feend he drough, as noght ne were,
Ful prively, and rouned in his ere:
' Herkne, my brother, herkne, by thy feith;
Herestow nat how that the carter seith?
Hent it anon, for he hath yeve it thee,
Bothe hey and cart, and eek hise caples three.'
    ' Nay,' quod the devel, ' god wot, never a deel;
It is nat his entente, trust me weel.
Axe him thy-self, if thou nat trowest me,
Or elles stint a while, and thou shalt see.'
    This carter thakketh his hors upon the croupe,
And they bigonne drawen and to-stoupe;
' Heyt, now! ' quod he, ' ther Jesu Christ yow blesse,
And al his handwerk, bothe more and lesse!
That was wel twight, myn owene lyard boy!
I pray god save thee and sëynt Loy!
Now is my cart out of the slow, pardee! '
    ' Lo! brother,' quod the feend, ' what tolde I thee?
Heer may ye see, myn owene dere brother,
The carl spak oo thing, but he thoghte another.

And I will keep my faith for good or evil.
For though thou shouldst be Sathanas the devil,
Still will I hold my compact with my brother
As I am sworn, and each of us to other,
To be true brother to thee by my troth.
So go we now to get our profit both.
Take thou thy part, whatever men will give;
I shall take mine: so both of us shall live.
Should either one have more than hath the other,
Let him be true and share it with his brother."

    "Now by my faith," the fiend said, "I agree."
So on their way they rode forth speedily,
And as they reached the edges of the village
Whither this summoner was bent on pillage,
They came upon a cart heaped high with hay,
There where the carter drove it on its way.
The road beneath the cart was deep and bad;
The carter whipped and cried as he was mad:
"Hi! Brook! Hi! Scot! What! Stop ye for the stones?
Now the fiend take you, body, blood and bones
As clean as ever I helped to rid the mare of you!
God knows the way I suffer from the pair of you!
The devil take all now, horse, cart and hay!"

    This summoner said, "Now shall we have some play!"
And all as not a thought were going through him,
He edged towards the fiend and whispered to him:
"Listen, my brother; listen upon my faith!
Dost thou not hear this thing the carter saith?
Seize it at once, for he hath given it thee—
The hay and cart and horses—all the three."

    "Nay," said the devil, "God knows—never a jot!
The fellow says it, but he means it not.
Ask him thyself if thou hast doubt of me,
Or wait a little while and thou shalt see."

    The carter pats his horses till again
They stoop with sudden strength, and tug and strain.
"Hi there!" cries he, "Christ bless you now, and all
The creatures he hath made, both great and small!
That was well-pulled and true, mine own grey boy!
I pray God that He save you, and Saint Loy!
By God, my cart is safely through the slough!"

    "What said I, brother—was my word not true?"
Questioned the fiend. "Here may ye see, dear brother,
The fellow said one thing but thought another.

Lat us go forth abouten our viage;
Heer winne I no-thing up-on cariage.'
   Whan that they comen som-what out of toune,
This Somnour to his brother gan to roune,
' Brother,' quod he, 'heer woneth an old rebekke,
That hadde almost as lief to lese hir nekke
As for to yeve a peny of hir good.
I wol han twelf pens, though that she be wood,
Or I wol sompne hir un-to our offyce;
And yet, god woot, of hir knowe I no vyce.
But for thou canst nat, as in this contree,
Winne thy cost, tak heer ensample of me.'
   This Somnour clappeth at the widwes gate.
' Com out,' quod he, ' thou olde viritrate!
I trowe thou hast some frere or preest with thee! '
   ' Who clappeth? ' seyde this widwe, ' *ben'cite*!
God save you, sire, what is your swete wille? '
   ' I have,' quod he, ' of somonce here a bille;
Up peyne of cursing, loke that thou be
To-morn bifore the erchedeknes knee
T'answere to the court of certeyn thinges.'
   ' Now, lord,' quod she, ' Crist Jesu, king of kinges,
So wisly helpe me, as I ne may.
I have been syk, and that ful many a day.
I may nat go so fer,' quod she, ' ne ryde,
But I be deed, so priketh it in my syde.
May I nat axe a libel, sir Somnour,
And answere there, by my procutour,
To swich thing as men wol opposen me? '
   ' Yis,' quod this Somnour, ' pay anon, lat se,
Twelf pens to me, and I wol thee acquyte.
I shall no profit han ther-by but lyte;
My maister hath the profit, and nat I.
Com of, and lat me ryden hastily;
Yif me twelf pens, I may no lenger tarie.'
   ' Twelf pens,' quod she, ' now lady Seinte Marie
So wisly help me out of care and sinne,
This wyde world thogh that I shoulde winne,
Ne have I nat twelf pens with-inne myn hold.
Ye knowen wel that I am povre and old;
Kythe your almesse on me povre wrecche.'
   ' Nay than,' quod he, ' the foule feend me fecche
If I th'excuse, though thou shul be spilt!'
   'Alas' quod she, 'god woot, I have no gilt.'

Let us along and make no more delay;
Here win I nothing I can cart away."
When they were somewhat out of town again,
This summoner to his brother whispered then:
"Here, brother," said he, " doth an old hag live
Would almost lose her neck ere she would give
A penny from her store. Yet will I sever
Full twelve pence from her, be she mad as never,
Or I will summon her to our chapter hall;
And yet I know no fault in her at all.
But since in these parts it is hard for thee
To make thy living, take a look at me!"

This summoner knocketh at the widow's gate.
"Come out," he cried, " Come out, thou old grey-pate;
Art thou within there with some priest or friar?"
"Who knocks?" this widow cried. " God save you, sire!
Benedicite! Sir, what is your sweet will?"
"I have," said he, " of summons here a bill;
On penalty of curse, look that thou be
To-morrow morn at the archdeacon's knee
To answer to the court for certain things."
"Now, lord," said she, " Christ Jesu, King of Kings,
Give me His help who have no other way.
I have been sick, and that for many a day.
I cannot go so far," she said, " nor ride,
But I shall die, such pain is in my side.
May I not have a brief, sir summoner,
And by my proctor make my answer there
Unto such things as men may say of me?"
He said, " Yes. Pay at once—um—let me see—
Twelve pence to me—and thou shalt have acquittal.
My profit in the matter will be little;
My master gets it—nothing comes to me.
Pay up, and let me ride off speedily;
Give me twelve pence: I cannot longer tarry."
"Twelve pence!" she cried. " Now as our holy Mary
May help me out of sorrow and of sin,
Though all this wide world I should thereby win,
I could not find twelve pence inside my door!
Ye know it well that I am old and poor—
Then show to me, poor wretch, your charity!"
"Nay, may the foul fiend fetch me," answered he,
"If I excuse thee, though thou fall down dead."
"Alas! God knows I have no guilt," she said.

'Pay me,' quod he, 'or by the swete seinte Anne,
As I wol bere awey thy newe panne
For dette, which that thou owest me of old,
Whan that thou madest thyn housbond cokewold,
I payde at hoom for thy correccioun.'

'Thou lixt,' quod she, 'by my savacioun!
Ne was I never er now, widwe ne wyf,
Somoned un-to your court in al my lyf;
Ne never I nas but of my body trewe!
Un-to the devel blak and rough of hewe
Yeve I thy body and my panne also!'

And whan the devel herde hir cursen so
Up-on hir knees, he seyde in this manere,
'Now Mabely, myn owene moder dere,
Is this your wil in ernest, that ye seye?'

'The devel,' quod she, 'so fecche him er he deye,
And panne and al, but he wol him repente!'

'Nay, olde stot, that is nat myn entente,'
Quod this Somnour, 'for to repente me,
For any thing that I have had of thee;
I wolde I hadde thy smok and every clooth!'

'Now, brother,' quod the devel, 'be nat wrooth;
Thy body and this panne ben myne by right.
Thou shalt with me to helle yet to-night,
Where thou shalt knowen of our privetee
More than a maister of divinitee;'
And with that word this foule feend him hente;
Body and soule, he with the devel wente
Wher-as that somnours han hir heritage.
And god, that maked after his image
Mankinde, save and gyde us alle and some;
And leve this Somnour good man to bicome!

" Pay me," cried he, " or by the sweet St. Anne,
I shall bear off with me thy newest pan
For debt, which thou hast owed me since the time
Thou mad'st thy husband cuckold—for that crime
I paid thy fine and saved thy reputation."
   " Thou liest," she said, " as I shall win salvation!
Never was I, as widow or as wife,
Summoned unto your court in all my life
Till now, nor with my body was untrue.
Unto the devil, shaggy and black of hue,
May both my pan and thy vile body go! "
   And when the fiend heard how she cursed him so
Upon her knees, as hard as she was able,
He said to her: " Mine own dear mother Mabel,
Is this your will in earnest, what ye cry? "
   " The devil," said she, " fetch him before he die
And pan and all, unless he shall repent! "
   " Nay then, old mare, that is not mine intent,"
This summoner said, " to rue the least success
I win with thee. I would I had thy dress
And every rag thou hast—yea, the last shred."
   " Now, brother, be not wroth," the devil said.
" Thy body and this pan are mine by right;
Thou go'st along to hell with me to-night,
Where thou shalt know of our deep privacy
More than a master of divinity! "
And with that word the foul fiend gripped him strong;
Body and soul. So went this wretch along
To where indeed all summoners may find
Their heritage. And God, who made mankind
In his own image, save us, as he can,
And let this summoner change to a good man!
                              (*Translated by Frank Ernest Hill*)

BALADE OF BON COUNSEILL

Flee fro the prees, and dwelle with sothfastnesse,
Suffyce unto thy good, though hit be smal;
For hord hath hate, and climbing tikelnesse,
Prees hath envye, and wele blent overal;
Savour no more than thee bihove shal;
Werk wel thy-self, that other folk canst rede;
And trouthe shal delivere, hit is no drede.

Tempest thee noght al croked to redresse,
In trust of hir that turneth as a bal:
Gret reste stant in litel besinesse;
And eek be war to sporne ageyn an al;
Stryve noght, as doth the crokke with the wal.
Daunte thy-self, that dauntest otheres dede;
And trouthe shal delivere, hit is no drede.

That thee is sent, receyve in buxumnesse,
The wrastling for this worlde axeth a fal.
Her nis non hoom, her nis but wildernesse:
Forth, pilgrim, forth! Forth, beste, out of thy stal!
Know thy contree, look up, thank God of al;
Hold the hye wey, and lat thy gost thee lede:
And trouthe shal delivere, hit is no drede.

ENVOY

Therfore, thou vache, leve thyn old wrecchednesse
Unto the worlde; leve now to be thral;
Crye him mercy that of his hy goodnesse
Made thee of noght, and in especial
Draw unto him, and pray in general
For thee, and eek for other, hevenlich mede
And trouthe shal delivere, hit is no drede.

BALLADE OF GOOD COUNSEL

Flee from the crowd and dwell with truthfulness:
　　Suffice thee with thy goods, tho' they be small:
To hoard brings hate, to climb brings giddiness;
　　The crowd has envy, and success blinds all;
　　Desire no more than to thy lot may fall;
Work well thyself to counsel others clear,
And Truth shall make thee free, there is no fear!

Torment thee not all crooked to redress,
　　Nor put thy trust in fortune's turning ball;
Great peace is found in little busy-ness
　　And war but kicks against a sharpened awl;
　　Strive not, thou earthen pot, to break the wall;
Subdue thyself, and others thee shall hear;
And Truth shall make thee free, there is no fear!

What God doth send, receive in gladsomeness;
　　To wrestle for this world foretells a fall.
Here is no home, here is but wilderness:
　　Forth, pilgrim, forth; up, beast, and leave thy stall!
　　Know thy country, look up, thank God for all:
Hold the high way, thy soul the pioneer,
And Truth shall make thee free, there is no fear!

ENVOY

Therefore, poor beast, forsake thy wretchedness;
　　No longer let the vain world be thy stall.
His mercy seek who in his mightiness
　　Made thee of naught, but not to be a thrall.
　　Pray freely for thyself and pray for all
Who long for larger life and heavenly cheer;
And Truth shall make thee free, there is no fear!

　　　　　　　　　　　(*Modern version by Henry Van Dyke*)

JOHN SKELTON

1460 (?) - 1529

THE PRELATES

from " Colin Clout "

My name is Colin Clout.
I purpose to shake out
All my cunning bag
Like a clerkly hag;
For, though my rhyme be ragged,
Tattered and jagged,
Rudely rain-beaten,
Rusty and moth-eaten,
If ye take well therewith
It hath in it some pith.
For, as far as I can see,
It is wrong with each degree,
The temporal
Accuseth the spiritual;
The spiritual again
Doth grudge and complain
Upon the temporal men.
Thus each raiseth a pother,
One against the other.
Alas, they make me shudder!
For (do not say it loud!)
The prelates are so proud,
They say, and look so high
As though they would fly
Above the starry sky.
Laymen say indeed
How they take no heed
Their silly sheep to feed,
But pluck away and pull
The fleeces of their wool;
Scarcely they leave a lock
Of wool among their flock.
And as for their cunning,
A-humming and mumming,
They make of it a jape.

They gasp and they gape
All to have promotion—
That is their whole devotion!

STEPHEN HAWES

(?) - 1523 (?)

EPITAPH

O mortal folk, you may behold and see
How I lie here, sometime a mighty knight.
The end of joy and all prosperity
Is death at last—thorough his course and might
After the day there cometh the dark night:
For though the day be never so long,
At last the bell ringeth to evensong.

HENRY VIII

1491 - 1547

GOOD COMPANY

Pastime with good company
I love, and shall until I die.
Grouch who list, but none deny,
So God be pleased, thus live will I.
For my pastànce,[1]
Hunt, sing, and dance,
My heart is set;
All goodly sport
For my comfòrt,
Who shall me let?

Youth must have some dalliance,
Of good or ill some pastànce;
Company, methinks, then best
All thoughts and fancies to digest.
For idleness is chief mistress
Of vices all; then who can say
But mirth and play
Is best of all?

[1] Pastime.

Company with honesty
Is virtue, vice to flee;
Company is good and ill,
But every man hath his free will.
The best ensue,
The worst eschew;
My mind shall be,—
Virtue to use,
Vice to refuse,
Thus shall I use me.

THOMAS WYATT

1503 - 1542

DESCRIPTION OF THE CONTRARIOUS PASSIONS IN A LOVER

I find no peace, and all my war is done;
I fear and hope, I burn and freeze like ice;
I fly aloft yet can I not arise;
And nought I have, and all the world I seize on,
That locks nor loseth, holdeth me in prison,
And holds me not, yet can I scape no wise:
Nor letteth me live, nor die at my devise,
And yet of death it giveth me occasion.
Without eye I see; without tongue I plain:
I wish to perish yet I ask for health;
I love another, and I hate myself;
I feed me in sorrow, and laugh in all my pain.
    Lo, thus displeaseth me both death and life;
    And my delight is causer of this strife.

THE LOVER SHOWETH HOW HE IS FORSAKEN OF SUCH AS HE SOMETIME ENJOYED

They flee from me, that sometime did me seek,
With naked foot stalking within my chamber;
Once have I seen them gentle, tame, and meek,
That now are wild, and do not once remember,
That sometime they have put themselves in danger
To take bread at my hand; and now they range
Busily seeking in continual change.

Thanks be to Fortune, it hath been otherwise
Twenty times better; but once especial,
In thin array, after a pleasant guise,
When her loose gown did from her shoulders fall,
And she me caught in her arms long and small,
And therewithal so sweetly did me kiss,
And softly said, " Dear heart, how like you this? "

It was no dream; for I lay broad awaking:
But all is turned now through my gentleness
Into a bitter fashion of forsaking,
And I have leave to go of her goodness,
And she also to use new-fangledness.
But since that I unkindly so am served:
" How like you this," what hath she now deserved?

THE LOVER REJOICETH THAT HE HATH BROKEN THE SNARES OF LOVE

Tangled was I in Love's snare,
Oppressed with pain, torment with care;
Of grief right sure, of joy quite bare,
Clean in despair by cruelty.
But ha! ha! ha! full well is me,
For I am now at liberty.

The woeful days so full of pain,
The weary nights all spent in vain,
The labour lost for so small gain,
To write them all it will not be.
But ha! ha! ha! full well is me,
For I am now at liberty.

With feignèd words which were but wind
To long delays was I assigned;
Her wily looks my wits did blind;
Whate'er she would I would agree.
But ha! ha! ha! full well is me,
For I am now at liberty.

Was never bird tangled in lime
That broke away in better time,
Than I, that rotten boughs did climb

And had no hurt but 'scapèd free.
Now ha! ha! ha! full well is me,
For I am now at liberty.

HENRY HOWARD

Earl of Surrey

1518 - 1547

VOW TO LOVE FAITHFULLY

Set me whereas the sun doth parch the green,
Or where his beams do not dissolve the ice,
In temperate heat where he is felt and seen;
In presence 'prest of people, mad or wise;
Set me in high or yet in low degree,
In longest night or in the shortest day,
In clearest sky or where clouds thickest be,
In lusty youth or when my hairs are grey.
Set me in heaven, in earth, or else in hell;
In hill, or dale, or in the foaming flood;
Thrall or at large, alive, whereso I dwell,
Sick or in health, in evil fame or good;
Hers will I be, and only with this thought
Content myself although my chance be nought.

FRAIL BEAUTY

Brittle beauty that nature made so frail,
Whereof the gift is small, and short the season,
Flow'ring to-day, to-morrow apt to fail,
Tickle treasure, abhorrèd of reason,
Dangerous to deal with, vain, of none avail,
Costly in keeping, passed not worth two peason,[1]
Slippery in sliding as an eelès tail,
Hard to attain, once gotten not geason,[2]
Jewel of jeopardy that peril doth assail,
False and untrue, enticèd oft to treason,
Enemy to youth (that most may I bewail!),
Ah, bitter sweet! infecting as the poison,
Thou farest as fruit that with the frost is taken:
To-day ready ripe, to-morrow all too shaken.

[1] Not worth two peas.   [2] No longer wonderful.

NICHOLAS BRETON

1548 (?) - 1626 (?)

A PASTORAL

On a hill there grows a flower,
  Fair befall the dainty sweet!
By that flower there is a bower
  Where the heavenly Muses meet.

In that bower there is a chair
  Fringèd all about with gold,
Where doth sit the fairest fair
  That did ever eye behold.

It is Phillis fair and bright,
  She that is the shepherds' joy,
She that Venus did despite
  And did blind her little boy.

This is she, the wise, the rich,
  All the world desires to see;
This is *ipsa quae* the which
  There is none but only she.

Who would not this face admire?
  Who would not this saint adore?
Who would not this sight desire,
  Though he thought to see no more?

O fair eyes, yet let me see!
  One good look, and I am gone,
Look on me, for I am he—
  Thy poor silly Coridon.

Thou that art the shepherds' queen,
  Look upon thy silly swain;
By thy comfort have been seen
  Dead men brought to life again.

PHILLIDA AND CORIDON

In the merry month of May,
In a morn by break of day
Forth I walked by the wood-side,
When as May was in his pride.
There I spièd, all alone,
Phillida and Coridon.
Much ado there was, God wot,
He would love and she would not.
She said, " Never man was true."
He said, " None was false to you."
He said he had loved her long.
She said, " Love should have no wrong."
Coridon would kiss her then.
She said maids must kiss no men
Till they did for good and all.
Then she made the shepherd call
All the heavens to witness truth,
Never loved a truer youth.
Thus, with many a pretty oath,
Yea and nay, and faith and troth,
Such as silly shepherds use
When they will not love abuse,
Love which had been long deluded
Was with kisses sweet concluded.
And Phillida with garlands gay
Was made the lady of the May.

WALTER RALEIGH

1552 (?) - 1618

THE WOOD, THE WEED, THE WAG

TO HIS SON

Three things there be that prosper all apace
And flourish while they grow asunder far;
But on a day, they meet all in a place,
And when they meet, they one another mar.

And they be these: the wood, the weed, the wag.
The wood is that which makes the gallows tree;
The weed is that which strings the hangman's bag;
The wag, my pretty knave, betokens thee.

Now mark, dear boy, while these assemble not,
Green springs the tree, hemp grows, the wag is wild;
But when they meet, it makes the timber rot,
It frets the halter, and it chokes the child.

Then bless thee, and beware, and let us pray
We part not with thee at this meeting day.

HIS EPITAPH

Even such is Time, which takes in trust
Our youth, our joys, and all we have,
And pays us but with age and dust,
Who, in the dark and silent grave,
When we have wandered all our ways,
Shuts up the story of our days.
   Yet from this earth, and grave, and dust,
   The Lord shall raise me up I trust.

THE PASSIONATE MAN'S PILGRIMAGE

SUPPOSED TO BE WRITTEN BY ONE AT THE POINT
OF DEATH

Give me my scallop-shell of quiet,
My staff of faith to walk upon,
My scrip of joy, immortal diet,
My bottle of salvatiòn,
My gown of glory, hope's true gage,
And thus I'll take my pilgrimage.

Blood must be my body's balmer,
No other balm will there be given,
Whilst my soul, like a white palmer,
Travels to the land of heaven,
Over the silver mountains,
Where spring the nectar fountains;

And there I'll kiss
The bowl of bliss,
And drink my eternal fill
On every milken hill.
My soul will be a-dry before,
But, after, it will ne'er thirst more.

And by the happy blissful way
More peaceful pilgrims I shall see,
That have shook off their gowns of clay
And go apparelled fresh like me.
I'll bring them first
To slake their thirst,
And then to taste those nectar suckets,
At the clear wells
Where sweetness dwells,
Drawn up by saints in crystal buckets.

And when our bottles and all we
Are filled with immortality,
Then the holy paths we'll travel,
Strewed with rubies thick as gravel,
Ceilings of diamonds, sapphire floors,
High walls of coral, and pearl bowers.
From thence to heaven's bribeless hall
Where no corrupted voices brawl,
No conscience molten into gold,
Nor forged accusers bought and sold,
No cause deferred, nor vain-spent journey,
For there Christ is the king's attorney,
Who pleads for all without degrees,
And he hath angels, but no fees.

When the grand twelve million jury
Of our sins and sinful fury,
'Gainst our souls black verdicts give,
Christ pleads his death, and then we live.
Be thou my speaker, taintless pleader,
Unblotted lawyer, true proceeder,
Thou movest salvation even for alms,
Not with a bribèd lawyer's palms.

And this is my eternal plea
To him that made heaven, earth, and sea,
Seeing my flesh must die so soon,
And want a head to dine next noon,
Just at the stroke when my veins start and spread,
Set on my soul an everlasting head.
Then am I ready, like a palmer fit,
To tread those blest paths which before I writ.

THE NYMPH'S REPLY TO THE SHEPHERD[1]

If all the world and love were young,
And truth in every shepherd's tongue,
These pretty pleasures might me move,
To live with thee and be thy love.

Time drives the flocks from field to fold,
When rivers rage, and rocks grow cold;
And Philomel becometh dumb;
The rest complains of cares to come.

The flowers do fade, and wanton fields
To wayward winter reckoning yields;
A honey tongue, a heart of gall,
Is fancy's spring, but sorrow's fall.

Thy gowns, thy shoes, thy beds of roses,
Thy cap, thy kirtle, and thy posies,
Soon break, soon wither, soon forgotten;
In folly ripe, in reason rotten.

Thy belt of straw and ivy buds,
Thy coral clasps and amber studs,
All these in me no means can move,
To come to thee and be thy love.

But could youth last, and love still breed,
Had joys no date, nor age no need,
Then these delights my mind might move
To live with thee and be thy love.

[1] A reply to Marlow's poem on page 148.

THE LIE

Go, soul, the body's guest,
    Upon a thankless arrant.[1]
Fear not to touch the best;
    The truth shall be thy warrant.
    Go, since I needs must die,
    And give the world the lie.

Say to the court, it glows
    And shines like rotten wood;
Say to the church, it shows
    What's good, and doth no good.
    If church and court reply,
    Then give them both the lie.

Tell potentates, they live
    Acting by others' action,
Not loved unless they give,
    Not strong but by affection.
    If potentates reply,
    Give potentates the lie.

Tell men of high condition
    That manage the estate,
Their purpose is ambition,
    Their practice only hate;
    And if they once reply,
    Then give them all the lie.

Tell them that brave it most,
    They beg for more by spending,
Who, in their greatest cost,
    Like nothing but commending;
    And if they make reply,
    Then give them all the lie

Tell zeal it wants devotion;
    Tell love it is but lust;
Tell time it meets but motion;
    Tell flesh it is but dust;
            [1] Errand or mission.

And wish them not reply,
For thou must give the lie.

Tell age it daily wasteth;
  Tell honour how it alters;
Tell beauty how she blasteth;
  Tell favour how it falters;
  And as they shall reply,
  Give every one the lie.

Tell wit how much it wrangles
  In tickle-points of niceness;
Tell wisdom she entangles
  Herself in over-wiseness;
  And when they do reply,
  Straight give them both the lie.

Tell physic of her boldness;
  Tell skill it is prevention;
Tell charity of coldness;
  Tell law it is contention;
  And as they do reply,
  So give them still the lie.

Tell fortune of her blindness;
  Tell nature of decay;
Tell friendship of unkindness;
  Tell justice of delay;
  And if they will reply,
  Then give them all the lie.

Tell arts they have no soundness,
  But vary by esteeming;
Tell schools they want profoundness,
  And stand too much on seeming;
  If arts and schools reply,
  Give arts and schools the lie.

Tell faith it's fled the city;
  Tell how the country erreth;
Tell manhood shakes off pity,
  Tell virtue least preferrèd;
  And if they do reply,
  Spare not to give the lie.

So when thou hast, as I
   Commanded thee, done blabbing;
Because to give the lie
   Deserves no less than stabbing.
   Stab at thee he that will—
   No stab thy soul can kill.

EDMUND SPENSER

1552 (?) - 1599

SONNETS FROM " AMORETTI "

HIS LOVE'S RICHES

Ye tradeful Merchants, that, with weary toil,
Do seek most precious things to make your gain,
And both the Indias of their treasure spoil,
What needeth you to seek so far in vain?
For lo! my Love doth in herself contain
All this world's riches that may far be found:
If sapphires, lo! her eyes be sapphires plain;
If rubies, lo! her lips be rubies sound;
If pearls, her teeth be pearls, both pure and round;
If ivory, her forehead ivory ween;
If gold, her locks are finest gold on ground;
If silver, her fair hands are silver sheen:
   But that which fairest is but few behold:
   Her mind, adorned with virtues manifold.

ICE AND FIRE

My Love is like to ice, and I to fire:
How comes it then that this her cold so great
Is not dissolved through my so hot desire,
But harder grows the more I her entreat?
Or how comes it that my exceeding heat
Is not allayed by her heart-frozen cold,
But that I burn much more in boiling sweat,
And feel my flames augmented manifold?
What more miraculous thing may be told,
That fire, which all things melts, should harden ice,
And ice, which is congealed with senseless cold,
Should kindle fire by wonderful device?
   Such is the power of love in gentle mind,
   That it can alter all the course of kind.

ANOTHER ELEMENT

So oft as I her beauty do behold,
And therewith do her cruelty compare,
I marvel of what substance was the mould
The which her made at once so cruel fair.
Not earth; for her high thoughts more heavenly are:
Not water; for her love doth burn like fire:
Not air; for she is not so light or rare:
Not fire; for she doth freeze with faint desire.
Then needs another element enquire
Whereof she might be made; that is, the sky.
For to the heaven her haughty looks aspire,
And eke her love is pure immortal high.
    Then since to heaven ye likened are the best,
    Be like in mercy as in all the rest.

THE GOLDEN HOOK

Trust not the treason of those smiling looks,
Until ye have their guileful trains well tried!
For they are like but unto golden hooks,
That from the foolish fish their baits do hide:
So she with flatt'ring smiles weak hearts doth guide
Unto her love, and tempt to their decay;
Whom, being caught, she kills with cruel pride,
And feeds at pleasure on the wretched prey.
Yet even whilst her bloody hands them slay,
Her eyes look lovely, and upon them smile,
That they take pleasure in their cruel play,
And, dying, do themselves of pain beguile.
    O mighty charm! which makes men love their bane,
    And think they die with pleasure, live with pain.

THE TAMED DEER

Like as a huntsman after weary chase,
Seeing the game from him escaped away,
Sits down to rest him in some shady place,
With panting hounds, beguilèd of their prey:
So, after long pursuit and vain assay,
When I all weary had the chase forsook,
The gentle deer returned the self-same way,
Thinking to quench her thirst at the next brook.

There she, beholding me with milder look,
Sought not to fly, but fearless still did bide,
Till I in hand her yet half trembling took,
And with her own good-will her firmly tied.
　　Strange thing, me seemed, to see a beast so wild
　　So goodly won, with her own will beguiled.

YOUR POWER

More than most fair, full of the living fire
Kindled above unto the Maker near:
No eyes, but joys, in which all powers conspire,
That to the world naught else be counted dear:
Through your bright beams doth not the blinded guest
Shoot out his darts to base affection's wound;
But angels come, to lead frail minds to rest.
In chaste desires, on heavenly beauty bound.
You frame my thoughts, and fashion me within,
You stop my tongue, and teach my heart to speak,
You calm the storm that passion did begin,
Strong through your cause, but by your virtue weak.
　　Dark is the world where your light shinèd never;
　　Well is he born that may behold you ever.

SO LET US LOVE

Most glorious Lord of life! that on this day
Didst make thy triumph over death and sin,
And, having harrowed hell, didst bring away
Captivity thence captive, us to win:
This joyous day, dear Lord, with joy begin;
And grant that we, for whom thou diddest die,
Being, with thy dear blood, clean washed from sin,
May live for ever in felicity;
And that thy love we weighing worthily,
May likewise love thee for the same again;
And for thy sake, that all like dear didst buy,
With love may one another entertain.
　　So let us love, dear Love, like as we ought:
　　Love is the lesson which the Lord us taught.

JOHN LYLY

1553 (?) - 1606

CUPID AND CAMPASPE

Cupid and my Campaspe played
At cards for kisses; Cupid paid;
He stakes his quiver, bow and arrows,
His mother's doves, and team of sparrows;
Loses them too; then down he throws
The coral of his lip, the rose
Growing on's cheek (but none knows how);
With these, the crystal of his brow,
And then the dimple of his chin.
All these did my Campaspe win.
At last he set her both his eyes.
She won, and Cupid blind did rise.
    O Love! has she done this to thee?
    What shall, alas! become of me?

LOVE'S SCHOOLING

O Cupid! monarch over kings,
Wherefore hast thou feet and wings?
It is to show how swift thou art,
When thou woundest a tender heart!
Thy wings being clipped, and feet held still,
Thy bow so many could not kill.

It is all one in Venus' wanton school,
Who highest sits, the wise man or the fool.
    Fools in love's college
    Have far more knowledge
    To read a woman over,
    Than a neat prating lover:
    Nay, 'tis confessed
    That fools please women best.

PHILIP SIDNEY

1554 - 1586

MY TRUE-LOVE HATH MY HEART

My true-love hath my heart, and I have his,
By just exchange one for another given:
I hold his dear, and mine he cannot miss,
There never was a better bargain driven:
   My true-love hath my heart, and I have his.

His heart in me keeps him and me in one,
My heart in him his thoughts and senses guides:
He loves my heart, for once it was his own,
I cherish his because in me it bides:
   My true-love hath my heart, and I have his.

SONNETS FROM "ASTROPHEL AND STELLA"

"WITH HOW SAD STEPS, O MOON"

With how sad steps, O moon, thou climb'st the skies;
How silently and with how wan a face.
What! May it be that even in heav'nly place
That busy archer his sharp arrows tries?
Sure, if that long-with-love-acquainted eyes
Can judge of love, thou feel'st a lover's case;
I read it in thy looks, thy languished grace,
To me, that feel the like, thy state decries.

Then even of fellowship, O moon, tell me:
Is constant love deemed there but want of wit?
Are beauties there as proud as here they be?
Do they above love to be loved, and yet
Those lovers scorn whom that love doth possess?
Do they call virtue there ungratefulness?

MAGPIES AND SWANS

Because I breathe not love to every one,
Nor do not use set colours for to wear,
Nor nourish special locks of vowèd hair,

Nor give each speech the full point of a groan;
The courtly nymphs, acquainted with the moan
Of them who on their lips love's standard bear—
" What! he? " say they of me. " Now I dare swear
He cannot love. No, no; let him alone."

And think so still, so Stella know my mind;
Profess indeed I do not Cupid's art;
But you, fair maids, at length this true shall find,
That his right badge is worn but in the heart.
Dumb swans, not chattering pies, do lovers prove:
They love indeed who quake to say they love.

CONDITIONAL SURRENDER

Oh, joy too high for my low style to show!
Oh, bliss fit for a nobler state than me!
Envy, put out thine eyes, lest thou do see
What oceans of delight in me do flow!
My friend, that oft saw, through all masks, my woe,
Come, come, and let me pour myself on thee.
Gone is the winter of my misery!
My spring appears, oh, see what here doth grow.
For Stella hath, with words where faith doth shine,
Of her high heart giv'n me the monarchy;
I, I, oh, I may say that she is mine!
And though she gives but thus condition'ly
This realm of bliss, while virtuous course I take,
No kings be crowned but they some covenants make.

COME, SLEEP

Come sleep, O sleep, the certain knot of peace,
The baiting place of wit, the balm of woe,
The poor man's wealth, the prisoner's release,
The indifferent judge between the high and low.
With shield of proof shield me from out the press[1]
Of those fierce darts despair at me doth throw:
Oh, make in me those civil wars to cease;
I will good tribute pay if thou do so.

---

[1] The rhyme is more exact in the original, " press " having been
prease."

Take thou of me smooth pillows, sweetest bed,
A chamber deaf to noise, and blind to light,
A rosy garland and a weary head.
And if these things, as being thine by right,
Move not thy heavy grace, thou shalt in me
Livelier than elsewhere Stella's image see.

THOMAS LODGE

1558 (?) - 1625

ROSALINE

Like to the clear in highest sphere
Where all imperial glory shines,
Of selfsame colour is her hair
Whether unfolded, or in twines:
    Heigh ho, fair Rosaline!
Her eyes are sapphires set in snow
Resembling heaven by every wink;
The Gods do fear whenas they glow,
And I do tremble when I think,
    Heigh ho, would she were mine!

Her cheeks are like the blushing cloud
That beautifies Aurora's face,
Or like the silver crimson shroud
That Phœbus' smiling looks doth grace:
    Heigh ho, fair Rosaline!
Her lips are like two budded roses
Whom ranks of lilies neighbour nigh,
Within which bounds she balm encloses
Apt to entice a deity:
    Heigh ho, would she were mine!

Her neck is like a stately tower
Where Love himself imprisoned lies,
To watch for glances every hour
From her divine and sacred eyes:
    Heigh ho, fair Rosaline!
Her paps are centres of delight,
Her breasts are orbs of heavenly frame,
Where Nature moulds the dew of light
To feed perfection with the same:
    Heigh ho, would she were mine!

With orient pearl, with ruby red,
With marble white, with sapphire blue
Her body every way is fed,
Yet soft in touch and sweet in view:
    Heigh ho, fair Rosaline!
Nature herself her shape admires;
The Gods are wounded in her sight;
And Love forsakes his heavenly fires
And at her eyes his brand doth light:
    Heigh ho, would she were mine!

Then muse not, Nymphs, though I bemoan
The absence of fair Rosaline,
Since for a fair there's fairer none,
Nor for her virtues so divine:
    Heigh ho, fair Rosaline;
Heigh ho, my heart! would God that she were mine!

ROSALIND'S MADRIGAL

Love in my bosom like a bee
    Doth suck his sweet;
Now with his wings he plays with me,
    Now with his feet.
Within mine eyes he makes his nest,
His bed amidst my tender breast;
My kisses are his daily feast,
And yet he robs me of my rest.
    Ah, wanton, will ye?

And if I sleep, then percheth he
    With pretty flight,
And makes his pillow of my knee
    The livelong night.
Strike I my lute, he tunes the string;
He music plays if so I sing;
He lends me every lovely thing;
Yet cruel he my heart doth sting.
    Whist, wanton, still ye!

Else I with roses every day
    Will whip you hence
And bind you, when you long to play,
    For your offence.

I'll shut mine eyes to keep you in,
I'll make you fast it for your sin,
I'll count your power not worth a pin.
Alas, what hereby shall I win,
   If he gainsay me?

What if I beat the wanton boy
   With many a rod?
He will repay me with annoy,
   Because a god.
Then sit thou safely on my knee,
Then let thy bower my bosom be;
Lurk in mine eyes, I like of thee.
O Cupid, so thou pity me,
   Spare not, but play thee.

GEORGE PEELE

1558 - 1597 (?)

HARVESTER'S SONG

All ye that lovely lovers be,
Pray you for me:
Lo, here we come a-sowing, a-sowing,
And sow sweet fruits of love;
In your sweet hearts well may it prove!

Lo, here we come a-reaping, a-reaping, a-reaping,
To reap our harvest-fruit!
And thus we pass the year so long,
And never be we mute.

BETHSABE, BATHING, SINGS

Hot sun, cool fire, tempered with sweet air,
Black shade, fair nurse, shadow my white hair:
Shine, sun; burn, fire; breathe, air, and ease me;
Black shade, fair nurse, shroud me, and please me:
Shadow, my sweet nurse, keep me from burning,
Make not my glad cause cause of mourning,
     Let not my beauty's fire
     Inflame unstaid desire,
     Nor pierce any bright eye
     That wandereth lightly.

ROBERT SOUTHWELL

1561 - 1595

THE BURNING BABE

As I in hoary winter's night stood shivering in the snow,
Surprised I was with sudden heat which made my heart to glow;
And lifting up a fearful eye to view what fire was near,
A pretty babe all burning bright did in the air appear;
Who, scorchèd with excessive heat, such floods of tears did shed
As though his floods should quench his flames which with his tears
    were fed.
" Alas," quoth he, " but newly born in fiery heats I fry,
Yet none approach to warm their hearts or feel my fire but I!
My faultless breast the furnace is; the fuel, wounding thorns;
Love is the fire, and sighs the smoke; the ashes, shame and scorns;
The fuel justice layeth on, and mercy blows the coals;
The metal in this furnace wrought are men's defilèd souls,
For which, as now on fire I am to work them to their good;
So will I melt into a bath to wash them in my blood."
With this he vanished out of sight and swiftly shrunk away,—
And straight I callèd unto mind that it was Christmas Day.

SAMUEL DANIEL

1562 - 1619

SLEEP

Care-charmer Sleep, son of the sable Night,[1]
Brother to Death, in silent darkness born,
Relieve my languish, and restore the light;
With dark forgetting of my care return.

And let the day be time enough to mourn
The shipwreck of my ill-adventured youth:
Let waking eyes suffice to wail their scorn,
Without the torment of the night's untruth.

[1] Compare the poem by Fletcher on page 170.

Cease, dreams, the images of day-desires,
To model forth the passions of the morrow;
Never let rising sun approve you liars,
To add more grief to aggravate my sorrow:
Still let me sleep, embracing clouds in vain,
And never wake to feel the day's disdain.

THEN AND NOW

When men shall find thy flower, thy glory, pass,
And thou, with careful brow sitting alone,
Receivèd hast this message from thy glass,
That tells the truth and says that all is gone;
Fresh shalt thou see in me the wounds thou madest,
Though spent thy flame, in me the heat remaining;
I that have loved thee thus before thou fadest,
My faith shall wax when thou art in thy waning.

The world shall find this miracle in me,
That fire can burn when all the matter's spent;
Then what my faith hath been, thyself shall see,
And that thou wast unkind, thou mayst repent.
Thou mayst repent that thou hast scorned my tears,
When winter snows upon thy sable hairs.

MICHAEL DRAYTON

1563 - 1631

THE PARTING

Since there's no help, come, let us kiss and part;
Nay, I have done, you get no more of me;
And I am glad, yea glad with all my heart
That thus so cleanly I myself can free.

Shake hands for ever, cancel all our vows,
And, when we meet at any time again,
Be it not seen in either of our brows
That we one jot of former love retain.

Now at the last gasp of Love's latest breath,
When, his pulse failing, Passion speechless lies,
When Faith is kneeling by his bed of death,
And Innocence is closing up his eyes—
    Now if thou wouldst, when all have given him over,
    From death to life thou might'st him yet recover.

GIVE ME MY SELF

You're not alone when you are still alone;
O God! from you that I could private be!
Since you one were, I never since was one,
Since you in me, myself since out of me.
Transported from myself into your being,
Though either distant, present yet to either;
Senseless with too much joy, each other seeing
And only absent when we are together.

Give me my self, and take your self again!
Devise some means by how I may forsake you!
So much is mine that doth with you remain,
That taking what is mine, with me I take you.
    You do bewitch me! O that I could fly
    From my self you, or from your own self I!

LAUGHING AT FORTUNE

I hear some say, " This man is not in love! "
" Who! can he love? a likely thing! " they say.
" Read but his verse, and it will easily prove! "
O judge not rashly, gentle sir, I pray!
Because I loosely trifle in this sort,
As one that fain his sorrows would beguile,
You now suppose me, all this time, in sport,
And please yourself with this conceit the while.

Ye shallow Censures! sometimes, see ye not.
In greatest perils some men pleasant be?
Where Fame by death is only to be got,
They resolute! So stands the case with me.
    Where other men in depth of passion cry,
    I laugh at Fortune, as in jest to die!

THE PARADOX

When first I ended, then I first began;
Then more I travelled further from my rest.
Where most I lost, there most of all I won;
Pinèd with hunger, rising from a feast.
Methinks I fly, yet want I legs to go;
Wise in conceit, in act a very sot;
Ravished with joy amidst a hell of woe;
What most I seem that surest I am not.

I build my hopes a world above the sky,
Yet with the mole I creep into the earth;
In plenty, I am starved with penury,
And yet I surfeit in the greatest dearth.
  I have, I want; despair, and yet desire;
  Burned in a sea of ice, and drowned amidst a fire.

THE SIXTEENTH CENTURY

SECOND HALF

SHAKESPEARE AND THE RENAISSANCE

The age commonly known as Elizabethan set the key for the succeeding era in its division of the intellectual and the emotional nature. Sometimes—at its highest pitch in Shakespeare—the two were combined, and the expression was as direct as the feeling that impelled it. But frequently the attitude was prescribed, and the diction, though delicate, became inflexibly mannered. Poets were evidently forced by their profession to be—or profess to be—determined and far from private lovers, and the objects of their love were a succession of lay figures, each resembling the other to the last physical detail. The England of 1600 —if one is to trust the picture presented by *England's Helicon*—seemed populated entirely by lightly wanton, rhyme-turning shepherds; and the affairs of state were, seemingly, less important than the affairs of Corydon and his Phillis. Every true gentleman occupied himself with the fashioning of falsely naïve pastoral ditties, bucolics bearing the same relation to the soil as did Marie Antoinette's dresden-china milkmaids. In this agreeable world of amorous extravagance and unreality, of appealing languors and (apparently) no labour, the poet's lady— whether a court nymph or a country Nell—was celebrated in no wise for anything mental or spiritual, but always and only for her softness or her hardness, her kindness or her coyness, her redness or her whiteness. Even these qualities were hymned in a limited vocabulary of metaphors, images repeated so often and with so little variety that they were stereotypes even in their own day. Shakespeare mockingly summed up the catalogue of conceits in the sonnet beginning, " My Mistress' eyes are nothing like the sun," and as early as 1578, Barnabe Riche satirised the users of them. " If he be learned," wrote Riche, " and that he be able to write a verse, then his penne must plie to paint his mistresse prayse; she must then be a *Pallas* for her witte, a *Diana* for her chastitie, a *Venus* for her face; then shee shall be praysed for her proportion: first her Haires are wires of golde, her Cheekes are made of Lilies and red Roses, her Browes be arches, her eyes Saphires, her lookes lightnings, her mouth Corall, her teeth Pearles, her pappes Alabaster balles, her bodye streight, her belly softe, from thence downwarde to her knees, I thinke, is made of Sugar Candie, her hands, her fingers, her legges, her feete, and all the reste of her bodie shall be so perfect, and so pure, that of my conscience, the worst parte they will leave in her, shall be her soule."

It must, however, be added that this monotonous prettifying did not prevent Nashe and Webster and, especially, Campion from developing a rare and almost perfect lyricism. The various energies of the Renaissance could not be confined; they broke through patterns of sentiment and style, permitting certain other poets, notably Marlowe, Jonson and

Fletcher, to attain an eloquence of such richness that it is surpassed only by Shakespeare's.

Contrasted with the latter half of the sixteenth century, the period immediately preceding seems, for all its singers, sparse. Within fifty years English poetry flowered with a splendour comparable to the glory stretched over two centuries of Italian painting. Depths of passion were sounded; heights of rhetoric achieved. The temper as well as the tone of the period came to one kind of climax—an intense if tortured outcry —in Donne, who stands midway between the Elizabethan lyricists and the metaphysicians of the next division. And in Shakespeare this many-sided, almost over-vitalised, age found a complete and spontaneous release.

WILLIAM SHAKESPEARE

1564 - 1616

SONGS FROM THE PLAYS

SILVIA

Who is Silvia? What is she,
    That all our swains commend her?
Holy, fair, and wise is she;
    The heaven such grace did lend her,
That she might admirèd be.

Is she kind as she is fair?
    For beauty lives with kindness.
Love doth to her eyes repair,
    To help him of his blindness;
And, being helped, inhabits there.

Then to Silvia let us sing,
    That Silvia is excelling;
She excels each mortal thing,
    Upon the dull earth dwelling:
To her let us garlands bring.

FAIRY SONGS

I

Over hill, over dale,
    Thorough bush, thorough brier,
Over park, over pale,
    Thorough flood, thorough fire,
I do wander everywhere,
Swifter than the moonès sphere;

And I serve the fairy queen,
To dew her orbs upon the green.
The cowslips tall her pensioners be;
In their gold coats spots you see,
Those be rubies, fairy favours,
In those freckles live their savours:
I must go seek some dewdrops here,
And hang a pearl in every cowslip's ear.

2

You spotted snakes with double tongue,
    Thorny hedge-hogs, be not seen;
Newts and blind-worms, do no wrong;
    Come not near our fairy queen:
        Philomel, with melody,
        Sing in our sweet lullaby;
Lulla, lulla, lullaby, lulla, lulla, lullaby.

Never harm, nor spell, nor charm,
Come our lovely lady nigh;
So, good night, with lullaby.

Weaving spiders, come not here:
    Hence, you long-legged spinners, hence!
Beetles black, approach not near;
    Worm, nor snail, do no offence.
        Philomel, with melody,
        Sing in our sweet lullaby;
Lulla, lulla, lullaby, lulla, lulla, lullaby.

3

Now the hungry lion roars,
    And the wolf behowls the moon;
Whilst the heavy ploughman snores,
    All with weary task fordone.
Now the wasted brands do glow,
    Whilst the screech-owl, screeching loud,
Puts the wretch that lies in woe
    In remembrance of a shroud.
Now it is the time of night
    That the graves, all gaping wide,
Every one lets forth his sprite,
    In the churchway paths to glide:

And we fairies, that do run
　By the triple Hecate's team,
From the presence of the sun,
　Following darkness like a dream,
Now are frolic; not a mouse
Shall disturb this hallowed house:
I am sent with broom before,
To sweep the dust behind the door.

Through the house give glimmering light,
　By the dead and drowsy fire;
Every elf and fairy sprite
　Hop as light as bird from brier;
And this ditty, after me,
Sing, and dance it, trippingly.
First rehearse your song by rote,
To each word a warbling note:
Hand in hand, with fairy grace.
Will we sing, and bless this place.

THE FRAUD OF MEN

Sigh no more, ladies, sigh no more;
　Men were deceivers ever;
One foot in sea, and one on shore,
　To one thing constant never:
Then sigh not so, but let them go,
　And be you blithe and bonny,
Converting all your sounds of woe
　Into Hey nonny nonny.

Sing no more ditties, sing no moe,
　Of dumps so dull and heavy;
The fraud of men was ever so,
　Since summer first was leavy:
Then sigh not so, but let them go,
　And be you blithe and bonny,
Converting all your sounds of woe
　Into Hey nonny, nonny.

WINTER

When icicles hang by the wall
　And Dick the shepherd blows his nail,
And Tom bears logs into the hall,
　And milk comes frozen home in pail;

When blood is nipt, and ways be foul,
Then nightly sings the staring owl
Tu-whoo!
To-whit, Tu-whoo! A merry note!
While greasy Joan doth keel the pot.

When all about the wind both blow,
    And coughing drowns the parson's saw,
And birds sit brooding in the snow,
    And Marian's nose looks red and raw;
When roasted crabs hiss in the bowl—
Then nightly sings the staring owl
Tu-whoo!
To-whit, Tu-whoo! A merry note!
While greasy Joan doth keel the pot.

SEALS OF LOVE

Take, O take those lips away
That so sweetly were forsworn,
And those eyes, the break of day,
Lights that do mislead the morn.
But my kisses bring again,
        Bring again—
Seals of love, but sealed in vain,
        Sealed in vain!

COME AWAY, DEATH

Come away, come away, Death,
And in sad cypres[1] let me be laid;
Fly away, fly away, breath;
I am slain by a fair cruel maid.
My shroud of white, stuck all with yew,
        O prepare it!
My part of death no one so true
        Did share it.

Not a flower, not a flower sweet
On my black coffin let there be strown;
Not a friend, not a friend greet
My poor corpse, where my bones shall be thrown;
A thousand thousand sighs to save,
        Lay me, O where
Sad true lover never find my grave,
        To weep there.

[1] Cypres: crêpe.

SEA DIRGE

Full fathom five thy father lies:
    Of his bones are coral made;
Those are pearls that were his eyes:
    Nothing of him that doth fade,
But doth suffer a sea-change
Into something rich and strange.
Sea-nymphs hourly ring his knell:
    Hark! now I hear them,—
        Ding, dong, bell.

MORNING SONG

Hark! hark! the lark at heaven's gate sings,
    And Phœbus 'gins arise,
His steeds to water at those springs
    On chaliced flowers that lies;
And winking, Mary-buds begin
    To ope their golden eyes;
With every thing that pretty is,
    My lady sweet, arise;
        Arise, arise!

LOVERS LOVE THE SPRING

It was a lover and his lass
    With a hey, and a ho, and a hey nonino,
That o'er the green corn-field did pass
    In the spring-time, the only pretty ring-time,
When birds do sing, hey ding a ding, ding;
    Sweet lovers love the spring.

Between the acres of the rye,
    With a hey and a ho, and a hey nonino,
These pretty country folks would lie,
    In the spring-time, the only pretty ring-time,
When birds do sing, hey ding a ding, ding;
    Sweet lovers love the spring.

This carol they began that hour,
    With a hey, and a ho, and a hey nonino,
How that a life was but a flower
    In the spring-time, the only pretty ring-time,
When birds do sing, hey ding a ding, ding;
    Sweet lovers love the spring.

And therefore take the present time,
 With a hey, and a ho, and a hey nonino,
For love is crownèd with the prime
 In the spring-time, the only pretty ring-time,
When birds do sing, hey ding a ding, ding;
 Sweet lovers love the spring.

BITTER SONG

Blow, blow, thou winter wind,
Thou art not so unkind
As man's ingratitude;
Thy tooth is not so keen
Because thou art not seen,
Although thy breath be rude.
Heigh ho! sing heigh ho! unto the green holly:
Most friendship is feigning, most loving mere folly:
Then, heigh ho! the holly!
This life is most jolly.

Freeze, freeze, thou bitter sky,
Thou dost not bite so nigh
As benefits forgot:
Though thou the waters warp,
Thy sting is not so sharp
As friend remembered not.
Heigh ho! sing heigh ho! unto the green holly:
Most friendship is feigning, most loving mere folly:
Then, heigh ho! the holly!
This life is most jolly.

FEAR NO MORE

Fear no more the heat o' the sun
 Nor the furious winter's rages:
Thou thy worldly task hast done,
 Home art gone and ta'en thy wages:
Golden lads and girls all must,
As chimney-sweepers, come to dust.

Fear no more the frown o' the great,
 Thou art past the tyrant's stroke;
Care no more to clothe and eat;
 To thee the reed is as the oak:
The sceptre, learning, physic, must
All follow this, and come to dust.

Fear no more the lightning-flash
  Nor the all-dreaded thunder-stone;
Fear not slander, censure rash;
  Thou hast finished joy and moan:
All lovers young, all lovers must
Consign to thee, and come to dust.

FANCY

Tell me where is Fancy bred,
Or in the heart, or in the head?
How begot, how nourishèd?
        Reply, reply.

It is engendered in the eyes;
With gazing fed; and Fancy dies
In the cradle where it lies.
Let us all ring Fancy's knell;
I'll begin it:—Ding, dong, bell.
        —Ding, dong, bell.

UNDER THE GREENWOOD TREE

Under the greenwood tree
Who loves to lie with me,
And tune his merry note
Unto the sweet bird's throat—
Come hither, come hither, come hither!
        Here shall he see
        No enemy
But winter and rough weather.

Who doth ambition shun
And loves to live i' the sun,
Seeking the food he eats
And pleased with what he gets—
Come hither, come hither, come hither!
        Here shall he see
        No enemy
But winter and rough weather.

CRABBÈD AGE AND YOUTH[1]

Crabbèd Age and Youth
Cannot live together:
Youth is full of pleasance,
Age is full of care;

[1] This was printed in *The Passionate Pilgrim*, not in any of the plays, and some editors believe it to be by another hand than Shakespeare's.

Youth like summer morn,
Age like winter weather;
Youth like summer brave,
Age like winter bare:
Youth is full of sport,
Age's breath is short;
Youth is nimble, Age is lame:
Youth is hot and bold,
Age is weak and cold;
Youth is wild, and Age is tame:—
Age, I do abhor thee,
Youth, I do adore thee.
O! my love, my love is young!
Age, I do defy thee—
O sweet shepherd, hie thee,
For methinks thou stay'st too long.

O MISTRESS MINE

O Mistress mine, where are you roaming?
O stay and hear! your true-love's coming
    That can sing both high and low;
Trip no further, pretty sweeting,
Journeys end in lovers' meeting—
    Every wise man's son doth know.

What is love? 'tis not hereafter;
Present mirth hath present laughter;
    What's to come is still unsure:
In delay there lies no plenty,—
Then come kiss me, Sweet-and-twenty,
    Youth's a stuff will not endure.

MUSIC[1]

Orpheus with his lute made trees,
And the mountain-tops that freeze,
    Bow themselves when he did sing:
To his music plants and flowers
Ever sprung; as sun and showers
    There had made a lasting spring.

[1] This song, from *Henry VIII*, has sometimes been assigned to Fletcher, who collaborated with Shakespeare in the writing of the play. Since it is impossible to determine what parts were written by either poet, and since the accent of the verse seems Shakespearean, the editor is not shifting the ascription.

Everything that heard him play,
Ev'n the billows of the sea,
  Hung their heads, and then lay by.
In sweet music is such art:
Killing care ånd grief of heart
  Fall asleep, or, hearing, die.

SONNETS

ETERNAL SUMMER

Shall I compare thee to a summer's day?
Thou art more lovely and more temperate;
Rough winds do shake the darling buds of May,
And summer's lease hath all too short a date:
Sometimes too hot the eye of heaven shines,
And often is his gold complexion dimmed:
And every fair from fair sometime declines,
By chance, or nature's changing course, untrimmed:

But thy eternal summer shall not fade
Nor lose possession of that fair thou owest;
Nor shall Death brag thou wanderest in his shade
When in eternal lines to time thou growest.
So long as men can breathe, or eyes can see
So long lives this, and this gives life to thee.

FORTUNE AND MEN'S EYES

When in disgrace with fortune and men's eyes
I all alone beweep my outcast state,
And trouble deaf heaven with my bootless cries,
And look upon myself, and curse my fate;
Wishing me like to one more rich in hope,
Featured like him, like him with friends possest,
Desiring this man's art, and that man's scope,
With what I most enjoy contented least;

Yet in these thoughts myself almost despising,
Haply I think on thee—and then my state,
Like to the lark at break of day arising
From sullen earth, sings hymns at heaven's gate;
For thy sweet love remembered, such wealth brings
That then I scorn to change my state with kings.

REMEMBRANCE OF THINGS PAST

When to the sessions of sweet silent thought
I summon up remembrance of things past,
I sigh the lack of many a thing I sought,
And with old woes new wail my dear time's waste;
Then can I drown an eye, unused to flow,
For precious friends hid in death's dateless night,
And weep afresh love's long-since-cancelled woe,
And moan the expense of many a vanished sight.

Then can I grieve at grievances foregone,
And heavily from woe to woe tell o'er
The sad account of fore-bemoanèd moan,
Which I new pay as if not paid before.
—But if the while I think on thee, dear friend,
All losses are restored, and sorrows end.

THESE LINES

If Thou survive my well-contented day
When that churl Death my bones with dust shall cover.
And shalt by fortune once more re-survey
These poor rude lines of thy deceasèd lover;
Compare them with the bettering of the time,
And though they be outstripped by every pen,
Reserve them for my love, not for their rhyme
Exceeded by the height of happier men.

O then vouchsafe me but this loving thought—
"Had my friend's muse grown with this growing age,
A dearer birth than this his love had brought,
To march in ranks of better equipage:
But since he died, and poets better prove,
Theirs for their style I'll read, his for his love."

SUNS AND CLOUDS

Full many a glorious morning have I seen
Flatter the mountain-tops with sovereign eye,
Kissing with golden face the meadows green,
Gilding pale streams with heavenly alchemy;
Anon permit the basest clouds to ride
With ugly rack on his celestial face,
And from the forlorn world his visage hide,
Stealing unseen to west with this disgrace.

Even so my sun one early morn did shine
With all-triumphant splendour on my brow;
But out, alack! he was but one hour mine,
The region cloud hath masked him from me now.
Yet him for this my love no whit disdaineth;
Suns of the world may stain when heaven's sun staineth.

TIME

Like as the waves make towards the pebbled shore,
So do our minutes hasten to their end;
Each changing place with that which goes before,
In sequent toil all forwards do contend.
Nativity, once in the main of light,
Crawls to maturity, wherewith being crowned,
Crooked eclipses 'gainst his glory fight,
And Time that gave, doth now his gift confound.

Time doth transfix the flourish set on youth,
And delves the parallels in beauty's brow;
Feeds on the rarities of nature's truth,
And nothing stands but for his scythe to mow:—
And yet, to times in hope, my verse shall stand
Praising Thy worth, despite his cruel hand.

TIRED WITH ALL THESE

Tired with all these, for restful death I cry—
As, to behold desert a beggar born,
And needy nothing trimmed in jollity,
And purest faith unhappily forsworn,
And gilded honour shamefully misplaced,
And maiden virtue rudely strumpeted,
And right perfection wrongfully disgraced,
And strength by limping sway disablèd,
And art made tongue-tied by authority,
And folly, doctor-like, controlling skill,
And simple truth miscalled simplicity,
And captive Good attending captain Ill:—
Tired with all these, from these would I be gone,
Save that, to die, I leave my love alone.

TWILIGHT OF LOVE

That time of year thou may'st in me behold
When yellow leaves, or none, or few, do hang
Upon those boughs which shake against the cold—
Bare ruined choirs, where late the sweet birds sang.

In me thou seest the twilight of such day
As after sunset fadeth in the west,
Which by-and-by black night doth take away,
Death's second self, that seals up all in rest:

In me thou seest the glowing of such fire
That on the ashes of his youth doth lie,
As the death-bed whereon it must expire,
Consumed with that which it was nourished by.
This thou perceiv'st, which makes thy love more strong,
To love that well which thou must leave ere long.

FAREWELL

Farewell! thou art too dear for my possessing,
And like enough thou know'st thy estimate:
The charter of thy worth gives thee releasing;
My bonds in thee are all determinate.
For how do I hold thee but by thy granting?
And for that riches where is my deserving?
The cause of this fair gift in me is wanting,
And so my patent back again is swerving.

Thyself thou gav'st, thy own worth then not knowing,
Or me, to whom thou gav'st it, else mistaking;
So thy great gift, upon misprision growing,
Comes home again, on better judgment making.
Thus have I had thee as a dream doth flatter,
In sleep, a king; but waking, no such matter.

LILIES THAT FESTER

They that have power to hurt, and will do none,
That do not do the thing they most do show,
Who, moving others, are themselves as stone,
Unmovèd, cold, and to temptation slow,—
They rightly do inherit heaven's graces,
And husband nature's riches from expense;
They are the lords and owners of their faces,
Others, but stewards of their excellence.

The summer's flower is to the summer sweet
Though to itself it only live and die;
But if that flower with base infection meet,
The basest weed outbraves his dignity:
For sweetest things turn sourest by their deeds;
Lilies that fester smell far worse than weeds.

CHRONICLE OF WASTED TIME

When in the chronicle of wasted time
I see descriptions of the fairest wights,
And beauty making beautiful old rhyme
In praise of ladies dead, and lovely knights;
Then in the blazon of sweet beauty's best
Of hand, of foot, of lip, of eye, of brow,
I see their antique pen would have exprest
Ev'n such a beauty as you master now.

So all their praises are but prophecies
Of this our time, all, you prèfiguring;
And for they looked but with divining eyes,
They had not skill enough your worth to sing!
For we, which now behold these present days,
Have eyes to wonder, but lack tongues to praise.

LOVE IS NOT LOVE WHICH ALTERS

Let me not to the marriage of true minds
Admit impediments. Love is not love
Which alters when it alteration finds,
Or bends with the remover to remove:—
O no! it is an ever-fixèd mark
That looks on tempests, and is never shaken;
It is the star to every wandering bark.
Whose worth's unknown, although his height be taken.

Love's not Time's fool, though rosy lips and cheeks
Within his bending sickle's compass come;
Love alters not with his brief hours and weeks,
But bears it out ev'n to the edge of doom.
If this be error, and upon me proved,
I never writ, nor no man ever loved.

DESPITE TIME

No, Time, thou shalt not boast that I do change:
Thy pyramids built up with newer might,
To me are nothing novel, nothing strange;
They are but dressings of a former sight.
Our dates are brief, and therefore we admire
What thou dost foist upon us that is old,
And rather make them born to our desire
Than think that we before have heard them told.

Thy registers and thee I both defy,
Not wondering at the present nor the past;
For thy records and what we see do lie,
Made more or less by thy continual haste.
This I do vow, and this shall ever be,
I will be true, despite thy scythe and thee.

PAST REASON

The expense of spirit in a waste of shame
Is lust in action; and till action lust
Is perjured, murderous, bloody, full of blame,
Savage, extreme, rude, cruel, not to trust;
Enjoyed no sooner but despisèd straight;
Past reason hunted; and no sooner had,
Past reason hated, as a swallowed bait,
On purpose laid to make the taker mad:
Mad in pursuit, and in possession so;
Had, having, and in quest to have, extreme;
A bliss in proof,—and proved, a very woe;
Before, a joy proposed; behind, a dream.
All this the world well knows; yet none knows well
To shun the heaven that leads men to this hell.

BODY AND SOUL

Poor Soul, the centre of my sinful earth,
Fooled by those rebel powers that thee array,
Why dost thou pine within, and suffer dearth,
Painting thy outward walls so costly gay?
Why so large cost, having so short a lease,
Dost thou upon thy fading mansion spend?
Shall worms, inheritors of this excess,
Eat up thy charge? is this thy body's end?

Then, Soul, live thou upon thy servant's loss,
And let that pine to aggravate thy store;
Buy terms divine in selling hours of dross;
Within be fed, without be rich no more:—
So shalt thou feed on Death, that feeds on men,
And Death once dead, there's no more dying then.

CHRISTOPHER MARLOWE

1564 - 1593

THE PASSIONATE SHEPHERD TO HIS LOVE[1]

Come live with me and be my Love,
And we will all the pleasures prove
That hills and valleys, dale and field,
And all the craggy mountains yield.

There will we sit upon the rocks
And see the shepherds feed their flocks,
By shallow rivers, to whose falls
Melodious birds sing madrigals.

There will I make thee beds of roses
And a thousand fragrant posies,
A cap of flowers, and a kirtle
Embroidered all with leaves of myrtle.

A gown made of the finest wool,
Which from our pretty lambs we pull,
Fair linèd slippers for the cold,
With buckles of the purest gold.

A belt of straw and ivy buds
With coral clasps and amber studs:
And if these pleasures may thee move,
Come live with me and be my Love.

Thy silver dishes for thy meat
As precious as the gods do eat,
Shall on an ivory table be
Prepared each day for thee and me.

The shepherd swains shall dance and sing
For thy delight each May-morning:
If these delights thy mind may move,
Then live with me and be my Love.

[1] Walter Raleigh's " Reply " is on page 117.

FIRST SIGHT

from " Hero and Leander "

It lies not in our power to love or hate,
For will in us is overruled by fate.
When two are stripped, long ere the course begin
We wish that one should lose, the other win;
And one especially do we affect
Of two gold ingots, like in each respect.
The reason no man knows, let it suffice,
What we behold is censured by our eyes.
Where both deliberate, the love is slight;
Who ever loved, that loved not at first sight?

THOMAS NASHE

1567 - 1601

SPRING

Spring, the sweet Spring, is the year's pleasant king;
Then blooms each thing, then maids dance in a ring,
Cold doth not sting, the pretty birds do sing,
   Cuckoo, jug-jug, pu-we, to-witta-woo!

The palm and may make country houses gay,
Lambs frisk and play, the shepherds pipe all day,
And we hear aye birds tune this merry lay,
   Cuckoo, jug-jug, pu-we, to-witta-woo!

The fields breathe sweet, the daisies kiss our feet,
Young lovers meet, old wives a-sunning sit,
In every street these tunes our ears do greet,
   Cuckoo, jug-jug, pu-we, to-witta-woo!
      Spring! the sweet Spring!

WINTER, PLAGUE AND PESTILENCE

Autumn hath all the summer's fruitful treasure;
Gone is our sport, fled is our Corydon's pleasure!
Short days, sharp days, long nights come on apace:
Ah, who shall hide us from the winter's face?

Cold doth increase, the sickness will not cease,
And here we lie, God knows, with little ease.
  From winter, plague, and pestilence, good Lord, deliver us!

London doth mourn, Lambeth is quite forlorn!
Trades cry, woe worth that ever they were born!
The want of term is town and city's harm;
Close chambers we do want to keep us warm.
Long banished must we live from all our friends:
This low-built house will bring us to our ends.
  From winter, plague, and pestilence, good Lord, deliver us!

THOMAS CAMPION

1567 - 1620

LOST FREEDOM

Kind are her answers,
  But her performance keeps no day;
Breaks time, as dancers
  From their own music when they stray:
  All her free favours
And smooth words wing my hopes in vain.
O did ever voice so sweet but only feign?
  Can true love yield such delay,
  Converting joy to pain?

Lost is our freedom,
  When we submit to women so:
Why do we need them,
  When in their best they work our woe?
  There is no wisdom
Can alter ends, by Fate prefixed.
O why is the good of man with evil mixed?
  Never were days yet called two,
  But one night went betwixt.

THERE IS A GARDEN IN HER FACE

There is a garden in her face,
Where roses and white lilies grow;
  A heav'nly paradise is that place,
Wherein all pleasant fruits do flow.

There cherries grow which none may buy
Till " cherry-ripe " themselves do cry.

Those cherries fairly do enclose
Of orient pearls a double row,
  Which when her lovely laughter shows,
They look like rosebuds filled with snow.
  Yet them nor peer nor prince can buy,
Till " cherry-ripe " themselves do cry.

Her eyes like angels watch them still;
Her brows like bended bows do stand,
  Threat'ning with piercing frowns to kill
All that attempt with eye or hand
  Those sacred cherries to come nigh,
Till " cherry-ripe " themselves do cry.

ROSE-CHEEKED LAURA

Rose-cheeked Laura, come,
Sing thou smoothly with thy beauty's
Silent music, either other
    Sweetly gracing.

Lovely forms do flow
From concent[1] divinely framèd;
Heav'n is music, and thy beauty's
    Birth is heavenly.

These dull notes we sing
Discords need for helps to grace them;
Only beauty purely loving
    Knows no discord,

But still moves delight,
Like clear springs renewed by flowing,
Ever perfect, ever in them-
    Selves eternal.

IT SHALL SUFFICE

Follow your saint, follow with accents sweet!
Haste you, sad notes, fall at her flying feet!
There, wrapped in clouds of sorrow, pity move,
And tell the ravisher of my soul I perish for her love:

[1] Harmony; concord of tones.

But, if she scorns my never-ceasing pain,
Then burst with sighing in her sight and ne'er return again.

All that I sang still to her praise did tend,
Still she was first, still she my songs did end;
Yet she my love and music both doth fly,
The music that her echo is and beauty's sympathy.
Then let my notes pursue her scornful flight!
It shall suffice that they were breathed and died for her delight.

HIS LOVER'S TRIUMPHS

When thou must home to shades of underground,
And there arrived, a new admirèd guest,
The beauteous spirits do engirt thee round,
White Iope, blithe Helen and the rest,
To hear the stories of thy finished love
From that smooth tongue whose music hell can move:
Then wilt thou speak of banqueting delights,
Of masques and revels which sweet youth did make,
Of tourneys and great challenges of knights,
And all these triumphs for thy beauty's sake.
When thou hast told these honours done to thee,
Then tell, O tell, how thou didst murder me.

BEAUTY UNBOUND

Give beauty all her right!
She's not to one form tied;
Each shape yields fair delight
Where her perfections bide:
Helen, I grant, might pleasing be,
And Rosamond was as sweet as she.

Some the quick eye commends,
Some swelling lips and red;
Pale looks have many friends,
Through sacred sweetness bred:
Meadows have flowers that pleasures move,
Though roses are the flowers of love.

Free beauty is not bound
To one unmovèd clime;
She visits every ground
And favours every time.
Let the old loves with mine compare;
My sovereign is as sweet and fair.

HENRY WOTTON

1568 - 1639

CHARACTER OF A HAPPY LIFE

How happy is he born and taught
That serveth not another's will;
Whose armour is his honest thought
And simple truth his utmost skill!

Whose passions not his masters are,
Whose soul is still prepared for death,
Not tied unto the world with care
Of public fame, or private breath;

Who envies none that chance doth raise,
Or vice; who never understood
How deepest wounds are given by praise;
Nor rules of state, but rules of good:

Who hath his life from rumours freed,
Whose conscience is his strong retreat;
Whose state can neither flatterers feed,
Nor ruin make oppressors great;

Who God doth late and early pray
More of his grace than gifts to lend;
And entertains the harmless day
With a well-chosen book or friend;

—This man is freed from servile bands
Of hope to rise, or fear to fall;
Lord of himself, though not of lands;
And having nothing, yet hath all.

ON THE DEATH
OF SIR ALBERT MORTON'S WIFE

He first deceased—she, for a little, tried
To live without him, liked it not and died.

JOHN DAVIES

1569 - 1626

THE VIRGIN QUEEN

AN ANAGRAM

E arly before the day doth spring
L et us awake, my Muse, and sing,
I t is no time to slumber;
S o many joys this time doth bring
A s time will fail to number.

B ut whereto shall we bend our lays?
E ven up to heaven, again to raise
T he maid which, thence descended,
H ath brought again the golden days
A nd all the world amended.

R udeness itself she doth refine,
E 'en like an alchemist divine,
G ross times of iron turning
I nto the purest form of gold,
N ot to corrupt till heaven wax old,
A nd be refined with burning.

BEN JONSON

1572 - 1637

SHORT MEASURES

FROM AN ODE

It is not growing like a tree
In bulk, doth make man better be;
Or standing long an oak, three hundred year,
To fall a log at last, dry, bald, and sere:

A lily of a day
Is fairer far in May,
Although it fall and die that night—
It was the plant and flower of light.
In small proportions we just beauties see;
And in short measures life may perfect be.

HYMN TO DIANA

Queen and Huntress, chaste and fair
Now the sun is laid to sleep,
Seated in thy silver chair
State in wonted manner keep:
Hesperus entreats thy light,
Goddess excellently bright.

Earth, let not thy envious shade
Dare itself to interpose;
Cynthia's shining orb was made
Heaven to clear when day did close:
Bless us then with wishèd sight,
Goddess excellently bright.

Lay thy bow of pearl apart
And thy crystal-shining quiver;
Give unto the flying hart
Space to breathe, how short soever:
Thou that mak'st a day of night.
Goddess excellently bright!

TO CELIA

Drink to me only with thine eyes,
And I will pledge with mine;
Or leave a kiss but in the cup
And I'll not look for wine.
The thirst that from the soul doth rise
Doth ask a drink divine;
But might I of Jove's nectar sup,
I would not change for thine.

I sent thee late a rosy wreath,
Not so much honouring thee
As giving it a hope that there
It could not withered be;

But thou thereon didst only breathe
   And sent'st it back to me;
Since when it grows, and smells, I swear,
   Not of itself but thee!

SWEET NEGLECT

Still to be neat, still to be drest,
As you were going to a feast:
Still to be powdered, still perfumed:
Lady, it is to be presumed.
Though art's hid causes are not found,
All is not sweet, all is not sound.

Give me a look, give me a face
That makes simplicity a grace;
Robes loosely flowing, hair as free:
Such sweet neglect more taketh me,
Than all th' adulteries of art,
That strike mine eyes, but not my heart.

DIRGE FOR NARCISSUS

Slow, slow, fresh fount, keep time with my salt tears;
   Yet slower, yet; O faintly, gentle springs;
List to the heavy part the music bears,
   Woe weeps out her division when she sings.

   Droop, herbs and flowers;
   Fall, grief, in showers,
   Our beauties are not ours;
     O, I could still,
Like melting snow upon some craggy hill,
   Drop, drop, drop, drop,
Since nature's pride is now a withered daffodil.

FORTUNATE FOOL

Fools, they are the only nation
Worth men's envy or admiration;
Free from care or sorrow-taking,
Selves and others merry making:

All they speak or do is sterling.
Your fool, he is your great man's darling,
And your ladies' sport and pleasure;
Tongue and bauble are his treasure.
Ev'n his face begetteth laughter,
And he speaks truth free from slaughter
He's the grace of every feast,
And sometimes the chiefest guest;
Hath his trencher and his stool,
When wit waits upon the fool.
    O, who would not be
      He, he, he?

THOMAS HEYWOOD

1573 (?) - 1641

WELCOME TO DAY

Pack, clouds, away, and welcome day,
    With night we banish sorrow;
Sweet air, blow soft, mount, larks, aloft
    To give my Love good-morrow!
Wings from the wind to please her mind
    Notes from the lark I'll borrow;
Bird, prune thy wing, nightingale, sing.
    To give my Love good-morrow;
      To give my Love good-morrow
      Notes from them both I'll borrow.

Wake from thy nest, Robin-red-breast,
    Sing, birds, in every furrow!
And from each hill, let music shrill
    Give my fair Love good-morrow!
Blackbird and thrush in every bush,
    Stare, linnet, and cock-sparrow!
You pretty elves, amongst yourselves
    Sing my fair Love good-morrow;
      To give my fair Love good-morrow
      Sing, birds, in every furrow!

JOHN DONNE

1573 - 1631

THE GOOD-MORROW

I wonder, by my troth, what thou and I
Did, till we loved? were we not weaned till then?
But sucked on country pleasures, childishly?
Or snorted we in the Seven Sleepers' den?
'Twas so; but this, all pleasures fancies be;
If ever any beauty I did see,
Which I desired, and got, 'twas but a dream of thee.

And now good-morrow to our waking souls,
Which watch not one another out of fear;
For love all love of other sights controls,
And makes one little room an everywhere.
Let sea-discoverers to new worlds have gone;
Let maps to other worlds on worlds have shown;
Let us possess one world; each hath one, and is one.

My face in thine eye, thine in mine appears,
And true plain hearts do in the faces rest;
Where can we find two better hemispheres
Without sharp north, without declining west?
Whatever dies, was not mixed equally;
If our two loves be one, or thou and I
Love so alike that none can slacken, none can die.

THE SUN RISING

Busy old fool, unruly Sun,
　　Why dost thou thus,
Through windows, and through curtains, call on us?
Must to thy motions lovers' seasons run?
　　Saucy pedantic wretch, go chide
　　Late school-boys and sour prentices,
　Go tell court-huntsmen that the king will ride,
　Call country ants to harvest offices;
Love, all alike, no season knows nor clime,
Nor hours, days, months, which are the rags of time.

Thy beams so reverend and strong
    Why shouldst thou think?
I could eclipse and cloud them with a wink,
But that I would not lose her sight so long.
    If her eyes have not blinded thine,
      Look, and to-morrow late tell me,
   Whether both th' Indias of spice and mine
    Be where thou left'st them, or lie here with me.
Ask for those kings whom thou saw'st yesterday,
And thou shalt hear, " All here in one bed lay."

    She's all states, and all princes I:
      Nothing else is;
Princes do but play us; compared to this,
All honour's mimic, all wealth alchemy.
    Thou, Sun, art half as happy as are we,
      In that the world's contracted thus;
   Thine age asks ease, and since thy duties be
    To warm the world, that's done by warming us.
Shine here to us, and thou art everywhere;
This bed thy centre is, these walls thy sphere.

THE ECSTASY

    Where, like a pillow on a bed,
      A pregnant bank swelled up, to rest
The violet's reclining head,
      Sat we two, one another's best.

Our hands were firmly cèmented
      By a fast balm, which thence did spring,
Our eye-beams twisted, and did thread
      Our eyes upon one double string.

So to engraft our hands, as yet
      Was all the means to make us one;
And pictures in our eyes to get
      Was all our propagation.

As, 'twixt two equal armies, Fate
      Suspends uncertain victory,
Our souls—which to advance their state,
      Were gone out—hung 'twixt her and me.

And whilst our souls negotiate there,
  We like sepulchral statues lay;
All day, the same our postures were,
  And we said nothing, all the day.

If any, so by love refined,
  That he soul's language understood,
And by good love were grown all mind,
  Within convenient distance stood,

He—though he knew not which soul spake,
  Because both meant, both spoke the same—
Might thence a new concoction take,
  And part far purer than he came.

This ecstasy doth unperplex
  (We said) and tell us what we love;
We see by this, it was not sex;
  We see, we saw not, what did move:

But as all several souls contain
  Mixture of things they know not what,
Love these mixed souls doth mix again,
  And makes both one, each this and that.

A single violet transplant,
  The strength, the colour, and the size—
All which before was poor and scant—
  Redoubles still, and multiplies.

When love with one another so
  Interinanimates two souls,
That abler soul, which thence doth flow,
  Defects of loneliness controls.

We then, who are this new soul, know,
  Of what we are composed and made,
For th'atomies of which we grow
  Are souls, whom no change can invade.

But, O alas! so long, so far,
  Our bodies why do we forbear?
They are ours, though they're not we; we are
  Th'intelligences, they the spheres.

We owe them thanks, because they thus
    Did us, to us, at first convey,
Yielded their forces, sense, to us,
    Nor are dross to us, but allay.

On man heaven's influence works not so,
    But that it first imprints the air;
So soul into the soul may flow,
    Though it to body first repair.

As our blood labours to beget
    Spirits, as like souls as it can,
Because such fingers need to knit
    That subtle knot, which makes us man:

So must pure lovers' souls descend
    To affections, and to faculties,
Which sense may reach and apprehend,
    Else a great prince in prison lies.

To our bodies turn we then, that so
    Weak men on love revealed may look;
Love's mysteries in souls do grow,
    But yet the body is his book.

And if some lover, such as we,
    Have heard this dialogue of one,
Let him still mark us, he shall see
    Small change when we're to bodies gone.

THE CANONIZATION

For God's sake hold your tongue, and let me love,
    Or chide my palsy, or my gout,
My five grey hairs, or ruined fortune flout;
    With wealth your state, your mind with arts improve,
        Take you a course, get you a place,
        Observe his honour, or his grace;
Or the king's real, or his stampèd face
    Contemplate; what you will, approve,
    So you will let me love.

Alas, alas, who's injured by my love?
  What merchants' ships have my sighs drowned?
Who says my tears have overflowed his ground?
  When did my colds a forward spring remove?
    When did the heats which my veins fill
    Add one more to the plaguy bill?
Soldiers find wars, and lawyers find out still
  Litigious men, which quarrels move,
  Though she and I do love.

We can die by it, if not live by love,
  And if unfit for tombs and hearse
Our legend be, it will be fit for verse;
  And if no piece of chronicle we prove,
    We'll build in sonnets pretty rooms;
    As well a well-wrought urn becomes
The greatest ashes as half-acre tombs,
  And by these hymns, all shall approve
  Us canonized for love,

And thus invoke us: You whom reverend love
  Made one another's hermitage;
You, to whom love was peace, that now is rage;
  Who did the whole world's soul contract, and drove
    Into the glasses of your eyes—
    So made such mirrors and such spies
That they did all to you epitomize,—
  Countries, towns, courts; beg from above
  A pattern of your love!

THE UNDERTAKING

I have done one braver thing
Than all the worthies did;
And yet a braver thence doth spring,
Which is, to keep that hid.

It were but madness now to impart
The skill of specular stone,
When he, which can have learned the art
To cut it, can find none.

So, if I now should utter this,
Others—because no more
Such stuff to work upon there is—
Would love but as before.

But he who loveliness within
Hath found, all outward loathes,
For he who colour loves, and skin,
Loves but their oldest clothes.

If, as I have, you also do
Virtue in woman see,
And dare love that, and say so too,
And forget the He and She;

And if this love, though placèd so,
From profane men you hide,
Which will no faith on this bestow,
Or, if they do, deride;

Then you have done a braver thing
Than all the worthies did;
And yet a braver thence will spring,
Which is, to keep that hid.

SONG

Sweetest love, I do not go
    For weariness of thee,
Nor in hope the world can show
    A fitter love for me;
        But since that I
Must die at last, 'tis best,
To use myself in jest
    Thus by feigned deaths to die.

Yesternight the sun went hence,
    And yet is here to-day;
He hath no desire nor sense,
    Nor half so short a way;
        Then fear not me,
But believe that I shall make
Speedier journeys, since I take
    More wings and spurs than he.

Oh, how feeble is man's power,
   That if good fortune fall,
Cannot add another hour,
   Nor a lost hour recall!
      But come bad chance,
And we join to it our strength,
And we teach it art and length,
   Itself o'er us to advance.

When thou sigh'st, thou sigh'st not wind,
   But sigh'st my soul away;
When thou weep'st, unkindly kind,
   My life's blood doth decay.
      It cannot be
That thou lov'st me, as thou say'st,
If in thine my life thou waste;
   Thou art the best of me.

Let not thy divining heart
   Forethink me any ill,
Destiny may take thy part,
   And may thy fears fulfil;
      But think that we
Are but turned aside to sleep;
They who one another keep
   Alive, ne'er parted be.

PRAYER FOR VIOLENCE

DIVINE POEM

Batter my heart, three-personed God; for you
As yet but knock, breathe, shine, and seek to mend.
That I may rise and stand, o'erthrow me and bend
Your force to break, blow, burn and make me new.
I, like an usurped town, to another due,
Labour to admit you, but, oh, to no end;
Reason, your viceroy in me, me should defend,
But is captived and proves weak or untrue.
Yet dearly I love you and would be loved fain,
But am betrothed unto your enemy:
Divorce me, untie or break that knot again,
Take me to you, imprison me, for I,
Except you enthrall me, never shall be free,
Nor ever chaste, except you ravish me.

DEATH, BE NOT PROUD

Death, be not proud, though some have callèd thee
Mighty and dreadful, for thou art not so;
For those whom thou think'st thou dost overthrow
Die not, poor Death; nor yet canst thou kill me.
From Rest and Sleep, which but thy picture be,
Much pleasure; then from thee much more must flow;
And soonest our best men with thee do go—
Rest of their bones and souls' delivery!
Thou'rt slave to fate, chance, kings, and desperate men,
And dost with poison, war, and sickness dwell;
And poppy or charms can make us sleep as well
And better than thy stroke. Why swell'st thou then?
One short sleep past, we wake eternally,
And Death shall be no more: Death, thou shalt die!

THOMAS DEKKER

1570 (?) - 1641 (?)

LULLABY

Golden slumbers kiss your eyes;
Smiles awake you when you rise.
Sleep, pretty wantons, do not cry,
And I will sing a lullaby:
Rock them, rock them, lullaby.

Care is heavy, therefore sleep you;
You are care, and care must keep you.
Sleep, pretty wantons, do not cry,
And I will sing a lullaby:
Rock them, rock them, lullaby.

O SWEET CONTENT

Art thou poor, yet hast thou golden slumbers?
O sweet content!
Art thou rich, yet is thy mind perplexèd?
O punishment!

Dost thou laugh to see how fools are vexèd
To add to golden numbers, golden numbers?
O sweet content! O sweet, O sweet content!
  Work apace, apace, apace, apace;
  Honest labour bears a lovely face;
Then hey nonny nonny, hey nonny nonny!

Canst drink the waters of the crispèd spring?
          O sweet content!
Swimm'st thou in wealth, yet sink'st in thine own tears?
          O punishment!
Then he that patiently want's burden bears
No burden bears, but is a king, a king!
O sweet content! O sweet, O sweet content!
  Work apace, apace, apace, apace;
  Honest labour bears a lovely face;
Then hey nonny nonny, hey nonny nonny!

RICHARD BARNEFIELD

1574 - 1627

THE NIGHTINGALE

As it fell upon a day,
In the merry month of May,
Sitting in a pleasant shade,
Which a grove of myrtles made,
Beasts did leap, and birds did sing,
Trees did grow, and plants did spring:
Every thing did banish moan,
Save the nightingale alone.
She (poor bird) as all forlorn,
Leaned her breast up-till a thorn,
And there sung the dolefulst ditty,
That to hear it was great pity.
Fie, fie, fie, now would she cry
Teru teru, by and by:
That to hear her so complain,
Scarce I could from tears refrain:
For her grief so lively shown,
Made me think upon mine own.
Ah (thought I) thou mournst in vain;
None takes pity on thy pain:

Senseless trees, they cannot hear thee:
Ruthless beasts, they will not cheer thee.
King Pandion, he is dead:
All thy friends are lapped in lead.
All thy fellow birds do sing,
Careless of thy sorrowing.
Whilst as fickle fortune smiled,
Thou and I, were both beguiled.
Every one that flatters thee,
Is no friend in misery:
Words are easy, like the wind;
Faithful friends are hard to find:
Every man will be thy friend
Whilst thou hast wherewith to spend:
But if store of crowns be scant,
No man will supply thy want.
If that one be prodigal,
Bountiful, they will him call:
And with such-like flattering,
Pity but he were a king.
If he be addict to vice,
Quickly him they will entice.
If to women he be bent,
They have at commandement.
But if fortune once do frown,
Then farewell his great renown:
They that fawned on him before,
Use his company no more.
He that is thy friend indeed,
He will help thee in thy need:
If thou sorrow, he will weep;
If thou wake, he cannot sleep:
Thus of every grief, in heart
He, with thee doth bear a part.
These are certain signs, to know
Faithful friend, from flatt'ring foe.

JOHN MARSTON

1575 (?) - 1634

OBLIVION

from " The Scourge of Villainy "

Thou mighty gulf, insatiate cormorant,
Deride me not, though I seem petulant
To fall into thy chops. Let others pray
Forever their fair poems flourish may;
But as for me, hungry Oblivion,
Devour me quick, accept my orison,
   My earnest prayers, which do importune thee
   With gloomy shade of thy still empery,
   To veil both me and my rude poesy.

Far worthier lines in silence of thy state
   Do sleep securely, free from love or hate,
From which this, living, ne'er can be exempt,
But whilst it breathes will hate and fury tempt.
Then close his eyes with thy all-dimming hand,
Which not right glorious actions can withstand.
Peace, hateful tongues, I now in silence pace;
Unless some hound do wake me from my place,
   I with the sharp, yet well-meant poesy,
   Will sleep secure, right free from injury
   Of cankered hate or rankest villainy.

JOHN FLETCHER

1579 - 1625

MOURN NO MORE

Weep no more, nor sigh, nor groan,
Sorrow calls no time that's gone:
Violets plucked the sweetest rain
Makes not fresh nor grow again.
Trim thy locks, look cheerfully;
Fate's hid ends eyes cannot see.

Joys as wingèd dreams fly fast;
Why should sadness longer last?
Grief is but a wound to woe:
Gentlest fair, mourn, mourn no moe!

ASPATIA'S SONG

Lay a garland on my hearse,
    Of the dismal yew:
Maidens, willow branches bear;
    Say, I dièd true.

My love was false, but I was firm
    From my hour of birth.
Upon my buried body lie
    Lightly, gentle earth!

TO PAN

All ye woods, and trees, and bowers,
All ye virtues and ye powers
That inhabit in the lakes,
In the pleasant springs or brakes,
        Move your feet
            To our sound
        Whilst we greet
            All this ground
With his honour and his name
That defends our flocks from blame.

He is great, and he is just,
He is ever good, and must
Thus be honoured. Daffadillies,
Roses, pinks, and lovèd lilies,
        Let us fling,
        Whilst we sing,
        Ever holy,
        Ever holy,
Ever honoured, ever young!
Thus great Pan is ever sung.

CARE-CHARMING SLEEP[1]

Care-charming Sleep, thou easer of all woes,
Brother to Death, sweetly thyself dispose
On this afflicted prince. Fall like a cloud
In gentle showers. Give nothing that is loud,
Or painful to his slumbers; easy, light,
And as a purling stream, thou son of Night,
Pass by his troubled senses. Sing his pain,
Like hollow murmuring wind or silver rain.
Into this prince gently, oh, gently slide.
And kiss him into slumbers like a bride.

JOHN WEBSTER

1580 (?) - 1625 (?)

NETS TO CATCH THE WIND

All the flowers of the spring
Meet to perfume our burying;
These have but their growing prime,
And man does flourish but his time.
Survey our progress from our birth—
We are set, we grow, we turn to earth
Courts adieu, and all delights,
All bewitching appetites!
Sweetest breath and clearest eye
Like perfumes go out and die;
And consequently this is done
As shadows wait upon the sun.
Vain the ambition of kings
Who seek by trophies and dead things
To leave a living name behind,
And weave but nets to catch the wind.

A LAND DIRGE

Call for the robin-redbreast and the wren,
Since o'er shady groves they hover,
And with leaves and flowers do cover
The friendless bodies of unburied men.

[1] Compare the poem by Daniel on page 129.

Call unto his funeral dole
The ant, the field-mouse, and the mole,
To rear him hillocks that shall keep him warm,
And (when gay tombs are robbed) sustain no harm;
But keep the wolf far thence, that's foe to men,
For with his nails he'll dig them up again.

RICHARD CORBET

Bishop of Oxford and Norwich

1582 - 1635

THE FAIRIES' FAREWELL

Farewell, rewards and fairies,
　Good housewives now may say,
For now foul sluts in dairies
　Do fare as well as they.
And though they sweep their hearths no less
　Than maids were wont to do,
Yet who of late, for cleanliness,
　Finds sixpence in her shoe?

Lament, lament, old Abbeys,
　The fairies' lost command;
They did not change priests' babies,
　But some have changed your land!
And all your children sprung from thence
　Are now grown Puritans,
Who live as changelings ever since,
　For love of your domains.

At morning and at evening both
　You merry were and glad;
So little care of sleep or sloth
　These pretty ladies had;
When Tom came home from labour,
　Or Ciss to milking rose,
Then merrily went their tabor
　And nimbly went their toes.

Witness those rings and roundelays
   Of theirs, which yet remain,
Were footed in Queen Mary's days
   On many a grassy plain;
But since of late, Elizabeth
   And, later, James came in,
They never danced on any heath
   As when the time hath been.

By which we note the fairies
   Were of the old profession;
Their songs were *Ave-Maries*,
   Their dances were procession.
But now, alas! they all are dead,
   Or gone beyond the seas;
Or farther for religion fled;
   Or else they take their ease.

A tell-tale in their company
   They never could endure;
And whoso kept not secretly
   Their mirth, was punished sure;
It was a most just Christian deed
   To pinch such black and blue:
Oh, how the Commonwealth doth need
   Such justices as you!

FRANCIS BEAUMONT

1584 - 1616

A DANCE

Shake off your heavy trance!
   And leap into a dance
Such as no mortals use to tread:
   Fit only for Apollo
To play to, for the moon to lead,
   And all the stars to follow!

MIRTH

'Tis mirth that fills the veins with blood,
More than wine, or sleep, or food;
Let each man keep his heart at ease;
No man dies of that disease!
He that would his body keep
From diseases, must not weep;
But whoever laughs and sings,
Never he his body brings
Into fevers, gouts, or rheums,
Or lingeringly his lungs consumes;
Or meets with ague in his bone,
Or catarrhs, or griping stone:
But contented lives for aye;
The more he laughs, the more he may!

ON THE TOMBS IN WESTMINSTER ABBEY

Mortality, behold and fear
What a change of flesh is here!
Think how many royal bones
Sleep within this heap of stones;
Here they lie, had realms and lands,
Who now want strength to stir their hands,
Where from their pulpits sealed with dust
They preach, " In greatness is no trust."
Here's an acre sown indeed
With the richest royallest seed
That the earth did e'er suck in
Since the first man died for sin:
Here the bones of birth have cried
" Though gods they were, as men they died! "
Here are sands, ignoble things,
Dropt from the ruined sides of kings:
Here's a world of pomp and state
Buried in dust, once dead by fate.

GEORGE WITHER

1588 - 1667

FAREWELL, SWEET GROVES

from " Fair-Virtue "

Farewell,
Sweet groves to you;
You hills, that highest dwell,
And all you humble vales, adieu.
You wanton brooks and solitary rocks,
My dear companions all, and you, my tender flocks!
Farewell, my pipe, and all those pleasing songs, whose moving strains
Delighted once the fairest nymphs that dance upon the plains;
You discontents, whose deep and over-deadly smart,
Have, without pity, broke the truest heart;
Sighs, tears, and every sad annoy,
That erst did with me dwell,
And all other's joy,
Farewell!

Adieu,
Fair shepherdesses:
Let garlands of sad yew
Adorn your dainty golden tresses.
I, that loved you, and often with my quill
Made music that delighted fountain, grove, and hill:
I, whom you loved so, and with a sweet and chaste embrace.
(Yea, with a thousand rarer favours) would vouchsafe to grace,
I, now must leave you all alone, of love to plain;
And never pipe, nor never sing again.
I must, for evermore, be gone,
And therefore bid I you,
And every one,
Adieu.

WHAT CARE I?

Shall I, wasting in despair,
Die because a woman's fair?
Or my cheeks make pale with care
'Cause another's rosy are?
Be she fairer than the day
Or the flowery meads in May—
     If she be not so to me,
     What care I how fair she be?

Shall my foolish heart be pined
'Cause I see a woman kind?
Or a well disposèd nature
Joinèd with a lovely feature?
Be she meeker, kinder, than
Turtle-dove or pelican,
    If she be not so to me,
      What care I how kind she be?

Shall a woman's virtues move
Me to perish for her love?
Or her merits' value known
Make me quite forget mine own?
Be she with that goodness blest
Which may gain her name of Best;
    If she seem not such to me,
      What care I how good she be?

'Cause her fortune seems too high,
Shall I play the fool and die?
Those that bear a noble mind
Where they want of riches find,
Think what with them they would do
Who without them dare to woo;
    And unless that mind I see,
      What care I how great she be!

Great or good, or kind or fair,
I will ne'er the more despair;
If she love me, this believe,
I will die ere she shall grieve;
If she slight me when I woo,
I can scorn and let her go;
    For if she be not for me,
      What care I for whom she be?

THE SEVENTEENTH CENTURY

CAVALIERS, PURITANS, METAPHYSICIANS

All previous strains of English poetry reached a sudden amplification in the seventeenth century. Diverse political movements, new alignments in religion were reflected in swift cultural changes and in an enlarging literature. The gamut ranged from the extreme of delicacy to the height of sublimity; every creative impulse, from the minute to the magnificent, flourished in unprecedented variety. The Elizabethan courtliness was continued, even more nimbly turned, by the cavaliers Suckling, Lovelace and Waller; Herrick took the artfully artless lyric from Ben Jonson and surpassed his master in charm and craftsmanship. Dryden, changing the spirit as well as the versification at the end of the century, was the poet of transition, bridging the Renaissance and the Restoration. Far different and deeper harmonies were sounded by the metaphysical poets, poets in the combined rôles of ministers, " angels and earthly creatures." It was a curious music; lightly or ironically meditative in Marvell, gravely speculative in Vaughan and King, innocent and affirmative in Traherne, suffused with a most radiant simplicity (not a mere " quaintness ") in Herbert.

Milton towered above the literature of his day, and his age became as definitely " the age of Milton " as the preceding epoch was " the age of Shakespeare." Writing of *Paradise Lost*, Samuel Johnson, whose reactions to poetry were by turns invaluable and incredible, once concluded: " such is the power of Milton's poetry, that his will is obeyed without resistance; the reader feels himself in captivity to a higher and a nobler mind, and criticism sinks in admiration." Yet Johnson could not see (or hear) the magic in " Lycidas," an elegy which is one of Milton's finest, though, superficially, one of his most " difficult " poems. Johnson, like many others, was probably disturbed by the mounting periods, nonplussed by the remote allusions and the strange mixture of " heathen fictions " and " sacred truths." Yet " Lycidas " —certain schoolmen to the contrary—is not a scholar's exercise. As the late poet laureate, Robert Bridges, wrote, " It was not Dr. Johnson's ignorance or deficient education that made him dislike ' Lycidas.' It was his unpoetic mind that was at fault, and his taste in music or painting would probably have been at the same level. Moreover, children do not resent what they cannot understand in poetry, and they generally have a keener sense for beauty than Dr. Johnson had—indeed, if he would have become again as a little child, he might have liked ' Lycidas ' very well."

The difficulties dwindle if they do not disappear as one reads Milton. The pagan myths, the mythological references, the " remote allusions " are not the poetry but merely the properties, properties which, nevertheless, become an integral part of the poem. It is sheer rapture that lifts the line—whether in the happy running couplets of " L'Allegro " or the immediate orchestral surge of the first book of " Paradise Lost " —and it is nothing but this magic which is needed to translate

" Lycidas " to any reader who cares to listen. Here the poet has com-
bined his memories and his emotions and " the practical aspects of life
into a dreamy passionate flux " and, to quote Bridges again, " all is so
heightened and inspired that we do not wonder to find embedded
therein the clear prophecy of a conspicuous historical event: though
the whole literature can scarcely show any comparable example."

I have said so much (comparatively) of Milton because I have quoted
so much less than I would have chosen. Though my excuse is the
strictly limited space, I feel guilty because of the omission of the hymn
" On the Morning of Christ's Nativity " (which may be found in
practically every anthology), even though I have used the pages for the
full-length picture of Satan, a composite from " Paradise Lost."
I apologise for such condensation, rather than for the few textual
changes in spelling and punctuation.

ROBERT HERRICK

1591 - 1674

THE ARGUMENT OF HIS BOOK

I sing of Brooks, of Blossoms, Birds, and Bowers:
Of April, May, of June, and July-Flowers.
I sing of May-poles, Hock-carts, Wassails, Wakes,
Of Bride-grooms, Brides, and of their Bridal-cakes.
I write of Youth, of Love, and have access
By these, to sing of cleanly-wantonness.
I sing of Dews, of Rains, and piece by piece
Of Balm, of Oil, of Spice, and Amber-Greece.
I sing of Times trans-shifting; and I write
How Roses first came red, and Lilies white.
I write of Groves, of Twilights, and I sing
The Court of Mab, and of the Fairy-King.
I write of Hell; I sing (and ever shall)
Of Heaven, and hope to have it after all.

TO THE VIRGINS, TO MAKE MUCH OF TIME

Gather ye rose-buds while ye may,
    Old Time is still a-flying:
And this same flower that smiles to-day,
    To-morrow will be dying.

The glorious lamp of heaven, the Sun,
    The higher he's a-getting,
The sooner will his race be run,
    And nearer he's to setting.

That age is best which is the first,
    When youth and blood are warmer;
But being spent, the worse, and worst
    Times, still succeed the former.

Then be not coy, but use your time,
    And while ye may, go marry;
For having lost but once your prime,
    You may for ever tarry.

TO DAFFODILS

Fair daffodils, we weep to see
    You haste away so soon:
As yet the early-rising Sun
    Has not attained his noon.
        Stay, stay,
    Until the hasting day
        Has run
    But to the evensong;
And, having prayed together, we
    Will go with you along.

We have short time to stay, as you,
    We have as short a Spring!
As quick a growth to meet decay
    As you, or any thing.
        We die,
    As your hours do, and dry
        Away
    Like to the Summer's rain;
Or as the pearls of morning's dew
    Ne'er to be found again.

THE MAD MAID'S SONG

Good morrow to the day so fair;
    Good morning, sir, to you:
Good morrow to mine own torn hair
    Bedabbled with the dew.

Good morning to this primrose, too;
    Good morrow to each maid
That will with flowers the tomb bestrew,
    Wherein my love is laid.

Ah! woe is me; woe, woe is me!
    Alack and welladay!
For pity, sir, find out that bee,
    Which bore my love away.

I'll seek him in your bonnet brave;
    I'll seek him in your eyes;
Nay, now I think they've made his grave
    I' the bed of strawberries.

I'll seek him there; I know, ere this,
The cold, cold earth doth shake him;
But I will go, or send a kiss
    By you, sir, to awake him.

Pray hurt him not; though he be dead,
    He knows well who do love him,
And who with green-turfs rear his head,
    And who do rudely move him.

He's soft and tender (pray take heed),
    With bands of cowslips bind him;
And bring him home. But 'tis decreed,
    That I shall never find him.

TO DAISIES, NOT TO SHUT SO SOON

Shut not so soon; the dull-eyed night
    Has not as yet begun
To make a seizure on the light,
    Or to seal up the sun.

No marigolds yet closèd are;
    No shadows great appear;
Nor doth the early shepherd's star
    Shine like a spangle here.

Stay but till my Julia close
    Her life-begetting eye;
And let the whole world then dispose
    Itself to live or die.

UPON LOVE

Love brought me to a silent grove,
　　And showed me there a tree,
Where some had hanged themselves for love,
　　And gave a twist to me.

The halter was of silk and gold,
　　That he reacht forth unto me:
No otherwise, than if he would
　　By dainty things undo me.

He bade me then that necklace use;
　　And told me too, he maketh
A glorious end by such a noose,
　　His death for love that taketh.

'Twas but a dream. But had I been
　　There rèally alone,
My desperate fears, in love, had seen
　　Mine executiòn.

OBERON'S FEAST

Shapcot! to thee the Fairy State
I, with discretion, dedicate.
Because thou prizest things that are
Curious, and unfamiliar.
Take first the feast; these dishes gone;
We'll see the Fairy-Court anon.

A little mushroom-table spread,
After short prayers, they set on bread;
A moon-parcht grain of purest wheat,
With some small glitt'ring grit, to eat
His choice bits with; then in a trice
They make a feast less great than nice.
But all this while his eye is served,
We must not think his ear was starved:
But that there was in place to stir
His spleen, the chirring grasshopper;
The merry cricket, puling fly,
The piping gnat for minstrelsy.

And now, we must imagine first,
The elves present to quench his thirst
A pure seed-pearl of infant dew,
Brought and besweetened in a blue
And pregnant violet; which done,
His catlike eyes begin to run
Quite through the table, where he spies
The horns of papery butterflies:
Of which he eats, and tastes a little
Of that we call the cuckoo's spittle.
A little fuzz-ball pudding stands
By, yet not blessèd by his hands,
That was too coarse. But then, forthwith,
He ventures boldly on the pith
Of sugared rush, and eats the sag
And well bestrutted bee's sweet bag,
Gladding his palate with some store
Of emmets' eggs. What would he more?
But beards of mice, a newt's stewed thigh,
A bloated earwig, and a fly,
With the red-capped worm that's shut
Within the concave of a nut,
Brown as his tooth. A little moth,
Late fattened in a piece of cloth:
With withered cherries; mandrake's ears;
Moles' eyes; to these, the slain stag's tears:
The unctuous dewlaps of a snail;
The broke' heart of a nightingale
O'ercome in music; with a wine,
Ne'er ravisht from the flattering vine,
But gently prest from the soft side
Of the most sweet and dainty bride,
Brought in a dainty daisy, which
He fully quaffs up to bewitch
His blood to height. This done, commended
Grace by his priest. *The feast is ended.*

HIS PRAYER TO BEN JONSON

When I a verse shall make,
Know I have prayed thee,
For old religion's sake,
Saint Ben, to aid me.

Make the way smooth for me,
When I, thy Herrick,
Honouring thee, on my knee
Offer my lyric.

Candles I'll give to thee,
And a new altar;
And thou, Saint Ben, shalt be
Writ in my psalter.

TO ANTHEA WHO MAY COMMAND HIM ANYTHING

Bid me to live, and I will live
    Thy protestant to be:
Or bid me love, and I will give
    A loving heart to thee.

A heart as soft, a heart as kind,
    A heart as sound and free
As in the whole world thou canst find,
    That heart I'll give to thee.

Bid that heart stay, and it will stay,
    To honour thy decree:
Or bid it languish quite away,
    And 't shall do so for thee.

Bid me to weep, and I will weep
    While I have eyes to see:
And having none, yet I will keep
    A heart to weep for thee.

Bid me despair, and I'll despair,
    Under that cypress tree:
Or bid me die, and I will dare
    E'en Death, to die for thee.

Thou art my life, my love, my heart,
    The very eyes of me,
And hast command of every part,
    To live and die for thee.

DELIGHT IN DISORDER

A sweet disorder in the dress
Kindles in clothes a wantonness:
A lawn about the shoulders thrown
Into a fine distractiòn.
An erring lace, which here and there
Enthrals the crimson stomacher,
A cuff neglectful, and thereby
Ribbands to flow confusedly,
A winning wave (deserving note)
In the tempestuous petticoat,
A careless shoe-string, in whose tie
I see a wild civility,
Do more bewitch me, than when art
Is too precise in every part.

UPON JULIA'S CLOTHES

Whenas in silks my Julia goes
Then, then (methinks) how sweetly flows
That liquefaction of her clothes.

Next, when I cast mine eyes and see
That brave vibration each way free;
O how that glittering taketh me!

HENRY KING

1592 - 1669

THE SURRENDER

My once dear Love; hapless that I no more
Must call thee so: the rich affections' store
That fed our hopes, lies now exhaust and spent,
Like sums of treasure unto bankrupts lent.

We that did nothing study but the way
To love each other, with which thoughts the day
Rose with delight to us, and with them set,
Must learn the hateful art, how to forget.

We that did nothing wish that Heav'n could give
Beyond ourselves, nor did desire to live
Beyond that wish, all these now cancel must
As if not writ in faith, but words and dust.

Yet witness those clear vows which lovers make;
Witness the chaste desires that never break
Into unruly heats; witness that breast
Which in thy bosom anchored his whole rest.
'Tis no default in us, I dare acquit
Thy maiden faith, thy purpose fair and white
As thy pure self. Cross planets did envy
Us to each other, and Heaven did untie
Faster than vows could bind. O that the stars,
When lovers meet, should stand opposed in wars!

Since then some higher Destinies command.
Let us not strive, nor labour to withstand
What is past help. The longest date of grief
Can never yield a hope of our relief;
And though we waste ourselves in moist laments,
Tears may drown us, but not our discontents.

Fold back our arms, take home our fruitless loves,
That must new fortunes try, like turtle doves
Dislodgèd from their haunts. We must in tears
Unwind a love knit up in many years.
In this last kiss I here surrender thee
Back to thyself, so thou again art free.
Thou in another, sad as that, resend
The truest heart that lover ere did lend.

Now turn from each. So fare our severed hearts
As the divorced soul from her body parts.

A CONTEMPLATION UPON FLOWERS

Brave flowers—that I could gallant it like you,
　　And be so little vain!
You come abroad, and make a harmless show,
　　And to your beds of earth again.
You are not proud: you know your birth:
For your embroidered garments are from earth.

You do obey your months and times, but I
  Would have it ever Spring:
My fate would know no Winter, never die,
  Nor think of such a thing.
O that I could my bed of earth but view
And smile, and look as cheerfully as you!

O teach me to see Death and not to fear,
  But rather to take truce!
How often have I seen you at a bier,
  And there look fresh and spruce!
You fragrant flowers, then teach me, that my breath
Like yours may sweeten and perfume my death.

OF HUMAN LIFE

Like to the falling of a star,
Or as the flights of eagles are,—
Or like the fresh spring's gaudy hue,
Or silver drops of morning dew;
Or like a wind that chafes the flood,
Or bubbles which on water stood:
Even such a man, whose borrowed light
Is straight called in, and paid to night.
The wind blows out, the bubble dies;
The spring entombed in autumn lies;
The dew dries up, the star is shot;
The flight is past—and man forgot.

GEORGE HERBERT

1593 - 1633

THE PULLEY

When God at first made man,
Having a glass of blessings standing by—
Let us (said he) pour on him all we can;
Let the world's riches, which dispersèd lie,
  Contract into a span.

So strength first made a way,
Then beauty flowed, then wisdom, honour, pleasure:
When almost all was out, God made a stay,
Perceiving that, alone of all his treasure,
    Rest in the bottom lay.

    For if I should (said he)
Bestow this jewel also on my creature,
He would adore my gifts instead of me,
And rest in nature, not the God of nature,
    So both should losers be.

    Yet let him keep the rest,
But keep them with repining restlessness;
Let him be rich and weary, that at least,
If goodness lead him not, yet weariness
    May toss him to my breast.

DISCIPLINE

Throw away thy rod,
Throw away thy wrath;
    O my God,
Take the gentle path.

For my heart's desire
Unto thine is bent;
    I aspire
To a full consent.

Not a word or look
I affect to own,
    But by book,
And thy book alone.

Though I fail, I weep;
Though I halt in pace,
    Yet I creep
To the throne of grace.

Then let wrath remove;
Love will do the deed;
    For with love
Stony hearts will bleed.

Love is swift of foot;
Love's a man of war,
    And can shoot,
And can hit from far.

Who can 'scape his bow?
That which wrought on thee,
    Brought thee low,
Needs must work on me.

Throw away thy rod:
Though man frailties hath,
    Thou art God;
Throw away thy wrath.

PARADISE

I bless thee, Lord, because I GROW
Among the trees, which in a ROW
To thee both fruit and order OW.[1]

What open force, or hidden CHARM
Can blast my fruit, or bring me HARM,
While the inclosure is thine ARM:

Inclose me still for fear I START;
Be to me rather sharp and TART,
Than let me want thy hand and ART.

When thou dost greater judgments SPARE,
And with thy knife but prune and PARE,
Even fruitful trees more fruitful ARE:

Such sharpness shows the sweetest FREND,[1]
Such cuttings rather heal than REND,
And such beginning touch their END.

[1] The old spelling is retained in order to preserve Herbert's ingenious construction: furnishing new rhymes by the dropping of a single letter at a time.

HEAVEN

O, who will show me those delights on high?
                                        Echo: *I.*
Thou Echo, thou art mortal, all men know.
                                        Echo: *No.*
Wert thou not born among the trees and leaves?
                                        Echo: *Leaves.*
And are there any leaves that still abide?
                                        Echo: *Bide.*
What leaves are they? impart the matter wholly.
                                        Echo: *Holy.*
Are holy leaves the Echo, then, of bliss?
                                        Echo: *Yes.*
Then tell me, what is that supreme delight?
                                        Echo: *Light.*
Light to the mind; what shall the will enjoy?
                                        Echo: *Joy.*
But are there cares and business with the pleasure?
                                        Echo: *Leisure.*
Light, joy, and leisure; but shall they persèver?
                                        Echo: *Ever.*

MAN

My God, I heard this day
That none doth build a stately habitation,
  But he that means to dwell therein.
  What house more stately hath there been,
Or can be, than is man? to whose creation
  All things are in decay.

For man is everything,
And more: He is a tree, yet bears more fruit;[1]
  A beast, yet is, or should be, more:
  Reason and speech we only bring;
Parrots may thank us, if they are not mute,
  They go upon the score.

[1] This line usually reads:
        And more: he is a tree, yet bears no fruit;
which contradicts the sense and is at complete variance with Herbert's
evident intention. The Williams Manuscript has "mo," which certain
transcribers took to be "no," and most editions have perpetuated the
error.

Man is all symmetry,
Full of proportions, one limb to another,
    And all to all the world besides;
    Each part may call the furthest brother,
For head with foot hath private amity,
        And both with moons and tides.

    Nothing hath got so far,
But man hath caught and kept it as his prey;
    His eyes dismount the highest star;
    He is in little all the sphere;
Herbs gladly cure our flesh, because that they
        Find their acquaintance there.

    For us the winds do blow;
The earth doth rest, heaven move, and fountains flow;
    Nothing we see but means our good,
    As our delight or as our treasure.
The whole is either our cupboard of food,
        Or cabinet of pleasure.

    The stars have us to bed;
Night draws the curtain, which the sun withdraws;
    Music and light attend our head.
    All things unto our flesh are kind
In their descent and being; to our mind
        In their ascent and cause.

    Each thing is full of duty:
Waters united are our navigation;
    Distinguishèd, our habitation.
    Below, our drink; above, our meat;
Both are our cleanliness. Hath one such beauty?
        Then how are all things neat!

    More servants wait on man
Than he'll take notice of: in every path
    He treads down that which doth befriend him
    When sickness makes him pale and wan.
O mighty love! Man is one world, and hath
        Another to attend him.

Since then, my God, thou hast
So brave a palace built, O dwell in it,
   That it may dwell with thee at last!
   Till then afford us so much wit,
That, as the world serves us, we may serve thee,
   And both thy servants be.

THE ELIXIR

   Teach me, my God and King,
     In all things thee to see,
And what I do in anything
     To do it as for thee.

   Not rudely, as a beast,
     To run into an action;
But still to make thee prepossest,
     And give it his perfection.

   A man that looks on glass,
     On it may stay his eye;
Or, if he pleaseth, through it pass,
     And then the Heaven espy.

   All may of thee partake:
     Nothing can be so mean
Which with his tincture, (for thy sake)
     Will not grow bright and clean.

   A servant with this clause
     Makes drudgery divine;
Who sweeps a room, as for thy laws,
     Makes that and the action fine.

   This is the famous stone
     That turneth all to gold;
For that which God doth touch and own
     Cannot for less be told.

VIRTUE

Sweet day, so cool, so calm, so bright—
The bridal of the earth and sky;
The dew shall weep thy fall to-night;
     For thou must die.

Sweet rose, whose hue, angry and brave,
Bids the rash gazer wipe his eye,
Thy root is ever in its grave.
    And thou must die.

Sweet springs, full of sweet days and roses,
A box where sweets compacted lie,
My music shows ye have your closes,
    And all must die.

Only a sweet and virtuous soul,
Like seasoned timber, never gives;
But though the whole world turn to coal,
    Then chiefly lives.

LOVE

Love bade me welcome; yet my soul drew back,
    Guilty of dust and sin.
But quick-eyed Love, observing me grow slack
    From my first entrance in,
Drew nearer to me, sweetly questioning
    If I lacked anything.

" A guest," I answered, " worthy to be here."
    Love said, " You shall be he."
" I, the unkind, the ungrateful? Ah, my dear,
    I cannot look on Thee."
Love took my hand, and smiling, did reply,
    " Who made the eyes but I? "

" Truth, Lord, but I have marred them: let my shame
    Go where it doth deserve."
" And know you not," says Love, " who bore the blame? "
    " My dear, then I will serve."
" You must sit down," says Love, " and taste my meat."
    So I did sit and eat.

JAMES SHIRLEY

1596 - 1666

THE LEVELLING DUST

The glories of our blood and state
   Are shadows, not substantial things;
There is no armour against fate;
   Death lays his icy hand on kings:
      Sceptre and Crown
      Must tumble down,
And in the dust be equal made
With the poor crooked scythe and spade.

Some men with swords may reap the field,
   And plant fresh laurels where they kill:
But their strong nerves at last must yield;
   They tame but one another still:
      Early or late
      They stoop to fate,
And must give up their murmuring breath
When they, pale captives, creep to death.

The garlands wither on your brow;
   Then boast no more your mighty deeds;
Upon Death's purple altar now
   See where the victor-victim bleeds:
      Your heads must come
      To the cold tomb;
Only the actions of the just
Smell sweet, and blossom in their dust.

MORE WAYS TO KILL

Victorious men of earth, no more
   Proclaim how wide your empires are:
Though you bind-in every shore
   And your triumphs reach as far
      As night or day,
   Yet you, proud monarchs, must obey
And mingle with forgotten ashes, when
Death calls ye to the crowd of common men.

Devouring Famine, Plague, and War,
  Each able to undo mankind,
Death's servile emissaries are;
  Nor to these alone confined,
    He hath at will
  More quaint and subtle ways to kill;
A smile or kiss, as he will use the art,
Shall have the cunning skill to break a heart.

THOMAS CAREW

1598 - 1638

EPITAPH ON A YOUNG GIRL

  This little vault, this narrow room,
Of love and beauty is the tomb;
The dawning beam, that 'gan to clear
Our clouded sky lies darkened here,
For ever set to us: by Death
Sent to enflame the world beneath.
  'Twas but a bud, yet did contain
More sweetness than shall spring again;
A budding star, that might have grown
Into a sun when it had blown.
This hopeful beauty did create
New life in love's declining state;
But now his empire ends, and we
From fire and wounding darts are free.
  His brand, his bow, let no man fear:
  The flames, the arrows, all lie here.

NEVER-DYING FIRE

He that loves a rosy cheek
  Or a coral lip admires,
Or from star-like eyes doth seek
  Fuel to maintain his fires;
As old Time makes these decay,
So his flames must waste away.

But a smooth and steadfast mind,
   Gentle thoughts, and calm desires,
Hearts with equal love combined,
   Kindle never-dying fires:—
Where these are not, I despise
Lovely cheeks or lips or eyes.

WILLIAM DAVENANT

1606 - 1668

AWAKE! AWAKE!

The lark now leaves his watery nest,
   And, climbing, shakes his dewy wings.
He takes this window for the East,
   And to implore your light he sings—
Awake! awake! The morn will never rise
Till she can dress her beauty at your eyes.

The merchant bows unto the seaman's star,
   The ploughman from the sun his season takes;
But still the lover wonders what they are
   Who look for day before his mistress wakes.
Awake! awake! Break thro' your veils of lawn!
Then draw your curtains, and begin the dawn!

EDMUND WALLER

1606 - 1687

THE DANCER

Behold the brand of beauty tossed!
See how the motion does dilate the flame!
Delighted love his spoils does boast,
And triumph in this game.
Fire, to no place confined,
Is both our wonder and our fear;
Moving the mind,
As lightning hurled through air.

High heaven the glory does increase
Of all her shining lamps, this artful way;
The sun in figures, such as these,
Joys with the moon to play.
To the sweet strains they all advance,
Which do result from their own spheres,
As this nymph's dance
Moves with the numbers which she hears.

GO, LOVELY ROSE

Go, lovely Rose!
Tell her, that wastes her time and me,
That now she knows,
When I resemble her to thee,
How sweet and fair she seems to be.

Tell her that's young
And shuns to have her graces spied,
That hadst thou sprung
In deserts, where no men abide,
Thou must have uncommended died.

Small is the worth
Of beauty from the light retired.
Bid her come forth,
Suffer herself to be desired,
And not blush so to be admired.

Then die! that she,
The common fate of all things rare
May read in thee:
How small a part of time they share
They are so wondrous sweet and fair!

ON A GIRDLE

That which her slender waist confined
Shall now my joyful temples bind.
No monarch but would give his crown
His arms might do what this has done.

It was my heaven's extremest sphere,
The pale which held that lovely deer;
My joy, my grief, my hope, my love
Did all within this circle move.

A narrow compass! and yet there
Dwelt all that's good, and all that's fair.
Give me but what this ribband bound,
Take all the rest the sun goes round.

JOHN MILTON

1608 - 1674

ON SHAKESPEARE

What needs my Shakespeare for his honoured bones
The labour of an age in pilèd stones?
Or that his hallowed reliques should be hid
Under a stary-pointing pyramid?
Dear son of memory, great heir of fame,
What need'st thou such weak witness of thy name?
Thou in our wonder and astonishment
Hast built thyself a livelong monument.
For whilst, to the shame of slow-endeavouring art,
Thy easy numbers flow, and that each heart
Hath from the leaves of thy unvalued book
Those Delphic lines with deep impression took,
Then thou, our fancy of itself bereaving,
Dost make us marble with too much conceiving,
And so sepùlchred in such pomp dost lie
That kings for such a tomb would wish to die.

ON HIS BLINDNESS

When I consider how my light is spent
Ere half my days in this dark world and wide,
And that one talent which is death to hide
Lodged with me useless, though my soul more bent
To serve therewith my Maker, and present
My true account, lest He returning chide,
" Doth God exact day-labour, light denied? "
I fondly ask. But Patience, to prevent

That murmur, soon replies, " God doth not need
Either man's work or his own gifts. Who best
Bear his mild yoke, they serve him best. His state
Is kingly: thousands at his bidding speed,
And post o'er land and ocean without rest;
They also serve who only stand and wait."

SONG ON MAY MORNING

Now the bright morning star, Day's harbinger,
Comes dancing from the east, and leads with her
The flowery May, who from her green lap throws
The yellow cowslip and the pale primrose.
  Hail, bounteous May, that does inspire
  Mirth, and youth, and warm desire!
  Woods and groves are of thy dressing;
  Hill and dale doth boast thy blessing.
  Thus we salute thee with our early song,
  And welcome thee, and wish thee long.

L'ALLEGRO

Hence, loathèd Melancholy,
  Of Cerberus and blackest Midnight born
In Stygian cave forlorn
  'Mongst horrid shapes, and shrieks, and sights unholy!
Find out some uncouth cell
  Where brooding Darkness spreads his jealous wings
And the night-raven sings;
  There under ebon shades, and low-browed rocks
As ragged as thy locks,
  In dark Cimmerian desert ever dwell.
But come, thou goddess fair and free,
In heaven yclept Euphrosyne,
And by men, heart-easing Mirth,
Whom lovely Venus at a birth
With two sister Graces more
To ivy-crownèd Bacchus bore;
Or whether (as some sages sing)
The frolic wind that breathes the spring,
Zephyr, with Aurora playing,
As he met her once a-Maying—

There on beds of violets blue
And fresh-blown roses washed in dew
Filled her with thee, a daughter fair,
So buxom, blithe, and debonair.
 Haste thee, Nymph, and bring with thee
Jest and youthful jollity,
Quips and cranks and wanton wiles,
Nods and becks and wreathèd smiles,
Such as hang on Hebe's cheek
And love to live in dimple sleek;
Sport that wrinkled Care derides,
And Laughter holding both his sides.
Come, and trip it as you go
On the light fantastic toe;
And in thy right hand lead with thee
The mountain-nymph, sweet Liberty;
And if I give thee honour due
Mirth, admit me of thy crew,
To live with her, and live with thee
In unreprovèd pleasures free;
To hear the lark begin his flight
And singing startle the dull night
From his watch-tower in the skies,
Till the dappled dawn doth rise;
Then to come, in spite of sorrow,
And at my window bid good-morrow
Through the sweetbrier, or the vine,
Or the twisted eglantine:
While the cock with lively din
Scatters the rear of darkness thin,
And to the stack, or the barn-door,
Stoutly struts his dames before:
Oft listening how the hounds and horn
Cheerly rouse the slumbering morn,
From the side of some hoar hill,
Through the high wood echoing shrill;
Sometime walking, not unseen,
By hedge-row elms, on hillocks green,
Right against the eastern gate
Where the great Sun begins his state
Robed in flames and amber light,
The clouds in thousand liveries dight;
While the ploughman, near at hand,
Whistles o'er the furrowed land,
And the milkmaid singeth blithe,

And the mower whets his scythe,
And every shepherd tells his tale
Under the hawthorn in the dale.

   Straight mine eye hath caught new pleasures
Whilst the landscape round it measures;
Russet lawns, and fallows gray,
Where the nibbling flocks do stray;
Mountains, on whose barren breast
The labouring clouds do often rest;
Meadows trim with daisies pied,
Shallow brooks, and rivers wide;
Towers and battlements it sees
Bosomed high in tufted trees,
Where perhaps some beauty lies,
The cynosure of neighbouring eyes.

   Hard by, a cottage chimney smokes
From betwixt two aged oaks,
Where Corydon and Thyrsis, met,
Are at their savoury dinner set
Of herbs, and other country messes
Which the neat-handed Phillis dresses;
And then in haste her bower she leaves
With Thestylis to bind the sheaves;
Or, if the earlier season lead,
To the tanned haycock in the mead.

   Sometimes with secure delight
The upland hamlets will invite,
When the merry bells ring round,
And the jocund rebecks sound
To many a youth and many a maid,
Dancing in the chequered shade;
And young and old come forth to play
On a sun-shine holy-day,
Till the live-long day-light fail:
Then to the spicy nut-brown ale,
With stories told of many a feat,
How faery Mab the junkets eat:—
She was pinched, and pulled, she said;
And he, by friar's lantern led,
Tells how the drudging Goblin sweat,
To earn his cream-bowl duly set,
When in one night, ere glimpse of morn,
His shadowy flail hath threshed the corn
That ten day-labourers could not end;
Then lies him down the lubber fiend,

And, stretched out all the chimney's length,
Basks at the fire his hairy strength;
And crop-full out of doors he flings,
Ere the first cock his matin rings.
Thus done the tales, to bed they creep,
By whispering winds soon lulled asleep.
  Towered cities please us then
And the busy hum of men,
Where throngs of knights and barons bold,
In weeds[1] of peace, high triumphs hold,
With store of ladies, whose bright eyes
Rain influence, and judge the prize
Of wit or arms, while both contend
To win her grace, whom all commend.
There let Hymen oft appear
In saffron robe, with taper clear,
And pomp, and feast, and revelry,
With mask, and antique pageantry;
Such sights as youthful poets dream
On summer eves by haunted stream.
Then to the well-trod stage anon,
If Jonson's learnèd sock be on,
Or sweetest Shakespeare, Fancy's child,
Warble his native wood-notes wild.
  And ever against eating cares
Lap me in soft Lydian airs
Married to immortal verse,
Such as the meeting soul may pierce
In notes, with many a winding bout
Of linkèd sweetness long drawn out,
With wanton heed and giddy cunning,
The melting voice through mazes running,
Untwisting all the chains that tie
The hidden soul of harmony;
That Orpheus' self may heave his head
From golden slumber, on a bed
Of heaped Elysian flowers, and hear
Such strains as would have won the ear
Of Pluto, to have quite set free
His half-regained Eurydice.
  These delights if thou canst give,
Mirth, with thee I mean to live.

---

[1] Weeds: apparel. Some editions make this "weeks of peace," but "weeds" is evidently the correct form.

IL PENSEROSO

Hence, vain deluding Joys,
   The brood of Folly without father bred!
How little you bestead
   Or fill the fixèd mind with all your toys!
Dwell in some idle brain,
   And fancies fond with gaudy shapes possess
As thick and numberless
   As the gay motes that people the sunbeams,
Or likest hovering dreams,
   The fickle pensioners of Morpheus' train.
But hail, thou goddess sage and holy.
Hail, divinest Melancholy!
Whose saintly visage is too bright
To hit the sense of human sight,
And therefore to our weaker view
O'erlaid with black, staid Wisdom's hue;
Black, but such as in esteem
Prince Memnon's sister might beseem,
Or that starred Ethiop queen that strove
To set her beauty's praise above
The sea-nymphs, and their powers offended.
Yet thou art higher far descended:
Thee bright-haired Vesta, long of yore,
To solitary Saturn bore;
His daughter she; in Saturn's reign
Such mixture was not held a stain:
Oft in glimmering bowers and glades
He met her, and in secret shades
Of woody Ida's inmost grove,
While yet there was no fear of Jove.
   Come, pensive Nun, devout and pure,
Sober, steadfast, and demure,
All in a robe of darkest grain
Flowing with majestic train,
And sable stole of cypres lawn
Over thy decent shoulders drawn.
Come, but keep thy wonted state,
With even step, and musing gait,
And looks commercing with the skies,
Thy rapt soul sitting in thine eyes;
There, held in holy passion still,

Forget thyself to marble, till
With a sad leaden downward cast
Thou fix them on the earth as fast:
And join with thee calm Peace, and Quiet,
Spare Fast, that oft with gods doth diet,
And hears the Muses in a ring
Aye round about Jove's altar sing:
And add to these retirèd Leisure
That in trim gardens takes his pleasure:—
But first and chiefest, with thee bring
Him that yon soars on golden wing
Guiding the fiery-wheelèd throne,
The cherub Contemplatìon;
And the mute Silence hist along,
'Less Philomel will deign a song
In her sweetest saddest plight,
Smoothing the rugged brow of Night,
While Cynthia checks her dragon yoke
Gently o'er the accustomed oak.
Sweet bird, that shunn'st the noise of folly,
Most musical, most melancholy!
Thee, chauntress, oft, the woods among
I woo, to hear thy even-song;
And missing thee, I walk unseen
On the dry smooth-shaven green,
To behold the wandering Moon
Riding near her highest noon,
Like one that had been led astray
Through the heaven's wide pathless way,
And oft, as if her head she bowed,
Stooping through a fleecy cloud.
    Oft, on a plat of rising ground
I hear the far-off curfew sound
Over some wide-watered shore,
Swinging slow with sullen roar:
Or, if the air will not permit,
Some still removèd place will fit,
Where blowing embers through the room
Teach light to counterfeit a gloom,
Far from all resort of mirth,
Save the cricket on the hearth,
Or the bellman's drowsy charm
To bless the doors from nightly harm.
    Or let my lamp at midnight hour
Be seen in some high lonely tower,

Where I may oft out-watch the Bear
With thrice-great Hermes, or unsphe
The spirit of Plato, to unfold
What worlds or what vast regions hol
The immortal mind that hath forsook
Her mansion in this fleshly nook:
And of those demons that are found
In fire, air, flood, or under ground,
Whose power hath a true consent
With planet, or with element.
Sometime let gorgeous Tragedy
In sceptred pall come sweeping by,
Presenting Thebes, or Pelops' line,
Or the tale of Troy divine;
Or what (though rare) of later age
Ennobled hath the buskined stage.
    But, O sad Virgin, that thy power,
Might raise Muaesus from his bower,
Or bid the soul of Orpheus sing
Such notes as, warbled to the string,
Drew iron tears down Pluto's cheek
And made Hell grant what Love did seek! . . .
    Thus, Night, oft see me in thy pale career,
Till civil-suited Morn appear,
Not tricked and frounced as she was wont
With the Attic Boy to hunt,
But kerchiefed in a comely cloud
While rocking winds are piping loud,
Or ushered with a shower still,
When the gust hath blown his fill,
Ending on the rustling leaves
With minute drops from off the eaves.
And when the sun begins to fling
His flaring beams, me, goddess, bring
To archèd walks of twilight groves,
And shadows brown, that Sylvan loves,
Of pine, or monumental oak,
Where the rude axe, with heavèd stroke,
Was never heard the nymphs to daunt
Or fright them from their hallowed haunt.
There in close covert by some brook
Where no profaner eye may look,
Hide me from day's garish eye,
While the bee with honeyed thigh,
That at her flowery work doth sing,

And the waters murmuring,
With such consort as they keep,
Entice the dewy-feathered Sleep;
And let some strange mysterious dream
Wave at his wings in airy stream
Of lively portraiture displayed,
Softly on my eyelids laid:
And, as I wake, sweet music breathe
Above, about, or underneath,
Sent by some spirit to mortals good,
Or the unseen Genius of the wood.
    But let my due feet never fail
To walk the studious cloister's pale
And love the high-embowèd roof,
With antique pillars massy proof
And storied windows richly dight,
Casting a dim religious light:
There let the pealing organ blow
To the full-voiced quire below
In service high and anthems clear,
As may with sweetness, through mine ear,
Dissolve me into ecstasies,
And bring all Heaven before mine eyes.
    And may at last my weary age
Find out the peaceful hermitage,
The hairy gown and mossy cell
Where I may sit and rightly spell
Of every star that heaven doth shew,
And every herb that sips the dew;
Till old experience do attain
To something like prophetic strain.
    These pleasures, Melancholy, give,
And I with thee will choose to live.

ON TIME

Fly, envious Time, till thou run out thy race:
Call on the lazy, leaden-stepping hours,
Whose speed is but the heavy plummet's pace;
And glut thyself with what thy womb devours,
Which is no more than what is false and vain,
And merely mortal dross;
So little is our loss,

So little is thy gain!
For, when as each thing bad thou hast entombed,
And, last of all, thy greedy self consumed,
Then long Eternity shall greet our bliss
With an individual kiss,
And Joy shall overtake us as a flood;
When every thing that is sincerely good,
And perfectly divine,
With Truth, and Peace, and Love, shall ever shine
About the supreme throne
Of him, to whose happy-making sight alone
When once our heavenly-guided soul shall climb,
Then, all this earthly grossness quit,
Attired with stars we shall for ever sit,
Triumphing over Death, and Chance, and thee, O Time!

SONGS

from " Arcades "

O'er the smooth enamelled green,
Where no print of step hath been,
  Follow me, as I sing
  And touch the warbled string;
Under the shady roof
Of branching elm star-proof
    Follow me.
I will bring you where she sits,
Clad in splendour as befits
      Her deity.
Such a rural Queen
All Arcadia hath not seen.

from " Comus "

I

Sweet Echo, sweetest nymph, that liv'st unseen
    Within thy airy shell
  By slow Meander's margent green,
And in the violet-embroidered vale
    Where the love-lorn nightingale
Nightly to thee her sad song mourneth well:
Canst thou not tell me of a gentle pair

That likest thy Narcissus are?
   O, if thou have
Hid them in some flowery cave,
   Tell me but where,
Sweet Queen of Parley, Daughter of the Sphere!
So may'st thou be translated to the skies,
And give resounding grace to all Heaven's harmonies!

2

The star that bids the shepherd fold
Now the top of heaven doth hold;
And the gilded car of day
His glowing axle doth allay
In the steep Atlantic stream;
And the slope sun his upward beam
Shoots against the dusky pole,
Pacing toward the other goal
Of his chamber in the east.
Meanwhile, welcome joy and feast,
Midnight shout and revelry,
Tipsy dance and jollity.
Braid your locks with rosy twine,
Dropping odours, dropping wine.
Rigour now is gone to bed;
And Advice with scrupulous head,
Strict Age, and sour Severity,
With their grave saws, in slumber lie.
We, that are of purer fire,
Imitate the starry quire,
Who, in their nightly watchful spheres,
Lead in swift round the months and years.
The sounds and seas, with all their finny drove,
Now to the moon in wavering morrice move;
And on the tawny sands and shelves
Trip the pert fairies and the dapper elves.
By dimpled brook and fountain-brim,
The wood-nymphs, decked with daisies trim.
Their merry wakes and pastimes keep:
What hath night to do with sleep?
Night hath better sweets to prove;
Venus now wakes, and wakens Love.
Come, let us our rites begin;
'Tis only daylight that makes sin. . . .
Come, knit hands, and beat the ground
In a light fantastic round.

3

To the ocean now I fly,
And those happy climes that lie
Where day never shuts his eye,
Up in the broad fields of the sky.
There I suck the liquid air,
All amidst the gardens fair
Of Hesperus, and his daughters three
That sing about the golden tree.
Along the crispèd shades and bowers
Revels the spruce and jocund Spring;
The Graces and the rosy-bosomed Hours
Thither all their bounties bring.
There eternal Summer dwells,
And west winds with musky wing
About the cedarn alleys fling
Nard and cassia's balmy smells.
Iris there with humid bow
Waters the odorous banks, that blow
Flowers of more mingled hue
Than her purfled scarf can shew,
And drenches with Elysian dew
(List, mortals, if your ears be true)
Beds of hyacinth and roses,
Where young Adonis oft reposes,
Waxing well of his deep wound,
In slumber soft, and on the ground
Sadly sits the Assyrian queen.
But far above, in spangled sheen,
Celestial Cupid, her famed son, advanced,
Holds his dear Psyche, sweet entranced
After her wandering labours long,
Till free consent the gods among
Make her his eternal bride,
And from her fair unspotted side
Two blissful twins are to be born,
Youth and Joy; so Jove hath sworn.

But now my task is smoothly done:
I can fly, or I can run
Quickly to the green earth's end,
Where the bowed welkin slow doth bend,
And from thence can soar as soon
     To the corners of the moon.

Mortals, that would follow me,
Love Virtue; she alone is free.
She can teach ye how to climb
Higher than the sphery chime;
Or, if Virtue feeble were,
Heaven itself would stoop to her.

SATAN

from " Paradise Lost," Book I

           . . . His pride
Had cast him out from Heaven, with all his host
Of rebel Angels, by whose aid, aspiring
To set himself in glory above his peers,
He trusted to have equalled the Most High,
If he opposed, and, with ambitious aim
Against the throne and monarchy of God,
Raised impious war in Heaven and battle proud,
With vain attempt. Him the Almighty Power
Hurled headlong flaming from the ethereal sky,
With hideous ruin and combustion, down
To bottomless perdition, there to dwell
In adamantine chains and penal fire,
Who durst defy the Omnipotent to arms.
   Nine times the space that measures day and night
To mortal men, he, with his horrid crew,
Lay vanquished, rolling in the fiery gulf,
Confounded, though immortal. But his doom
Reserved him to more wrath; for now the thought
Both of lost happiness and lasting pain
Torments him: round he throws his baleful eyes,
That witnessed huge affliction and dismay,
Mixed with obdurate pride and steadfast hate.
At once, as far as Angels ken, he views
The dismal situation waste and wild.
A dungeon horrible, on all sides round,
As one great furnace flamed; yet from those flames
No light; but rather darkness visible
Served only to discover sights of woe,
Regions of sorrow, doleful shades, where peace
And rest can never dwell, hope never comes
That comes to all, but torture without end
Still urges, and a fiery deluge, fed
With ever burning sulphur unconsumed.

Such place Eternal Justice had prepared
For those rebellious; here their prison ordained
In utter darkness, and their portion set,
As far removed from God and light of Heaven
As from the centre thrice to the utmost pole.
Oh, how unlike the place from whence they fell!
There the companions of his fall, o'erwhelmed
With floods and whirlwinds of tempestuous fire,
He soon discerns; and, weltering by his side,
One next himself in power, and next in crime,
Long after known in Palestine, and named
Beëlzebub. To whom the Arch-Enemy,
And thence in Heaven called Satan, with bold words
Breaking the horrid silence, thus began:—
    " If thou beest he—but, Oh, how fallen! how changed
From him!—who, in the happy realms of light,
Clothed with transcendent brightness, didst outshine
Myriads, though bright—if he whom mutual league,
United thoughts and counsels, equal hope
And hazard in the glorious enterprise,
Joined with me once, now misery hath joined
In equal ruin; into what pit thou seest
From what height fallen: so much the stronger proved
He with his thunder: and till then who knew
The force of those dire arms? Yet not for those,
Nor what the potent Victor in his rage
Can else inflict, do I repent, or change,
Though changed in outward lustre, that fixed mind,
And high disdain from sense of injured merit,
That with the Mightiest raised me to contend,
And to the fierce contentions brought along
Innumerable force of Spirits armed,
That durst dislike his reign, and, me preferring,
His utmost power with adverse power opposed
In dubious battle on the plains of Heaven,
And shook his throne. What though the field be lost!
All is not lost—the unconquerable will,
And study of revenge, immortal hate,
And courage never to submit or yield:
And what is else not to be overcome."

    °   °   °   °   °   °

    Thus Satan, talking to his nearest mate,
With head uplift above the wave, and eyes
That sparkling blazed; his other parts besides

Prone on the flood, extended long and large,
Lay floating many a rood, in bulk as huge
As whom the fables name of monstrous size,
Titanian or Earth-born, that warred on Jove,
Briareos or Typhon, whom the den
By ancient Tarsus held, or that sea-beast
Leviathan, which God of all his works
Created hugest that swim the ocean-stream;
Him, haply slumbering on the Norway foam,
The pilot of some small night-foundered skiff,
Deeming some island, oft, as seamen tell,
With fixèd anchor in his scaly rind,
Moors by his side under the lee, while night
Invests the sea, and wishèd morn delays.
So stretched out huge in length the Arch-fiend lay,
Chained on the burning lake; nor ever thence
Had risen, or heaved his head, but that the will
And high permission of all-ruling heaven
Left him at large to his own dark designs. . . .

Forthwith upright he rears from off the pool
His mighty stature; on each hand the flames
Driven backward slope their pointing spires, and, rolled
In billows, leave i' the midst a horrid vale.
Then with expanded wings he steers his flight
Aloft, incumbent on the dusky air,
That felt unusual weight; till on dry land
He lights—if it were land that ever burned
With solid, as the lake with liquid fire,
And such appeared in hue as when the force
Of subterranean wind transports a hill
Torn from Pelorus, or the shattered side
Of thundering Ætna, whose combustible
And fuelled entrails, thence conceiving fire,
Sublimed with mineral fury, aid the winds,
And leave a singèd bottom all involved
With stench and smoke.

        .   .   .   .   .   .

He scarce had ceased when the superior Fiend
Was moving toward the shore; his ponderous shield,
Ethereal temper, massy, large, and round,
Behind him cast. The broad circumference
Hung on his shoulders like the moon, whose orb

Through optic glass the Tuscan artist views[1]
At evening, from the top of Fiesolè,
Or in Valdarno, to descry new lands,
Rivers, or mountains, in her spotty globe.
His spear—to equal which the tallest pine
Hewn on Norwegian hills, to be the mast
Of some great admiral, were but a wand—
He walked with, to support uneasy steps
Over the burning marle, not like those steps
On Heaven's azure; and the torrid clime
Smote on him sore besides, vaulted with fire.
Nathless he so endured, till on the beach
Of that inflamèd sea he stood, and called
His legions. . . . " Princes, Potentates,
Warriors, the flower of Heaven—once yours; now lost,
If such astonishment as this can seize
Eternal Spirits! Or have ye chosen this place
After the toil of battle to repose
Your wearied virtue, for the ease you find
To slumber here, as in the vales of Heaven?
Or in this abject posture have ye sworn
To adore the Conqueror, who now beholds
Cherub and Seraph rolling in the flood
With scattered arms and ensigns, till anon
His swift pursuers from Heaven-gates discern
The advantage, and, descending, tread us down
Thus drooping, or with linkèd thunderbolts
Transfix us to the bottom of this gulf?—
Awake, arise, or be for ever fallen! "
     They heard, and were abashed, and up they sprung
Upon the wing, as when men wont to watch,
On duty sleeping found by whom they dread,
Rouse and bestir themselves ere well awake.
Nor did they not perceive the evil plight
In which they were, or the fierce pains not feel;
Yet to their General's voice they soon obeyed
Innumberable. As when the potent rod
Of Amram's son, in Egypt's evil day,
Waved round the coast, up-called a pitchy cloud
Of locusts, warping on the eastern wind,
That o'er the realm of impious Pharaoh hung
Like Night, and darkened all the land of Nile;

[1] The reference is to the astonomer Galileo whom Milton had visited.
Fiesolè is a town near Florence; Valdarno is the valley of the river
Arno.

So numberless were those bad Angels seen
Hovering on wing under the cope of Hell.

.   .   .   .   .   .

   All these and more came flocking; but with looks
Downcast and damp; yet such wherein appeared
Obscure some glimpse of joy to have found their Chief
Not in despair, to have found themselves not lost
In loss itself; which on his countenance cast
Like doubtful hue. But he, his wonted pride
Soon recollecting, with high word, that bore
Semblance of worth, not substance, gently raised
Their fainting courage, and dispelled their fears:
Then straight commands that, at the warlike sound
Of trumpets loud and clarions, be upreared
His mighty standard. That proud honour claimed
Azazel as his right, a Cherub tall:
Who forthwith from the glittering staff unfurled
The imperial ensign; which, full high advanced,
Shone like a meteor streaming to the wind,
With gems and golden lustre rich emblazed,
Seraphic arms and trophies; all the while
Sonorous metal blowing martial sounds:
At which the universal host up-sent
A shout that tore Hell's concave, and beyond
Frighted the reign of Chaos and old Night.

EVE AND THE SERPENT

from " Paradise Lost," Book IX

As one who, long in populous city pent,[1]
Where houses thick and sewers annoy the air,
Forth issuing on a summer's morn, to breathe
Among the pleasant villages and farms
Adjoined, from each thing met conceives delight—
The smell of grain, or tedded grass, or kine,
Or dairy, each rural sight, each rural sound—
If chance with nymph-like step fair virgin pass,
What pleasing seemed, for her now pleases more,
She most, and in her look sums all delight:
Such pleasure took the Serpent to behold
This flowery plat, the sweet recess of Eve

[1] See the sonnet by Keats beginning " To one who has been long in
city pent " on page 373.

Thus early, thus alone. Her heavenly form
Angelic, but more soft and feminine,
Her graceful innocence, her every air
Of gesture or least action, overawed
His malice, and with rapine sweet bereaved
His fierceness of the fierce intent it brought.
That space the Evil One abstracted stood
From his own evil, and for the time remained
Stupidly good, of enmity disarmed,
Of guile, of hate, of envy, of revenge.
But the hot hell that always in him burns,
Though in mid Heaven, soon ended his delight
And tortures him now more the more he sees
Of pleasure not for him ordained. Then soon
Fierce hate he recollects, and all his thoughts
Of mischief, gratulating, thus excites:—
  " Thoughts, whither have ye led me? with what sweet
Compulsion thus transported to forget
What hither brought us? hate, not love, nor hope
Of Paradise for Hell, hope here to taste
Of pleasure, but all pleasure to destroy,
Save what is in destroying; other joy
To me is lost. Then let me not let pass
Occasion which now smiles. Behold alone
The Woman, opportune to all attempts—
Her husband, for I view far round, not nigh,
Whose higher intellectual more I shun,
And strength, of courage haughty, and of limb
Heroic built, though of terrestrial mould;
Foe not informidable, exempt from wound—
I not; so much hath Hell debased, and pain
Enfeebled me, to what I was in Heaven.
She fair, divinely fair, fit love for Gods,
Not terrible, though terror be in love,
And beauty, not approached by stronger hate,
Hate stronger under show of love well feigned—
The way which to her ruin now I tend."
  So spake the Enemy of Mankind, enclosed
In serpent, inmate bad, and toward Eve
Addressed his way—not with indented wave,
Prone on the ground, as since, but on his rear,
Circular base of rising folds, that towered
Fold above fold, a surging maze; his head
Crested aloft, and carbuncle his eyes;
With burnished neck of verdant gold, erect

Amidst his circling spires, that on the grass
Floated redundant. . . . With track oblique
At first, as one who sought access but feared
To interrupt, sidelong he works his way.
As when a ship, by skilful steersman wrought
Nigh river's mouth, or foreland, where the wind
Veers oft, as oft so steers, and shifts her sail,
So varied he, and of his tortuous train
Curled many a wanton wreath in sight of Eve,
To lure her eye. She, busied, heard the sound
Of rustling leaves, but minded not, as used
To such disport before her through the field
From every beast, more duteous at her call
Than at Circean call the herd disguised.
He, bolder now, uncalled, before her stood,
But as in gaze admiring. Oft he bowed
His turret crest and sleek enamelled neck,
Fawning, and licked the ground whereon she trod.

LYCIDAS[1]

Yet once more, O ye laurels, and once more,
Ye myrtles brown, with ivy never sere,
I come to pluck your berries harsh and crude,
And with forced fingers rude
Shatter your leaves before the mellowing year.
Bitter constraint and sad occasion dear
Compels me to disturb your season due:
For Lycidas is dead, dead ere his prime,
Young Lycidas, and hath not left his peer:
Who would not sing for Lycidas? he knew
Himself to sing, and build the lofty rhyme.
He must not float upon his watery bier
Unwept, and welter to the parching wind,
Without the meed of some melodious tear.

Begin then, Sisters of the sacred well
That from beneath the seat of Jove doth spring;
Begin, and somewhat loudly sweep the string;

[1] In this Monody the author bewails a learned friend unfortunately
drowned in his passage from Chester on the Irish Seas, 1637; and, by
occasion, foretells the ruin of the corrupted Clergy, then in their height.

Hence, with denial vain and coy excuse.
So may some gentle Muse
With lucky words favour my destined urn;
And as he passes, turn
And bid fair peace be to my sable shroud.

For we were nursed upon the self-same hill,
Fed the same flock by fountain, shade, and rill.
Together both, ere the high lawns appeared
Under the opening eye-lids of the Morn,
We drove a-field, and both together heard
What time the grey-fly winds her sultry horn,
Battening our flocks with the fresh dews of night;
Oft till the star, that rose at evening bright,
Toward heaven's descent had sloped his westering wheel.
Meanwhile the rural ditties were not mute,
Tempered to the oaten flute;
Rough Satyrs danced, and Fauns with cloven heel
From the glad sound would not be absent long;
And old Damœtas loved to hear our song.

But, O the heavy change, now thou art gone,
Now thou art gone, and never must return!
Thee, Shepherd, thee the woods and desert caves
With wild thyme and the gadding vine o'ergrown,
And all their echoes, mourn:
The willows and the hazel copses green
Shall now no more be seen
Fanning their joyous leaves to thy soft lays:—
As killing as the canker to the rose,
Or taint-worm to the weanling herds that graze,
Or frost to flowers, that their gay wardrobe wear
When first the white-thorn blows;
Such, Lycidas, thy loss to shepherd's ear.

Where were ye, Nymphs, when the remorseless deep
Closed o'er the head of your loved Lycidas?
For neither were ye playing on the steep
Where your old bards, the famous Druids, lie,
Nor on the shaggy top of Mona high,
Nor yet where Deva spreads her wizard stream.
Ay me! I fondly dream—
Had ye been there—for what could that have done,

What could the Muse herself that Orpheus bore,
The Muse herself, for her enchanting son,
Whom universal nature did lament,
When by the rout that made the hideous roar
His gory visage down the stream was sent,
Down the swift Hebrus to the Lesbian shore?

Alas! what boots it with incessant care
To tend the homely, slighted, shepherd's trade
And strictly meditate the thankless Muse?
Were it not better done, as others use,
To sport with Amaryllis in the shade,
Or with the tangles of Neæra's hair?
Fame is the spur that the clear spirit doth raise
(That last infirmity of noble mind)
To scorn delights, and live laborious days;
But the fair guerdon when we hope to find,
And think to burst out into sudden blaze,
Comes the blind Fury with the abhorrèd shears
And slits the thin-spun life. " But not the praise,"
Phœbus replied, and touched my trembling ears.
" Fame is no plant that grows on mortal soil,
Nor in the glistering foil
Set off to the world, nor in broad rumour lies:
But lives and spreads aloft by those pure eyes
And perfect witness of all-judging Jove;
As he pronounces lastly on each deed,
Of so much fame in heaven expect thy meed."

O fountain Arethuse, and thou honoured flood,
Smooth-sliding Mincius, crowned with vocal reeds!
That strain I heard was of a higher mood:
But now my oat proceeds,
And listens to the herald of the sea
That came in Neptune's plea;
He asked the waves, and asked the felon winds,
What hard mishap hath doomed this gentle swain?
And questioned every gust of rugged wings
That blows from off each beakèd promontory:
They knew not of his story;
And sage Hippotadès their answer brings,
That not a blast was from his dungeon strayed;
The air was calm, and on the level brine
Sleek Panopè, with all her sisters played.

It was that fatal and perfidious bark
Built in the eclipse, and rigged with curses dark,
That sunk so low that sacred head of thine.

Next Camus, reverend sire, went footing slow,
His mantle hairy, and his bonnet sedge
Inwrought with figures dim, and on the edge
Like to that sanguine flower inscribed with woe:
" Ah! who hath reft," quoth he, " my dearest pledge! "
Last came, and last did go
The Pilot of the Galilean lake;
Two massy keys he bore of metals twain
(The golden opes, the iron shuts amain);
He shook his mitred locks, and stern bespake:
" How well could I have spared for thee, young swain,
Enow of such, as for their bellies' sake
Creep and intrude and climb into the fold!
Of other care they little reckoning make
Than how to scramble at the shearers' feast,
And shove away the worthy bidden guest;
Blind mouths! that scarce themselves know how to hold
A sheep-hook, or have learned aught else the least
That to the faithful herdman's art belongs!
What recks it them? What need they? They are sped;
And when they list, their lean and flashy songs
Grate on their scrannel pipes of wretched straw;
The hungry sheep look up, and are not fed,
But swol'n with wind and the rank mist they draw
Rot inwardly, and foul contagion spread:
Besides what the grim wolf with privy paw
Daily devours apace, and nothing said:
—But that two-handed engine at the door
Stands ready to smite once, and smite no more."
Return, Alpheus; the dread voice is past
That shrunk thy streams; return, Sicilian Muse,
And call the vales, and bid them hither cast
Their bells and flowerets of a thousand hues.
Ye valleys low, where the mild whispers use
Of shades, and wanton winds, and gushing brooks
On whose fresh lap the swart star sparely looks;
Throw hither all your quaint enamelled eyes
That on the green turf suck the honeyed showers
And purple all the ground with vernal flowers.
Bring the rathe primrose that forsaken dies,

The tufted crow-toe, and pale jessamine,
The white pink, and the pansy freaked with jet,
The glowing violet,
The musk-rose, and the well-attired woodbine,
With cowslips wan that hang the pensive head,
And every flower that sad embroidery wears:
Bid amaranthus all his beauty shed,
And daffadillies fill their cups with tears
To strew the laureate hearse where Lycid lies.
For so to interpose a little ease,
Let our frail thoughts dally with false surmise.
Ay me! whilst thee the shores and sounding seas
Wash far away,—where'er thy bones are hurled,
Whether beyond the stormy Hebrides
Where thou, perhaps, under the whelming tide,
Visitest the bottom of the monstrous world;
Or whether thou, to our moist vows denied,
Sleep'st by the fable of Bellerus old
Where the great Vision of the guarded mount
Looks toward Namancos and Bayona's hold,
—Look homeward, Angel, now, and melt with ruth:
—And, O ye dolphins, waft the hapless youth!

    Weep no more, woeful shepherds, weep no more,
For Lycidas, your sorrow, is not dead,
Sunk though he be beneath the watery floor;
So sinks the day-star in the ocean bed,
And yet anon repairs his drooping head
And tricks his beams, and with new-spangled ore
Flames in the forehead of the morning sky:
So Lycidas sunk low, but mounted high
Through the dear might of Him that walked the waves;
Where, other groves and other streams along,
With nectar pure his oozy locks he laves,
And hears the unexpressive nuptial song
In the blest kingdoms meek of joy and love.
There entertain him all the saints above
In solemn troops, and sweet societies
That sing, and singing in their glory move,
And wipe the tears for ever from his eyes.
Now, Lycidas, the shepherds weep no more;
Henceforth thou art the Genius of the shore
In thy large recompense, and shalt be good
To all that wander in that perilous flood.

Thus sang the uncouth swain to the oaks and rills,
While the still morn went out with sandals gray;
He touched the tender stops of various quills,
With eager thought warbling his Doric lay:
And now the sun had stretched out all the hills,
And now was dropt into the western bay:
At last he rose, and twitched his mantle blue:
To-morrow to fresh woods, and pastures new.

JOHN SUCKLING

1609 - 1642

WHY SO PALE AND WAN?

Why so pale and wan, fond lover?
    Prithee, why so pale?
Will, when looking well can't move her,
    Looking ill prevail?
    Prithee, why so pale?

Why so dull and mute, young sinner?
    Prithee, why so mute?
Will, when speaking well can't win her,
    Saying nothing do 't?
    Prithee, why so mute?

Quit, quit for shame! This will not move;
    This cannot take her.
If of herself she will not love,
    Nothing can make her.
    The devil take her!

THE BRIDE

from " A Ballad upon a Wedding "

Her feet beneath her petticoat,
Like little mice, stole in and out,
    As if they feared the light:
But O she dances such a way!
No sun upon an Easter-day
    Is half so fine a sight.

Her finger was so small, the ring
Would not stay on, which they did bring,
   It was too wide a peck:
And to say truth (for out it must)
It looked like the great collar, just,
   About our young colt's neck.

Her cheeks so rare a white was on,
No daisy makes comparison;
   Who sees them is undone;
For streaks of red were mingled there,
Such as are on a Catherine pear,
   The side that's next the sun.

Her lips were red, and one was thin,
Compared to that was next her chin
   (Some bee had stung it newly)
But, Dick, her eyes so guard her face;
I durst no more upon them gaze
   Than on the sun in July.

Her mouth so small, when she does speak,
Thou'dst swear her teeth her words did break,
   That they might passage get;
But she so handled still the matter,
They came as good as ours, or better,
   And are not spent a whit. . . .

THE CONSTANT LOVER

Out upon it, I have loved
   Three whole days together!
And am like to love three more,
   If it prove fair weather.

Time shall moult away his wings
   Ere he shall discover
In the whole wide world again
   Such a constant lover.

But the spite on't is, no praise
   Is due at all to me:
Love with me had made no stays,
   Had it any been but she.

Had it any been but she,
  And that very face,
There had been at least ere this
  A dozen in her place.

RICHARD CRASHAW

1613 - 1649

AN EPITAPH UPON HUSBAND AND WIFE

WHO DIED AND WERE BURIED TOGETHER

To those whom death again did wed
This grave's the second marriage-bed.
For though the hand of Fate could force
'Twixt soul and body a divorce,
It could not sever man and wife,
Because they both lived but one life.
Peace, good reader, do not weep;
Peace; the lovers are asleep.

They, sweet turtles, folded lie
In the last knot that love could tie.
Let them sleep, let them sleep on,
Till the stormy night be gone,
And the eternal morrow dawn;
Then the curtains will be drawn,
And they wake into a light
Whose day shall never die in night.

CHRIST CRUCIFIED

Thy restless feet now cannot go
  For us and our eternal good,
As they were ever wont. What though
  They swim, alas! in their own flood?

Thy hands to give Thou canst not lift,
  Yet will Thy hand still giving be;
It gives, but O, itself's the gift!
  It gives tho' bound, tho' bound 'tis free!

ST. TERESA

O thou undaunted daughter of desires!
By all thy dower of lights and fires;
By all the eagle in thee, all the dove;
By all thy lives and deaths of love;
By thy large draughts of intellectual day,
And by thy thirsts of love more large than they;
By all thy brim-filled bowls of fierce desire,
By thy last morning's draught of liquid fire;
By the full kingdom of that final kiss
That seized thy parting soul, and sealed thee His;
By all the Heaven thou hast in Him
(Fair sister of the seraphim!);
By all of Him we have in thee;
Leave nothing of myself in me.
Let me so read thy life that I
Unto all life of mine may die!

WISHES FOR THE SUPPOSED MISTRESS

Whoe'er she be,
That not impossible She
That shall command my heart and me;

Where'er she lie,
Locked up from mortal eye
In shady leaves of destiny:

Till that ripe birth
Of studied Fate stand forth,
And teach her fair steps tread our earth:

Till that divine
Idea take a shrine
Of crystal flesh, through which to shine:

Meet you her, my wishes,
Bespeak her to my blisses,
And be ye called my absent kisses.

I wish her beauty
That owes not all its duty
To gaudy tire, or glist'ring shoe-tie:

A face that's best
By its own beauty drest,
And can alone commend the rest . . .

Whate'er delight
Can make day's forehead bright
Or give down to the wings of night.

Soft silken hours,
Open suns, shady bowers;
'Bove all, nothing within that lowers.

Days, that need borrow
No part of their good morrow
From a fore-spent night of sorrow:

Days, that in spite
Of darkness, by the light
Of a clear mind are day all night.

Life, that dares send
A challenge to his end,
And when it comes, say, " Welcome, friend."

I wish her store
Of worth may leave her poor
Of wishes; and I wish—no more.

Now, if Time knows,
That Her, whose radiant brows
Weave them a garland of my vows;

Her that dares be
What these lines wish to see:
I seek no further, it is She.

'Tis She, and here
Lo! I unclothe and clear
My wishes' cloudy character . . .

Such worth as this is
Shall fix my flying wishes,
And determine them to kisses.

Let her full glory,
My fancies, fly before ye;
Be ye my fictions—but her story.

RICHARD LOVELACE

1618 - 1658

TO LUCASTA, ON GOING TO THE WARS

Tell me not, Sweet, I am unkind
   That from the nunnery
Of thy chaste breast and quiet mind,
   To war and arms I fly.

True, a new mistress now I chase,
   The first foe in the field;
And with a stronger faith embrace
   A sword, a horse, a shield.

Yet this inconstancy is such
   As you too shall adore;
I could not love thee, dear, so much,
   Loved I not honour more.

TO ALTHEA FROM PRISON

When Love with unconfinèd wings
   Hovers within my gates,
And my divine Althea brings
   To whisper at the grates;
When I lie tangled in her hair
   And fettered to her eye,
The birds that wanton in the air
   Know no such liberty.

When flowing cups run swiftly round
   With no allaying Thames,
Our careless heads with roses crowned,
   Our hearts with loyal flames;

When thirsty grief in wine we steep,
  When healths and draughts go free,
Fishes that tipple in the deep
  Know no such liberty. . . .

Stone walls do not a prison make,
  Nor iron bars a cage;
Minds innocent and quiet take
  That for an hermitage;
If I have freedom in my love
  And in my soul am free,
Angels alone, that soar above,
  Enjoy such liberty.

TO AMARANTHA

THAT SHE WOULD DISHEVEL HER HAIR

Amarantha, sweet and fair,
Ah, braid no more that shining hair!
As my curious hand or eye
Hovering round thee, let it fly!

Let it fly as unconfined
As its calm ravisher the wind,
Who hath left his darling East
To wanton o'er that spicy nest.

Every tress must be confest,
But neatly tangled at the best;
Like a clue of golden thread
Most excellently ravellèd.

Do not, then, wind up that light
In ribbands, and o'ercloud in night,
Like the Sun in's early ray;
But shake your head, and scatter day!

ABRAHAM COWLEY

1618 - 1667

THE PROPHET

Teach me to Love? Go teach thy self more wit:
  I chief professor am of it.
  Teach craft to Scots, and thrift to Jews,
  Teach boldness to the stews;
In tyrant's courts teach supple flattery,
Teach Jesuits, that have travelled far, to lie.
  Teach fire to burn, and winds to blow,
  Teach restless fountains how to flow,
  Teach the dull earth, fixt, to abide.
Teach woman-kind inconstancy and pride.
See if your diligence here will useful prove;
  But, pr'ithee, teach me not to love.

The god of love, if such a thing there be,
  May learn to love from me;
  He who does boast that he has been
  In every heart since Adam's sin;
I'll lay my life, nay, mistress on't, that's more,
I'll teach him things he never knew before;
  I'll teach him a receipt to make
  Words that weep, and tears that speak,
  I'll teach him sighs, like those in death,
At which the souls go out too with the breath:
Still the soul stays, yet still does from me run;
  As light and heat does with the sun.

'Tis I who love's Columbus am; 'tis I.
  Who must new worlds in it descry:
  Rich worlds, that yield of treasure more
  Than all that has been known before.
And yet like his (I fear) my fate must be,
To find them out for others; not for me.
  Me, times to come (I know it) shall
  Love's last and greatest prophet call.
  But, ah, what's that, if she refuse
To hear the wholesome doctrines of my Muse?
If to my share the prophet's fate must come,
  Hereafter fame, here martyrdom.

BEAUTY

Beauty, thou wild fantastic ape,
Who dost in ev'ry country change thy shape!
Here black, there brown, here tawny, and there white;
Thou flatt'rer which compli'st with every sight!
    Thou Babel which confound'st the eye
With unintelligible variety!
    Who hast no certain What, nor Where,
But vari'st still, and dost thy self declare
Inconstant, as thy she-possessors are.

Beauty, love's scene and masquerade,
So gay by well-placed lights, and distance made!
False coin, with which th' impostor cheats us still;
The stamp and colour good, but metal ill!
    Which light, or base we find, when we
Weigh by enjoyment, and examine thee!
    For though thy being be but show,
'Tis chiefly night which men to thee allow:
And choose t' enjoy thee, when thou least art thou.

Beauty, thou active, passive ill!
Which diest thy self as fast as thou dost kill!
Thou tulip, who thy stock in paint dost waste,
Neither for physic good, nor smell, nor taste,
    Beauty, whose flames but meteors are,
Short-lived and low, though thou wouldst seem a star,
    Who dar'st not thine own home descry,
Pretending to dwell richly in the eye,
When thou, alas, dost in the fancy lie.

THE WISH

Well then! I now do plainly see
This busy world and I shall ne'er agree.
The very honey of all earthly joy
Does of all meats the soonest cloy;
    And they, methinks, deserve my pity
Who for it can endure the stings,
The crowd and buzz and murmurings
    Of this great hive, the city.

Ah, yet, ere I descend to th' grave
May I a small house and large garden have;
And a few friends, and many books, both true.
Both wise, and both delightful too!
    And since love ne'er will from me flee,
A mistress moderately fair,
And good as guardian angels are,
    Only beloved and loving me.

O fountains! when in you shall I
Myself eased of unpeaceful thoughts espy?
O fields! O woods! when, when shall I be made
The happy tenant of your shade?
    Here's the spring-head of Pleasure's flood:
Here's wealthy Nature's treasury,
Where all the riches lie that she
    Has coined and stamped for good.

Pride and Ambition here
Only in far-fetched metaphors appear;
Here nought but winds can hurtful murmurs scatter,
And nought but Echo flatter.
    The gods, when they descended, hither
From heaven did always choose their wa
And therefore we may boldly say
    That 'tis the way, too, thither.

How happy here should I
And one dear She live, and embracing ᴏɴ
She who is all the world, and can exclude
In deserts solitude.
    I should have then this only fear;
Lest men, when they my pleasure see,
Should hither throng to live like me,
    And make a city here.

ANDREW MARVELL

1621 - 1678

TO HIS COY MISTRESS

Had we but world enough, and time.
This coyness, lady, were no crime.
We would sit down, and think which way
To walk, and pass our long love's day.

Thou by the Indian Ganges' side
Should'st rubies find: I by the tide
Of Humber would complain. I would
Love you ten years before the Flood,
And you should, if you please, refuse
Till the conversion of the Jews.
My vegetable love should grow
Vaster than empires, and more slow
An hundred years should go to praise
Thine eyes, and on thy forehead gaze:
Two hundred to adore each breast;
But thirty thousand to the rest;
An age at least to every part,
And the last age should show your heart.
For, lady, you deserve this state,
Nor would I love at lower rate.

But at my back I always hear
Time's wingèd chariot hurrying near:
And yonder all before us lie
Deserts of vast eternity.
Thy beauty shall no more be found;
Nor, in thy marble vault, shall sound
My echoing song: then worms shall try
That long-preserved virginity,
And your quaint honour turn to dust,
And into ashes all my lust.
The grave's a fine and private place,
But none, I think, do there embrace.

Now, therefore, while the youthful hue
Sits on thy skin like morning dew,
And while thy willing soul transpires
At every pore with instant fires,
Now let us sport us while we may;
And now, like amorous birds of prey,
Rather at once our Time devour,
Than languish in his slow-chapt power.
Let us roll all our strength and all
Our sweetness up into one ball,
And tear our pleasures with rough strife
Thorough the iron gates of life.
Thus, though we cannot make our Sun
Stand still, yet we will make him run.

THE GARDEN

How vainly men themselves amaze
To win the palm, the oak, or bays;
And their incessant labours see
Crowned from some single herb, or tree,
Whose short and narrow-vergèd shade
Does prudently their toils upbraid;
While all flow'rs and all trees do close
To weave the garlands of repose.

Fair Quiet, have I found thee here,
And Innocence, thy sister dear?
Mistaken long, I sought you then
In busy companies of men.
Your sacred plants, if here below,
Only among the plants will grow;
Society is all but rude
To this delicious solitude.

No white nor red was ever seen
So amorous as this lovely green.
Fond lovers, cruel as their flame,
Cut in these trees their mistress' name:
Little, alas! they know or heed
How far these beauties hers exceed!
Fair trees! wheres'e'er your barks I wound
No name shall but your own be found.

When we have run our passion's heat,
Love hither makes his best retreat.
The Gods, that mortal beauty chase,
Still in a tree did end their race;
Apollo hunted Daphne so,
Only that she might laurel grow;
And Pan did after Syrinx speed,
Not as a nymph, but for a reed.

What wondrous life is this I lead!
Ripe apples drop about my head;
The luscious clusters of the vine
Upon my mouth do crush their wine;

The nectarine, and curious peach,
Into my hands themselves do reach;
Stumbling on melons, as I pass,
Insnared with flowers, I fall on grass.

Meanwhile, the mind, from pleasure less,
Withdraws into its happiness:
The mind, that ocean where each kind
Does straight its own resemblance find;
Yet it creates, transcending these,
Far other worlds, and other seas;
Annihilating all that's made
To a green thought in a green shade.

Here at the fountain's sliding foot,
Or at some fruit-tree's mossy root,
Casting the body's vest aside,
My soul into the boughs does glide;
There like a bird it sits, and sings,
Then whets and claps its silver wings;
And, till prepared for longer flight,
Waves in its plumes the various light.

Such was that happy garden-state,
While man there walked without a mate:
After a place so pure and sweet,
What other help could yet be meet!
But 'twas beyond a mortal's share
To wander solitary there:
Two paradises 'twere in one,
To live in Paradise alone.

How well the skilful gardener drew
Of flowers, and herbs, this dial new;
Where, from above, the milder sun
Does through a fragrant zodiac run;
And, as it works, the industrious bee
Computes its time as well as we.
How could such sweet and wholesome hours
Be reckoned but with herbs and flowers!

THE DEFINITION OF LOVE

My Love is of a birth as rare
As 'tis, for object, strange and high:
It was begotten by despair
Upon impossibility.

Magnanimous despair alone
Could show me so divine a thing,
Where feeble hope could ne'er have flown
But vainly flapped its tinsel wing.

And yet I quickly might arrive
Where my extended soul is fixt,
But Fate does iron wedges drive,
And always crowds itself betwixt.

For Fate with jealous eye does see
Two perfect loves; nor lets them close:
Their union would her ruin be,
And her tyrannic power depose.

And therefore her decrees of steel
Us as the distant poles have placed,
(Though love's whole world on us doth wheel)
Not by themselves to be embraced.

Unless the giddy heaven fall,
And earth some new convulsion tear;
And, us to join, the world should all
Be cramped into a planisphere.

As lines so love's oblique may well
Themselves in every angle greet:
But ours, so truly parallel,
Though infinite, can never meet.

Therefore the love which us doth bind,
But Fate so enviously debars,
Is the conjunction of the mind,
And opposition of the stars.

HENRY VAUGHAN

1622 - 1695

THE REVIVAL

Unfold, unfold! take in his light,
Who makes thy cares more short than night,
The joys which with his day-star rise
He deals to all but drowsy eyes;
And (what the men of this world miss)
Some drops and dews of future bliss.

Hark, how his winds have changed their note,
And with warm whispers call thee out.
The frosts are past, the storms are gone,
And backward life at last comes on.
The lofty groves in express joys
Reply unto the turtle's voice;
And here in dust and dirt, O here
The lilies of his love appear!

THE WORLD

I saw Eternity the other night,
Like a great Ring of pure and endless light,
    All calm, as it was bright;
And round beneath it, Time in hours, days, years,
    Driven by the spheres
Like a vast shadow moved; in which the world
    And all her train were hurled.

The doting lover in his quaintest strain
    Did there complain;
Near him, his lute, his fancy, and his flights,
    Wit's sour delights,
With gloves, and knots, the silly snares of pleasure,
    Yet his dear treasure,
All scattered lay, while he his eyes did pour
    Upon a flower.

The darksome statesman, hung with weights and woe,
Like a thick midnight-fog, moved there so slow,
    He did not stay, nor go;
Condemning thoughts—like sad eclipses—scowl
    Upon his soul,
And clouds of crying witnesses without
    Pursued him with one shout.
Yet digged the mole, and lest his ways be found,
    Worked under ground,
Where he did clutch his prey; (But one did see
    That policy;)
Churches and altars fed him: perjuries
    Were gnats and flies;
It rained about him blood and tears; but he
    Drank them as free.

The fearful miser on a heap of rust
Sate pining all his life there, did scarce trust
    His own hands with the dust,
Yet would not place one piece above, but lives
    In fear of thieves.
Thousands there were as frantic as himself
    And hugged each one his pelf,
The downright epicure placed heaven in sense
    And scorned pretence,
While others, slipped into a wide excess,
    Said little less;
The weaker sort slight, trivial wares enslave,
    Who think them brave;
And poor, despisèd Truth sat counting by
    Their victory.

Yet some, who all this while did weep and sing,
And sing, and weep, soared up into the Ring;
    But most would use no wing.
O fools (said I) thus to prefer dark night
    Before true light!
To live in grots and caves, and hate the day
    Because it shows the way,
The way, which from this dead and dark abode
    Leads up to God,
A way where you might tread the sun, and be
    More bright than he.

But as I did their madness so discuss,
    One whispered thus,
" This Ring the Bridegroom did for none provide,
    But for his bride."

THE RETREAT

Happy those early days, when I
Shined in my Angel-infancy!
Before I understood this place
Appointed for my second race,
Or taught my soul to fancy aught
But a white, celestial thought;
When yet I had not walked above
A mile or two from my first Love,
And looking back, at that short space
Could see a glimpse of His bright face;
When, on some gilded cloud or flower
My gazing soul would dwell an hour,
And in those weaker glories spy
Some shadows of eternity;
Before I taught my tongue to wound
My conscience with a sinful sound,
Or had the black art to dispense
A several sin to every sense,
But felt through all this fleshly dress
Bright shoots of everlastingness.

O how I long to travel back,
And tread again that ancient track!
That I might once more reach that plain
Where first I felt my glorious train;
From whence th' enlightened spirit sees
That shady City of palm trees!
But ah! my soul with too much stay
Is drunk, and staggers in the way.
Some men a forward motion love,
But I by backward steps would move;
And when this dust falls to the urn,
In that state I came, return.

JOHN DRYDEN

1631 - 1700

ALEXANDER'S FEAST, OR, THE POWER OF MUSIC

'Twas at the royal feast for Persia won
By Philip's warlike son—
Aloft in awful state
The godlike hero sate
On his imperial throne;
His valiant peers were placed around,
Their brows with roses and with myrtles bound,
(So should desert in arms be crowned);
The lovely Thais by his side
Sat like a blooming eastern bride
In flower of youth and beauty's pride:—
Happy, happy, happy pair!
None but the brave
None but the brave
None but the brave deserves the fair!

Timotheus, placèd on high
Amid the tuneful choir,
With flying fingers touched the lyre:
The trembling notes ascend the sky
And heavenly joys inspire.
The song began from Jove
Who left his blissful seats above—
Such is the power of mighty love!
A dragon's fiery form belied the god;
Sublime on radiant spires he rode
When he to fair Olympia prest,
And while he sought her snowy breast,
Then round her slender waist he curled,
And stamped an image of himself, a sovereign of the world.
—The listening crowd admire the lofty sound!
A present deity! they shout around:
A present deity! the vaulted roofs rebound!

With ravished ears
The monarch hears,
Assumes the god;
Affects to nod
And seems to shake the spheres.
The praise of Bacchus then the sweet musician sung,
Of Bacchus ever fair and ever young:
The jolly god in triumph comes!
Sound the trumpets, beat the drums!
Flushed with a purple grace
He shows his honest face;
Now give the hautboys breath. He comes! he comes!
Bacchus, ever fair and young,
Drinking joys did first ordain;
Bacchus' blessings are a treasure,
Drinking is the soldier's pleasure:
Rich the treasure,
Sweet the pleasure,
Sweet is pleasure after pain.

Soothed with the sound, the king grew vain;
Fought all his battles o'er again,
And thrice he routed all his foes, and thrice he slew the
    slain!
The master saw the madness rise,
His glowing cheeks, his ardent eyes;
And while he heaven and earth defied
Changed his hand and checked his pride.
He chose a mournful Muse
Soft pity to infuse:
He sung Darius great and good,
By too severe a fate
Fallen, fallen, fallen, fallen,
Fallen from his high estate,
And weltering in his blood;
Deserted at his utmost need
By those his former bounty fed;
On the bare earth exposed he lies
With not a friend to close his eyes.
—With downcast looks the joyless victor sat,
Revolving in his altered soul
The various turns of chance below;
And now and then a sigh he stole,
And tears began to flow.

The mighty master smiled to see
That love was in the next degree;
'Twas but a kindred sound to move,
For pity melts the mind to love.
Softly sweet, in Lydian measures
Soon he soothed his soul to pleasures.
War, he sung, is toil and trouble,
Honour but an empty bubble;
Never ending, still beginning,
Fighting still, and still destroying;
If the world be worth thy winning,
Think, O think, it worth enjoying:
Lovely Thais sits beside thee,
Take the good the gods provide thee!

—The many rend the skies with loud applause;
So Love was crowned, but Music won the cause.
The prince, unable to conceal his pain,
Gazed on the fair
Who caused his care,
And sighed and looked, sighed and looked again:
Sighed and looked, and sighed again:
At length with love and wine at once opprest
The vanquished victor sunk upon her breast.

Now strike the golden lyre again:
A louder yet, and yet a louder strain!
Break his bands of sleep asunder
And rouse him like a rattling peal of thunder.
Hark! hark! the horrid sound
Has raisèd up his head:
As awakèd from the dead
And amazed he stares around.
" Revenge, revenge," Timotheus cries,
" See the Furies arise!
See the snakes that they rear!
How they hiss in their hair,
And the sparkles that flash from their eyes!
Behold a ghastly band,
Each a torch in his hand!
Those are Grecian ghosts, that in battle were slain
And unburied remain
Inglorious on the plain:
Give the vengeance due
To the valiant crew!

Behold how they toss their torches on high,
How they point to the Persian abodes
And glittering temples of their hostile gods."
—The princes applaud with a furious joy:
And the King seized a flambeau with zeal to destroy;
Thais led the way
To light him to his prey,
And like another Helen, fired another Troy!

—Thus, long ago,
Ere heaving bellows learned to blow,
While organs yet were mute,
Timotheus, to his breathing flute
And sounding lyre
Could swell the soul to rage, or kindle soft desire.
At last divine Cecilia came,
Inventress of the vocal frame;
The sweet enthusiast from her sacred store
Enlarged the former narrow bounds,
And added length to solemn sounds,
With Nature's mother-wit, and arts unknown before.

Let old Timotheus yield the prize
Or both divide the crown;
He raised a mortal to the skies;
She drew an angel down!

THE INSTRUMENTS

from "A Song for St. Cecilia's Day"

The trumpet's loud clangour
    Excites us to arms
With shrill notes of anger
    And mortal alarms.

The double, double, double beat
    Of the thundering drum
    Cries, " Hark! the foes come!
Charge! charge! 'tis too late to retreat! "

    The soft complaining flute
    In dying notes discovers
    The woes of hopeless lovers,
Whose dirge is whispered by the warbling lute.

Sharp violins proclaim
Their jealous pangs and desperation,
Fury, frantic indignation,
Depth of pain and height of passion,
 For the fair, disdainful dame.

But oh! what art can teach,
What human voice can reach
 The sacred organ's praise?
 Notes inspiring holy love,
Notes that wing their heavenly ways
 To mend the choirs above. . . .

As from the power of sacred lays
 The spheres began to move,
And sung the great Creator's praise
 To all the Blest above;
So, when the last and dreadful hour
This crumbling pageant shall devour,
The trumpet shall be heard on high,
The dead shall live, the living die,
And Music shall untune the sky.

MILTON

Three poets, in three distant ages born,
Greece, Italy, and England did adorn.
The first in loftiness of thought surpassed,
The next in majesty, in both the last.
The force of Nature could no further go—
To make a third she joined the other two.

THOMAS TRAHERNE

1636 (?) - 1674

EDEN

A learnèd and a happy ignorance
        Divided me
    From all the vanity,
From all the sloth, care, sorrow, that advance
    The madness and the misery
Of men. No error, no distraction, I
Saw cloud the earth, or overcast the sky.

I knew not that there was a serpent's sting,
        Whose poison, shed
    On men, did overspread
The world; nor did I dream of such a thing
    As sin, in which mankind lay dead.
They all were brisk and living things to me,
Yea, pure, and full of immortality. . . .

Only what Adam in his first estate
        Did I behold;
    Hard silver and dry gold
As yet lay underground: my happy fate
    Was more acquainted with the old
And innocent delights which he did see
In his original simplicity.

Those things which first his Eden did adorn,
        My infancy
    Did crown: simplicity
Was my protection when I first was born.
    Mine eyes those treasures first did see
Which God first made: the first effects of love
My first enjoyments upon earth did prove,

And were so great and so divine, so pure,
        So fair and sweet,
    So true; when I did meet
Them here at first, they did my soul allure,
    And drew away mine infant feet
Quite from the works of men, that I might see
The glorious wonders of the Deity.

WALKING

To walk abroad is, not with eyes,
But thoughts, the fields to see and prize;
   Else may the silent feet,
     Like logs of wood,
Move up and down, and see no good,
   Nor joy nor glory meet.

Ev'n carts and wheels their place do change,
But cannot see; though very strange
   The glory that is by:
     Dead puppets may
Move in the bright and glorious day,
   Yet not behold the sky.

And are not men than they more blind,
Who having eyes yet never find
   The bliss in which they move:
     Like statues dead
They up and down are carried,
   Yet neither see nor love. . . .

Observe those rich and glorious things;
The rivers, meadows, woods, and springs,
   The fructifying sun;
     To note from far
The rising of each twinkling star
   For us his race to run.

A little child these well perceives,
Who, tumbling in green grass and leaves,
   May rich as kings be thought.
     But there's a sight
Which perfect manhood may delight,
   To which we shall be brought.

While in those pleasant paths we talk
'Tis that towards which at last we walk;
   For we may by degrees
     Wisely proceed
Pleasures of love and praise to heed,
   From viewing herbs and trees.

MEASURE

All music, sauces, feasts, delights, and pleasures,
Games, dancing, arts, consist in governed measures;
Much more do words and passions of the mind
In temperance their sacred beauty find.

JOHN WILMOT
Earl of Rochester

1647-1680

LOVE AND LIFE

All my past life is mine no more;
    The flying hours are gone,
Like transitory dreams given o'er,
Whose images are kept in store
    By memory alone.

The time that is to come is not;
    How can it then be mine?
The present moment's all my lot;
And that, as fast as it is got,
    Phillis, is only thine.

Then talk not of inconstancy,
    False hearts, and broken vows;
If I by miracle can be
This live-long minute true to thee,
    'Tis all that Heaven allows.

EPITAPH ON CHARLES II

Here lies our Sovereign Lord the King,
　　Whose word no man relies on,
Who never said a foolish thing,
　　Nor ever did a wise one.

UPON NOTHING

Nothing! thou elder brother ev'n to Shade,
Thou hadst a being ere the world was made,
And (well fixt) art alone of ending not afraid.

Ere time and place were, time and place were not,
When primitive Nothing something straight begot,
Then all proceeded from the great united—What.

Something the general attribute of all,
Severed from thee, its sole original,
Into thy boundless self must undistinguished fall.

Yet something did thy mighty pow'r command,
And from thy fruitful emptiness's hand,
Snatched men, beasts, birds, fire, air and land.

Matter, the wickedest off-spring of thy race,
By Form assisted, flew from thy embrace,
And rebel Light obscured thy reverend dusky face.

With Form, and Matter, Time and Place did join,
Body, thy foe, with thee did leagues combine,
To spoil thy peaceful realm, and ruin all thy line.

But turn-coat Time assists the foe in vain,
And, bribed by thee, assists thy short-lived reign,
And to thy hungry womb drives back thy slaves again.

THE EIGHTEENTH CENTURY

THE RESTORATION AND REVIVAL OF CLASSICISM

The eighteenth century is usually identified with a revival of classicism, a scientific detachment, and, more specifically, with the clipped precisions of Pope. In reality, the century witnessed two distinct tendencies: the literature of the town which was (generally) polished and so pointed as to be barbed; and the more rounded if less reasoned literature of the country-side. Pope, refining the tone dictated by Dryden, almost refined poetry out of it; his witty rationalism influenced an entire generation which turned from passionate, or natural, poetry to a high species of social verse and thence, logically enough, to prose. But the fashion, like all conventions, forced the revolt. The revulsion from the elegantly artificial was as swift as it was inevitable. Even so great an admirer (and, in form, a follower) of Pope's as Lady Winchelsea was out of sympathy with the prevailing mode of thought, and her lovely if little known " Petition for Absolute Retreat " is the expression of a wholly different spirit.

Thus the purely intellectual note was not as continuous as is frequently assumed. The elaborate classical detachment was interrupted by simple romantic affection; the malicious urban brilliance of Pope and the *vers de société* of Prior were met, if not matched, by the rural sincerities of Gray and Goldsmith and Collins and Ramsay, who were already sounding that strain of unaffected love of Nature which flowered, soon after, in Burns and, fifty years later, in Wordsworth. Nor was the age without its flashes of wild genius. The boy Chatterton, dead by his own hand in his eighteenth year, appeared suddenly in the literary heavens and burned out in his own meteoric flame; Christopher Smart's " A Song to David " stands forth as a completely noble poem in a century of wit. As Hugh l'Anson Fausset has put it, " Viewed from this standpoint, the poetry of the eighteenth century has a double appeal. It is both an expression of cultured and very English sobriety, of sanity untouched by fanaticism, and of social elegance, and it trembles with the first vibrations of a new life of vast potentialities."

The very combination of two opposed idioms—the courtly and the common—is typical of this transitional period. The discovery of the law of gravitation affected not only religion, but the arts. Pope's tribute is, in both senses, illuminating:

> Nature and Nature's laws lay hid in night:
> God said, " Let Newton be! " and all was light.

It is no exaggeration to repeat that the influence of Science is as apparent in the carefully turned couplets of Pope as the spirit of chivalry in the sonnets of Sidney or the Elizabethan luxuriance in the plays of Shakespeare. Profound changes were imminent; men were conscious of complex questions for which they had few answers.

Nevertheless, though the romantic reflex of the eighteenth century should be noted instead of neglected, it should not be overstressed. In the main, the period followed Dryden's precept that poetry should resemble natural truth, but it should be ethical. Thus the clue to the Augustans' conception of poetry lies, as Jean Stewart declares, " in the strong sense of the unity and continuity of human nature." Despite the idyllic cross-currents, it was an era of innuendo and subtlety, in which reason and artifice were skilfully integrated.

ANNE, COUNTESS OF WINCHELSEA

1661 - 1720

PETITION FOR ABSOLUTE RETREAT

Give me, O indulgent fate!
Give me yet, before I die,
A sweet, but absolute retreat,
'Mongst paths so lost, and trees so high,
That the world may ne'er invade
Through such windings and such shade
My unshaken liberty.

No intruders thither come,
Who visit but to be from home!
None who their vain moments pass
Only studious of their glass;
News, that charm to list'ning ears,
That false alarm to hopes and fears,
That common theme of every fop,
From the statesmen to the shop,
In those coverts ne'er be spread
Of who's deceased, or who's to wed;
Be no tidings thither brought
But silent as a midnight thought:
Where the world may ne'er invade
Be those windings and that shade.

Courteous fate! afford me there
A table spread, without my care,
With what the neighb'ring fields impart.
Whose cleanliness be all its art.
When of old the calf was dressed
(Tho' to make an angel's feast)
In the plain, unstudied sauce,
Nor truffle, nor morillia was;

Nor could the mighty patriarch's board
One far-fetched ortolan afford.
Courteous fate, then give me there
Only plain and wholesome fare.
Fruits indeed would Heaven bestow,
All that did in Eden grow,
All, but the Forbidden Tree,
Would be coveted by me:
Grapes with juice so crowded up,
As breaking thro' the native cup,
Figs, yet growing, candied o'er
By the sun's attracting power,
Cherries, with the downy peach
All within my easy reach,
While creeping near the humble ground,
Should the strawberry be found,
Springing wheresoe'er I strayed,
Thro' those windings and that shade.

    o   o   o   •   o

Give me there (since heaven has shown
It was not good to be alone)
A partner suited to my mind,
Solitary, pleased, and kind;
Who, partially, may something see
Preferred to all the world in me,
Slighting, by my humble side,
Fame and splendour, wealth and pride.
When but two the earth possessed,
'Twas their happiest days and best:
They by bus'ness, nor by wars,
They by no domestic cares,
From each other e'er were drawn,
But in some grove, or flow'ry lawn
Spent the swiftly flying time,
Spent their own and nature's prime
In love—that only passion given
To perfect man, whilst friends with heaven.
Rage, and jealousy, and hate,
Transports of this sullen state
(When by Satan's wiles betrayed)
Fly those windings and that shade!

    o   o   o   o   •

Let me then, indulgent fate!
Let me still in my retreat
From all roving thoughts be freed,
Or aims that may contention breed:
Nor be my endeavours led
By goods that perish with the dead!
Fitly might the life of man
Be indeed esteemed a span,
If the present moment were
Of delight his only share:
If no other joys he knew
Than what round about him grew.
But as those who stars would trace
From a subterranean place,
Through some engine lift their eyes
To the outward, glorious skies:
So th' immortal spirit may,
When descended to our clay,
From a rightly governed frame
View the height from whence she came:
To her paradise be caught,
And things unutterable taught.
Give me then, in that retreat,
Give me, O indulgent fate!
For all pleasures left behind
Contemplations of the mind.
Let the fair, the gay, the vain
Courtship and applause obtain;
Let th' ambitious rule the earth;
Let the giddy fool have mirth;
Give the epicure his dish,
Ev'ry one their sev'ral wish,
Whilst my transports I employ
On that more extensive joy:
When all heaven shall be surveyed
From those windings and that shade.

A SONG

'Tis strange, this heart within my breast,
   Reason opposing, and her pow'rs,
Cannot one gentle moment rest
   Unless it knows what's done in yours.

In vain I ask it of your eyes,
    Which subtly would my fears control:
For art has taught them to disguise
    Which nature made t' explain the soul.

In vain that sound your voice affords,
    Flatters sometimes my easy mind;
But of too vast extent are words
    In them the jewel truth to find.

Then let my fond inquiries cease,
    And so let all my troubles end:
For sure, that heart shall ne'er know peace
    Which on another's does depend.

THE SOLDIER'S DEATH

Trail all your pikes, dispirit every drum,
March in a slow procession from afar,
Ye silent, ye dejected men of war!
Be still the hautboys, and the flute be dumb!
Display no more, in vain, the lofty banner.
For see! where on the bier before ye lies
The pale, the fall'n, th' untimely sacrifice
To your mistaken shrine, to your false idol Honour.

THE GREATER TRIAL

Wretched Amintor with a flame
    Too strong to be subdued,
A nymph above his rank and name
    Still eagerly pursued.

To gain her ev'ry art he tried,
    But no return procured,
Mistook her prudence for her pride,
    Nor guessed what she endured.

Till prostrate at her feet one day
    Urging in deep despair,
Thus softly was she heard to say,
    Or sighed it to the air:

Witness ye secret cares I prove,
  Which is the greater trial,
To sue for unrewarded love,
  Or die by self-denial.

MATTHEW PRIOR

1664 - 1721

SONG

The merchant, to secure his treasure,
  Conveys it in a borrowed name:
Euphelia serves to grace my measure,
  But Cloe is my real flame.

My softest verse, my darling lyre
  Upon Euphelia's toilet lay—
When Cloe noted her desire
  That I should sing, that I should play.

My lyre I tune, my voice I raise,
  But with my numbers mix my sighs;
And whilst I sing Euphelia's praise,
  I fix my soul on Cloe's eyes.

Fair Cloe blushed; Euphelia frowned:
  I sung, and gazed; I played, and trembled:
And Venus to the Loves around
  Remarked how ill we all dissembled.

A REASONABLE AFFLICTION

On his death-bed poor Lubin lies:
  His spouse is in despair;
With frequent cries, and mutual sighs,
  They both express their care.

" A different cause," says Parson Sly,
  " The same effect may give:
Poor Lubin fears that he may die;
  His wife, that he may live."

ISAAC WATTS

1674 - 1748

MAN FRAIL AND GOD ETERNAL

Our God, our Help in Ages past,
　　Our Hope for Years to come,
Our Shelter from the Stormy Blast,
　　And our eternal Home.

Under the Shadow of thy Throne
　　Thy Saints have dwelt secure;
Sufficient is thine Arm alone,
　　And our Defence is sure.

Before the Hills in order stood,
　　Or Earth receiv'd her Frame,
From everlasting Thou art God,
　　To endless years the same.

Thy Word commands our Flesh to Dust,
　　Return ye sons of Men:
All Nations rose from Earth at first,
　　And turn to Earth again.

A thousand ages in thy Sight
　　Are like an Evening gone:
Short as the Watch that ends the Night
　　Before the rising Sun.

The busy Tribes of Flesh and Blood
　　With all their Lives and Cares
Are carried downwards by thy Flood,
　　And lost in following Years.

Time like an ever-rolling Stream
　　Bears all its Sons away;
They fly forgotten as a Dream
　　Dies at the opening Day.

Like flow'ry Fields the Nations stand
    Pleas'd with the Morning-light;
The Flowers beneath the Mower's Hand
    Ly withering e'er 'tis Night.

Our God, our Help in Ages past,
    Our Hope for Years to come,
Be thou our Guard while Troubles last,
    And our eternal Home.

ALEXANDER POPE

1688 - 1744

THE RAPE OF THE LOCK[1]

CANTO I

What dire offence from amorous causes springs,
What mighty contests rise from trivial things,
I sing—This verse to Caryl, Muse! is due:
This, even Belinda may vouchsafe to view:
Slight is the subject, but not so the praise,
If she inspire, and he approve my lays.
    Say what strange motive, Goddess! could compel
A well-bred lord to assault a gentle belle?
O say what stranger cause, yet unexplored,
Could make a gentle belle reject a lord?
In tasks so bold, can little men engage,
And in soft bosoms dwells such mighty rage?
    Sol through white curtains shot a timorous ray,
And oped those eyes that must eclipse the day:
Now lap-dogs give themselves the rousing shake,
And sleepless lovers, just at twelve, awake:
Thrice rung the bell, the slipper knocked the ground,
And the pressed watch returned a silver sound.

[1] This condensed arrangement is a compromise between Pope's first
version (consisting of two cantos of less than three hundred and fifty
lines) and the final form of the poem in which Pope found a subject
on the precise level of his genius as a delineator of manners. The first
canto of these mock-heroic verses (here reduced to the original draft)
immediately achieves a parody of the epic.

CANTO II

Not with more glories, in the ethereal plain,
The sun first rises o'er the purpled main,
Than, issuing forth, the rival of his beams
Launched on the bosom of the silver Thames.
Fair nymphs, and well-dressed youths around her shone,
But every eye was fixed on her alone.
On her white breast a sparkling cross she wore,
Which Jews might kiss, and infidels adore.
Her lively looks a sprightly mind disclose,
Quick as her eyes, and as unfixed as those:
Favours to none, to all she smiles extends;
Oft she rejects, but never once offends.
Bright as the sun, her eyes the gazers strike,
And, like the sun, they shine on all alike.
Yet graceful ease, and sweetness void of pride,
Might hide her faults, if belles had faults to hide:
If to her share some female errors fall,
Look on her face, and you'll forget 'em all.
    This nymph, to the destruction of mankind,
Nourished two locks, which graceful hung behind
In equal curls, and well conspired to deck
With shining ringlets the smooth iv'ry neck.
Love in these labyrinths his slaves detains,
And mighty hearts are held in slender chains.
With hairy springes[1] we the birds betray,
Slight lines of hair surprise the finny prey,
Fair tresses man's imperial race ensnare,
And beauty draws us with a single hair.
    The adventurous Baron the bright locks admired;
He saw, he wished, and to the prize aspired.
Resolved to win, he meditates the way,
By force to ravish, or by fraud betray;
For when success a lover's toil attends,
Few ask, if fraud or force attained his ends.
    For this, ere Phœbus rose, he had implored
Propitious heaven, and every Power adored,
But chiefly Love—to Love an altar built,
Of twelve vast French romances neatly gilt.
There lay three garters, half a pair of gloves;
And all the trophies of his former loves;
With tender billet-doux he lights the pyre,
And breathes three amorous sighs to raise the fire.

---

[1] Snares made of horse-hair.

Then prostrate falls, and begs with ardent eyes
Soon to obtain, and long possess the prize:
The Powers gave ear, and granted half his prayer,
The rest the winds dispersed in empty air.
　　But now secure the painted vessel glides,
The sun-beams trembling on the floating tides:
While melting music steals upon the sky,
And softened sounds along the waters die;
Smooth flow the waves, the zephyrs gently play,
Belinda smiled, and all the world was gay.
All but the sylph—with careful thoughts oppressed,
The impending woe sat heavy on his breast.
He summons straight his denizens of air;
The lucid squadrons round the sails repair:
Soft o'er the shrouds aërial whispers breathe,
That seemed but zephyrs to the train beneath.
Some to the sun their insect-wings unfold,
Waft on the breeze, or sink in clouds of gold;
Transparent forms, too fine for mortal sight,
Their fluid bodies half dissolved in light,
Loose to the wind their airy garments flew,
Thin glittering textures of the filmy dew,
Dipt in the richest tincture of the skies,
Where light disports in ever-mingling dyes,
While every beam new transient colours flings,
Colours that change whene'er they wave their wings.
Amid the circle, on the gilded mast,
Superior by the head, was Ariel placed;
His purple pinions opening to the sun,
He raised his azure wand, and thus begun:
　　" Ye sylphs and sylphids, to your chief give ear!
Fays, fairies, genii, elves, and demons, hear!
Ye know the spheres and various tasks assigned
By laws eternal to the aërial kind.
Some in the fields of purest ether play,
And bask and whiten in the blaze of day.
Some guide the course of wandering orbs on high,
Or roll the planets through the boundless sky.
Some less refined, beneath the moon's pale light
Pursue the stars that shoot athwart the night,
Or suck the mists in grosser air below,
Or dip their pinions in the painted bow,
Or brew fierce tempests on the wintry main,
Or o'er the glebe distil the kindly rain.

Others on earth o'er human race preside,
Watch all their ways, and all their actions guide:
Of these the chief the care of nations own,
And guard with arms divine the British throne.

    Our humbler province is to tend the fair,
Not a less pleasing, though less glorious care;
To save the powder from too rude a gale,
Nor let the imprisoned essences exhale;
To draw fresh colours from the vernal flowers;
To steal from rainbows ere they drop in showers
A brighter wash; to curl their waving hairs,
Assist their blushes, and inspire their airs;
Nay oft, in dreams, invention we bestow,
To change a flounce, or add a furbelow.

    This day, black omens threat the brightest fair,
That e'er deserved a watchful spirit's care;
Some dire disaster, or by force, or slight;
But what, or where, the fates have wrapt in night.
Whether the nymph shall break Diana's law,
Or some frail china jar receive a flaw;
Or stain her honour or her new brocade;
Forget her prayers, or miss a masquerade;
Or lose her heart, or necklace, at a ball;
Or whether Heaven has doomed that Shock[1] must fall.
Haste, then, ye spirits! to your charge repair:
The fluttering fan be Zephyretta's care;
The drops to thee, Brillante, we consign;
And, Momentilla, let the watch be thine;
Do thou, Crispissa, tend her favourite lock;
Ariel himself shall be the guard of Shock.

    To fifty chosen sylphs, of special note,
We trust th' important charge, the petticoat:
Oft have we known that seven-fold fence to fail,
Though stiff with hoops, and armed with ribs of whale:
Form a strong line about the silver bound,
And guard the wide circumference around. . . ."

    He spoke; the spirits from the sails descend;
Some, orb in orb, around the nymph extend;
Some thrid the mazy ringlets of her hair;
Some hang upon the pendants of her ear:
With beating hearts the dire event they wait,
Anxious, and trembling for the birth of Fate.

---

[1] Shock was Belinda's lap dog.

CANTO III

Close by those meads, for ever crowned with flowers,
Where Thames with pride surveys his rising towers,
There stands a structure of majestic frame,
Which from the neighb'ring Hampton[1] takes its name.
Here Britain's statesmen oft the fall foredoom
Of foreign tyrants and of nymphs at home;
Here thou, great Anna! whom three realms obey,
Dost sometimes counsel take—and sometimes tea.
    Hither the heroes and the nymphs resort,
To taste awhile the pleasures of a court;
In various talk the instructive hours they passed,
Who gave the ball, or paid the visit last;
One speaks the glory of the British queen,
And one describes a charming Indian screen;
A third interprets motions, looks, and eyes.
At every word a reputation dies.
Snuff, or the fan, supply each pause of chat,
With singing, laughing, ogling, and all that.
    Meanwhile, declining from the noon of day,
The sun obliquely shoots his burning ray;
The hungry judges soon the sentence sign,
And wretches hang that jury-men may dine;
The merchant from the Exchange returns in peace,
And the long labours of the toilet cease. . . .
    For lo! the board with cups and spoons is crowned,
The berries crackle, and the mill turns round;[2]
On shining altars of Japan they raise
The silver lamp; the fiery spirits blaze:
From silver spouts the grateful liquors glide,
While China's earth receives the smoking tide:
At once they gratify their scent and taste,
And frequent cups prolong the rich repast.
Straight hover round the fair her airy band;
Some, as she sipped, the fuming liquor fanned,
Some o'er her lap their careful plumes displayed,
Trembling, and conscious of the rich brocade.
Coffee (which makes the politician wise,
And see through all things with his half-shut eyes)
Sent up in vapours to the Baron's brain
New stratagems, the radiant lock to gain. . . .

---

[1] Hampton Court, the most famous of English palaces.
[2] The coffee-beans (or berries) were roasted as well as ground on a sideboard by the ladies themselves.

But when to mischief mortals bend their will,
How soon they find fit instruments of ill!
Just then, Clarissa drew with tempting grace
A two-edged weapon from her shining case:
So ladies in romance assist their knight,
Present the spear, and arm him for the fight.
He takes the gift with reverence, and extends
The little engine on his fingers' ends;
This just behind Belinda's neck he spread,
As o'er the fragrant steam she bends her head.
Swift to the lock a thousand sprites repair,
A thousand wings, by turns, blow back the hair;
And thrice they twitched the diamond in her ear;
Thrice she looked back, and thrice the foe drew near.
Just in that instant, anxious Ariel sought
The close recesses of the virgin's thought;
As on the nosegay in her breast reclined,
He watched the ideas rising in her mind,
Sudden he viewed, in spite of all her art,
An earthly lover lurking at her heart.
Amazed, confused, he found his power expired,
Resigned to fate, and with a sigh retired.
    The peer now spreads the glittering forfex[1] wide,
To inclose the lock; now joins it, to divide. . . .
The meeting points the sacred hair dissever
From the fair head, for ever, and for ever!
    Then flashed the living lightning from her eyes,
And screams of horror rend the affrighted skies.
Not louder shrieks to pitying heaven are cast,
When husbands, or when lap-dogs breathe their last;
Or when rich China vessels fallen from high,
In glittering dust and painted fragments lie!
    Let wreaths of triumph now my temples twine
(The victor cried), the glorious prize is mine!
While fish in streams, or birds delight in air,
Or in a coach and six the British fair. . . .
While visits shall be paid on solemn days,
When numerous wax-lights in bright order blaze,
While nymphs take treats, or assignations give,
So long my honour, name, and praise shall live!
What time would spare, from steel receives its date,
And monuments, like men, submit to fate!
Steel could the labour of the Gods destroy,
And strike to dust the imperial towers of Troy;

[1] Shears.

Steel could the works of mortal pride confound,
And hew triumphal arches to the ground.
What wonder then, fair nymph! thy hairs should feel
The conquering force of unresisted steel?

.   .   .   .   .

CANTO V

" To arms, to arms! " the fierce virago cries,
And swift as lightning to the combat flies.
All side in parties, and begin the attack;
Fans clap, silks rustle, and tough whalebones crack;
Heroes' and heroines' shouts confusedly rise,
And bass and treble voices strike the skies.
No common weapons in their hands are found,
Like gods they fight, nor dread a mortal wound.

So when bold Homer makes the gods engage,
And heavenly breasts with human passions rage;
'Gainst Pallas, Mars; Latona, Hermes arms,
And all Olympus rings with loud alarms;
Jove's thunder roars, heaven trembles all around,
Blue Neptune storms, the bellowing deeps resound:
Earth shakes her nodding towers, the ground gives way,
And the pale ghosts start at the flash of day!

Triumphant Umbriel on a sconce's height
Clapped his glad wings, and sate to view the fight;
Propped on their bodkin spears, the sprites survey
The growing combat, or assist the fray. . . .

A beau and witling perished in the throng;
One died in metaphor, and one in song.
" O cruel nymph! a living death I bear,"
Cried Dapperwit, and sunk beside his chair.
A mournful glance Sir Fopling upwards cast,
" Those eyes are made so killing "—was his last.
Thus on Mæander's flowery margin lies
The expiring swan, and as he sings he dies.

When bold Sir Plume had drawn Clarissa down,
Chloe stepped in, and killed him with a frown;
She smiled to see the doughty hero slain,
But, at her smile, the beau revived again.

Now Jove suspends his golden scales in air,
Weighs the men's wits against the lady's hair;
The doubtful beam long nods from side to side;
At length the wits mount up, the hairs subside.

See, fierce Belinda on the Baron flies,
With more than usual lightning in her eyes:
Nor feared the chief the unequal fight to try,
Who sought no more than on his foe to die.
But this bold lord with manly strength endued,
She with one finger and a thumb subdued:
Just where the breath of life his nostrils drew,
A charge of snuff the wily virgin threw;
The gnomes direct, to every atom just,
The pungent grains of titillating dust.
Sudden, with starting tears each eye o'erflows,
And the high dome re-echoes to his nose.
   "Now meet thy fate," incensed Belinda cried,
And drew a deadly bodkin from her side.
   "Boast not my fall" (he cried), "insulting foe!
Thou by some other shalt be laid as low,
Nor think, to die dejects my lofty mind:
All that I dread is leaving you behind!
Rather than so, ah, let me still survive,
And burn in Cupid's flames—but burn alive."
   "Restore the lock!" she cries; and all around
"Restore the lock!" the vaulted roofs rebound.
Not fierce Othello in so loud a strain
Roared for the handkerchief that caused his pain.
But see how oft ambitious aims are crossed,
And chiefs contend till all the prize is lost!
The lock, obtained with guilt, and kept with pain,
In every place is sought, but sought in vain:
With such a prize no mortal must be blest,
So heaven decrees! with heaven who can contest?
   Some thought it mounted to the lunar sphere,
Since all things lost on earth are treasured there.
There heroes' wits are kept in ponderous vases,
And beaux in snuff-boxes and tweezer-cases.
There broken vows and death-bed alms are found,
And lovers' hearts with ends of ribband bound,
The courtier's promises, and sick men's prayers,
The smiles of harlots, and the tears of heirs,
Cages for gnats, and chains to yoke a flea,
Dried butterflies, and tomes of casuistry.
   But trust the Muse—she saw it upward rise,
Though marked by none but quick, poetic eyes:
A sudden star, it shot through liquid air,
And drew behind a radiant trail of hair.

Not Berenice's locks[1] first rose so bright
The heavens bespangling with dishevelled light.
The sylphs behold it kindling as it flies,
And, pleased, pursue its progress through the skies.
    This the beau monde shall from the Mall survey,
And hail with music its propitious ray.
This the blest lover shall for Venus take,
And send up vows from Rosamonda's lake.[2] . . .
        Then cease, bright nymph! to mourn thy ravished
            hair,
Which adds new glory to the shining sphere!
Not all the tresses that fair head can boast,
Shall draw such envy as the lock you lost.
For, after all the murders of your eye,
When, after millions slain, yourself shall die:
When those fair suns shall set, as set they must,
And all those tresses shall be laid in dust,
This lock, the Muse shall consecrate to fame,
And 'midst the stars inscribe Belinda's name.

MAN

Selections from "An Essay on Man"

Know then thyself, presume not God to scan,
The proper study of mankind is man.
Placed on this isthmus of a middle state,
A being darkly wise, and rudely great:
With too much knowledge for the sceptic side,
With too much weakness for the stoic's pride,
He hangs between; in doubt to act, or rest;
In doubt to deem himself a God, or beast;
In doubt his mind or body to prefer;
Born but to die, and reasoning but to err;
Alike in ignorance, his reason such,
Whether he thinks too little or too much:
Chaos of thought and passion, all confused;
Still by himself abused or disabused;
Created half to rise and half to fall;
Great lord of all things, yet a prey to all;

[1] The constellation of seven twinkling stars.

[2] A pond in St. James's Park " consecrated to disastrous love and elegiac poetry."

Sole judge of truth, in endless error hurled:
The glory, jest, and riddle of the world!

       o   o   •   o   o

Whate'er the passion—knowledge, fame, or pelf,
Not one will change his neighbour with himself.
The learned is happy nature to explore,
The fool is happy that he knows no more;
The rich is happy in the plenty given,
The poor contents him with the care of Heaven.
See the blind beggar dance, the cripple sing,
The sot a hero, lunatic a king;
The starving chemist in his golden views
Supremely blest, the poet in his muse.
See some strange comfort every state attend,
And pride bestowed on all, a common friend;
See some fit passion every age supply,
Hope travels through nor quits us when we die.
  Behold the child, by nature's kindly law,
Pleased with a rattle, tickled with a straw:
Some livelier play-thing gives his youth delight,
A little louder, but as empty quite:
Scarfs, garters, gold, amuse his riper stage,
And beads and prayer-books are the toys of age:
Pleased with this bauble still, as that before;
Till tired he sleeps, and life's poor play is o'er.

       o   o   o   o   o

  Honour and shame from no condition rise;
Act well your part, there all the honour lies.
Fortune in men has some small difference made,
One flaunts in rags, one flutters in brocade;
The cobbler aproned, and the parson gowned,
The friar hooded, and the monarch crowned.
" What differ more [you cry] than crown and cowl! "
I'll tell you, friend! a wise man and a fool.
You'll find, if once the monarch acts the monk,
Or, cobbler-like, the parson will be drunk,
Worth makes the man, and want of it the fellow;
The rest is all but leather or prunella.[1]

[1] Prunella was the material of which the parson's gown was made,
meaning that the rest is only a matter of clothing.

THE CRAFT OF VERSE

from "An Essay on Criticism"

True ease in writing comes from art, not chance,
As those move easiest who have learned to dance.
   'Tis not enough no harshness gives offence,
The sound must seem an echo to the sense.
Soft is the strain when zephyr gently blows,
And the smooth stream in smoother numbers flows;
But when loud surges lash the sounding shore,
The hoarse, rough verse should like the torrent roar:
When Ajax strives some rock's vast weight to throw,
The line too labours, and the words move slow;
Not so, when swift Camilla scours the plain,
Flies o'er the unbending corn, and skims along the main.

ON A CERTAIN LADY AT COURT

I know the thing that's most uncommon
(Envy be silent, and attend!);
I know a reasonable woman,
Handsome and witty, yet a friend.
Not warped by passion, awed by rumour,
Not grave thro' pride, or gay thro' folly,
An equal mixture of good humour,
And sensible soft melancholy.
" Has she no faults then [Envy says], Sir? "
Yes, she has one, I must aver:
When all the world conspires to praise her,
The woman's deaf, and does not hear.

SOLITUDE[1]

Happy the man, whose wish and care
A few paternal acres bound,
Content to breathe his native air
    In his own ground.

[1] This, according to Pope, was written when he was about twelve years old.

Whose herds with milk, whose fields with bread,
Whose flocks supply him with attire;
Whose trees in summer yield him shade,
        In winter fire.

Blest, who can unconcernedly find
Hours, days, and years, slide soft away
In health of body, peace of mind;
        Quiet by day.

Sound sleep by night; study and ease
Together mixed, sweet recreation,
And innocence, which most does please
        With meditation.

Thus let me live, unseen, unknown;
Thus unlamented let me die;
Steal from the world, and not a stone
        Tell where I lie.

SAMUEL JOHNSON

1709 - 1784

from " The Vanity of Human Wishes "

When first the college rolls receive his name,
The young enthusiast quits his ease for fame;
Through all his veins the fever of renown
Burns from the strong contagion of the gown;
O'er Bodley's dome his future labours spread,
And Bacon's mansion trembles o'er his head.
Are these thy views? proceed, illustrious youth,
And virtue guard thee to the throne of Truth!
Yet should thy soul indulge the gen'rous heat,
Till captive Science yields her last retreat;
Should Reason guide thee with her brightest ray,
And pour on misty Doubt resistless day;
Should no false Kindness lure to loose delight,
Nor Praise relax, nor Difficulty fright;
Should tempting Novelty thy cell refrain,
And Sloth effuse her opiate fumes in vain;
Should Beauty blunt on fops her fatal dart,
Nor claim the triumph of a letter'd heart;

Should no Disease thy torpid veins invade,
Nor Melancholy's phantoms haunt thy shade;
Yet hope not life from grief or danger free,
Nor think the doom of man revers'd for thee:
Deign on the passing world to turn thine eyes,
And pause awhile from letters, to be wise;
There mark what ills the scholar's life assail,
Toil, envy, want, the patron, and the jail.
See nations slowly wise, and meanly just,
To buried merit raise the tardy bust.
If dreams yet flatter, once again attend,
Hear Lydiat's life, and Galileo's end.

    Nor deem, when learning her last prize bestows,
The glitt'ring eminence exempt from foes;
See when the vulgar 'scape, despis'd or aw'd,
Rebellion's vengeful talons seize on Laud.
From meaner minds, tho' smaller fines content.
The plunder'd palace or sequester'd rent;
Mark'd out by dangerous parts he meets the shock,
And fatal Learning leads him to the block:
Around his tomb let Art and Genius weep,
But hear his death, ye blockheads, hear and sleep.

    The festal blazes, the triumphal show,
The ravish'd standard, and the captive foe,
The senate's thanks, the gazette's pompous tale,
With force resistless o'er the brave prevail.
Such bribes the rapid Greek o'er Asia whirl'd,
For such the steady Romans shook the world;
For such in distant lands the Britons shine,
And stain with blood the Danube or the Rhine;
This pow'r has praise, that virtue scarce can warm
Till fame supplies the universal charm.
Yet Reason frowns on War's unequal game,
Where wasted nations raise a single name,
And mortgag'd states their grandsires wreaths regret
From age to age in everlasting debt;
Wreaths which at last the dear-bought right convey
To rust on medals, or on stones decay.

    On what foundation stands the warrior's pride,
How just his hopes let Swedish Charles decide;
A frame of adamant, a soul of fire,
No dangers fright him, and no labours tire;
O'er love, o'er fear, extends his wide domain,
Unconquer'd lord of pleasure and of pain;

No joys to him pacific scepters yield,
War sounds the trump, he rushes to the field:
Behold surrounding kings their pow'r combine,
And one capitulate, and one resign;
Peace courts his hand, but spreads her charms in vain;
" Think nothing gain'd," he cries, " till nought remain.
On Moscow's walls till Gothic standards fly,
And all be mine beneath the polar sky."
The march begins in military state,
And nations on his eye suspended wait;
Stern Famine guards the solitary coast,
And Winter barricades the realms of Frost;
He comes, not want and cold his course delay;—
Hide, blushing Glory, hide Pultowa's day:
The vanquish'd hero leaves his broken bands,
And shows his miseries in distant lands;
Condemn'd a needy supplicant to wait,
While ladies interpose, and slaves debate.
But did not Chance at length her error mend?
Did no subverted empire mark his end?
Did rival monarchs give the fatal wound?
Or hostile millions press him to the ground?
His fall was destin'd to a barren strand,
A petty fortress and a dubious hand;
He left the name, at which the world grew pale,
To point a moral, or adorn a tale.

THOMAS GRAY

1716 - 1771

ELEGY

WRITTEN IN A COUNTRY CHURCHYARD

The curfew tolls the knell of parting day,
The lowing herd winds slowly o'er the lea,
The ploughman homeward plods his weary way,
And leaves the world to darkness and to me.

Now fades the glimmering landscape on the sight,
And all the air a solemn stillness holds,
Save where the beetle wheels his droning flight,
And drowsy tinklings lull the distant folds:

Save where from yonder ivy-mantled tower
The moping owl does to the moon complain
Of such as, wandering near her secret bower,
Molest her ancient solitary reign.

Beneath those rugged elms, that yew-tree's shade
Where heaves the turf in many a mouldering heap,
Each in his narrow cell for ever laid,
The rude forefathers of the hamlet sleep.

The breezy call of incense-breathing morn,
The swallow twittering from the straw-built shed,
The cock's shrill clarion, or the echoing horn,
No more shall rouse them from their lowly bed.

For them no more the blazing hearth shall burn
Or busy housewife ply her evening care:
No children run to lisp their sire's return,
Or climb his knees the envied kiss to share.

Oft did the harvest to their sickle yield,
Their furrow oft the stubborn glebe has broke;
How jocund did they drive their team afield!
How bowed the woods beneath their sturdy stroke!

Let not ambition mock their useful toil,
Their homely joys, and destiny obscure;
Nor grandeur hear with a disdainful smile
The short and simple annals of the poor.

The boast of heraldry, the pomp of power,
And all that beauty, all that wealth e'er gave
Awaits alike th' inevitable hour:—
The paths of glory lead but to the grave.

Nor you, ye proud, impute to these the fault
If memory o'er the tomb no trophies raise,
Where through the long-drawn aisle and fretted vault
The pealing anthem swells the note of praise.

Can storied urn or animated bust
Back to its mansion call the fleeting breath?
Can honour's voice provoke the silent dust,
Or flattery soothe the dull, cold ear of death?

Perhaps in this neglected spot is laid
Some heart once pregnant with celestial fire;
Hands, that the rod of empire might have swayed,
Or waked to ecstasy the living lyre:

But knowledge to their eyes her ample page,
Rich with the spoils of time, did ne'er unroll;
Chill penury repressed their noble rage,
And froze the genial current of the soul.

Full many a gem of purest ray serene
The dark unfathomed caves of ocean bear:
Full many a flower is born to blush unseen,
And waste its sweetness on the desert air.

Some village-Hampden, that with dauntless breast
The little tyrant of his fields withstood,
Some mute inglorious Milton here may rest,
Some Cromwell, guiltless of his country's blood.

Th' applause of listening senates to command,
The threats of pain and ruin to despise,
To scatter plenty o'er a smiling land,
And read their history in a nation's eyes.

Their lot forbade: nor circumscribed alone
Their growing virtues, but their crimes confined;
Forbade to wade through slaughter to a throne,
And shut the gates of mercy on mankind;

The struggling pangs of conscience truth to hide,
To quench the blushes of ingenuous shame,
Or heap the shrine of luxury and pride
With incense kindled at the Muse's flame.

Far from the madding crowd's ignoble strife
Their sober wishes never learned to stray;
Along the cool sequestered vale of life
They kept the noiseless tenor of their way.

Yet e'en these bones from insult to protect
Some frail memorial still erected nigh,
With uncouth rhymes and shapeless sculpture decked,
Implores the passing tribute of a sigh.

Their name, their years, spelt by th' unlettered Muse,
The place of fame and elegy supply:
And many a holy text around she strews,
That teach the rustic moralist to die.

For who, to dumb forgetfulness a prey,
This pleasing anxious being e'er resigned,
Left the warm precincts of the cheerful day,
Nor cast one longing lingering look behind?

On some fond breast the parting soul relies,
Some pious drops the closing eye requires;
E'en from the tomb the voice of Nature cries,
E'en in our ashes live their wonted fires.

For thee, who, mindful of th' unhonoured dead,
Dost in these lines their artless tale relate;
If chance, by lonely contemplation led,
Some kindred spirit shall enquire thy fate,—

Haply some hoary-headed swain may say,
" Oft have we seen him at the peep of dawn
Brushing with hasty steps the dews away,
To meet the sun upon the upland lawn;

" There at the foot of yonder nodding beech
That wreathes its old fantastic roots so high,
His listless length at noon-tide would he stretch,
And pore upon the brook that babbles by.

" Hard by yon wood, now smiling as in scorn,
Muttering his wayward fancies he would rove;
Now drooping, woeful-wan, like one forlorn,
Or crazed with care, or crossed in hopeless love.

" One morn I missed him on the 'customed hill,
Along the heath, and near his favourite tree;
Another came; nor yet beside the rill,
Nor up the lawn, nor at the wood was he;

" The next with dirges due in sad array
Slow through the church-way path we saw him borne,—
Approach and read for thou canst read the lay
Graved on the stone beneath yon aged thorn."

THE EPITAPH

Here rests his head upon the lap of earth
A youth, to fortune and to fame unknown;
Fair science frowned not on his humble birth
And melancholy marked him for her own.

Large was his bounty, and his soul sincere;
Heaven did a recompense as largely send.
He gave to misery all he had, a tear;
He gained from heaven ('twas all he wished) a friend.

No farther seek his merits to disclose,
Or draw his frailties from their dread abode,
(There they alike in trembling hope repose)
The bosom of his Father and his God.

WILLIAM COLLINS

1721 - 1759

"HOW SLEEP THE BRAVE"

How sleep the brave, who sink to rest,
By all their country's wishes blest!
When Spring, with dewy fingers cold,
Returns to deck their hallowed mould,
She there shall dress a sweeter sod,
Than Fancy's feet have ever trod.

By fairy hands their knell is rung,
By forms unseen their dirge is sung;
There Honour comes, a pilgrim grey,
To bless the turf that wraps their clay,
And Freedom shall a-while repair,
To dwell a weeping hermit there!

ODE TO EVENING

If ought of oaten stop or pastoral song
May hope, O pensive Eve, to soothe thine ear,
   Like thy own solemn springs,
   Thy springs, and dying gales,
O nymph reserved, while now the bright-haired sun
Sits in yon western tent, whose cloudy skirts,
   With brede ethereal wove,
   O'erhang his wavy bed:

Now air is hushed, save where the weak-eyed bat,
With short shrill shriek, flits by on leathern wing,
   Or where the beetle winds
   His small but sullen horn,
As oft he rises 'midst the twilight path,
Against the pilgrim born in heedless hum:
   Now teach me, maid composed,
   To breathe some softened strain,
Whose numbers stealing thro' thy darkening vale,
May not unseemly with its stillness suit,
   As, musing slow, I hail
   Thy genial loved return!

For when thy folding-star arising shows
His paly circlet, at his warning lamp
   The fragrant hours, and elves
   Who slept in buds the day,
And many a nymph who wreaths her brows with sedge,
And sheds the fresh'ning dew, and lovelier still,
   The pensive pleasures sweet
   Prepare thy shadowy ear.

Then let me rove some wild and heathy scene,
Or find some ruin 'midst its dreary dells,
   Whose walls more awful nod
   By thy religious gleams.
Or if chill blust'ring winds, or driving rain,
Prevent my willing feet, be mine the hut,
   That from the mountain's side,
   Views wilds, and swelling floods,
And hamlets brown, and dim-discovered spires,
And hears their simple bell, and marks o'er all
   Thy dewy fingers draw
   The gradual dusky veil.

While Spring shall pour his showers, as oft he wont,
And bathe thy breathing tresses, meekest Eve!
   While Summer loves to sport
   Beneath thy lingering light;
While sallow autumn fills thy lap with leaves;
Or winter, yelling through the troublous air,
   Affrights thy shrinking train
   And rudely rends thy robes;
So long, regardful of thy quiet rule,
Shall fancy, friendship, science, smiling peace,
   Thy gentlest influence own,
   And love thy favourite name!

CHRISTOPHER SMART

1722 - 1771

from "A Song to David"

He sang of God—the mighty source
Of all things—the stupendous force
On which all strength depends;
From whose right arm, beneath whose eyes,
All period, power, and enterprise
Commences, reigns and ends.

Angels—their ministry and meed,
Which to and fro with blessings speed,
Or with their citherns wait;
Where Michael, with his millions, bows,
Where dwell the search and his spouse,
The cherub and her mate.

Of man—the semblance and effect
Of God and love—the saint elect
For infinite applause—
To rule the land, and briny broad,
To be laborious in his laud,
And heroes in his cause.

The world—the clustering spheres he made;
The glorious light, the soothing shade,
Dale, champaign, grove, and hill;
The multitudinous abyss,
Where Secrecy remains in bliss,
And Wisdom hides her skill.

Trees, plants, and flowers—of virtuous root;
Gem-yielding blossom, yielding fruit,
Choice gums and precious balm;
Bless ye the nosegay in the vale,
And with the sweetness of the gale
Enrich the thankful psalm.

Of fowl—e'en every beak and wing
Which cheer the winter, hail the spring,
That live in peace, or prey;
They that make music, or that mock,
The quail, the brave domestic cock,
The raven, swan, and jay.

Of fishes—every size and shape,
Which nature frames of light escape,
Devouring man to shun;
The shells are in the weedy deep,
The shoals upon the surface leap,
And love the glancing sun.

Of beasts—the beaver plods his task;
While the sleek tigers roll and bask,
Nor yet the shades arouse:
Her cave the mining coney scoops;
Where o'er the mead the mountain stoops,
The kids exult and browse.

Of gems—their virtue and their price,
Which hid in earth from man's device,
Their darts of lustre sheathe;
The jasper of the master's stamp,
The topaz blazing like a lamp
Among the mines beneath.

    o   o   o   o   o

Strong is the horse upon his speed;
Strong in pursuit the rapid glede,[1]
Which makes at once his game;
Strong the tall ostrich on the ground;
Strong through the turbulent profound
Shoots xiphias[2] to his aim.

Strong is the lion—like a coal
His eyeball,—like a bastion's mole
His chest against the foes;
Strong the gier-eagle on his sail;
Strong against tide the enormous whale
Emerges as he goes.

But stronger still, in earth and air,
And in the sea, the man of prayer,
And far beneath the tide!
And in the seat to faith assigned,
Where ask is have, where seek is find,
Where knock is open wide.

Beauteous the fleet before the gale;
Beauteous the multitudes in mail,
Ranked arms and crested heads:
Beauteous the garden's umbrage mild,
Walk, water, meditated wild,
And all the bloomy beds.

Beauteous the moon full on the lawn;
And beauteous, when the veil's withdrawn,
The virgin to her spouse;
Beauteous the temple decked and filled,
When to the heaven of heavens they build
Their heart-directed vows.

Beauteous, yea, beauteous, more than these,
The shepherd-king upon his knees,
For his momentous trust;
With wish of infinite conceit,
For man, beast, mute, the small and great,
And prostrate dust to dust.

    °   °   °   °   °

Glorious the sun in mid career;
Glorious the assembled fires appear;

[1] The kite.   [2] The sword-fish.

Glorious the comet's train;
Glorious the trumpet and alarm;
Glorious the almighty stretched-out arm;
Glorious the enraptured main.

Glorious the northern lights astream;
Glorious the song when God's the theme;
Glorious the thunder's roar;
Glorious hosannas from the den;
Glorious the catholic Amen;
Glorious the martyr's gore.

Glorious, more glorious is the crown
Of Him that brought salvation down
By meekness, called the Son.
Thou at stupendous truth believed,
And now the matchless deed's achieved,
Determined, dared, and done.

OLIVER GOLDSMITH

1730 (?) - 1774

from " The Deserted Village "

O blest retirement, friend to life's decline,
Retreats from care that never must be mine,
How happy he who crowns, in shades like these,
A youth of labour with an age of ease;
Who quits a world where strong temptations try,
And, since 'tis hard to combat, learns to fly!
For him no wretches, born to work and weep,
Explore the mine, or tempt the dangerous deep;
No surly porter stands in guilty state
To spurn imploring famine from the gate,
But on he moves to meet his latter end,
Angels around befriending virtue's friend;
Bends to the grave with unperceived decay,
While resignation gently slopes the way;
And, all his prospects brightening to the last,
His Heaven commences ere the world be past!
  Sweet was the sound when oft at evening's close,
Up yonder hill the village murmur rose;

There, as I past with careless steps and slow,
The mingling notes came soften'd from below;
The swain responsive as the milk-maid sung,
The sober herd that lowed to meet their young,
The noisy geese that gabbled o'er the pool,
The playful children just let loose from school,
The watch-dog's voice that bayed the whispering wind,
And the loud laugh that spoke the vacant mind,
These all in sweet confusion sought the shade,
And filled each pause the nightingale had made.
But now the sounds of population fail,
No cheerful murmurs fluctuate in the gale,
No busy steps the grass-grown foot-way tread,
For all the bloomy flush of life is fled.
All but yon widowed, solitary thing
That feebly bends beside the plashy spring;
She, wretched matron, forced in age, for bread,
To strip the brook with mantling cresses spread,
To pick her wintry faggot from the thorn,
To seek her nightly shed, and weep till morn;
She only left of all the harmless train,
The sad historian of the pensive plain.
   Near yonder copse, where once the garden smiled,
And still where many a garden-flower grows wild;
There, where a few torn shrubs the place disclose,
The village preacher's modest mansion rose.
A man he was, to all the country dear,
And passing rich with forty pounds a year;
Remote from towns he ran his godly race,
Nor e'er had changed, nor wished to change his place;
Unpractised he to fawn, or seek for power,
By doctrines fashioned to the varying hour;
Far other aims his heart had learned to prize,
More skilled to raise the wretched than to rise.
His house was known to all the vagrant train,
He chid their wanderings, but relieved their pain;
The long-remembered beggar was his guest,
Whose beard descending swept his aged breast;
The ruined spendthrift, now no longer proud,
Claim'd kindred there, and had his claims allowed;
The broken soldier, kindly bade to stay,
Sate by his fire, and talked the night away;
Wept o'er his wounds, or, tales of sorrow done,
Shouldered his crutch, and shewed how fields were won

Pleased with his guests, the good man learned to glow,
And quite forgot their vices in their woe;
Careless their merits, or their faults to scan,
His pity gave ere charity began.

Thus to relieve the wretched was his pride,
And even his failings leaned to Virtue's side;
But in his duty prompt at every call,
He watched and wept, he prayed and felt, for all.
And, as a bird each fond endearment tries,
To tempt its new-fledged offspring to the skies;
He tried each art, reproved each dull delay,
Allured to brighter worlds, and led the way.

Beside the bed where parting life was layed,
And sorrow, guilt, and pain, by turns, dismayed
The reverend champion stood. At his control,
Despair and anguish fled the struggling soul;
Comfort came down the trembling wretch to raise,
And his last faultering accents whispered praise.

At church, with meek and unaffected grace,
His looks adorned the venerable place;
Truth from his lips prevailed with double sway,
And fools, who came to scoff, remained to pray.
The service past, around the pious man,
With steady zeal, each honest rustic ran;
Even children followed, with endearing wile,
And plucked his gown, to share the good man's smile.
His ready smile a parent's warmth exprest,
Their welfare pleased him, and their cares distrest;
To them his heart, his love, his griefs were given,
But all his serious thoughts had rest in Heaven.
As some tall cliff that lifts its awful form,
Swells from the vale, and midway leaves the storm,
Tho' round its breast the rolling clouds are spread,
Eternal sunshine settles on its head.

Beside yon straggling fence that skirts the way.
With blossomed furze unprofitably gay,
There, in his noisy mansion, skill'd to rule,
The village master taught his little school;
A man severe he was, and stern to view,
I knew him well, and every truant knew;
Well had the boding tremblers learned to trace
The day's disasters in his morning face;
Full well they laughed, with counterfeited glee,
At all his jokes, for many a joke had he:

Full well the busy whisper circling round,
Conveyed the dismal tidings when he frowned;
Yet he was kind, or if severe in aught,
The love he bore to learning was in fault;
The village all declared how much he knew;
'Twas certain he could write, and cypher too;
Lands he could measure, terms and tides presage,
And even the story ran that he could gauge.
In arguing too, the parson owned his skill,
For even tho' vanquished, he could argue still;
While words of learned length and thundering sound,
Amazed the gazing rustics ranged around;
And still they gazed, and still the wonder grew,
That one small head could carry all he knew.

WILLIAM COWPER

1731 - 1800

ALONE

VERSES SUPPOSED TO BE WRITTEN BY ALEXANDER SELKIRK,
DURING HIS SOLITARY ABODE IN THE ISLAND OF JUAN
FERNANDEZ

I am monarch of all I survey,
　　My right there is none to dispute;
From the centre all round to the sea,
　　I am lord of the fowl and the brute.
O Solitude! where are the charms
　　That sages have seen in thy face?
Better dwell in the midst of alarms
　　Than reign in this horrible place.

I am out of humanity's reach,
　　I must finish my journey alone,
Never hear the sweet music of speech,
　　I start at the sound of my own.
The beasts that roam over the plain
　　My form with indifference see;
They are so unacquainted with man,
　　Their tameness is shocking to me.

Society, friendship and love,
  Divinely bestowed upon man,
O, had I the wings of a dove,
  How soon would I taste you again!
My sorrows I then might assuage,
  In the ways of religion and truth,
Might learn from the wisdom of age,
  And be cheer'd by the sallies of youth.

Religion! what treasure untold
  Lies hid in that heavenly word!
More precious than silver or gold,
  Or all that this earth can afford.
But the sound of the church-going bell,
  These valleys and rocks never heard,
Never sigh'd at the sound of a knell,
  Or smiled when a sabbath appear'd.

Ye winds that have made me your sport,
  Convey to this desolate shore
Some cordial, endearing report
  Of a land I shall visit no more.
My friends, do they now and then send
  A wish or a thought after me?
O, tell me I yet have a friend,
  Though a friend I am never to see.

How fleet is a glance of the mind!
  Compar'd with the speed of its flight,
The tempest himself lags behind
  And the swift-winged arrows of light.
When I think of my own native land,
  In a moment I seem to be there;
But, alas! recollection at hand
  Soon hurries me back to despair.

But the sea-fowl is gone to her nest,
  The beast is laid down in his lair;
Even here is a season of rest,
  And I to my cabin repair.
There's mercy in every place,
  And mercy, encouraging thought,
Gives even affliction a grace,
  And reconciles man to his lot.

LIGHT SHINING OUT OF DARKNESS

God moves in a mysterious way
  His wonders to perform;
He plants his footsteps in the sea,
  And rides upon the storm.

Deep in unfathomable mines,
  With never-failing skill,
He treasures up his bright designs,
  And works his sovereign will.

Ye fearful saints, fresh courage take;
  The clouds ye so much dread
Are big with mercy, and shall break
  In blessings on your head.

Judge not the Lord by feeble sense,
  But trust him for his grace;
Behind a frowning providence
  He hides a smiling face.

His purposes will ripen fast,
  Unfolding every hour;
The bud may have a bitter taste,
  But sweet will be the flower.

Blind unbelief is sure to err,
  And scan his work in vain;
God is his own interpreter,
  And he will make it plain.

JOHN PHILPOT CURRAN

1750 - 1817

LET US BE MERRY

If sadly thinking, with spirits sinking,
Could, more than drinking, my cares compose
A cure for sorrow from sighs I'd borrow,
And hope to-morrow would end my woes.

But as in wailing, there's nought availing,
And Death unfailing will strike the blow;
Then for that reason, and for a season,
Let us be merry before we go.

To joy a stranger, a wayworn ranger,
In every danger my course I've run;
Now hope all ending, and death befriending,
His last aid lending, my cares are done.
No more a rover, or hapless lover,
My griefs are over—my glass runs low;
Then for that reason, and for a season,
Let us be merry before we go.

THOMAS CHATTERTON

1752 - 1770

MINSTREL'S SONG

from "Aella"

Oh! sing unto my roundelay;
    Oh! drop the briny tear with me;
Dance no more at holiday;
    Like a running river be.
        My love is dead,
        Gone to his death-bed,
        All under the willow-tree.

Black his hair as the winter night,
    White his skin as the summer snow,
Red his face as the morning light;
    Cold he lies in the grave below.
        My love is dead,
        Gone to his death-bed,
        All under the willow-tree.

Sweet his tongue as the throstle's note,
    Quick in dance as thought can be,
Deft his tabour, cudgel stout;
    Oh! he lies by the willow-tree.
        My love is dead,
        Gone to his death-bed,
        All under the willow-tree.

See! the white moon shines on high,
  Whiter is my true love's shroud,
Whiter than the morning sky,
  Whiter than the evening cloud.
    My love is dead,
    Gone to his death-bed,
    All under the willow-tree.

Come, with acorn-cup and thorn,
  Drain my own heart's blood away;
Life and all its good I scorn,
  Dance by night, or feast by day.
    My love is dead,
    Gone to his death-bed,
    All under the willow-tree.

FREEDOM'S WAR-SONG

Chorus from " Goddwyn "

When Freedom, dressed in bloodstained vest,
  To every knight her war-song sung,
Upon her head wild weeds were spread
  A gory sword-blade by her hung.
    She dancèd on the heath,
    She heard the voice of death.

Pale-eyed Affright, his heart of silver hue,
  In vain assailed her bosom to acale.[1]
She heard, unmoved, the shrieking voice of woe,
  And sadness in the owlet shake the dale,
    She shook the armèd spear,
      On high she raised her shield;
    Her foemen all appear,
      And fly along the field.

Power, with head stretchèd into the skies,
  His spear a sunbeam, and his shield a star;
Alike two flaming meteors, rolls his eyes,
  Stamps with his iron feet, and sounds to war.
    She sits upon a rock,
      She bends before his spear,
    She rises from the shock,
      Wielding her own in air.
        [1] Acale: chill.

Hard as the thunder doth she drive it on;
   Wit, closely mantled, guides it to his crown;
His long sharp spear, his spreading shield is gone,
   He falls, and, falling, rolleth thousands down.
War, gore-faced War, by Envy armed, arist,[1]
   His fiery helmet nodding to the air,
Ten bloody arrows in his straining fist!

GEORGE CRABBE

1754 - 1832

JONAS KINDRED'S HOUSEHOLD

from " Tales "

Fix'd were their habits; they arose betimes,
Then pray'd their hour, and sang their party-rhymes:
Their meals were plenteous, regular, and plain;
The trade of Jonas brought him constant gain;
Vendor of hops and malt, of coals and corn—
And, like his father, he was merchant born:
Neat was their house; each table, chair, and stool,
Stood in its place, or moving moved by rule;
No lively print or picture graced the room;
A plain brown paper lent its decent gloom;
But here the eye, in glancing round, survey'd
A small recess that seem'd for china made;
Such pleasing pictures seem'd this pencill'd ware,
That few would search for nobler objects there—
Yet, turn'd by chosen friends, and there appear'd
His stern strong features, whom they all revered;
For there in lofty air was seen to stand
The bold protector of the conquer'd land;
Drawn in that look with which he wept and swore,
Turn'd out the members, and made fast the door,
Ridding the house of every knave and drone,
Forced, though it grieved his soul, to rule alone.
The stern still smile each friend approving gave,
Then turn'd the view, and all again were grave.
   There stood a clock, though small the owner's need,
For habit told when all things should proceed;

[1] Arist: arisen.

Few their amusements, but when friends appear'd,
They with the world's distress their spirits cheer'd;
The nation's guilt, that would not long endure
The reign of men so modest and so pure:
Their town was large, and seldom pass'd a day
But some had fail'd, and others gone astray;
Clerks had absconded, wives eloped, girls flown
To Gretna-Green, or sons rebellious grown;
Quarrels and fires arose;—and it was plain
The times were bad; the saints had ceased to reign!
A few yet lived to languish and to mourn
For good old manners never to return.

THE NINETEENTH CENTURY

FIRST HALF

ROMANCE AND PROPHECY

Category has again been disturbed by placing Blake and Burns at the beginning of this section rather than at the end of the preceding one. Yet it is obvious that the mingled purity and passion of their songs spring from the romantic faith which characterises the nineteenth century rather than the scientific scepticism which we attribute to the eighteenth. With the passing of Pope, melody again resumed control, and the impulse to sing—an impulse alien to Pope's spirit of deliberate inquiry—was nowhere more lavishly gratified than in the earthly tunes of Burns and the super-terrestrial and symbolic lyrics of Blake.

The change was dramatic. The revival of the musical " tone " in poetry, quickened by a revulsion from versified pedantry, brought about not only a new set of concepts but another vocabulary. Instead of the stiff couplets and clenched quatrains, the poets fashioned a more flexible line, varied the rhythms, rediscovered the sonnet, revivified the ballad form, amplified the almost forgotten Spenserian stanza. Turning from the archaic inversions and mythological allusions, the language became richer and, at the same time, more real. Byron was the link between the two periods. He extended the tradition of the eighteenth century, which to-day seems far more remote to us than the seventeenth, and added a tradition of his own. Byron's contemporaries approved of his songs though they deprecated his morals, while we—such is the mutability of taste—excuse if we do not applaud his morals and condemn his songs. Byron may be said to persist not by virtue of the lyrics by which he set great store, but by the narratives and " set pieces " that embellish the longer poems.

In programme and practice, however, no one contributed more towards the new poetic language than Wordsworth. The " advertisement " to the *Lyrical Ballads*, which spoke up for a more vivid and even vulgar speech, still serves as a credo for those who wish to keep poetry from too much literature and too little life. In his effort to ascertain " how far the language of conversation is adapted to the purposes of poetic pleasure," Wordsworth accomplished more than he intended. His " natural piety " intensified a natural if sometimes too naïve idiom; it enabled him to restore freshness to a diction that had become affected and false, and it gave, as his collaborator Coleridge said, " the charm of novelty to things of every day . . . awakening the mind's attention from the lethargy of custom and directing it to the wonders of the world before us."

If we look for likenesses between Wordsworth and those who immediately followed him, we must look for spiritual affinities rather than for direct influences. The principles of liberty expressed through political revolutions on both sides of the Atlantic, the boldness of the

American experiment, the disparate movements towards a wide humanitarianism were reflected in the work of the younger poets. New currents agitated every surface—explicit in the case of Byron, implicit in Shelley. In Shelley the fiery soul leaped uppermost, the poetry was enriched with a more rebellious and resonant timbre. In Keats, possibly the " purest " poet who ever wrote in English, the effect was of continuous ecstasy—the odes being maintained on the perilous pitch of high, extended songs. In these two poets (Keats and Shelley) as with the prophetic Blake—and Wordsworth at his best—the moving syllables proceed not only from deeper wells of sound, but from an almost soundless depth of spirit.

WILLIAM BLAKE

1757 - 1827

THE TYGER

Tyger! Tyger! burning bright
In the forests of the night,
What immortal hand or eye
Could frame thy fearful symmetry?

In what distant deeps or skies
Burnt the fire of thine eyes?
On what wings dare he aspire?
What the hand dare seize the fire?

And what shoulder, and what art,
Could twist the sinews of thy heart?
And when thy heart began to beat,
What dread hand? and what dread feet?

What the hammer? what the chain?
In what furnace was thy brain?
What the anvil? what dread grasp
Dare its deadly terrors clasp?

When the stars threw down their spears
And watered heaven with their tears,
Did he smile his work to see?
Did he who made the Lamb make thee?

Tyger! Tyger! burning bright
In the forests of the night,
What immortal hand or eye
Dare frame thy fearful symmetry?

THE LAMB

Little Lamb, who made thee?
   Dost thou know who made thee?
Gave thee life and bid thee feed
By the stream and o'er the mead;
Gave thee clothing of delight,
Softest clothing, woolly, bright;
Gave thee such a tender voice
Making all the vales rejoice?
   Little Lamb, who made thee?
   Dost thou know who made thee?

Little Lamb, I'll tell thee,
   Little Lamb, I'll tell thee:
He is callèd by thy name,
For he calls himself a Lamb.
He is meek and he is mild;
He became a little child.
I a child and thou a lamb,
We are callèd by his name.
   Little Lamb, God bless thee.
   Little Lamb, God bless thee.

THE FLY

Little Fly,
Thy summer's play
My thoughtless hand
Has brushed away.

Am not I
A fly like thee?
Or art not thou
A man like me?

For I dance
And drink and sing,
Till some blind hand
Shall brush my wing.

If thought is life
And strength and breath,
And the want
Of thought is death,

Then am I
A happy fly
If I live
Or if I die.

THE SUN-FLOWER

Ah, Sun-flower! weary of time,
Who countest the steps of the Sun,
Seeking after that sweet golden clime
Where the traveller's journey is done:

Where the Youth pined away with desire,
And the pale Virgin shrouded in snow,
Arise from their graves and aspire
Where my Sun-flower wishes to go.

THE SICK ROSE

O rose, thou art sick:
The invisible worm
That flies in the night
In the howling storm,

Has found out thy bed
Of crimson joy,
And his dark secret love
Does thy life destroy.

SONG

How sweet I roamed from field to field
    And tasted all the summer's pride,
Till I the prince of love beheld
    Who in the sunny beams did glide!

He showed me lilies for my hair,
  And blushing roses for my brow;
He led me through his gardens fair
  Where all his golden pleasures grow.

With sweet May dews my wings were wet,
  And Phœbus fired my vocal rage;
He caught me in his silken net,
  And shut me in his golden cage.

He loves to sit and hear me sing,
  Then, laughing, sports and plays with me;
Then stretches out my golden wing,
  And mocks my loss of liberty.

INFANT SORROW

My mother groaned, my father wept;
Into the dangerous world I leapt;
Helpless, naked, piping loud,
Like a fiend hid in a cloud.

Struggling in my father's hands,
Striving against my swaddling-bands,
Bound and weary, I thought best
To sulk upon my mother's breast.

INJUNCTION

The Angel that presided o'er my birth
Said, " Little creature, formed of joy and mirth,
Go, love, without the help of anything on earth."

MY SILKS AND FINE ARRAY

My silks and fine array,
  My smiles and languished air,
By love are driven away;
  And mournful lean Despair
Brings me yew to deck my grave;
Such end true lovers have.

His face is fair as heaven
    When springing buds unfold;
Oh, why to him was't given,
    Whose heart is wintry cold?
His breast is Love's all-worshipped tomb
Where all Love's pilgrims come.

Bring me an axe and spade,
    Bring me a winding sheet;
When I my grave have made,
    Let winds and tempests beat:
Then down I'll lie, as cold as clay.
True love doth pass away!

MORNING

To find the Western path,
Right thro' the Gates of Wrath
I urge my way.
Sweet Mercy leads me on;
With soft repentant moan
I see the break of day.

The war of swords and spears,
Melted by dewy tears,
Exhales on high.
The Sun is freed from fears,
And with soft grateful tears
Ascends the sky.

AUGURIES OF INNOCENCE

To see a World in a Grain of Sand
And a Heaven in a Wild Flower,
Hold Infinity in the palm of your hand
And Eternity in an hour.

A Robin Redbreast in a Cage
Puts all Heaven in a rage.

A Dove-house filled with Doves and Pigeons
Shudders Hell thro' all its regions.

A Dog starved at his Master's Gate
Predicts the ruin of the State.

A Horse misused upon the Road
Calls to Heaven for human blood.

Each outcry of the hunted Hare
A fibre from the Brain does tear.

A Skylark wounded in the wing,
A Cherubim does cease to sing.

The Game Cock clipped and armed for fight
Does the Rising Sun affright.

Every Wolf's and Lion's howl
Raises from Hell a human Soul.

The wild Deer wand'ring here and there
Keeps the human Soul from Care.

The Lamb misused breeds public strife
And yet forgives the Butcher's Knife.

The Bat that flits at close of Eve
Has left the Brain that won't believe.

The Owl that calls upon the Night
Speaks the Unbeliever's fright.

He who shall hurt the little Wren
Shall never be beloved by Men.

He who the Ox to wrath had moved
Shall never be by Woman loved.

The wanton Boy that kills the Fly
Shall feel the Spider's enmity.

He who torments the Chafer's sprite
Weaves a Bower in endless Night.

The Caterpillar on the Leaf
Repeats to thee thy Mother's grief.

Kill not the Moth nor Butterfly
For the Last Judgement draweth nigh.

．　　．　　．　　．　　．

He who mocks the Infant's Faith
Shall be mocked in Age and Death.
He who shall teach the Child to Doubt
The rotting Grave shall ne'er get out.
He who respects the Infant's faith
Triumphs over Hell and Death.

The Child's Toys and the Old Man's Reasons
Are the Fruits of the Two seasons.

The Questioner who sits so sly
Shall never know how to Reply.
He who replies to words of Doubt
Doth put the Light of Knowledge out.

He who Doubts from what he sees
Will ne'er Believe, do what you please.
If the Sun and Moon should doubt,
They'd immediately go out.

To be in a Passion you Good may do,
But no Good if a Passion is in you.

The Whore and Gambler, by the State
Licensed, build that Nation's Fate.
The Harlot's cry from Street to Street
Shall weave Old England's winding Sheet.

The Winner's Shout, the Loser's Curse,
Dance before dead England's Hearse.

Every Night and every Morn
Some to Misery are Born.
Every Morn and every Night
Some are Born to sweet delight.

Some are Born to sweet delight,
Some are Born to Endless Night.

We are led to believe a Lie
When we see with, not thro' the Eye
Which was born in a Night, to perish in a Night,
When the Soul slept in Beams of Light.

God Appears, and God is Light
To those poor Souls who dwell in Night,
But does a Human Form display
To those who dwell in Realms of Day.

ETERNITY

He who binds to himself a joy
Does the wingèd life destroy;
But he who kisses the joy as it flies
Lives in eternity's sun-rise.

THE SWORD AND THE SICKLE

The sword sang on the barren heath;
The sickle in the fruitful field.
The sword he sang a song of death,
But could not make the sickle yield.

A NEW JERUSALEM

from "Milton"

And did those feet in ancient time
Walk upon England's mountains green?
And was the Holy Lamb of God
On England's pleasant pastures seen?

And did the countenance divine
Shine forth upon our clouded hills?
And was Jerusalem builded here
Among these dark satanic mills?

Bring me my bow of burning gold!
Bring me my arrows of desire!
Bring me my spear! O clouds, unfold!
Bring me my chariot of fire!

I will not cease from mental fight,
Nor shall my sword sleep in my hand,
Till we have built Jerusalem
In England's green and pleasant land.

TO THE MUSES

Whether on Ida's shady brow,
   Or in the chambers of the East,
The chambers of the sun that now
   From ancient melody have ceased;

Whether in heaven ye wander fair,
   Or the green corners of the earth,
Or the blue regions of the air,
   Where the melodious winds have birth;

Whether on crystal rocks ye rove,
   Beneath the bosom of the sea
Wandering in many a coral grove,
   Fair Nine, forsaking Poetry;

How have you left the ancient love
   That bards of old enjoyed in you!
The languid strings do scarcely move;
   The sound is forced, the notes are few!

LOVE'S SECRET

Never seek to tell thy love,
   Love that never told can be;
For the gentle wind does move
   Silently, invisibly.

I told my love, I told my love,
   I told her all my heart;
Trembling, cold, in ghastly fears,
   Ah! she did depart!

Soon as she was gone from me
   A traveller came by,
Silently, invisibly:
   He took her with a sigh.

ROBERT BURNS

1759 - 1796

THE BANKS O' DOON

Ye flowery banks o' bonie Doon,
    How can ye blume sae fair?
How can ye chant, ye little birds,
    And I sae fu' o' care!

Thou'll break my heart, thou bonie bird
    That sings upon the bough;
Thou minds me o' the happy days
    When my fause[1] Luve was true.

Thou'll break my heart, thou bonie bird
    That sings beside thy mate;
For sae I sat, and sae I sang,
    And wist na o' my fate.

Aft hae I roved by bonie Doon
    To see the woodbine twine,
And ilka[2] bird sang o' its love;
    And sae did I o' mine.

Wi' lightsome heart I pu'd a rose,
    Frae aff its thorny tree;
And my fause Luver staw[3] the rose,
    But left the thorn wi' me.

MARY MORISON

O Mary, at thy window be,
    It is the wished, the trysted hour!
Those smiles and glances let me see,
    That make the miser's treasure poor:
How blithely wad I bide the stour,[4]
    A weary slave frae sun to sun,
Could I the rich reward secure,
    The lovely Mary Morison.

[1] False.   [2] Every.   [3] Stole.   [4] Struggle.

Yestreen, when to the trembling string
   The dance gaed thro' the lighted ha',
To thee my fancy took its wing,
   I sat, but neither heard nor saw:
Tho' this was fair, and that was braw,
   And yon the toast of a' the town,
I sighed, and said amang them a',
   " Ye are na Mary Morison."

Oh, Mary, canst thou wreck his peace,
   Wha for thy sake wad gladly die?
Or canst thou break that heart of his,
   Whose only faut is loving thee?
If love for love thou wilt na gie,
   At least be pity to me shown;
A thought ungentle canna be
   The thought o' Mary Morison.

TO A MOUSE

ON TURNING HER UP IN HER NEST WITH THE PLOUGH

Wee, sleekit, cowrin, tim'rous beastie,
O, what a panic's in thy breastie!
Thou need na start awa sae hasty,
   Wi' bickering brattle!
I wad be laith to rin an' chase thee,
   Wi' murd'ring pattle![1]

I'm truly sorry man's dominion,
Has broken nature's social union,
An' justifies that ill opinion,
   Which makes thee startle
At me, thy poor, earth-born companion,
   An' fellow-mortal!

I doubt na, whiles, but thou may thieve;
What then? poor beastie, thou maun live!
A daimen icker in a thrave[2]

[1] Plough-stick.   [2] An odd ear of wheat in a shock of grain.

'S a sma' request;
I'll get a blessin wi' the lave,[1]
    An' never miss't!

Thy wee bit housie, too, in ruin!
It's silly wa's the winds are strewin!
An' naething, now, to big[2] a new ane,
    O' foggage[3] green!
An' bleak December's winds ensuin,
    Baith snell an' keen![4]

Thou saw the fields laid bare an' waste,
An' weary winter comin fast,
An' cozie here, beneath the blast,
    Thou thought to dwell—
Till crash! the cruel coulter past
    Out thro' thy cell.

That wee bit heap o' leaves an' stibble,
Has cost thee mony a weary nibble!
Now thou's turn'd out, for a' thy trouble,
    But house or hald,[5]
To thole[6] the winter's sleety dribble,
    An' cranreuch[7] cauld!

But, Mousie, thou art no thy lane,[8]
In proving foresight may be vain;
The best-laid schemes o' mice an men
    Gang aft agley,
An' lea'e us nought but grief an' pain,
    For promised joy!

Still thou art blest, compared wi' me;
The present only toucheth thee:
But och! I backward cast me e'e,
    On prospects drear!
An' forward, tho' I canna see,
    I guess an' fear!

[1] The leavings.   [2] Build.   [3] Moss.   [4] Sharp and bitter.
[5] Without house or home.   [6] Endure.   [7] Hoar-frost.
[8] Not the only one.

JOHN ANDERSON, MY JO

John Anderson, my jo, John,
　　When we were first acquent;
Your locks were like the raven,
　　Your bonie brow was brent;[1]
But now your brow is bald, John,
　　Your locks are like the snow;
But blessings on your frosty pow,[2]
　　John Anderson, my jo.

John Anderson, my jo, John,
　　We clamb the hill thegither;
And mony a cantie[3] day, John,
　　We've had wi' ane anither:
Now we maun totter down, John,
　　And hand in hand we'll go,
And sleep thegither at the foot,
　　John Anderson, my jo.

WHISTLE AN' I'LL COME TO YE, MY LAD

Chorus.—O whistle an' I'll come to ye, my lad,
　　O whistle an' I'll come to ye, my lad,
　　Tho' father an' mother an' a' should gae mad,
　　O whistle an' I'll come to ye, my lad.

But warily tent[4] when ye come to court me,
And come nae unless the back-yett be a-jee;[5]
Syne up the back-stile, and let naebody see,
And come as ye were na comin to me,
And come as ye were na comin to me.
　　　O whistle an' I'll come . . .

At kirk, or at market, whene'er ye meet me,
Gang by me as tho' that ye car'd na a flea;
But steal me a blink o' your bonie black e'e,
Yet look as ye were na lookin to me,
Yet look as ye were na lookin to me.
　　　O whistle an' I'll come . . .

[1] Smooth.　　[2] Head.　　[3] Lively.　　[4] Watch.
[5] . . . the back-gate be ajar.

Aye, vow and protest that ye care na for me,
And whiles ye may lightly my beauty a-wee;
But court na anither, tho' jokin ye be,
For fear that she wile your fancy frae me,
For fear that she wile your fancy frae me.
        O whistle an' I'll come . . .

TAM O' SHANTER

A TALE

" Of Brownyis and of Bogillis full is this Buke."
                                        GAWIN DOUGLAS.

When chapman billies[1] leave the street,
And drouthy neibors neibors meet;
As market days are wearing late,
And folk begin to tak the gate,
While we sit bousing at the nappy,[2]
An' getting fou and unco happy,
We think na on the lang Scots miles,
The mosses, water, slaps[3] and stiles,
That lie between us and our hame,
Where sits our sulky, sullen dame,
Gathering her brows like gathering storm,
Nursing her wrath to keep it warm.

        This truth fand honest Tam o' Shanter,
As he frae Ayr ae night did canter
(Auld Ayr, wham ne'er a town surpasses,
For honest men and bonie lasses).

        O Tam! had'st thou but been sae wise,
As taen thy ain wife Kate's advice!
She tauld thee weel thou was a skellum,[4]
A blethering, blustering, drunken blellum;[5]
That frae November till October,
Ae market-day thou was no sober;

        That ilka melder[6] wi' the Miller,
Thou sat as lang as thou had siller;[7]
That ev'ry naig was ca'd a shoe on[8]
The Smith and thee gat roarin fou on;

[1] Peddlers.   [2] Drinking-ale.   [3] Gaps.   [4] Rogue.   [5] Babbler.
[6] Corn-grinding.   [7] (Silver) Money.   [8] Every nag had a shoe driven on.

That at the Lord's house, ev'n on Sunday,
Thou drank wi' Kirkton Jean till Monday;
She prophesied that late or soon,
Thou wad be found, deep drowned in Doon,
Or catched wi' warlocks[1] in the mirk,
By Alloway's auld, haunted kirk.

Ah, gentle dames! it gars me greet,[2]
To think how mony counsels sweet,
How mony lengthened, sage advices,
The husband frae the wife despises!

But to our tale:—Ae market night,
Tam had got planted unco right,
Fast by an ingle, bleezing finely,[3]
Wi' reaming swats[4] that drank divinely;
And at his elbow, Souter Johnie,
His ancient, trusty, drouthy crony:
Tam lo'ed him like a very brither;[5]
They had been fou for weeks thegither.
The night drave on wi' sangs an clatter;
And aye the ale was growing better:
The Landlady and Tam grew gracious,
Wi' favours secret, sweet and precious:
The Souter tauld his queerest stories;
The Landlord's laugh was ready chorus:
The storm without might rair and rustle,
Tam did na mind the storm a whistle.

Care, mad to see a man sae happy,
E'en drowned himsel amang the nappy.
As bees flee hame wi' lades[6] o' treasure,
The minutes winged their way wi' pleasure:
Kings may be blest, but Tam was glorious,
O'er a' the ills o' life victorious!

But pleasures are like poppies spread,
You seize the flow'r, its bloom is shed;
Or like the snow falls in the river,
A moment white—then melts for ever;
Or like the borealis race,
That flit ere you can point their place;

---

[1] Male witches.   [2] Makes me weep.   [3] A blazing hearth.
[4] Foaming tankards.   [5] Brother.   [6] Loads.

Or like the rainbow's lovely form
Evanishing amid the storm.
Nae man can tether time or tide;—
The hour approaches Tam maun ride;
That hour, o' night's black arch the key-stane,
That dreary hour he mounts his beast in;
And sic a night he taks the road in,
As ne'er poor sinner was abroad in.

The wind blew as 'twad blawn its last;
The rattling showers rose on the blast;
The speedy gleams the darkness swallowed;
Loud, deep, and lang, the thunder bellowed:
That night, a child might understand,
The Deil[1] had business on his hand.

Weel mounted on his grey mare, Meg,
A better never lifted leg,
Tam skelpit[2] on through dub[3] and mire,
Despising wind, and rain, and fire;
Whiles holding fast his guid blue bonnet;
Whiles crooning o'er some auld Scots sonnet;
Whiles glowering round wi' prudent cares,
Lest bogles[4] catch him unawares;
Kirk Alloway was drawing nigh,
Whare ghaists and houlets[5] nightly cry.

By this time he was cross the ford,
Whare in the snaw the chapman smoored,[6]
And past the birks and meikle-stane,[7]
Whare drunken Charlie brak's neckbane;
And through the whins, and by the cairn,[8]
Whare hunters fand the murdered bairn;
And near the thorn, aboon the well,
Whare Mungo's mither hanged hersel.
Before him Doon pours all his floods;
The doubling storm roars through the woods;
The lightnings flash from pole to pole;
Near and more near the thunders roll:
When, glimmering thro' the groaning trees,
Kirk Alloway seemed in a bleeze;
Through ilka bore[9] the beams were glancing;
And loud resounded mirth and dancing.

[1] Devil.　　[2] Splashed.　　[3] Puddle.　　[4] Goblins.
[5] Ghosts and owls.　　[6] Smothered.　　[7] The large stone.
[8] Through brush by the stone-pile.　　[9] Every chink.

Inspiring bold John Barleycorn!
What dangers thou canst make us scorn!
Wi' tippenny,[1] we fear nae evil;
Wi' usquebae, [2] we'll face the Devil!
The swats sae reamed in Tammie's noddle,
Fair play, he cared na deils a boddle.[3]
But Maggie stood right sair astonished,
Till, by the heel and hand admonished,
She ventured forward on the light;
And, wow! Tam saw an unco sight!
Warlocks and witches in a dance;
Nae cotillion brent-new frae France,
But hornpipes, jigs, strathspeys, and reels,
Put life and mettle in their heels.
At winnock-bunker[4] in the east,
There sat auld Nick, in shape o' beast;
A towzie tyke,[5] black, grim, and large,
To gie them music was his charge:
He screwed the pipes and gart them skirl,[6]
Till roof and rafters a' did dirl.[7]—
Coffins stood round, like open presses,
That shawed the dead in their last dresses;
And by some devilish cantrip[8] sleight,
Each in its cauld hand held a light,—
By which heroic Tam was able
To note upon the haly table
A murderer's banes in gibbet-airns;[9]
Two span-lang, wee, unchristened bairns;
A thief, new-cutted frae a rape,[10]
Wi' his last gasp his gab[11] did gape;
Five tomahawks wi' blude red-rusted;
Five scimitars wi' murder crusted;
A garter which a babe had strangled;
A knife a father's throat had mangled,
Whom his ain son of life bereft,
The grey hairs sticking to the heft;
Wi' mair of horrible and awfu',
Which even to name wad be unlawfu'.

[1] Twopenny ale.　　　[2] Whisky.　　　[3] Cared not a copper.
[4] Window-seat.　　　[5] Shaggy cur.
[6] Played the bagpipes and made them scream.　　　[7] Rattle.
[8] Magic.　　　[9] Gallows-irons.　　　[10] Rope.　　　[11] Mouth.

As Tammie glowr'd, amazed and curious,
The mirth and fun grew fast and furious;
The Piper loud and louder blew,
The dancers quick and quicker flew,
They reeled, they set, they crossed, they cleekit,[1]
Till ilka carlin swat and reekit,[2]
And coost her duddies to the wark,[3]
And linkit at it in her sark![4]

.   .   .   .   .

But Tam kent what was what fu' brawlie;[5]
There was ae winsome wench and waulie[6]
That night enlisted in the core,[7]
Lang after ken'd on Carrick shore
(For mony a beast to dead she shot,
And perished mony a bonie boat,
And shook baith meikle corn and bear,
And kept the country-side in fear);
Her cutty sark,[8] o' Paisley harn,[9]
That while a lassie she had worn,
In longitude tho' sorely scanty,
It was her best, and she was vauntie.[10]
Ah! little ken'd thy reverend grannie,
That sark she coft[11] for her wee Nannie,
Wi' twa pund Scots ('twas a' her riches),
Wad ever graced a dance of witches!

But here my Muse her wing maun cower,
Sic flights are far beyond her power;
To sing how Nannie lap and flang
(A souple jade she was and strang).
And how Tam stood, like ane bewitched,
And thought his very een enriched:
Even Satan glowr'd, and fidg'd fu' fain,[12]
And hotched[13] and blew wi might and main:
Till first ae caper, syne anither,
Tam tint[14] his reason a' thegither,
And roars out, " Weel done, Cutty-sark! "
And in an instant all was dark:

[1] Joined hands.   [2] Till every old woman sweat and reeked.
[3] And cast off her clothes in the excitement.
[4] And danced in her shirt.   [5] Fine.   [6] Jolly.
[7] Corps, company.   [8] Short shirt.   [9] Linen.
[10] Vain, proud of it.   [11] Bought.   [12] Fidgeted eagerly.
[13] Squirmed.   [14] Lost.

And scarcely had he Maggie rallied,
When out the hellish legion sallied.

    As bees bizz out wi' angry fyke,[1]
When plundering herds assail their byke;[2]
As open pussie's[3] mortal foes,
When, pop! she starts before their nose;
As eager runs the market-crowd,
When " Catch the thief! " resounds aloud;
So Maggie runs, the witches follow,
Wi' mony an eldritch[4] skreich and hollo.

Ah, Tam! Ah, Tam! thou'll get thy fairin![5]
In hell they'll roast thee like a herrin!
In vain thy Kate awaits thy comin!
Kate soon will be a woefu' woman!
Now, do thy speedy utmost, Meg,
And win the key-stane o' the brig [6]
There, at them thou thy tail may toss,
A running stream they dare na cross;
But ere the key-stane she could make,
The fiend a tail she had to shake!
For Nannie, far before the rest,
Hard upon noble Maggie prest,
And flew at Tam wi' furious ettle;[7]
But little wist she Maggie's mettle!
Ae spring brought off her master hale,
But left behind her ain grey tail:
The carlin claught her by the rump,
And left poor Maggie scarce a stump.

    Now wha this tale o' truth shall read,
Ilk' man and mother's son, take heed,
Whene'er to drink you are inclined,
Or cutty-sarks run in your mind,
Think, ye may buy the joys o'er dear,
Remember Tam o' Shanter's mare!

[1] Fuss.   [2] Hive.   [3] The hare's.   [4] Unearthly.
[5] Reward.   [6] Bridge.   [7] Intent.

SWEET AFTON

Flow gently, sweet Afton! among thy green braes,
Flow gently, I'll sing thee a song in thy praise;
My Mary's asleep by thy murmuring stream,
Flow gently, sweet Afton, disturb not her dream.

Thou stock-dove whose echo resounds thro' the glen,
Ye wild whistling blackbirds in yon thorny den,
Thou green crested lapwing, thy screaming forbear,
I charge you, disturb not my slumbering Fair.

How lofty, sweet Afton, thy neighbouring hills,
Far marked with the courses of clear, winding rills;
There daily I wander as noon rises high,
My flocks and my Mary's sweet cot in my eye.

How pleasant thy banks and green valleys below,
Where, wild in the woodlands, the primroses blow;
There oft, as mild ev'ning weeps over the lea,
The sweet-scented birk[1] shades my Mary and me.

Thy crystal stream, Afton, how lovely it glides,
And winds by the cot where my Mary resides;
How wanton thy waters her snowy feet lave,
As, gathering sweet flowerets, she stems thy clear wave.

Flow gently, sweet Afton, among thy green braes,
Flow gently, sweet river, the theme of my lays;
My Mary's asleep by thy murmuring stream,
Flow gently, sweet Afton, disturb not her dream.

BRUCE'S MARCH TO BANNOCKBURN

Scots, wha hae wi' Wallace bled,
Scots, wham Bruce has aften led,
Welcome to your gory bed,
    Or to victorie!

[1] Birch.

Now's the day, and now's the hour;
See the front o' battle lour:
See approach proud Edward's power—
 Chains and slaverie!

Wha will be a traitor knave?
Wha can fill a coward's grave?
Wha sae base as be a slave?
 Let him turn and flee!

Wha, for Scotland's King and Law,
Freedom's sword will strongly draw,
Free-man stand, or Free-man fa',
 Let him on wi' me!

By oppression's woes and pains!
By your sons in servile chains!
We will drain our dearest veins,
 But they shall be free!

Lay the proud usurpers low!
Tyrants fall in every foe!
Liberty's in every blow!—
 Let us do or die!

MY LUVE

O my Luve is like a red, red rose,
 That's newly sprung in June:
O my Luve is like the melodie,
 That's sweetly played in tune.

As fair art thou, my bonie lass,
 So deep in luve am I;
And I will luve thee still, my dear,
 Till a' the seas gang dry.

Till a' the seas gang dry, my dear,
 And the rocks melt wi' the sun;
And I will luve thee still, my dear,
 While the sands o' life shall run.

And fare-thee-weel, my only Luve!
   And fare-thee-weel a while!
And I will come again, my Luve,
   Tho' it were ten thousand mile.

O WERT THOU IN THE CAULD BLAST

O wert thou in the cauld blast,
   On yonder lea, on yonder lea,
My plaidie to the angry airt,[1]
   I'd shelter thee, I'd shelter thee.
Or did misfortune's bitter storms
   Around thee blaw, around thee blaw,
Thy bield[2] should be my bosom,
   To share it a', to share it a'!

Or were I in the wildest waste,
   Sae black and bare, sae black and bare,
The desert were a Paradise,
   If thou wert there, if thou wert there;
Or were I monarch o' the globe,
   Wi' thee to reign, wi' thee to reign,
The brightest jewel in my crown
   Wad be my queen, wad be my queen!

WILLIAM WORDSWORTH

1770 - 1850

THE DAFFODILS

I wandered lonely as a cloud
That floats on high o'er vales and hills,
When all at once I saw a crowd,
A host of golden daffodils,
Beside the lake, beneath the trees,
Fluttering and dancing in the breeze.

Continuous as the stars that shine
And twinkle on the milky way,
They stretched in never-ending line
Along the margin of a bay:

[1] Wind.   [2] Shelter.

Ten thousand saw I at a glance
Tossing their heads in sprightly dance.

The waves beside them danced, but they
Out-did the sparkling waves in glee:
A poet could not but be gay
In such a jocund company!
I gazed—and gazed—but little thought
What wealth the show to me had brought.

For oft, when on my couch I lie
In vacant or in pensive mood,
They flash upon that inward eye
Which is the bliss of solitude;
And then my heart with pleasure fills,
And dances with the daffodils.

" MY HEART LEAPS UP WHEN I BEHOLD "

My heart leaps up when I behold
        A rainbow in the sky:
So was it when my life began;
So is it now I am a man;
So be it when I shall grow old,
        Or let me die!
The Child is father of the Man;
And I could wish my days to be
Bound each to each by natural piety.

WRITTEN IN MARCH

The cock is crowing,
The stream is flowing,
The small birds twitter,
The lake doth glitter,
The green field sleeps in the sun;
The oldest and youngest
Are at work with the strongest;
The cattle are grazing,
Their heads never raising;
There are forty feeding like one!

Like an army defeated
The snow hath retreated,
And now doth fare ill
On the top of the bare hill;
The ploughboy is whooping—anon—anon:
  There's joy in the mountains;
  There's life in the fountains;
  Small clouds are sailing,
  Blue sky prevailing;
The rain is over and gone!

TO THE CUCKOO

O blithe new-comer! I have heard,
I hear thee and rejoice:
O cuckoo! shall I call thee Bird,
Or but a wandering Voice?

While I am lying on the grass
Thy twofold shout I hear;
From hill to hill it seems to pass,
At once far off and near.

Though babbling only to the vale
Of sunshine and of flowers,
Thou bringest unto me a tale
Of visionary hours.

Thrice welcome, darling of the Spring!
Even yet thou art to me
No bird, but an invisible thing,
A voice, a mystery;

The same whom in my school-boy days
I listened to; that cry
Which made me look a thousand ways
In bush, and tree, and sky.

To seek thee did I often rove
Through woods and on the green;
And thou wert still a hope, a love;
Still longed for, never seen!

And I can listen to thee yet;
Can lie upon the plain
And listen, till I do beget
That golden time again.

O blessèd bird! the earth we pace
Again appears to be
An unsubstantial, fairy place,
That is fit home for thee!

THE WORLD

The world is too much with us; late and soon,
Getting and spending, we lay waste our powers:
Little we see in Nature that is ours;
We have given our hearts away, a sordid boon!
The sea that bares her bosom to the moon;
The winds that will be howling at all hours
And are up-gathered now like sleeping flowers;
For this, for everything, we are out of tune;
It moves us not.—Great God! I'd rather be
A pagan suckled in a creed outworn.
So might I, standing on this pleasant lea,
Have glimpses that would make me less forlorn;
Have sight of Proteus rising from the sea;
Or hear old Triton blow his wreathèd horn.

SLEEP

A flock of sheep that leisurely pass by,
One after one; the sound of rain, and bees
Murmuring; the fall of rivers, winds and seas,
Smooth fields, white sheets of water, and pure sky;
I have thought of all by turns, and yet do lie
Sleepless! and soon the small birds' melodies
Must hear, first uttered from my orchard trees;
And the first cuckoo's melancholy cry.
Even thus last night, and two nights more, I lay,
And could not win thee, Sleep! by any stealth:
So do not let me wear to-night away:
Without Thee what is all the morning's wealth?
Come, blessèd barrier between day and day,
Dear mother of fresh thoughts and joyous health!

UPON WESTMINSTER BRIDGE

Earth has not anything to show more fair:
Dull would he be of soul who could pass by
A sight so touching in its majesty:
This city now doth, like a garment, wear
The beauty of the morning; silent, bare,
Ships, towers, domes, theatres, and temples lie
Open unto the fields, and to the sky:
All bright and glittering in the smokeless air.
Never did sun more beautifully steep
In his first splendour, valley, rock, or hill;
Ne'er saw I, never felt, a calm so deep!
The river glideth at his own sweet will:
Dear God! the very houses seem asleep;
And all that mighty heart is lying still!

ENGLAND, 1802

O Friend! I know not which way I must look
For comfort, being, as I am, opprest,
To think that now our life is only drest
For show; mean handy-work of craftsman, cook,
Or groom! We must run glittering like a brook
In the open sunshine, or we are unblest:
The wealthiest man among us is the best:
No grandeur now in nature or in book
Delights us. Rapine, avarice, expense,
This is idolatry; and these we adore;
Plain living and high thinking are no more:
The homely beauty of the good old cause
Is gone; our peace, our fearful innocence,
And pure religion breathing household laws.

TO MILTON

(LONDON, 1802)

Milton! thou should'st be living at this hour:
England hath need of thee: she is a fen
Of stagnant waters: altar, sword, and pen,
Fireside, the heroic wealth of hall and bower,
Have forfeited their ancient English dower
Of inward happiness. We are selfish men.
Oh! raise us up, return to us again;
And give us manners, virtue, freedom, power.
Thy soul was like a star, and dwelt apart:
Thou hadst a voice whose sound was like the sea;
Pure as the naked heavens, majestic, free,
So didst thou travel on life's common way,
In cheerful godliness; and yet thy heart
The lowliest duties on herself did lay.

EVENING ON THE BEACH

It is a beauteous evening, calm and free;
The holy time is quiet as a nun
Breathless with adoration; the broad sun
Is sinking down in its tranquillity;
The gentleness of heaven is on the sea:
Listen! the mighty Being is awake,
And doth with his eternal motion make
A sound like thunder—everlastingly.
Dear child! dear girl! that walkest with me here,
If thou appear untouched by solemn thought
Thy nature is not therefore less divine:
Thou liest in Abraham's bosom all the year,
And worshipp'st at the Temple's inner shrine,
God being with thee when we know it not.

THE SONNET

Scorn not the Sonnet; critic, you have frowned,
Mindless of its just honours; with this key
Shakespeare unlocked his heart; the melody
Of this small lute gave ease to Petrarch's wound;
A thousand times this pipe did Tasso sound;
With it Camöens soothed an exile's grief;
The Sonnet glittered a gay myrtle leaf
Amid the cypress with which Dante crowned
His visionary brow: a glow-worm lamp,
It cheered mild Spenser, called from faeryland
To struggle through dark ways; and, when a damp
Fell round the path of Milton, in his hand
The thing became a trumpet; whence he blew
Soul-animating strains—alas, too few!

LUCY

I

She dwelt among the untrodden ways
   Beside the springs of Dove,
A maid whom there were none to praise
   And very few to love:

A violet by a mossy stone
   Half hidden from the eye!
Fair as a star, when only one
   Is shining in the sky.

She lived unknown, and few could know
   When Lucy ceased to be;
But she is in her grave, and, oh,
   The difference to me!

2

I travelled among unknown men,
   In lands beyond the sea;
Nor, England! did I know till then
   What love I bore to thee.

'Tis past, that melancholy dream!
  Nor will I quit thy shore
A second time; for still I seem
  To love thee more and more.

Among thy mountains did I feel
  The joy of my desire;
And she I cherished turned her wheel
  Beside an English fire.

Thy mornings showed, thy nights concealed
  The bowers where Lucy played;
And thine too is the last green field
  That Lucy's eyes surveyed.

3

A slumber did my spirit seal;
  I had no human fears:
She seemed a thing that could not feel
  The touch of earthly years.

No motion has she now, no force;
  She neither hears nor sees;
Rolled round in earth's diurnal course,
  With rocks, and stones, and trees.

CHARACTER OF THE HAPPY WARRIOR

Who is the happy Warrior? Who is he
That every man in arms should wish to be?
—It is the generous Spirit, who, when brought
Among the tasks of real life, hath wrought
Upon the plan that pleased his boyish thought:
Whose high endeavours are an inward light
That makes the path before him always bright:
Who, with a natural instinct to discern
What knowledge can perform, is diligent to learn;
Abides by this resolve, and stops not there,
But makes his moral being his prime care;
Who, doomed to go in company with pain,
And fear, and bloodshed, miserable train!
Turns his necessity to glorious gain;
In face of these doth exercise a power
Which is our human nature's highest dower;

Controls them and subdues, transmutes, bereaves
Of their bad influence, and their good receives:
By objects, which might force the soul to abate
Her feeling, rendered more compassionate;
Is placable—because occasions rise
So often that demand such sacrifice;
More skilful in self-knowledge, even more pure,
As tempted more; more able to endure,
As more exposed to suffering and distress;
Thence, also, more alive to tenderness.
—'Tis he whose law is reason; who depends
Upon that law as on the best of friends;
Whence, in a state where men are tempted still
To evil for a guard against worse ill,
And what in quality or act is best
Doth seldom on a right foundation rest,
He labours good on good to fix, and owes
To virtue every triumph that he knows . . .

SKY AFTER STORM

from " The Excursion," Book Two

A single step, that freed me from the skirts
Of the blind vapour, opened to my view
Glory beyond all glory ever seen
By waking sense or by the dreaming soul!
The appearance, instantaneously disclosed,
Was of a mighty city—boldly say
A wilderness of building, sinking far
And self-withdrawn into a boundless depth,
Far sinking into splendour—without end!
Fabric it seemed of diamond and of gold,
With alabaster domes, and silver spires,
And blazing terrace upon terrace, high
Uplifted; here, serene pavilions bright,
In avenues disposed; there, towers begirt
With battlements that on their restless fronts
Bore stars—illumination of all gems!
By earthly nature had the effect been wrought
Upon the dark materials of the storm
Now pacified; on them, and on the coves
And mountain-steeps and summits, whereunto
The vapours had receded, taking there
Their station under a cerulean sky.

Oh, 'twas an unimaginable sight!
Clouds, mists, streams, watery rocks and emerald turf,
Clouds of all tincture, rocks and sapphire sky,
Confused, commingled, mutually inflamed,
Molten together, and composing thus,
Each lost in each, that marvellous array
Of temple, palace, citadel, and huge
Fantastic pomp of structure without name,
In fleecy folds voluminous, enwrapped.
Right in the midst, where interspace appeared
Of open court, an object like a throne
Under a shining canopy of state
Stood fixed. . . .

THE SOLITARY REAPER

Behold her, single in the field,
Yon solitary highland lass!
Reaping and singing by herself;
Stop here, or gently pass!
Alone she cuts and binds the grain,
And sings a melancholy strain;
O listen! for the vale profound
Is overflowing with the sound.

No nightingale did ever chaunt
More welcome notes to weary bands
Of travellers in some shady haunt,
Among Arabian sands:
A voice so thrilling ne'er was heard
In spring-time from the cuckoo-bird,
Breaking the silence of the seas
Among the farthest Hebrides.

Will no one tell me what she sings?—
Perhaps the plaintive numbers flow
For old, unhappy, far-off things,
And battles long ago;
Or is it some more humble lay,
Familiar matter of to-day?
Some natural sorrow, loss, or pain,
That has been, and may be again?

Whate'er the theme, the maiden sang
As if her song could have no ending;
I saw her singing at her work,
And o'er the sickle bending;—
I listened, motionless and still;
And, as I mounted up the hill
The music in my heart I bore,
Long after it was heard no more.

ODE

INTIMATIONS OF IMMORTALITY

There was a time when meadow, grove, and stream,
        The earth, and every common sight,
            To me did seem
            Apparelled in celestial light,
The glory and the freshness of a dream.
It is not now as it hath been of yore—
        Turn wheresoe'er I may,
            By night or day,
The things which I have seen I now can see no more.

        The rainbow comes and goes,
        And lovely is the rose,
        The moon doth with delight
Look round her when the heavens are bare,
        Waters on a starry night
        Are beautiful and fair;
    The sunshine is a glorious birth;
    But yet I know, where'er I go,
That there hath passed away a glory from the earth.

Now, while the birds thus sing a joyous song,
    And while the young lambs bound
        As to the tabor's sound,
To me alone there came a thought of grief;
A timely utterance gave that thought relief,
        And I again am strong.
The cataracts blow their trumpets from the steep;
No more shall grief of mine the season wrong;
I hear the echoes through the mountains throng;
The winds come to me from the fields of sleep,

And all the earth is gay;
Land and sea
Give themselves up to jollity,
And with the heart of May
Doth every beast keep holiday—
Thou child of joy,
Shout round me, let me hear thy shouts, thou happy
shepherd-boy.

.   .   .   .   .

Our birth is but a sleep and a forgetting:
The soul that rises with us, our life's star,
Hath had elsewhere its setting,
And cometh from afar;
Not in entire forgetfulness,
And not in utter nakedness,
But trailing clouds of glory do we come
From God, who is our home.
Heaven lies about us in our infancy;
Shades of the prison-house begin to close
Upon the growing boy,
But he beholds the light, and whence it flows.
He sees it in his joy;
The youth, who daily farther from the east
Must travel, still is Nature's priest,
And by the vision splendid
Is on his way attended;
At length the man perceives it die away,
And fade into the light of common day.

Earth fills her lap with pleasures of her own;
Yearnings she hath in her own natural kind,
And, even with something of a mother's mind,
And no unworthy aim,
The homely nurse doth all she can
To make her foster child, her inmate man,
Forget the glories he hath known,
And that imperial palace whence he came.

Behold the child among his newborn blisses,
A six years' darling of a pygmy size!
See, where 'mid work of his own hand he lies,
Fretted by sallies of his mother's kisses,
With light upon him from his father's eyes!
See, at his feet, some little plan or chart,

Some fragment from his dream of human life,
Shaped by himself with newly learnèd art;
    A wedding or a festival,
    A mourning or a funeral;
      And this hath now his heart,
    And unto this he frames his song:
      Then will he fit his tongue
To dialogues of business, love, or strife;
    But it will not be long
    Ere this be thrown aside,
    And with new joy and pride
The little actor cons another part;
Filling from time to time his " humorous stage "
With all the persons, down to palsied age,
That life brings with her in her equipage;
    As if his whole vocation
    Were endless imitation.

     .   .   .   .   .

    O joy! that in our embers
    Is something that doth live,
    That nature yet remembers
    What was so fugitive!
The thought of our past years in me doth breed
Perpetual benediction: not indeed
For that which is most worthy to be blest—
Delight and liberty, the simple creed
Of childhood, whether busy or at rest,
With new-fledged hope still fluttering in his breast:—
    Not for these I raise
    The song of thanks and praise;
  But for those obstinate questionings
  Of sense and outward things,
  Fallings from us, vanishings;
  Blank misgivings of a creature
Moving about in worlds not realized,
High instincts before which our mortal nature
Did tremble like a guilty thing surprised:
    But for those first affections,
    Those shadowy recollections,
  Which, be they what they may,
Are yet the fountain light of all our day,
Are yet a master light of all our seeing;
    Uphold us, cherish, and have power to make
Our noisy years seem moments in the being

Of the eternal silence: truths that wake,
        To perish never;
Which neither listlessness, nor mad endeavour,
        Nor man nor boy,
Nor all that is at enmity with joy,
Can utterly abolish or destroy!
        Hence in a season of calm weather,
        Though inland far we be,
Our souls have sight of that immortal sea
        Which brought us hither,
        Can in a moment travel thither,
And see the children sport upon the shore,
And hear the mighty waters rolling evermore.

Then sing, ye birds! sing, sing a joyous song!
        And let the young lambs bound
        As to the tabor's sound!
    We in thought will join your throng,
        Ye that pipe and ye that play,
        Ye that through your hearts to-day
        Feel the gladness of the May!
What though the radiance which was once so bright
Be now for ever taken from my sight,
        Though nothing can bring back the hour
Of splendour in the grass, of glory in the flower;
        We will grieve not, rather find
        Strength in what remains behind;
        In the primal sympathy
        Which having been must ever be;
        In the soothing thoughts that spring
        Out of human suffering;
        In the faith that looks through death,
In years that bring the philosophic mind.

And oh, ye fountains, meadows, hills, and groves,
Forebode not any severing of our loves!
Yet in my heart of hearts I feel your might;
I only have relinquished one delight
To live beneath your more habitual sway.
I love the brooks which down their channels fret,
Even more than when I tripped lightly as they;
The innocent brightness of a newborn day
            Is lovely yet;
The clouds that gather round the setting sun

Do take a sober colouring from an eye
That hath kept watch o'er man's mortality;
Another race hath been, and other palms are won.
Thanks to the human heart by which we live,
Thanks to its tenderness, its joys, and fears,
To me the meanest flower that blows can give
Thoughts that do often lie too deep for tears.

TO A SKYLARK

Ethereal minstrel! pilgrim of the sky!
Dost thou despise the earth where cares abound?
Or, while the wings aspire, are heart and eye
Both with thy nest upon the dewy ground?
Thy nest which thou canst drop into at will,
Those quivering wings composed, that music still!
Leave to the nightingale her shady wood;
A privacy of glorious light is thine;
Whence thou dost pour upon the world a flood
Of harmony, with instinct more divine;
Type of the wise who soar, but never roam;
True to the kindred points of Heaven and home!

SIR WALTER SCOTT

1771 - 1832

PROUD MAISIE

Proud Maisie is in the wood,
    Walking so early;
Sweet Robin sits on the bush
    Singing so rarely.

" Tell me, thou bonny bird,
    When shall I marry me? "
" When six braw gentlemen
    Kirkward shall carry ye."

" Who makes the bridal bed,
    Birdie, say truly? "
" The grey-headed sexton
    That delves the grave duly.

" The glow-worm o'er grave and stone
    Shall light thee steady;
The owl from the steeple sing,
    ' Welcome, proud lady.' "

HUNTING SONG

Waken, lords and ladies gay,
On the mountain dawns the day;
All the jolly chase is here
With hawk and horse and hunting-spear;
Hounds are in their couples yelling,
Hawks are whistling, horns are knelling;
Merrily, merrily mingle they,
" Waken, lords and ladies gay."

Waken, lords and ladies gay,
The mist has left the mountain grey,
Springlets in the dawn are streaming,
Diamonds on the brake are gleaming;
And foresters have busy been
To track the buck in thicket green;
Now we come to chant our lay,
" Waken, lords and ladies gay."

Waken, lords and ladies gay,
To the greenwood haste away;
We can show you where he lies,
Fleet of foot and tall of size;
We can show the marks he made
When the oak his antlers frayed;
You shall see him brought to bay;
Waken, lords and ladies gay.

Louder, louder chant the lay,
Waken, lords and ladies gay!
Tell them youth and mirth and glee
Run a course as well as we;
Time, stern huntsman! who can baulk,
Staunch as hound and fleet as hawk;
Think of this, and rise with day,
Gentle lords and ladies gay!

SAMUEL TAYLOR COLERIDGE

1772 - 1834

KUBLA KHAN

In Xanadu did Kubla Khan
  A stately pleasure-dome decree:
Where Alph, the sacred river, ran
Through caverns measureless to man
  Down to a sunless sea.

So twice five miles of fertile ground
With walls and towers were girdled round:
And here were gardens bright with sinuous rills,
Where blossomed many an incense-bearing tree,
And here were forests ancient as the hills,
Enfolding sunny spots of greenery.

But oh! that deep romantic chasm which slanted
Down the green hill athwart a cedarn cover!
A savage place; as holy and enchanted
As e'er beneath a waning moon was haunted
By woman wailing for her demon-lover!
And from this chasm, with ceaseless turmoil seething,
As if this earth in fast thick pants were breathing,
A mighty fountain momently was forced,
Amid whose swift half-intermitted burst
Huge fragments vaulted like rebounding hail,
Or chaffy grain beneath the thresher's flail:
And 'mid these dancing rocks at once and ever
It flung up momently the sacred river.
Five miles meandering with a mazy motion
Through wood and dale the sacred river ran,
Then reached the caverns measureless to man,
And sank in tumult to a lifeless ocean:
And 'mid this tumult Kubla heard from far
Ancestral voices prophesying war!

    The shadow of the dome of pleasure
    Floated midway on the waves;
    Where was heard the mingled measure
    From the fountain and the caves.

It was a miracle of rare device,
A sunny pleasure-dome with caves of ice!

A damsel with a dulcimer
In a vision once I saw:
It was an Abyssinian maid,
And on her dulcimer she played,
Singing of Mount Abora.
Could I revive within me
Her symphony and song,
To such a deep delight 'twould win me,
That with music loud and long,
I would build that dome in air,
That sunny dome! those caves of ice!
And all who heard should see them there,
And all should cry, Beware! Beware!
His flashing eyes, his floating hair!
Weave a circle round him thrice,
And close your eyes with holy dread,
For he on honey dew hath fed,
And drunk the milk of Paradise.

THE RIME OF THE ANCIENT MARINER

PART I

An ancient Mariner meeteth three Gallants bidden to a wedding-feast, and detaineth one.

It is an ancient Mariner,
And he stoppeth one of three.
" By thy long grey beard and glittering eye,
Now wherefore stopp'st thou me?

The Bridegroom's doors are opened wide,
And I am next of kin;
The guests are met, the feast is set:
May'st hear the merry din."

The Wedding-Guest is spellbound by the old seafaring man, and constrained to hear his tale.

He holds him with his skinny hand,
" There was a ship," quoth he.
" Hold off! unhand me, grey-beard loon! "
Eftsoons his hand dropt he.

He holds him with his glittering eye—
The Wedding-Guest stood still,
And listens like a three years' child:
The mariner hath his will.

The Wedding-Guest sat on a stone:
He cannot choose but hear;
And thus spake on that ancient man,
The bright-eyed Mariner

" The ship was cheered, the harbour cleared,
Merrily did we drop
Below the kirk, below the hill,
Below the lighthouse top.

The Mari-
ner tells how
the ship
sailed south-
ward with a
good wind
and fair
weather, till
it reached
the Line.

The sun came up upon the left,
Out of the sea came he!
And he shone bright, and on the right
Went down into the sea.

Higher and higher every day,
Till over the mast at noon—"
The Wedding-Guest here beat his breast,
For he heard the loud bassoon.

The Wed-
ding-Guest
heareth the
bridal
music; but
the Mariner
continueth
his tale.

The bride hath paced into the hall,
Red as a rose is she;
Nodding their heads before her goes
The merry minstrelsy.

The Wedding-Guest he beat his breast,
Yet he cannot choose but hear;
And thus spake on that ancient man,
The bright-eyed Mariner.

The ship
drawn by a
storm
toward the
south pole.

" And now the Storm-blast came, and he
Was tyrannous and strong:
He struck with his o'ertaking wings,
And chased us south along.

With sloping masts and dipping prow,
As who pursued with yell and blow
Still treads the shadow of his foe,
And forward bends his head,
The ship drove fast, loud roared the blast,
And southward aye we fled.

And now there came both mist and snow,
And it grew wondrous cold:
And ice, mast-high, came floating by,
As green as emerald.

The land of
ice, and of
fearful
sounds
where no
living thing
was to be
seen.

And through the drifts the snowy clifts
Did send a dismal sheen:
Nor shapes of men nor beasts we ken—
The ice was all between.

The ice was here, the ice was there,
The ice was all around:
It cracked and growled, and roared and howled,
Like noises in a swound!

Till a great
sea-bird,
called the
Albatross,
came
through the
snow-fog,
and was re-
ceived with
great joy
and hos-
pitality.

At length did cross an Albatross,
Thorough the fog it came;
As if it had been a Christian soul,
We hailed it in God's name.

And lo! the
Albatross
proveth a
bird of good
omen, and
followeth
the ship as it
returned
northward
through fog
and floating
ice.

It ate the food it ne'er had eat,
And round and round it flew.
The ice did split with a thunder-fit;
The helmsman steered us through!

And a good south wind sprung up behind;
The Albatross did follow,
And every day, for food or play,
Came to the mariners' hollo!

In mist or cloud, on mast or shroud,
It perched for vespers nine;
Whiles all the night, through fog-smoke white,
Glimmered the white moon-shine."

The ancient
Mariner in-
hospitably
killeth the
pious bird of
good omen.

" God save thee, ancient Mariner!
From the fiends, that plague thee thus!—
Why look'st thou so? "—With my cross-bow
I shot the Albatross.

PART 2

The Sun now rose upon the right:
Out of the sea came he,
Still hid in mist, and on the left
Went down into the sea.

And the good south wind still blew behind,
But no sweet bird did follow,
Nor any day for food or play
Came to the mariners' hollo!

His ship-
mates cry
out against
the Mariner,
for killing
the bird
of
good luck.

And I had done a hellish thing,
And it would work 'em woe:
For all averred, I had killed the bird
That made the breeze to blow.
Ah wretch! said they, the bird to slay,
That made the breeze to blow!

But when
the fog
cleared off,
they justify
the same,
and thus
make them-
selves
accomplices
in the crime.

Nor dim nor red, like God's own head,
The glorious Sun uprist:
Then all averred, I had killed the bird
That brought the fog and mist.
'Twas right, said they, such birds to slay,
That bring the fog and mist.

The fair
breeze con-
tinues; the
ship enters
the Pacific
Ocean, and
sails north-
ward, even
till it
reaches the
Line.

The fair breeze blew, the white foam flew,
The furrow followed free;
We were the first that ever burst
Into that silent sea.

The ship
hath been
suddenly
becalmed.

Down dropt the breeze, the sails dropt down,
'Twas sad as sad could be;
And we did speak only to break
The silence of the sea!

All in a hot and copper sky,
The bloody Sun, at noon,
Right up above the mast did stand,
No bigger than the Moon.

Day after day, day after day,
We stuck, nor breath nor motion;
As idle as a painted ship
Upon a painted ocean.

And the
Albatross
begins to be
avenged.

Water, water, everywhere,
And all the boards did shrink;
Water, water, everywhere
Nor any drop to drink.

The very deep did rot: O Christ!
That ever this should be!
Yea, slimy things did crawl with legs
Upon the slimy sea.

About, about, in reel and rout
The death-fires danced at night;
The water, like a witch's oils,
Burnt green, and blue and white.

A Spirit had followed them; one of the invisible inhabitants of this planet, neither departed souls nor angels; concerning whom the learned Jew, Josephus, and the Platonic Constantinopolitan, Michael Psellus, may be consulted. They are very numerous, and there is no climate or element without one or more.

And some in dreams assurèd were
Of the Spirit that plagued us so,
Nine fathom deep he had followed us
From the land of mist and snow.

And every tongue, through utter drought,
Was withered at the root;
We could not speak, no more than if
We had been choked with soot.

The ship-mates, in their sore distress, would fain throw the whole guilt on the ancient Mariner: in sign whereof they hang the dead sea-bird round his neck.

Ah! well a-day! what evil looks
Had I from old and young!
Instead of the cross, the Albatross
About my neck was hung.

PART 3

There passed a weary time. Each throat
Was parched, and glazed each eye.
A weary time! a weary time!
How glazed each weary eye,

The ancient Mariner beholdeth a sign in the element afar off.

When looking westward, I beheld
A something in the sky.

At first it seemed a little speck,
And then it seemed a mist;
It moved and moved, and took at last
A certain shape, I wist.

A speck, a mist, a shape, I wist!
And still it neared and neared:
As if it dodged a water-sprite,
It plunged and tacked and veered.

At its nearer approach, it seemeth him to be a ship; and at a dear ransom he freeth his speech from the bonds of thirst.

With throats unslaked, with black lips baked,
We could nor laugh nor wail;
Through utter drought all dumb we stood!
I bit my arm, I sucked the blood,
And cried, A sail! a sail!

With throats unslaked, with black lips baked,
Agape they heard me call;
Gramercy! they for joy did grin,
And all at once their breath drew in,
As they were drinking all.

A flash of joy.

See! see! (I cried) she tacks no more!
Hither to work us weal;
Without a breeze, without a tide,
She steadies with upright keel!

And horror follows. For can it be a ship that comes onward without wind or tide?

The western wave was all a-flame.
The day was well nigh done!
Almost upon the western wave
Rested the broad bright Sun;
When that strange shape drove suddenly
Betwixt us and the Sun.

And straight the Sun was flecked with bars,
(Heaven's Mother send us grace!)
As if through a dungeon-grate he peered
With broad and burning face.

It seemeth him but the skeleton of a ship.

Alas! (thought I, and my heart beat loud)
How fast she nears and nears!
Are those her sails that glance in the Sun,
Like restless gossameres?

Are those her ribs through which the Sun
Did peer, as through a grate?
And is that Woman all her crew?
Is that a Death? and are there two?
Is Death that woman's mate?

And its ribs are seen as bars on the face of the setting Sun. The Spectre-Woman and her Death-mate, and no other on board the skeleton-ship. Like vessel, like crew!

Her lips were red, her looks were free,
Her locks were yellow as gold:
Her skin was as white as leprosy,
The nightmare Life-in-Death was she,
Who thicks man's blood with cold.

Death and Life-in-Death have diced for the ship's crew, and she (the latter) winneth the ancient Mariner.

The naked hulk alongside came,
And the twain were casting dice;
" The game is done! I've won! I've won! "
Quoth she, and whistles thrice.

No twilight within the courts of the Sun.

The Sun's rim dips; the stars rush out:
At one stride comes the dark;
With far-heard whisper, o'er the sea,
Off shot the spectre-bark.

At the rising of tne Moon,

We listened and looked sideways up!
Fear at my heart, as at a cup,
My life-blood seemed to sip!
The stars were dim, and thick the night,
The steersman's face by his lamp gleamed white;
From the sails the dew did drip—
Till clomb above the eastern bar
The hornèd Moon, with one bright star
Within the nether tip.

One after another,

One after one, by the star-dogged Moon,
Too quick for groan or sigh,
Each turned his face with a ghastly pang,
And cursed me with his eye.

His ship-mates drop down dead.

Four times fifty living men,
(And I heard nor sigh nor groan)
With heavy thump, a lifeless lump,
They dropped down one by one.

But Life-in-Death begins her work on the ancient Mariner.

The souls did from their bodies fly,—
They fled to bliss or woe!
And every soul, it passed me by,
Like the whizz of my cross-bow!

PART 4

The Wedding-Guest feareth that a Spirit is talking to him.

" I fear thee, ancient Mariner!
I fear thy skinny hand!
And thou art long, and lank, and brown,
As is the ribbed sea-sand.

But the ancient Mariner assureth him of his bodily life, and proceedeth to relate his horrible penance.

I fear thee and thy glittering eye,
And thy skinny hand, so brown."—
Fear not, fear not, thou Wedding-Guest!
This body dropt not down.

Alone, alone, all, all alone,
Alone on a wide, wide sea!
And never a saint took pity on
My soul in agony.

He despiseth
the creatures
of the calm.

The many men, so beautiful!
And they all dead did lie:
And a thousand thousand slimy things
Lived on; and so did I.

And envieth
that they
should live,
and so many
lie dead.

I looked upon the rotting sea,
And drew my eyes away;
I looked upon the rotting deck,
And there the dead men lay.

I looked to heaven, and tried to pray;
But or ever a prayer had gusht,
A wicked whisper came, and made
My heart as dry as dust.

I closed my lids, and kept them close,
And the balls like pulses beat;
For the sky and the sea, and the sea and
    the sky
Lay like a load on my weary eye,
And the dead were at my feet.

But the
curse liveth
for him in
the eye of
the dead
men.

The cold sweat melted from their limbs,
Nor rot nor reek did they:
The look with which they looked on me
Had never passed away.

An orphan's curse would drag to hell
A spirit from on high;
But oh! more horrible than that
Is the curse in a dead man's eye!
Seven days, seven nights, I saw that curse,
And yet I could not die.

In his loneliness and
fixedness he yearneth
towards the journeying
Moon, and the stars that
still sojourn, yet still
move onward; and every-
where the blue sky be-
longs to them, and is
their appointed rest, and
their native country, and
their own natural homes,
which they enter unan-
nounced, as lords that
are certainly expected
and yet there is a silent
joy at their arrival.

The moving Moon went up the sky,
And nowhere did abide:
Softly she was going up,
And a star or two beside—

Her beams bemocked the sultry main,
Like April hoar-frost spread;
But where the ship's huge shadow lay,
The charmèd water burnt alway
A still and awful red.

By the light of the
Moon he beholdeth
God's creatures of the
great calm.

Beyond the shadow of the ship,
I watched the water-snakes:
They moved in tracks of shining white,
And when they reared, the elfish light
Fell off in hoary flakes.

Within the shadow of the ship
I watched their rich attire:
Blue, glossy green, and velvet black,
They coiled and swam: and every track
Was a flash of golden fire.

Their beauty and
their happiness.

O happy living things! no tongue
Their beauty might declare:
A spring of love gushed from my heart,

He blesseth them in his
heart.

And I blessed them unaware:
Sure my kind saint took pity on me,
And I blessed them unaware.

The spell begins to
break.

The selfsame moment I could pray;
And from my neck so free
The Albatross fell off, and sank
Like lead into the sea.

PART 5

O sleep! it is a gentle thing,
Beloved from pole to pole!
To Mary Queen the praise be given!
She sent the gentle sleep from Heaven,
That slid into my soul.

By grace of
the holy
Mother, the
ancient
Mariner is
refreshed
with rain.

The silly buckets on the deck,
That had so long remained,
I dreamt that they were filled with dew;
And when I awoke, it rained.

My lips were wet, my throat was cold,
My garments all were dank;
Sure I had drunken in my dreams,
And still my body drank.

I moved, and could not feel my limbs;
I was so light—almost
I thought that I had died in sleep,
And was a blessèd ghost.

He heareth
sounds and
seeth strange
sights and
commotions
in the sky
and the
element.

And soon I heard a roaring wind:
It did not come anear;
But with its sound it shook the sails,
That were so thin and sere.

The upper air burst into life!
And a hundred fire-flags sheen,
To and fro they were hurried about!
And to and fro, and in and out,
The wan stars danced between.

And the coming wind did roar more loud,
And the sails did sigh like sedge;
And the rain poured down from one black cloud;
The Moon was at its edge.

The thick black cloud was cleft, and still
The Moon was at its side:
Like waters shot from some high crag,
The lightning fell with never a jag,
A river steep and wide.

The loud wind never reached the ship,
Yet now the ship moved on!
Beneath the lightning and the Moon
The dead men gave a groan.

The bodies
of the ship's
crew are in-
spired, and
the ship
moves on;

They groaned, they stirred, they all uprose,
Nor spake, nor moved their eyes;
It had been strange, even in a dream,
To have seen those dead men rise.

The helmsman steered, the ship moved on;
Yet never a breeze up blew;
The mariners all 'gan work the ropes,
Where they were wont to do;
They raised their limbs like lifeless tools—
We were a ghastly crew.

The body of my brother's son
Stood by me, knee to knee:
The body and I pulled at one rope
But he said nought to me.

But not by
the souls of
the men, nor
by dæmons
of earth or
middle air,
but by a
blessed
troop of
angelic
spirits, sent
down by the
invocation
of the
guardian
Saint.

" I fear thee, ancient Mariner! "
Be calm, thou Wedding-Guest!
'Twas not those souls that fled in pain,
Which to their corses came again,
But a troop of spirits blest:

For when it dawned—they dropped their arms,
And clustered round the mast;
Sweet sounds rose slowly through their mouths,
And from their bodies passed.

Around, around, flew each sweet sound,
Then darted to the Sun;
Slowly the sounds came back again,
Now mixed, now one by one.

Sometimes a-dropping from the sky
I heard the skylark sing;
Sometimes all little birds that are,
How they seemed to fill the sea and air
With their sweet jargoning!

And now 'twas like all instruments,
Now like a lonely flute;
And now it is an angel's song,
That makes the heavens be mute.

It ceased; yet still the sails made on
A pleasant noise till noon,
A noise like of a hidden brook
In the leafy month of June,
That to the sleeping woods all night
Singeth a quiet tune.

Till noon we quietly sailed on,
Yet never a breeze did breathe:
Slowly and smoothly went the ship,
Moved onward from beneath.

The lone-
some Spirit
from the
south-pole
carries on
the ship as
far as the
Line, in
obedience to
the angelic
troop, but
still
requireth
vengeance.

Under the keel nine fathom deep,
From the land of mist and snow,
The Spirit slid: and it was he
That made the ship to go.
The sails at noon left off their tune,
And the ship stood still also.

The Sun, right up above the mast,
Had fixed her to the ocean:
But in a minute she 'gan stir,
With a short uneasy motion—
Backwards and forwards half her length
With a short uneasy motion.

Then like a pawing horse let go,
She made a sudden bound:
It flung the blood into my head,
And I fell down in a swound.

The Polar Spirit's fellow-dæmons, the invisible inhabitants of the element, take part in his wrong; and two of them relate, one to the other, that penance long and heavy for the ancient Mariner has been accorded to the Polar Spirit, who returneth southward.

How long in that same fit I lay,
I have not to declare;
But ere my living life returned,
I heard and in my soul discerned
Two voices in the air.

" Is it he? " quoth one, " Is this the man?
By Him who died on cross,
With his cruel bow he laid full low
The harmless Albatross.

The Spirit who bideth by himself
In the land of mist and snow,
He loved the bird that loved the man
Who shot him with his bow."

The other was a softer voice,
As soft as honey-dew:
Quoth he, " The man hath penance done,
And penance more will do."

PART 6

First Voice

" But tell me, tell me! speak again,
Thy soft response renewing—
What makes that ship drive on so fast?
What is the ocean doing? "

Second Voice

" Still as a slave before his lord,
The ocean hath no blast;
His great bright eye most silently
Up to the moon is cast—

If he may know which way to go;
For she guides him smooth or grim.
See, brother, see! how graciously
She looketh down on him."

First Voice

" But why drives on that ship so fast,
Without or wave or wind? "

Second Voice

" The air is cut away before,
And closes from behind.

Fly, brother, fly! more high, more high! –
Or we shall be belated:
For slow and slow that ship will go,
When the Mariner's trance is abated."

I woke, and we were sailing on
As in a gentle weather:
'Twas night, calm night, the moon was high,
The dead men stood together.

All stood together on the deck,
For a charnel-dungeon fitter:
All fixed on me their stony eyes,
That in the moon did glitter.

The pang, the curse, with which they died,
Had never passed away:
I could not draw my eyes from theirs,
Nor turn them up to pray.

And now this spell was snapt: once more
I viewed the ocean green,
And looked far forth, yet little saw
Of what had else been seen—

Like one, that on a lonesome road
Doth walk in fear and dread,
And having once turned round walks on,
And turns no more his head;
Because he knows, a rightful fiend
Doth close behind him tread.

Margin notes:

The Mariner hath been cast into a trance; for the angelic power causeth the vessel to drive northward faster than human life could endure.

The supernatural motion is retarded; the Mariner awakes, and his penance begins anew.

The curse is finally expiated.

But soon there breathed a wind on me,
Nor sound nor motion made:
Its path was not upon the sea,
In ripple or in shade.

It raised my hair, it fanned my cheek
Like a meadow-gale of spring—
It mingled strangely with my fears,
Yet it felt like a welcoming.

Swiftly, swiftly flew the ship,
Yet she sailed softly too:
Sweetly, sweetly blew the breeze—
On me alone it blew.

And the ancient Mariner beholdeth his native country.

Oh! dream of joy! is this indeed
The lighthouse top I see?
Is this the hill? is this the kirk?
Is this mine own countree?

We drifted o'er the harbour-bar,
And I with sobs did pray—
O let me be awake, my God!
Or let me sleep alway.

The harbour-bay was clear as glass,
So smoothly it was strewn!
And on the bay the moonlight lay,
And the shadow of the moon.

The rock shone bright, the kirk no less,
That stands above the rock:
The moonlight steeped in silentness
The steady weathercock.

And the bay was white with silent light
Till rising from the same,
Full many shapes, that shadows were,
In crimson colours came.

The Angelic spirits leave the dead bodies,

A little distance from the prow
Those crimson shadows were:
I turned my eyes upon the deck—
Oh, Christ! what saw I there!

And appear
in their own
forms of
light.
Each corse lay flat, lifeless and flat,
And, by the holy rood!
A man all light, a seraph-man,
On every corse there stood.

This seraph-band, each waved his hand;
It was a heavenly sight!
They stood as signals to the land,
Each one a lovely light;

This seraph-band, each waved his hand,
No voice did they impart—
No voice; but oh! the silence sank
Like music on my heart.

But soon I heard the dash of oars,
I heard the Pilot's cheer;
My head was turning perforce away,
And I saw a boat appear.

The Pilot and the Pilot's boy,
I heard them coming fast:
Dear Lord in Heaven! it was a joy
The dead men could not blast.

I saw a third—I heard his voice:
It is the Hermit good!
He singeth loud his godly hymns
That he makes in the wood.
He'll shrieve my soul; he'll wash away
The Albatross's blood.

PART 7

The Hermit
of the Wood
This Hermit good lives in that wood
Which slopes down to the sea.
How loudly his sweet voice he rears!
He loves to talk with marineres
That come from a far countree.

He kneels at morn, and noon, and eve—
He hath a cushion plump:
It is the moss that wholly hides
The rotted old oak-stump.

The skiff-boat neared: I heard them talk,
' Why, this is strange, I trow!
Where are those lights so many and fair,
That signal made but now? "

Approacheth
the ship
with
wonder.

" Strange, by my faith! " the Hermit said—
" And they answered not our cheer!
The planks look warped! and see those sails,
How thin they are and sere!
I never saw aught like to them,
Unless perchance it were

Brown skeletons of leaves that lag
My forest-brook along;
When the ivy-tod is heavy with snow,
And the owlet whoops to the wolf below,
That eats the she-wolf's young."

" Dear Lord! it hath a fiendish look—
(The Pilot made reply)
I am a-feared "—" Push on, push on! "
Said the Hermit cheerily.

The boat came closer to the ship,
But I nor spake nor stirred;
The boat came close beneath the ship,
And straight a sound was heard.

The ship
suddenly
sinketh.

Under the water it rumbled on,
Still louder and more dread:
It reached the ship, it split the bay;
The ship went down like lead.

The ancient
Mariner is
saved in the
Pilot's boat.

Stunned by that loud and dreadful sound,
Which sky and ocean smote,
Like one that hath been seven days drowned
My body lay afloat;
But swift as dreams, myself I found
Within the Pilot's boat.

Upon the whirl, where sank the ship,
The boat spun round and round;
And all was still, save that the hill
Was telling of the sound.

I moved my lips—the Pilot shrieked
And fell down in a fit;
The holy Hermit raised his eyes,
And prayed where he did sit.

I took the oars: the Pilot's boy,
Who now doth crazy go,
Laughed loud and long, and all the while
His eyes went to and fro.
" Ha! ha! " quoth he, " full plain I see,
The Devil knows how to row."

And now, all in my own countree,
I stood on the firm land!
The Hermit stepped forth from the boat,
And scarcely he could stand.

The ancient
Mariner
earnestly
entreateth
the Hermit
to shrieve
him; and
the penance
of life falls
on him.

" O shrieve me, shrieve me, holy man! "
The Hermit crossed his brow.
" Say quick," quoth he, " I bid thee say—
What manner of man art thou?"

Forthwith this frame of mine was wrenched
With a woful agony,
Which forced me to begin my tale;
And then it left me free.

And ever
and anon
throughout
his future
life an agony
constraineth
him to travel
from land to
land.

Since then, at an uncertain hour,
That agony returns:
And till my ghastly tale is told,
This heart within me burns.

I pass, like night, from land to land;
I have strange power of speech;
That moment that his face I see,
I know the man that must hear me:
To him my tale I teach.

What loud uproar bursts from that door!
The Wedding-guests are there:
But in the garden-bower the bride
And bride-maids singing are:
And hark the little vesper bell
Which biddeth me to prayer!

O Wedding-Guest! this soul hath been
Alone on a wide, wide sea;
So lonely 'twas, that God himself
Scarce seemèd there to be.

O sweeter than the marriage-feast,
'Tis sweeter far to me,
To walk together to the kirk
With a goodly company!—

To walk together to the kirk,
And all together pray,
While each to his great Father bends,
Old men, and babes, and loving friends,
And youths and maidens gay!

Farewell, farewell! but this I tell
To thee, thou Wedding-Guest!
He prayeth well, who loveth well
Both man and bird and beast.

He prayeth best, who loveth best
All things both great and small;
For the dear God who loveth us,
He made and loveth all.

The Mariner, whose eye is bright,
Whose beard with age is hoar,
Is gone: and now the Wedding-Guest
Turned from the bridegroom's door.

He went like one that hath been stunned,
And is of sense forlorn:
A sadder and a wiser man,
He rose the morrow morn.

ROBERT SOUTHEY

1774 - 1843

AFTER BLENHEIM

It was a summer evening,
  Old Kaspar's work was done,
And he before his cottage door
  Was sitting in the sun;
And by him sported on the green
His little grandchild Wilhelmine.

She saw her brother Peterkin
  Roll something large and round
Which he beside the rivulet
  In playing there had found;
He came to ask what he had found
That was so large and smooth and round.

Old Kaspar took it from the boy
  Who stood expectant by;
And then the old man shook his head,
  And with a natural sigh,
" 'Tis some poor fellow's skull," said he,
" Who fell in the great victory.

" I find them in the garden,
  For there's many here about;
And often when I go to plough
  The ploughshare turns them out.
For many thousand men," said he,
" Were slain in that great victory."

" Now tell us what 'twas all about,"
  Young Peterkin he cries;
And little Wilhelmine looks up
  With wonder-waiting eyes;
" Now tell us all about the war,
And what they fought each other for."

" It was the English," Kaspar cried,
  " Who put the French to rout;
But what they fought each other for
  I could not well make out.
But everybody said," quoth he,
" That 'twas a famous victory.

" My father lived at Blenheim then,
  Yon little stream hard by;
They burnt his dwelling to the ground,
  And he was forced to fly:
So with his wife and child he fled,
Nor had he where to rest his head.

" With fire and sword the country round
  Was wasted far and wide,
And many a childing mother then
  And newborn baby died:
But things like that, you know, must be
At every famous victory.

" Great praise the Duke of Marlb'ro' won
  And our good Prince Eugene."
" Why 'twas a very wicked thing! "
  Said little Wilhelmine;
" Nay . . . nay . . . my little girl," quoth he,
" It was a famous victory.

" And everybody praised the Duke
  Who this great fight did win."
" But what good came of it at last? "
  Quoth little Peterkin:—
" Why, that I cannot tell," said he,
" But 'twas a famous victory."

WALTER SAVAGE LANDOR

1775 - 1864

MOTHER, I CANNOT MIND MY WHEEL

Mother, I cannot mind my wheel;
    My fingers ache, my lips are dry;
O, if you felt the pain I feel!
    But O, who ever felt as I?

No longer could I doubt him true—
    All other men may use deceit.
He always said my eyes were blue,
    And often swore my lips were sweet.

ROSE AYLMER

Ah, what avails the sceptred race!
    Ah, what the form divine!
What every virtue, every grace!
    Rose Aylmer, all were thine.

Rose Aylmer, whom these wakeful eyes
    May weep, but never see,
A night of memories and sighs
    I consecrate to thee.

AUTUMN

Mild is the parting year, and sweet
    The odour of the falling spray;
Life passes on more rudely fleet,
    And balmless is its closing day.

I wait its close, I court its gloom,
    But mourn that never must there fall
Or on my breast or on my tomb
    The tear that would have soothed it all.

IANTHE

From you, Ianthe, little troubles pass
    Like little ripples down a sunny river;
Your pleasures spring like daisies in the grass,
    Cut down, and up again as blithe as ever.

DIRCE

Stand close around, ye Stygian set,
    With Dirce in one boat conveyed,
Or Charon, seeing, may forget
    That he is old and she a shade.

ON HIS SEVENTY-FIFTH BIRTHDAY

I strove with none; for none was worth my strife.
Nature I loved and, next to Nature, Art;
I warmed both hands before the fire of life;
It sinks, and I am ready to depart.

VERSE

Past ruined Ilion Helen lives,
    Alcestis rises from the shades.
Verse calls them forth; 'tis verse that gives
    Immortal youth to mortal maids.

Soon shall oblivion's deepening veil
    Hide all the peopled hills you see,
The gay, the proud, while lovers hail
    These many summers you and me.

THOMAS MOORE

1779 - 1852

AT THE MID HOUR OF NIGHT

At the mid hour of night, when stars are weeping, I fly
To the lone vale we loved, when life shone warm in thine eye;
And I think oft, if spirits can steal from the regions of air
To revisit past scenes of delight, thou wilt come to me there
And tell me our love is remembered, even in the sky!

Then I sing the wild song it once was rapture to hear
When our voices, commingling, breathed like one on the ear;
And as echo far off through the vale my sad orison rolls,
I think, O my love! 'tis thy voice, from the kingdom of souls
Faintly answering still the notes that once were so dear.

OFT IN THE STILLY NIGHT

Oft in the stilly night
  Ere slumber's chain has bound me,
Fond memory brings the light
  Of other days around me:
    The smiles, the tears
    Of boyhood's years,
  The words of love then spoken;
    The eyes that shone,
    Now dimmed and gone,
  The cheerful hearts now broken!
Thus in the stilly night
  Ere slumber's chain has bound me,
Sad memory brings the light
  Of other days around me.

When I remember all
  The friends so linked together
I've seen around me fall
  Like leaves in wintry weather,
    I feel like one
    Who treads alone

Some banquet-hall deserted,
    Whose lights are fled,
    Whose garlands dead,
And all but he departed!
Thus in the stilly night
    Ere slumber's chain has bound me,
Sad memory brings the light
    Of other days around me.

LEIGH HUNT

1784 - 1859

JENNY KISSED ME

Jenny kissed me when we met,
    Jumping from the chair she sat in;
Time, you thief, who love to get
    Sweets into your list, put that in!
Say I'm weary, say I'm sad,
    Say that health and wealth have missed me,
Say I'm growing old, but add,
    Jenny kissed me.

GEORGE GORDON, LORD BYRON

1788 - 1824

SHE WALKS IN BEAUTY

from " Hebrew Melodies "

She walks in beauty, like the night
Of cloudless climes and starry skies,
And all that's best of dark and bright
Meet in her aspect and her eyes;
Thus mellowed to that tender light
Which heaven to gaudy day denies.

One shade the more, one ray the less,
Had half impaired the nameless grace
Which waves in every raven tress
Or softly lightens o'er her face,
Where thoughts serenely sweet express
How pure, how dear their dwelling-place.

And on that cheek and o'er that brow
So soft, so calm, yet eloquent,
The smiles that win, the tints that glow
But tell of days in goodness spent,
A mind at peace with all below,
A heart whose love is innocent.

WHEN WE TWO PARTED

When we two parted
In silence and tears,
Half broken-hearted,
To sever for years,
Pale grew thy cheek and cold,
Colder thy kiss;
Truly that hour foretold
Sorrow to this!

The dew of the morning
Sunk chill on my brow;
It felt like the warning
Of what I feel now.
Thy vows are all broken,
And light is thy fame:
I hear thy name spoken
And share in its shame.

They name thee before me,
A knell to mine ear;
A shudder comes o'er me—
Why wert thou so dear?
They know not I knew thee
Who knew thee too well:
Long, long shall I rue thee
Too deeply to tell.

In secret we met:
In silence I grieve
That thy heart could forget,
Thy spirit deceive.
If I should meet thee
After long years,
How should I greet thee?—
With silence and tears.

WE'LL GO NO MORE A-ROVING

So, we'll go no more a-roving
    So late into the night,
Though the heart be still as loving,
    And the moon be still as bright.

For the sword outwears its sheath,
    And the soul wears out the breast,
And the heart must pause to breathe,
    And love itself have rest.

Though the night was made for loving,
    And the day returns too soon,
Yet we'll go no more a-roving
    By the light of the moon.

THE DESTRUCTION OF SENNACHERIB

The Assyrian came down like the wolf on the fold,
And his cohorts were gleaming in purple and gold;
And the sheen of their spears was like stars on the sea,
When the blue wave rolls nightly on deep Galilee.

Like the leaves of the forest when summer is green,
That host with their banners at sunset were seen:
Like the leaves of the forest when autumn hath blown,
That host on the morrow lay withered and strown.

For the Angel of Death spread his wings on the blast,
And breathed in the face of the foe as he passed;
And the eyes of the sleepers waxed deadly and chill,
And their hearts but once heaved, and for ever grew still.

And there lay the steed with his nostril all wide,
But through it there rolled not the breath of his pride:
And the foam of his gasping lay white on the turf,
And cold as the spray of the rock-beating surf.

And there lay the rider distorted and pale,
With the dew on his brow, and the rust on his mail,
And the tents were all silent, the banners alone,
The lances unlifted, the trumpet unblown.

And the widows of Ashur are loud in their wail,
And the idols are broke in the temple of Baal;
And the might of the Gentile, unsmote by the sword,
Hath melted like snow in the glance of the Lord!

EVENING

from " Don Juan," Canto III

O Hesperus! thou bringest all good things—
    Home to the weary, to the hungry cheer,
To the young bird the parent's brooding wings,
    The welcome stall to the o'erlaboured steer:
Whate'er of peace about our hearthstone clings,
    Whate'er our household gods protect of dear,
Are gathered round us by thy look of rest;
Thou bring'st the child, too, to the mother's breast.

Soft hour! which wakes the wish and melts the heart
    Of those who sail the seas, on the first day
When they from their sweet friends are torn apart;
    Or fills with love the pilgrim on his way
As the far bell of vesper makes him start,
    Seeming to weep the dying day's decay;
Is this a fancy which our reason scorns?
Ah! surely nothing dies but something mourns.

WATERLOO

from " Childe Harold's Pilgrimage," Canto III

There was a sound of revelry by night,
And Belgium's capital had gathered then
Her beauty and her chivalry, and bright
The lamps shone o'er fair women and brave men;
A thousand hearts beat happily; and when
Music arose with its voluptuous swell,
Soft eyes looked love to eyes which spake again,
And all went merry as a marriage bell;
But hush! hark! a deep sound strikes like a rising knell!

Did ye not hear it?—No; 'twas but the wind,
Or the car rattling o'er the stony street;
On with the dance! let joy be unconfined;
No sleep till morn, when Youth and Pleasure meet

To chase the glowing hours with flying feet.—
But hark! that heavy sound breaks in once more,
As if the clouds its echo would repeat;
And nearer, clearer, deadlier than before!
Arm! arm! it is—it is—the cannon's opening roar!

Within a windowed niche of that high hall
Sate Brunswick's fated chieftain; he did hear
That sound the first amidst the festival,
And caught its tone with Death's prophetic ear,
And when they smiled because he deemed it near,
His heart more truly knew that peal too well
Which stretched his father on a bloody bier,
And roused the vengeance blood alone could quell.
He rushed into the field, and, foremost fighting, fell.

Ah! then and there was hurrying to and fro,
And gathering tears, and tremblings of distress,
And cheeks all pale, which but an hour ago
Blushed at the praise of their own loveliness;
And there were sudden partings, such as press
The life from out young hearts, and choking sighs
Which ne'er might be repeated: who could guess
If ever more should meet those mutual eyes,
Since upon night so sweet such awful morn could rise!

And wild and high the " Cameron's Gathering " rose,
The war-note of Lochiel, which Albyn's hills
Have heard, and heard, too, have her Saxon foes;
How in the noon of night that pibroch thrills
Savage and shrill! But with the breath which fills
Their mountain pipe, so fill the mountaineers
With the fierce native daring which instils
The stirring memory of a thousand years,
And Evan's, Donald's fame rings in each clansman's ears!

And Ardennes waves above them her green leaves,
Dewy with Nature's tear-drops, as they pass,
Grieving, if aught inanimate e'er grieves,
Over the unreturning brave—alas!
Ere evening to be trodden like the grass
Which now beneath them, but above shall grow
In its next verdure, when this fiery mass
Of living valour, rolling on the foe,
And burning with high hope, shall moulder cold and low.

Last noon beheld them full of lusty life,
Last eve in Beauty's circle proudly gay,
The midnight brought the signal-sound of strife,
The morn the marshalling arms—the day
Battle's magnificently stern array!
The thunder-clouds close o'er it, which when rent
The earth is covered thick with other clay,
Which her own clay shall cover, heaped and pent,
Rider and horse—friend, foe,—in one red burial blent!

OCEAN

from " Childe Harold's Pilgrimage," Canto IV

Roll on, thou deep and dark blue Ocean—roll!
Ten thousand fleets sweep over thee in vain;
Man marks the earth with ruin; his control
Stops with the shore; upon the watery plain
The wrecks are all thy deed, nor doth remain
A shadow of man's ravage, save his own,
When for a moment, like a drop of rain,
He sinks into thy depths with bubbling groan,
Without a grave, unknelled, uncoffined and unknown.

His steps are not upon thy paths—thy fields
Are not a spoil for him—thou dost arise
And shake him from thee; the vile strength he wields
For earth's destruction thou dost all despise,
Spurning him from thy bosom to the skies,
And send'st him, shivering in thy playful spray,
And howling, to his Gods, where haply lies
His petty hope in some near port or bay,
And dashest him again to earth—there let him lay.

The armaments which thunderstrike the walls
Of rock-built cities, bidding nations quake,
And monarchs tremble in their capitals,
The oak leviathans, whose huge ribs make
Their clay creator the vain title take
Of lord of thee, and arbiter of war;
These are thy toys and, as the snowy flake,
They melt into thy yeast of waves, which mar
Alike the Armada's pride, or spoils of Trafalgar.

Thy shores are empires, changed in all save thee—
Assyria, Greece, Rome, Carthage, what are they?
Thy waters washed them power while they were free,
And many a tyrant since: their shores obey
The stranger, slave or savage; their decay
Has dried up realms to deserts:—not so thou,
Unchangeable save to thy wild wave's play—
Time writes no wrinkle on thine azure brow—
Such as creation's dawn beheld, thou rollest now.

Thou glorious mirror, where the Almighty's form
Glasses itself in tempests: in all time,
Calm or convulsed—in breeze, or gale, or storm,
Icing the pole, or in the torrid clime
Dark-heaving; boundless, endless, and sublime—
The image of Eternity—the throne
Of the Invisible; even from out thy slime
The monsters of the deep are made; each zone
Obeys thee; thou goest forth, dread, fathomless, alone.

PERCY BYSSHE SHELLEY

1792 - 1822

TO NIGHT

Swiftly walk o'er the western wave,
    Spirit of Night!
Out of the misty eastern cave,
Where, all the long and lone day-light,
Thou wovest dreams of joy and fear,
Which make thee terrible and dear—
    Swift be thy flight!

Wrap thy form in a mantle grey,
    Star-inwrought!
Blind with thine hair the eyes of day;
Kiss her until she be wearied out,
Then wander o'er city, and sea, and land
Touching all with thine opiate wand—
    Come, long-sought!

When I arose and saw the dawn,
        I sighed for thee;
When light rode high, and the dew was gone,
And noon lay heavy on flower and tree,
And the weary day turned to his rest,
Lingering like an unloved guest,
        I sighed for thee.

Thy brother Death came, and cried,
        Wouldst thou me?
Thy sweet child Sleep, the filmy-eyed,
Murmured like a noontide bee,
Shall I nestle near thy side?
Wouldst thou me?—And I replied,
        No, not thee!

Death will come when thou art dead,
        Soon, too soon—
Sleep will come when thou art fled;
Of neither would I ask the boon
I ask of thee, belovèd Night—
Swift be thine approaching flight,
        Come soon, soon!

WINTER

A widow bird sat mourning for her love
        Upon a wintry bough;
The frozen wind crept on above,
        The freezing stream below.

There was no leaf upon the forest bare,
        No flower upon the ground,
And little motion in the air
        Except the mill-wheel's sound.

TO A SKYLARK

Hail to thee, blithe Spirit!
        Bird thou never wert,
That from heaven, or near it
        Pourest thy full heart
In profuse strains of unpremeditated art.

Higher still and higher
From the earth thou springest
Like a cloud of fire;
The blue deep thou wingest,
And singing still dost soar, and soaring ever singest.

In the golden lightning
Of the sunken sun
O'er which clouds are bright'ning
Thou dost float and run,
Like an unbodied joy whose race is just begun.

The pale purple even
Melts around thy flight;
Like a star of heaven
In the broad daylight
Thou art unseen, but yet I hear thy shrill delight:

Keen as are the arrows
Of that silver sphere,
Whose intense lamp narrows
In the white dawn clear
Until we hardly see—we feel that it is there.

All the earth and air
With thy voice is loud,
As, when night is bare,
From one lonely cloud
The moon rains out her beams, and heaven is overflowed.

What thou art we know not;
What is most like thee?
From rainbow clouds there flow not
Drops so bright to see
As from thy presence showers a rain of melody.

Like a poet hidden
In the light of thought,
Singing hymns unbidden,
Till the world is wrought
To sympathy with hopes and fears it heeded not:

Like a high-born maiden
    In a palace tower,
Soothing her love-laden
    Soul in secret hour
With music sweet as love, which overflows her bower:

Like a glow-worm golden
    In a dell of dew,
Scattering unbeholden
    Its aërial hue
Among the flowers and grass, which screen it from the view:

Like a rose embowered
    In its own green leaves,
By warm winds deflowered,
    Till the scent it gives
Makes faint with too much sweet these heavy-wingèd
    thieves.

Sound of vernal showers
    On the twinkling grass,
Rain-awakened flowers,
    All that ever was
Joyous, and clear, and fresh, thy music doth surpass.

Teach us, sprite or bird,
    What sweet thoughts are thine:
I have never heard
    Praise of love or wine
That panted forth a flood of rapture so divine.

Chorus hymeneal
    Or triumphant chaunt
Matched with thine, would be all
    But an empty vaunt—
A thing wherein we feel there is some hidden want.

What objects are the fountains
    Of thy happy strain?
What fields, or waves, or mountains?
    What shapes of sky or plain?
What love of thine own kind? what ignorance of pain?

With thy clear keen joyance
        Languor cannot be:
Shadow of annoyance
        Never came near thee:
Thou lovest, but ne'er knew love's sad satiety.

Waking or asleep,
        Thou of death must deem
Things more true and deep
        Than we mortals dream,
Or how could thy notes flow in such a crystal stream?

We look before and after,
        And pine for what is not:
Our sincerest laughter
        With some pain is fraught;
Our sweetest songs are those that tell of saddest thought.

Yet if we could scorn
        Hate, and pride, and fear;
If we were things born
        Not to shed a tear,
I know not how thy joy we ever should come near.

Better than all measures
        Of delightful sound,
Better than all treasures
        That in books are found,
Thy skill to poet were, thou scorner of the ground!

Teach me half the gladness
        That thy brain must know,
Such harmonious madness
        From my lips would flow
The world should listen then, as I am listening now!

THE INDIAN SERENADE

I arise from dreams of thee
In the first sweet sleep of night,
When the winds are breathing low,
And the stars are shining bright.
I arise from dreams of thee,
And a spirit in my feet
Hath led me—who knows how?
To thy chamber window, Sweet!

Thy wandering airs they faint
On the dark, the silent stream—
The champak odours fail
Like sweet thoughts in a dream;
The nightingale's complaint,
It dies upon her heart;
As I must on thine,
Belovèd as thou art!

O lift me from the grass!
I die! I faint! I fail!
Let thy love in kisses rain
On my lips and eyelids pale,
My cheek is cold and white, alas!
My heart beats loud and fast;—
Oh! press it close to thine again,
Where it will break at last.

THE DESIRE OF THE MOTH

One word is too often profaned
    For me to profane it,
One feeling too falsely disdained
    For thee to disdain it;
One hope is too like despair
    For prudence to smother,
And pity from thee more dear
    Than that from another.

I can give not what men call love;
    But wilt thou accept not
The worship the heart lifts above
    And the Heavens reject not:
The desire of the moth for the star,
    Of the night for the morrow,
The devotion to something afar
    From the sphere of our sorrow?

TO ——

Music, when soft voices die,
Vibrates in the memory—
Odours, when sweet violets sicken,
Live within the sense they quicken.

Rose leaves, when the rose is dead,
Are heaped for the belovèd's bed;
And so thy thoughts, when thou art gone,
Love itself shall slumber on.

FRAGMENT

To thirst and find no fill—to wail and wander
With short unsteady steps—to pause and ponder—
To feel the blood run through the veins and tingle
Where busy thought and blind sensation mingle;
To nurse the image of unfelt caresses
Till dim imagination just possesses
The half-created shadow, then all the night
Sick . . .

INVOCATION

TO THE SPIRIT OF DELIGHT

Rarely, rarely comest thou,
    Spirit of Delight!
Wherefore hast thou left me now
    Many a day and night?
Many a weary night and day
'Tis since thou art fled away.

How shall ever one like me
    Win thee back again?
With the joyous and the free
    Thou wilt scoff at pain.
Spirit false! thou hast forgot
All but those who need thee not.

As a lizard with the shade
    Of a trembling leaf,
Thou with sorrow art dismayed;
    Even the sighs of grief
Reproach thee, that thou art not near,
And reproach thou wilt not hear.

Let me set my mournful ditty
    To a merry measure;—
Thou wilt never come for pity,
    Thou wilt come for pleasure;—
Pity, thou wilt cut away
Those cruel wings, and thou wilt stay.

I love all that thou lovèst,
    Spirit of Delight!
The fresh Earth in new leaves drest
    And the starry night;
Autumn evening, and the morn
When the golden mists are born.

I love snow and all the forms
    Of the radiant frost;
I love waves, and winds, and storms,
    Everything almost
Which is Nature's, and may be
Untainted by man's misery.

I love tranquil solitude,
    And such society
As is quiet, wise, and good;
    Between thee and me
What diff'rence? but thou dost possess
The things I seek, nor love them less.

I love Love—though he has wings,
    And like light can flee,
But above all other things,
    Spirit, I love thee—
Thou art love and life! O come!
Make once more my heart thy home!

OZYMANDIAS

I met a traveller from an antique land,
Who said: Two vast and trunkless legs of stone
Stand in the desert. Near them, on the sand,
Half sunk, a shattered visage lies, whose frown
And wrinkled lip and sneer of cold command,
Tell that its sculptor well those passions read,
Which yet survive stamped on these lifeless things,
The hand that mocked them, and the heart that fed:
And on the pedestal these words appear:
" My name is Ozymandias, King of Kings:
Look on my works, ye Mighty, and despair! "
Nothing beside remains. Round the decay
Of that colossal wreck, boundless and bare
The lone and level sands stretch far away.

THE MOON

I

Art thou pale for weariness
Of climbing heaven, and gazing on the earth,
    Wandering companionless
Among the stars that have a different birth,—
And ever-changing, like a joyless eye
That finds no object worth its constancy?

2

And like a dying lady, lean and pale,
Who totters forth, wrapped in a gauzy veil,
Out of her chamber, led by the insane
And feeble wanderings of her fading brain,
The moon arose up in the murky East,
A white and shapeless mass—

A LAMENT

O world! O life! O time!
On whose last steps I climb,
    Trembling at that where I had stood before;
When will return the glory of your prime?
        No more—oh, never more!

Out of the day and night
A joy has taken flight;
   Fresh spring, and summer, and winter hoar,
Move my faint heart with grief, but with delight
     No more—oh, never more!

ODE TO THE WEST WIND

1

O Wild West Wind, thou breath of Autumn's being,
Thou, from whose unseen presence the leaves dead
Are driven, like ghosts from an enchanter fleeing,

Yellow, and black, and pale, and hectic red,
Pestilence-stricken multitudes! O thou,
Who chariotest to their dark wintry bed

The wingèd seeds, where they lie cold and low,
Each like a corpse within its grave, until
Thine azure sister of the Spring shall blow

Her clarion o'er the dreaming earth, and fill
(Driving sweet buds like flocks to feed in air)
With living hues and odours plain and hill:

Wild Spirit, which art moving everywhere;
Destroyer and preserver; hear, oh, hear!

2

Thou on whose stream, 'mid the steep sky's commotion,
Loose clouds like earth's decaying leaves are shed,
Shook from the tangled boughs of Heaven and Ocean,

Angels of rain and lightning: there are spread
On the blue surface of thine aery surge,
Like the bright hair uplifted from the head

Of some fierce Mænad, even from the dim verge
Of the horizon to the zenith's height,
The locks of the approaching storm. Thou dirge

Of the dying year, to which this closing night
Will be the dome of a vast sepulchre,
Vaulted with all thy congregated might

Of vapours, from whose solid atmosphere
Black rain, and fire, and hail will burst: oh, hear!

3

Thou who didst waken from his summer dreams
The blue Mediterranean, where he lay,
Lulled by the coil of his crystàlline streams,

Beside a pumice isle in Baiæ's bay,
And saw in sleep old palaces and towers
Quivering within the wave's intenser day,

All overgrown with azure moss and flowers
So sweet, the sense faints picturing them! Thou
For whose path the Atlantic's level powers

Cleave themselves into chasms, while far below
The sea-blooms and the oozy woods which wear
The sapless foliage of the ocean, know

Thy voice, and suddenly grow gray with fear,
And tremble and despoil themselves: oh, hear!

4

If I were a dead leaf thou mightest bear;
If I were a swift cloud to fly with thee;
A wave to pant beneath thy power, and share

The impulse of thy strength, only less free
Than thou, O uncontrollable! If even
I were as in my boyhood, and could be

The comrade of thy wanderings over Heaven,
As then, when to outstrip thy skiey speed
Scarce seemed a vision; I would ne'er have striven

As thus with thee in prayer in my sore need.
Oh, lift me as a wave, a leaf, a cloud!
I fall upon the thorns of life! I bleed!

A heavy weight of hours has chained and bowed
One too like thee: tameless, and swift, and proud.

5

Make me thy lyre, even as the forest is:
What if my leaves are falling like its own!
The tumult of thy mighty harmonies

Will take from both a deep, autumnal tone,
Sweet though in sadness. Be thou, Spirit fierce,
My spirit! Be thou me, impetuous one!

Drive my dead thoughts over the universe
Like withered leaves to quicken a new birth!
And, by the incantation of this verse,

Scatter, as from an unextinguished hearth
Ashes and sparks, my words among mankind!
Be through my lips to unawakened earth

The trumpet of a prophecy! O Wind,
If Winter comes, can Spring be far behind?

THE CLOUD

I bring fresh showers for the thirsting flowers,
    From the seas and the streams;
I bear light shade for the leaves when laid
    In their noonday dreams.
From my wings are shaken the dews that waken
    The sweet buds every one,
When rocked to rest on their mother's breast,
    As she dances about the sun,
I wield the flail of the lashing hail,
    And whiten the green plains under,
And then again I dissolve it in rain,
    And laugh as I pass in thunder.

I sift the snow on the mountains below,
    And their great pines groan aghast;
And all the night 'tis my pillow white,
    While I sleep in the arms of the blast.
Sublime on the towers of my skiey bowers,
    Lightning, my pilot, sits;
In a cavern under is fettered the thunder,
    It struggles and howls at fits;

Over earth and ocean, with gentle motion,
    This pilot is guiding me,
Lured by the love of the genii that move
    In the depths of the purple sea;
Over the rills, and the crags, and the hills,
    Over the lakes and the plains,
Wherever he dream, under mountain or stream,
    The Spirit he loves remains;
And I all the while bask in Heaven's blue smile,
    Whilst he is dissolving in rains.

The sanguine Sunrise, with his meteor eyes,
    And his burning plumes outspread,
Leaps on the back of my sailing rack,
    When the morning star shines dead;
As on the jag of a mountain crag,
    Which an earthquake rocks and swings,
An eagle alit one moment may sit
    In the light of its golden wings.
And when Sunset may breathe, from the lit sea beneath
    Its ardours of rest and of love,
And the crimson pall of eve may fall
    From the depth of Heaven above,
With wings folded I rest, on mine aery nest,
    As still as a brooding dove.

That orbèd maiden with white fire laden,
    Whom mortals call the Moon,
Glides glimmering o'er my fleece-like floor,
    By the midnight breezes strewn;
And wherever the beat of her unseen feet,
    Which only the angels hear,
May have broken the woof of my tent's thin roof,
    The stars peep behind her and peer;
And I laugh to see them whirl and flee,
    Like a swarm of golden bees,
When I widen the rent in my wind-built tent,
    Till the calm rivers, lakes, and seas,
Like strips of the sky fallen through me on high,
    Are each paved with the moon and these.

I bind the Sun's throne with a burning zone,
    And the Moon's with a girdle of pearl;
The volcanoes are dim, and the stars reel and swim
    When the whirlwinds my banner unfurl.

From cape to cape, with a bridge-like shape,
    Over a torrent sea,
Sunbeam-proof, I hang like a roof,—
    The mountains its columns be.
The triumphal arch through which I march
    With hurricane, fire, and snow,
When the Powers of the air are chained to my chair,
    Is the million-coloured bow;
The sphere-fire above its soft colours wove,
    While the moist Earth was laughing below.

I am the daughter of Earth and Water,
    And the nursling of the Sky;
I pass through the pores of the ocean and shores;
    I change, but I cannot die.
For after the rain when with never a stain
    The pavilion of Heaven is bare,
And the winds and sunbeams with their convex gleams
    Build up the blue dome of air,
I silently laugh at my own cenotaph,
    And out of the caverns of rain,
Like a child from the womb, like a ghost from the tomb,
    I arise and unbuild it again.

A NEW WORLD

Final Chorus from " Hellas "

The world's great age begins anew,
    The golden years return,
The earth doth like a snake renew
    Her winter weeds outworn:
Heaven smiles, and faiths and empires gleam,
Like wrecks of a dissolving dream.

A brighter Hellas rears its mountains
    From waves serener far;
A new Peneus rolls his fountains
    Against the morning star.
Where fairer Tempes bloom, there sleep
Young Cyclads on a sunnier deep.

A loftier Argo cleaves the main,
    Fraught with a later prize;
Another Orpheus sings again,
    And loves, and weeps, and dies.

A new Ulysses leaves once more
Calypso for his native shore.

Oh! write no more the tale of Troy,
    If earth Death's scroll must be!
Nor mix with Laian rage the joy
    Which dawns upon the free,
Altho' a subtler Sphinx renew
Riddles of death Thebes never knew.

Another Athens shall arise,
    And to remoter time
Bequeath, like sunset to the skies,
    The splendour of its prime;
And leave, if naught so bright may live,
All earth can take or heaven can give.

Saturn and Love their long repose
    Shall burst, more bright and good
Than all who fell, than One who rose,
    Than many unsubdued:
Not gold, not blood, their altar dowers,
But votive tears and symbol flowers.

Oh, cease! must hate and death return?
    Cease! must men kill and die?
Cease! drain not to its dregs the urn
    Of bitter prophecy.
The world is weary of the past.
Oh, might it die or rest at last!

JOHN CLARE

1793 - 1864

SONG'S ETERNITY

What is song's eternity?
Come and see.
Can it noise and bustle be?
Come and see.
Praises sung or praises said
Can it be?
Wait awhile and these are dead—
Sigh, sigh;
Be they high or lowly bred
They die.

What is song's eternity?
Come and see.
Melodies of ᴄarth and sky,
Here they be.
Song once sung to Adam's ears
Can it be?
Ballads of six thousand years
Thrive, thrive;
Song awakens with the spheres
Alive.

Mighty songs that miss decay,
What are they?
Crowds and cities pass away
Like a day.
Books are out and books are read;
What are they?
Years will lay them with the dead—
Sigh, sigh;
Trifles unto nothing wed,
They die.

Dreamers, mark the honey bee;
Mark the tree
Where the blue cap " *tootle tee* "
Sings a glee

Sung to Adam and to Eve—
Here they be.
When floods covered every bough,
Noah's ark
Heard that ballad singing now;
Hark, hark,

" *Tootle tootle tootle tee* "—
Can it be
Pride and fame must shadows be?
Come and see—
Every season owns her own;
Bird and bee
Sing creation's music on;
Nature's glee
Is in every mood and tone
Eternity.

CLOCK-O'-CLAY

In the cowslip pips I lie,
Hidden from the buzzing fly,
While green grass beneath me lies,
Pearled with dew like fishes' eyes,
Here I lie, a clock-o'-clay,
Waiting for the time o' day.

While the forest quakes surprise,
And the wild wind sobs and sighs,
My home rocks as like to fall,
On its pillar green and tall;
When the pattering rain drives by
Clock-o'-clay keeps warm and dry.

Day by day and night by night,
All the week I hide from sight;
In the cowslip pips I lie,
In the rain still warm and dry;
Day and night, and night and day,
Red, black-spotted clock-o'-clay.

My home shakes in wind and showers,
Pale green pillar topped with flowers,

Bending at the wild wind's breath,
Till I touch the grass beneath;
Here I live, lone clock-o'-clay,
Watching for the time of day.

JOHN KEATS

1795 - 1821

A THING OF BEAUTY

from " Endymion "

A thing of beauty is a joy for ever:
Its loveliness increases; it will never
Pass into nothingness; but still will keep
A bower quiet for us, and a sleep
Full of sweet dreams, and health, and quiet breathing.
Therefore, on every morrow, are we wreathing
A flowery band to bind us to the earth,
Spite of despondence, of the inhuman dearth
Of noble natures, of the gloomy days,
Of all the unhealthy and o'er-darkened ways
Made for our searching: yes, in spite of all,
Some shape of beauty moves away the pall
From our dark spirits. Such the sun, the moon,
Trees old and young, sprouting a shady boon
For simple sheep; and such are daffodils
With the green world they live in; and clear rills
That for themselves a cooling covert make
'Gainst the hot season; the mid-forest brake,
Rich with a sprinkling of fair musk-rose blooms:
And such too is the grandeur of the dooms
We have imagined for the mighty dead;
All lovely tales that we have heard or read:
An endless fountain of immortal drink,
Pouring unto us from the heaven's brink.

LA BELLE DAME SANS MERCI

" O what can ail thee, knight-at-arms,
    Alone and palely loitering?
The sedge has withered from the lake,
    And no birds sing.

" O what can ail thee, knight-at-arms,
    So haggard and so woe-begone?
The squirrel's granary is full,
    And the harvest's done.

" I see a lily on thy brow
    With anguish moist and fever dew,
And on thy cheeks a fading rose
    Fast withereth too."

I met a lady in the meads,
    Full beautiful—a faery's child,
Her hair was long, her foot was light,
    And her eyes were wild.

I made a garland for her head,
    And bracelets too, and fragrant zone,
She looked at me as she did love,
    And made sweet moan.

I set her on my pacing steed,
    And nothing else saw all day long,
For sidelong would she bend, and sing
    A faery's song.

She found me roots of relish sweet,
    And honey wild, and manna dew,
And sure in language strange she said—
    " I love thee true! "

She took me to her elfin grot,
    And there she wept and sighed full sore,
And there I shut her wild, wild eyes
    With kisses four.

And there she lullèd me asleep,
    And there I dreamed—ah! woe betide!
The latest dream I ever dreamed
    On the cold hill's side.

I saw pale kings and princes too,
    Pale warriors, death-pale were they all;
They cried—" La Belle Dame sans Merci
    Hath thee in thrall! "

I saw their starved lips in the gloam,
  With horrid warning gapèd wide,
And I awoke and found me here,
  On the cold hill's side.

And this is why I sojourn here,
  Alone and palely loitering,
Though the sedge is withered from the lake,
  And no birds sing.

MEG MERRILIES

Old Meg she was a gipsy;
  And lived upon the moors:
Her bed it was the brown heath turf,
  And her house was out of doors.
Her apples were swart blackberries,
  Her currants, pods o' broom;
Her wine was dew of the wild white rose,
  Her book a church-yard tomb.

Her brothers were the craggy hills,
  Her sisters larchen trees;
Alone with her great family
  She lived as she did please.
No breakfast had she many a morn,
  No dinner many a noon,
And, 'stead of supper, she would stare
  Full hard against the moon.

But every morn, of woodbine fresh
  She made her garlanding,
And, every night, the dark glen yew
  She wove, and she would sing.
And with her fingers, old and brown,
  She plaited mats of rushes,
And gave them to the cottagers
  She met among the bushes.

Old Meg was brave as Margaret Queen,
  And tall as Amazon;
An old red blanket cloak she wore,
  A chip-hat had she on.
God rest her aged bones somewhere!
  She died full long agone!

ON THE SEA

It keeps eternal whisperings around
   Desolate shores, and with its mighty swell
     Gluts twice ten thousand caverns, till the spell
Of Hecate leaves them their old shadowy sound.
Often 'tis in such gentle temper found,
   That scarcely will the very smallest shell
     Be moved for days from whence it sometime fell,
When last the winds of heaven were unbound.
O ye! who have your eye-balls vexed and tired,
   Feast them upon the wideness of the Sea;
   Oh ye! whose ears are dinned with uproar rude,
     Or fed too much with cloying melody,—
Sit ye near some old cavern's mouth, and brood
Until ye start, as if the sea-nymphs quired!

ON FIRST LOOKING INTO CHAPMAN'S HOMER

Much have I travelled in the realms of gold,
   And many goodly states and kingdoms seen;
   Round many western islands have I been
Which bards in fealty to Apollo hold.
Oft of one wide expanse had I been told,
   That deep-browed Homer ruled as his demesne:
   Yet did I never breathe its pure serene
Till I heard Chapman speak out loud and bold:
Then felt I like some watcher of the skies
   When a new planet swims into his ken;
Or like stout Cortez when with eagle eyes
   He stared at the Pacific—and all his men
Looked at each other with a wild surmise—
   Silent, upon a peak in Darien.

ON THE GRASSHOPPER AND CRICKET

The poetry of earth is never dead:
   When all the birds are faint with the hot sun,
   And hide in cooling trees, a voice will run
From hedge to hedge about the new-mown mead.

That is the grasshopper's—he takes the lead
   In summer luxury,—he has never done
   With his delights, for when tired out with fun,
He rests at ease beneath some pleasant weed.
The poetry of earth is ceasing never:
   On a lone winter evening, when the frost
Has wrought a silence, from the stove there shrills
The cricket's song, in warmth increasing ever,
   And seems to one, in drowsiness half-lost,
The grasshopper's among some grassy hills.

" TO ONE WHO HAS BEEN LONG IN CITY PENT "[1]

To one who has been long in city pent,
   'Tis very sweet to look into the fair
   And open face of heaven,—to breathe a prayer
Full in the smile of the blue firmament.
Who is more happy, when, with heart's content,
   Fatigued he sinks into some pleasant lair
   Of wavy grass, and reads a debonair
And gentle tale of love and languishment?
Returning home at evening, with an ear
   Catching the notes of Philomel,—an eye
Watching the sailing cloudlet's bright career,
   He mourns that day so soon has glided by,
E'en like the passage of an angel's tear
   That falls through the clear ether silently.

ON THE ELGIN MARBLES

My spirit is too weak; mortality
   Weighs heavily on me like unwilling sleep,
   And each imagined pinnacle and steep
Of godlike hardship tells me I must die
Like a sick eagle looking at the sky.
   Yet 'tis a gentle luxury to weep
   That I have not the cloudy winds to keep
Fresh for the opening of the morning's eye.
Such dim-conceivèd glories of the brain,
   Bring round the heart an indescribable feud;

[1] See the passage in Milton (on page 212) which suggested this.

So do these wonders a most dizzy pain,
　　That mingles Grecian grandeur with the rude
Wasting of old Time—with a billowy main—
　　A sun, a shadow of a magnitude.

ODE ON A GRECIAN URN

Thou still unravished bride of quietness!
　　Thou foster-child of Silence and slow Time,
Sylvan historian, who canst thus express
　　A flowery tale more sweetly than our rhyme:
What leaf-fringed legend haunts about thy shape
　　Of deities or mortals, or of both,
　　　In Tempe or the dales of Arcady?
　　What men or gods are these? What maidens loath?
What mad pursuit? What struggle to escape?
　　　What pipes and timbrels? What wild ecstasy?

Heard melodies are sweet, but those unheard
　　Are sweeter; therefore, ye soft pipes, play on;
Not to the sensual ear, but, more endeared,
　　Pipe to the spirit ditties of no tone:
Fair youth, beneath the trees, thou canst not leave
　　Thy song, nor ever can those trees be bare;
　　　Bold Lover, never, never canst thou kiss,
Though winning near the goal—yet, do not grieve;
　　　She cannot fade, though thou hast not thy bliss,
　　For ever wilt thou love, and she be fair!

Ah, happy, happy boughs! that cannot shed
　　Your leaves, nor ever bid the Spring adieu;
And, happy melodist, unwearièd,
　　For ever piping songs for ever new;
More happy love! more happy, happy love!
　　For ever warm and still to be enjoyed,
　　　For ever panting and for ever young;
All breathing human passion far above,
　　That leaves a heart high sorrowful and cloyed,
　　　A burning forehead, and a parching tongue.

Who are these coming to the sacrifice?
　　To what green altar, O mysterious priest,
Lead'st thou that heifer lowing at the skies,
　　And all her silken flanks with garlands drest?

What little town by river or sea-shore,
　Or mountain-built with peaceful citadel,
　　Is emptied of its folk, this pious morn?
And, little town, thy streets for evermore
　Will silent be; and not a soul to tell
　　Why thou art desolate, can e'er return.

O Attic shape! Fair attitude! with brede
　Of marble men and maidens overwrought,
With forest branches and the trodden weed;
　Thou, silent form, dost tease us out of thought
As doth eternity: Cold Pastoral!
　When old age shall this generation waste,
　　Thou shalt remain, in midst of other woe
Than ours, a friend to man, to whom thou say'st,
" Beauty is truth, truth beauty,—that is all
　　Ye know on earth, and all ye need to know."

ODE TO A NIGHTINGALE

My heart aches, and a drowsy numbness pains
　My sense, as though of hemlock I had drunk,
Or emptied some dull opiate to the drains
　One minute past, and Lethe-wards had sunk:
'Tis not through envy of thy happy lot,
　But being too happy in thy happiness,—
　　That thou, light-wingèd Dryad of the trees,
　　　In some melodious plot
Of beechen green, and shadows numberless,
　Singest of summer in full-throated ease.

O for a draught of vintage, that hath been
　Cooled a long age in the deep-delvèd earth,
Tasting of Flora and the country green,
　Dance, and Provençal song, and sun-burnt mirth!
O for a beaker full of the warm South,
　Full of the true, the blushful Hippocrene,
　　With beaded bubbles winking at the brim,
　　　And purple-stainèd mouth;
　That I might drink, and leave the world unseen,
　　And with thee fade away into the forest dim:

Fade far away, dissolve, and quite forget
   What thou among the leaves hast never known,
The weariness, the fever, and the fret
   Here, where men sit and hear each other groan;
Where palsy shakes a few, sad, last grey hairs,
    Where youth grows pale, and spectre-thin, and dies;
      Where but to think is to be full of sorrow
        And leaden-eyed despairs;
    Where beauty cannot keep her lustrous eyes,
      Or new love pine at them beyond to-morrow.

Away! away! for I will fly to thee,
   Not charioted by Bacchus and his pards,
But on the viewless wings of Poesy,
   Though the dull brain perplexes and retards:
Already with thee! tender is the night,
    And haply the Queen-Moon is on her throne,
      Clustered around by all her starry fays;
        But here there is no light,
    Save what from heaven is with the breezes blown
      Through verdurous glooms and winding mossy ways.

I cannot see what flowers are at my feet,
   Nor what soft incense hangs upon the boughs,
But, in embalmèd darkness, guess each sweet
   Wherewith the seasonable month endows
The grass, the thicket, and the fruit-tree wild;
    White hawthorn, and the pastoral eglantine;
      Fast-fading violets covered up in leaves;
        And mid-May's eldest child,
    The coming musk-rose, full of dewy wine,
      The murmurous haunt of flies on summer eves.

Darkling I listen; and for many a time
   I have been half in love with easeful Death,
Called him soft names in many a musèd rhyme,
   To take into the air my quiet breath;
Now more than ever seems it rich to die,
    To cease upon the midnight with no pain,
      While thou art pouring forth thy soul abroad
        In such an ecstasy!
    Still wouldst thou sing, and I have ears in vain—
      To thy high requiem become a sod.

Thou wast not born for death, immortal Bird!
    No hungry generations tread thee down;
The voice I hear this passing night was heard
    In ancient days by emperor and clown:
Perhaps the self-same song that found a path
    Through the sad heart of Ruth, when, sick for home,
        She stood in tears amid the alien corn;
            The same that oft-times hath
        Charmed magic casements, opening on the foam
        Of perilous seas, in faery lands forlorn.

Forlorn! the very word is like a bell
    To toll me back from thee to my sole self.
Adieu! the fancy cannot cheat so well
    As she is famed to do, deceiving elf.
Adieu! adieu! thy plaintive anthem fades
    Past the near meadows, over the still stream,
        Up the hill-side; and now 'tis buried deep
            In the next valley-glades:
        Was it a vision, or a waking dream?
        Fled is that music:—do I wake or sleep?

ODE TO AUTUMN

Season of mists and mellow fruitfulness!
    Close bosom-friend of the maturing sun;
Conspiring with him how to load and bless
    With fruit the vines that round the thatch-eaves run;
To bend with apples the mossed cottage-trees,
    And fill all fruit with ripeness to the core;
    To swell the gourd, and plump the hazel shells
    With a sweet kernel; to set budding more,
And still more, later flowers for the bees,
Until they think warm days will never cease,
    For summer has o'er-brimmed their clammy cells.

Who hath not seen thee oft amid thy store?
    Sometimes whoever seeks abroad may find
Thee sitting careless on a granary floor,
    Thy hair soft-lifted by the winnowing wind;
Or on a half-reaped furrow sound asleep,
    Drowsed with the fume of poppies, while thy hook
        Spares the next swath and all its twinèd flowers;

And sometime like a gleaner thou dost keep
　　Steady thy laden head across a brook;
　　Or by a cider-press, with patient look,
　　　Thou watchest the last oozings, hours by hours.

Where are the songs of Spring? Ay, where are they?
　　Think not of them, thou hast thy music too,
While barrèd clouds bloom the soft-dying day,
　　And touch the stubble-plains with rosy hue;
Then in a wailful choir, the small gnats mourn
　　Among the river sallows, borne aloft
　　　Or sinking as the light wind lives or dies;
And full-grown lambs loud bleat from hilly bourn;
　　Hedge-crickets sing; and now with treble soft
　　The redbreast whistles from a garden-croft,
　　　And gathering swallows twitter in the skies.

ODE ON MELANCHOLY

No, no! go not to Lethe, neither twist
　　Wolf's-bane, tight-rooted, for its poisonous wine;
Nor suffer thy pale forehead to be kissed
　　By nightshade, ruby grape of Proserpine;
Make not your rosary of yew-berries,
　　Nor let the beetle nor the death-moth be
　　　Your mournful Psyche, nor the downy owl
A partner in your sorrow's mysteries;
　　For shade to shade will come too drowsily
　　And drown the wakeful anguish of the soul.

But when the melancholy fit shall fall
　　Sudden from heaven like a weeping cloud,
That fosters the droop-headed flowers all,
　　And hides the green hill in an April shroud;
Then glut thy sorrow on a morning rose,
　　Or on the rainbow of the salt sand-wave,
　　　Or on the wealth of globèd peonies;
Or if thy mistress some rich anger shows,
　　Emprison her soft hand, and let her rave,
　　And feed deep, deep upon her peerless eyes.

She dwells with Beauty—Beauty that must die;
　　And Joy, whose hand is ever at his lips
Bidding adieu; and aching Pleasure nigh,
　　Turning to poison while the bee-mouth sips:

Ay, in the very temple of Delight
    Veiled Melancholy has her sovran shrine,
        Though seen of none save him whose strenuous tongue
Can burst Joy's grape against his palate fine:
His soul shall taste the sadness of her might,
    And be among her cloudy trophies hung.

THE EVE OF ST. AGNES

St. Agnes' Eve—ah, bitter chill it was!
The owl, for all his feathers, was a-cold;
The hare limped trembling through the frozen grass,
And silent was the flock in woolly fold:
Numb were the Beadsman's fingers while he told
His rosary, and while his frosted breath,
Like pious incense from a censor old,
Seemed taking flight for heaven without a death,
Past the sweet Virgin's picture, while his prayer he saith.

His prayer he said, this patient, holy man;
Then takes his lamp, and riseth from his knees,
And back returneth, meagre, barefoot, wan,
Along the chapel aisle by slow degrees:
The sculptured dead, on each side seem to freeze,
Emprisoned in black, purgatorial rails:
Knights, ladies, praying in dumb orat'ries,
He passeth by, and his weak spirit fails
To think how they may ache in icy hoods and mails.

Northward he turneth through a little door,
And scarce three steps, ere Music's golden tongue
Flattered to tears this aged man and poor.
But no—already had his death-bell rung;
The joys of all his life were said and sung:
His was harsh penance on St. Agnes' Eve:
Another way he went, and soon among
Rough ashes sat he for his soul's reprieve
And all night kept awake, for sinner's sake to grieve.

That ancient Beadsman heard the prelude soft;
And so it chanced, for many a door was wide,
From hurry to and fro. Soon, up aloft,
The silver, snarling trumpets 'gan to chide:
The level chambers, ready with their pride,

Were glowing to receive a thousand guests.
The carvèd angels, ever eager-eyed,
Stared, where upon their heads the cornice rests,
With hair blown back, and wings put crosswise on their
    breasts.

At length burst in the argent revelry,
With plume, tiara, and all rich array,
Numerous as shadows haunting fairily
The brain new-stuffed, in youth, with triumphs gay
Of old romance. These let us wish away,
And turn, sole-thoughted, to one Lady there,
Whose heart had brooded, all that wintry day,
On love, and winged St. Agnes' saintly care,
As she had heard old dames full many times declare.

They told her how, upon St. Agnes' Eve,
Young virgins might have visions of delight,
And soft adorings from their loves receive
Upon the honeyed middle of the night,
If ceremonies due they did aright;
As, supperless to bed they must retire,
And couch supine their beauties, lily white;
Nor look behind, nor sideways, but require
Of Heaven with upward eyes for all that they desire.

Full of this whim was thoughtful Madeline:
The music, yearning like a God in pain,
She scarcely heard: her maiden eyes divine,
Fixed on the floor, saw many a sweeping train
Pass by—she heeded not at all: in vain
Came many a tiptoe, amorous cavalier,
And back retired; not cooled by high disdain,
But she saw not: her heart was otherwhere;
She sighed for Agnes' dreams, the sweetest of the year.

She danced along with vague, regardless eyes,
Anxious her lips, her breathing quick and short:
The hallowed hour was near at hand: she sighs
Amid the timbrels, and the thronged resort
Of whisperers in anger or in sport;
'Mid looks of love, defiance, hate, and scorn,
Hoodwinked with faery fancy; all amort,
Save to St. Agnes and her lambs unshorn,
And all the bliss to be before to-morrow morn.

So, purposing each moment to retire,
She lingered still. Meantime, across the moors,
Had come young Porphyro, with heart on fire
For Madeline. Beside the portal doors,
Buttressed from moonlight, stands he, and implores
All saints to give him sight of Madeline,
But for one moment in the tedious hours,
That he might gaze and worship all unseen;
Perchance speak, kneel, touch, kiss—in sooth such things have
　　been.

He ventures in: let no buzzed whisper tell,
All eyes be muffed, or a hundred swords
Will storm his heart, Love's feverous citadel:
For him, those chambers held barbarian hordes,
Hyena foemen, and hot-blooded lords,
Whose very dogs would execration howl
Against his lineage; not one breast affords
Him any mercy in that mansion foul,
Save one old beldame, weak in body and in soul.

Ah, happy chance! the aged creature came,
Shuffling along with ivory-headed wand,
To where he stood, hid from the torch's flame,
Behind a broad hall pillar, far beyond
The sound of merriment and chorus bland.
He startled her: but soon she knew his face,
And grasped his fingers in her palsied hand,
Saying, " Mercy, Porphyro! hie thee from this place;
They are all here to-night, the whole blood-thirsty race!

" Get hence! get hence! there's dwarfish Hildebrand:
He had a fever late, and in the fit
He cursèd thee and thine, both house and land:
Then there's that old Lord Maurice, not a whit
More tame for his grey hairs—Alas me! flit!
Flit like a ghost away."—" Ah, Gossip dear,
We're safe enough; here in this arm-chair sit,
And tell me how—" " Good saints! not here, not here!
Follow me, child, or else these stones will be thy bier."

He followed through a lowly archèd way,
Brushing the cobwebs with his lofty plume;
And as she muttered " Well-a—well-a-day! "
He found him in a little moonlight room,

Pale, latticed, chill, and silent as a tomb.
" Now tell me where is Madeline," said he,
" O tell me, Angela, by the holy loom
Which none but secret sisterhood may see,
When they St. Agnes' wool are weaving piously."

" St. Agnes! Ah! it is St. Agnes' Eve—
Yet men will murder upon holy days.
Thou must hold water in a witch's sieve,
And be liege-lord of all the Elves and Fays
To venture so: it fills me with amaze
To see thee, Porphyro!—St. Agnes' Eve!
God's help! my lady fair the conjurer plays
This very night: good angels her deceive!
But let me laugh awhile,—I've mickle time to grieve."

Feebly she laugheth in the languid moon,
While Porphyro upon her face doth look,
Like puzzled urchin on an aged crone
Who keepeth closed a wondrous riddle-book,
As spectacled she sits in chimney nook.
But soon his eyes grew brilliant, when she told
His lady's purpose; and he scarce could brook
Tears at the thought of those enchantments cold,
And Madeline asleep in lap of legends old.

Sudden a thought came like a full-blown rose,
Flushing his brow, and in his painèd heart
Made purple riot: then doth he propose
A stratagem, that makes the beldame start:
" A cruel man and impious thou art!
Sweet lady, let her pray, and sleep and dream
Alone with her good angels, far apart
From wicked men like thee. Go, go! I deem
Thou canst not surely be the same that thou didst seem."

" I will not harm her, by all saints I swear! "
Quoth Porphyro: " O may I ne'er find grace
When my weak voice shall whisper its last prayer,
If one of her soft ringlets I displace,
Or look with ruffian passion in her face.
Good Angela, believe me, by these tears;
Or I will, even in a moment's space,
Awake, with horrid shout, my foemen's ears,
And beard them, though they be more fanged than wolves
    and bears."

" Ah! why wilt thou affright a feeble soul?
A poor, weak, palsy-stricken, churchyard thing,
Whose passing-bell may ere the midnight toll;
Whose prayers for thee, each morn and evening,
Were never missed." Thus plaining, doth she bring
A gentler speech from burning Porphyro;
So woeful, and of such deep sorrowing,
That Angela gives promise she will do
Whatever he shall wish, betide her weal or woe.

Which was, to lead him, in close secrecy,
Even to Madeline's chamber, and there hide
Him in a closet, of such privacy
That he might see her beauty unespied,
And win perhaps that night a peerless bride,
While legioned fairies paced the coverlet,
And pale enchantment held her sleepy-eyed.
Never on such a night have lovers met,
Since Merlin paid his Demon all the monstrous debt.

" It shall be as thou wishest," said the Dame:
" All cates and dainties shall be storèd there
Quickly on this feast-night: by the tambour frame
Her own lute thou wilt see: no time to spare,
For I am slow and feeble, and scarce dare
On such a catering trust my dizzy head.
Wait here, my child, with patience; kneel in prayer
The while. Ah! thou must needs the lady wed,
Or may I never leave my grave among the dead."

So saying she hobbled off with busy fear.
The lover's endless minutes slowly passed;
The dame returned, and whispered in his ear
To follow her; with aged eyes aghast
From fright of dim espial. Safe at last
Through many a dusky gallery, they gain
The maiden's chamber, silken, hushed and chaste
Where Porphyro took covert, pleased amain.
His poor guide hurried back with agues in her brain.

Her faltering hand upon the balustrade,
Old Angela was feeling for the stair,
When Madeline, St. Agnes' charmèd maid,
Rose, like a missioned spirit, unaware:

With silver taper's light, and pious care,
She turned, and down the aged gossip led
To a safe level matting. Now prepare,
Young Porphyro, for gazing on that bed;
She comes, she comes again, like ring-dove frayed and fled.

Out went the taper as she hurried in;
Its little smoke, in pallid moonshine, died:
She closed the door, she panted, all akin
To spirits of the air, and visions wide:
No uttered syllable, or, woe betide!
But to her heart, her heart was voluble,
Paining with eloquence her balmy side;
As though a tongueless nightingale should swell
Her throat in vain, and die, heart-stifled, in her dell.

A casement high and triple-arched there was,
All garlanded with carven imageries,
Of fruits and flowers, and bunches of knot-grass,
And diamonded with panes of quaint device,
Innumerable of stains and splendid dyes,
As are the tiger-moth's deep-damasked wings;
And in the midst, 'mong thousand heraldries,
And twilight saints, and dim emblazonings,
A shielded scutcheon blushed with blood of queens and kings.

Full on this casement shone the wintry moon,
And threw warm gules on Madeline's fair breast,
As down she knelt for Heaven's grace and boon;
Rose-bloom fell on her hands, together prest,
And on her silver cross soft amethyst,
And on her hair a glory, like a saint:
She seemed a splendid angel, newly drest,
Save wings, for heaven:—Porphyro grew faint:
She knelt, so pure a thing, so free from mortal taint.

Anon his heart revives: her vespers done,
Of all its wreathèd pearls her hair she frees;
Unclasps her warmèd jewels one by one;
Loosens her fragrant bodice; by degrees
Her rich attire creeps rustling to her knees:
Half-hidden, like a mermaid in sea-weed,
Pensive awhile she dreams awake, and sees,
In fancy, fair St. Agnes in her bed,
But dares not look behind, or all the charm is fled.

Soon, trembling in her soft and chilly nest,
In sort of wakeful swoon, perplexed she lay,
Until the poppied warmth of sleep oppressed
Her soothèd limbs, and soul fatigued away;
Flown, like a thought, until the morrow-day;
Blissfully havened both from joy and pain;
Clasped like a missal where swart Paynims pray;
Blinded alike from sunshine and from rain,
As though a rose should shut, and be a bud again.

Stol'n to this paradise, and so entranced,
Porphyro gazed upon her empty dress,
And listens to her breathing, if it chanced
To wake into a slumberous tenderness;
Which when he heard, that minute did he bless,
And breathed himself: then from the closet crept,
Noiseless as fear in a wide wilderness,
And over the hushed carpet, silent, stept,
And 'tween the curtains peeped, where, lo!—how fast she
    slept!

Then by the bed-side, where the faded moon
Made a dim, silver twilight, soft he set
A table, and half anguished, threw thereon
A cloth of woven crimson, gold, and jet:—
O for some drowsy Morphean amulet!
The boisterous, midnight, festive clarion,
The kettle-drum, and far-heard clarionet,
Affray his ears, though but in dying tone:—
The hall-door shuts again, and all the noise is gone.

And still she slept an azure-lidded sleep,
In blanchèd linen, smooth, and lavendered,
While he from forth the closet brought a heap
Of candied apple, quince, and plum, and gourd;
With jellies soother than the creamy curd,
And lucent syrops, tinct with cinnamon;
Manna and dates, in argosy transferred
From Fez; and spicèd dainties, every one
From silken Samarcand to cedared Lebanon.

These delicates he heaped with glowing hand
On golden dishes and in baskets bright
Of wreathèd silver: sumptuous they stand
In the retired quiet of the night,

Filling the chilly room with perfume light.—
" And now, my love, my seraph fair, awake!
Thou art my heaven, and I thine eremite:
Open thine eyes, for meek St. Agnes' sake,
Or I shall drowse beside thee, so my soul doth ache."

Thus whispering, his warm, unnervèd arm
Sank in her pillow. Shaded was her dream
By the dusk curtains:—'twas a midnight charm
Impossible to melt as icèd stream:
The lustrous salvers in the moonlight gleam;
Broad golden fringe upon the carpet lies:
It seemed he never, never could redeem
From such a steadfast spell his lady's eyes;
So mused awhile, entoiled in woofèd phantasies.

Awakening up, he took her hollow lute,—
Tumultuous,—and, in chords that tenderest be,
He played an ancient ditty, long since mute,
In Provence called " La belle dame sans mercy: "
Close to her ear touching the melody;—
Wherewith disturbed, she uttered a soft moan:
He ceased—she panted quick—and suddenly
Her blue affrayèd eyes wide open shone:
Upon his knees he sank, pale as smooth-sculptured stone.

Her eyes were open, but she still beheld,
Now wide awake, the vision of her sleep:
There was a painful change, that nigh expelled
The blisses of her dream so pure and deep.
At which fair Madeline began to weep,
And moan forth witless words with many a sigh,
While still her gaze on Porphyro would keep;
Who knelt, with joinèd hands and piteous eye,
Fearing to move or speak, she looked so dreamingly.

" Ah, Porphyro! " said she, " but even now
Thy voice was at sweet tremble in mine ear,
Made tunable with every sweetest vow;
And those sad eyes were spiritual and clear:
How changed thou art! how pallid, chill, and drear!
Give me that voice again, my Porphyro,
Those looks immortal, those complainings dear!
Oh, leave me not in this eternal woe,
For if thou diest, my Love, I know not where to go."

Beyond a mortal man impassioned far
At these voluptuous accents, he arose,
Ethereal, flushed, and like a throbbing star
Seen 'mid the sapphire heaven's deep repose;
Into her dream he melted, as the rose
Blendeth its odour with the violet,—
Solution sweet: meantime the frost-wind blows
Like Love's alarum, pattering the sharp sleet
Against the window-panes; St. Agnes' moon hath set.

'Tis dark: quick pattereth the flaw-blown sleet.
" This is no dream, my bride, my Madeline! "
'Tis dark: the icèd gusts still rave and beat:
" No dream, alas! alas! and woe is mine!
Porphyro will leave me here to fade and pine.
Cruel! what traitor could thee hither bring?
I curse not, for my heart is lost in thine,
Though thou forsakest a deceivèd thing;—
A dove forlorn and lost with sick unprunèd wing."

" My Madeline! sweet dreamer! lovely bride!
Say, may I be for aye thy vassal blest?
Thy beauty's shield, heart-shaped and vermeil-dyed?
Ah, silver shrine, here will I take my rest
After so many hours of toil and quest,
A famished pilgrim,—saved by miracle.
Though I have found, I will not rob thy nest,
Saving of thy sweet self; if thou think'st well
To trust, fair Madeline, to no rude infidel.

" Hark! 'tis an elfin storm from faery land,
Of haggard seeming, but a boon indeed:
Arise—arise! the morning is at hand;—
The bloated wassailers will never heed;—
Let us away, my love, with happy speed;
There are no ears to hear, or eyes to see,—
Drowned all in Rhenish and the sleepy mead.
Awake! arise! my love, and fearless be,
For o'er the southern moors I have a home for thee."

She hurried at his words, beset with fears,
For there were sleeping dragons all around
At glaring watch, perhaps, with ready spears.
Down the wide stairs a darkling way they found;

In all the house was heard no human sound.
A chain-drooped lamp was flickering by each door;
The arras, rich with horsemen, hawk, and hound,
Fluttered in the besieging wind's uproar;
And the long carpets rose along the gusty floor.

They glide, like phantoms, into the wide hall!
Like phantoms to the iron porch they glide,
Where lay the Porter, in uneasy sprawl,
With a huge empty flagon by his side:
The wakeful bloodhound rose, and shook his hide,
But his sagacious eye an inmate owns:
By one, and one, the bolts full easy slide:—
The chains lie silent on the footworn stones;
The key turns, and the door upon its hinges groans.

And they are gone: ay, ages long ago
These lovers fled away into the storm.
That night the Baron dreamt of many a woe,
And all his warrior-guests with shade and form
Of witch, and demon, and large coffin-worm,
Were long be-nightmared. Angela the old
Died palsy-twitched, with meagre face deform;
The Beadsman, after thousand aves told,
For aye unsought-for slept among his ashes cold.

LAST SONNET

Bright Star! would I were steadfast as thou art—
Not in lone splendour hung aloft the night,
And watching, with eternal lids apart,
Like Nature's patient sleepless Eremite,
The moving waters at their priest-like task
Of pure ablution round earth's human shores,
Or gazing on the new soft fallen mask
Of snow upon the mountains and the moors:
No—yet still steadfast, still unchangeable,
Pillowed upon my fair love's ripening breast
To feel for ever its soft fall and swell,
Awake for ever in a sweet unrest;
Still, still to hear her tender-taken breath,
And so live ever—or else swoon to death.

GEORGE DARLEY

1795 - 1846

THE MERMAIDS' VESPER-HYMN

Troop home to silent grots and caves!
Troop home! and mimic as you go
The mournful winding of the waves
Which to their dark abysses flow.

At this sweet hour, all things beside
In amorous pairs to covert creep:
The swans that brushed the evening tide
Homeward in snowy couples keep.

In his green den the murmuring seal
Close by his sleek companion lies;
While singly we to bedward steal,
And close in fruitless sleep our eyes.

In bowers of love men take their rest,
In loveless bowers we sigh alone,
With bosom-friends are others blest—
But we have none! but we have none!

PASSAGES FROM "NEPENTHE"

THE SEA

Hurry me, Nymphs, O, hurry me
Far above the grovelling sea,
Which, with blind weakness and base roar
Casting his white age on the shore,
Wallows along the slimy floor;
With his widespread webbèd hands
Seeking to climb the level sands,
And rejected still to rave
Alive in his uncovered grave.

THE PHOENIX

O blest unfabled Incense Tree,
That burns in glorious Araby,
With red scent chalicing the air,
Till earth-life grow Elysian there.

Half buried to her flaming breast
In this bright tree, she makes her nest,
Hundred-sunned Phœnix! when she must
Crumble at length to hoary dust!

Her gorgeous death-bed! her rich pyre
Burnt up with aromatic fire!
Her urn, sight high from spoiler men;
Her birth-place when self-born again!

The mountainless green wilds among,
Here ends she her unechoing song.
With amber tears and odorous sighs
Mourned by the desert where she dies.

THE NINETEENTH CENTURY
SECOND HALF
VICTORIANS AND AMERICANS

The second half of the nineteenth century is commonly referred to as Victorian and the reference is usually accompanied by a sneer. In fact there is scarcely a more destructive shot in the critic's arsenal, unless it is the adjective " mid-Victorian." Yet nothing could be more inaccurate than a blanket characterisation based on the assumption that all poets of the period wrote under the influence of a domesticated and moralising Muse bearing a strong family likeness to the buxom Queen. It is true that an over-emphasis on " sweetness and light " resulted in a great deal of mawkish versifying by the lesser poets and even, at times, by Tennyson. Yet no fifty years of English poetry displayed a greater variety than the half-century between 1850 and 1900. A composite picture of the proverbial, staid Victorian becomes an absurdity when we are confronted by the dramatic and challenging Browning, the calm but equally confident Patmore, the violent and rebellious Swinburne, the meditative Arnold, the high-pitched luxuriance of Francis Thompson, the subdued astringency of Hardy, the stern courage of Emily Brontë, the mediæval richness of Dante Gabriel Rossetti and the quiet-coloured warmth of his sister Christina.

Nor, in an age supposedly cowed by Science and the growing dominance of the machine, is there a lack of lyrical notes. The range of melody is all the way from the simple quatrains of A. E. Housman (whose " A Shropshire Lad " continues to ignore changing fashions and remains a collection of practically perfect songs) to the onrushing, image-crowded lines of Gerard Hopkins; it includes the nun-like serenity of Christina Rossetti and the forceful if unfamiliar acerbity of the " Northern Farmer " Tennyson, the long measures of George Meredith and the telegraphic concisions of Emily Dickinson.

A similar richness and variety is obvious in the American scene if examined with unprejudiced eyes. It becomes increasingly apparent that the poets of the famous New England group, overrated by their contemporaries and underrated by their successors, were both praised and blamed for the wrong thing. It was, in most cases, the same thing: the Sunday School lesson in easily remembered rhyme; the tag-end motto; the parade of exemplary village blacksmiths, alp-climbing youths and a moralising nautilus. This was the weaker work of genuine poets, the worst of which was too often interred in the textbooks of the past. In the light of unprejudiced reappraisal, Longfellow emerges as a ballad-writer of importance and a pioneer user of native material; Bryant stands out, not as " a smooth, silent iceberg," but as a prophet of dignity; Whittier impresses us as a genre painter in the manner of Burns, if Burns had been both a zealot and a Yankee; Emerson looms as a metaphysician without whom Whitman and Emily Dickinson—

highly original geniuses though they were—would have written far differently than they did. Nor will Poe, that self-driven, song-tortured Israfel, fit the tabulator's tight limitations. Like Whitman, Poe has passed beyond national borders. Poe's influence affected or, one might even say, effected a new literature abroad; Whitman's sometimes too inclusive affirmations, his attempted synthesis of life at every extreme— " immense in passion, impetuous with power "—spread a new gospel to remote corners of the world.

The keynote to the period, after all, was not so much righteousness (though the note was repeatedly struck) as richness.

WILLIAM CULLEN BRYANT

(A) 1794 - 1878

TO A WATERFOWL

Whither, 'midst falling dew,
While glow the heavens with the last steps of day,
Far, through their rosy depths, dost thou pursue
    Thy solitary way!

Vainly the fowler's eye
Might mark thy distant flight to do thee wrong,
As, darkly painted on the crimson sky,
    Thy figure floats along.

Seek'st thou the plashy brink
Of weedy lake, or marge of river wide,
Or where the rocking billows rise and sink
    On the chafed ocean side?

There is a power whose care
Teaches thy way along that pathless coast,—
The desert and illimitable air,—
    Lone wandering, but not lost.

All day thy wings have fanned,
At that far height, the cold, thin atmosphere,
Yet stoop not, weary, to the welcome land,
    Though the dark night is near.

And soon that toil shall end;
Soon shalt thou find a summer home, and rest,
And scream among thy fellows; reeds shall bend,
    Soon, o'er thy sheltered nest.

Thou'rt gone, the abyss of heaven
Hath swallowed up thy form; yet, on my heart
Deeply hath sunk the lesson thou hast given,
    And shall not soon depart.

    He who, from zone to zone,
Guides through the boundless sky thy certain flight,
In the long way that I must tread alone,
    Will lead my steps aright.

THANATOPSIS

To him who in the love of nature holds
Communion with her visible forms, she speaks
A various language; for his gayer hours
She has a voice of gladness, and a smile
And eloquence of beauty; and she glides
Into his darker musings, with a mild
And healing sympathy that steals away
Their sharpness ere he is aware. When thoughts
Of the last bitter hour come like a blight
Over thy spirit, and sad images
Of the stern agony, and shroud, and pall,
And breathless darkness, and the narrow house,
Make thee to shudder, and grow sick at heart;—
Go forth, under the open sky, and list
To Nature's teachings, while from all around—
Earth and her waters, and the depths of air—
Comes a still voice. Yet a few days, and thee
The all-beholding sun shall see no more. . . .
Yet not to thine eternal resting-place
Shalt thou retire alone, nor couldst thou wish
Couch more magnificent. Thou shalt lie down
With patriarchs of the infant world—with kings,
The powerful of the earth—the wise, the good,
Fair forms, and hoary seers, of ages past,
All in one mighty sepulchre. The hills
Rock-ribbed, and ancient as the sun, the vales
Stretching in pensive quietness between;
The venerable woods—rivers that move
In majesty, and the complaining brooks
That make the meadows green; and, poured round all,
Old ocean's grey and melancholy waste,—
Are but the solemn decorations all
Of the great tomb of man. . . .

So shalt thou rest,—and what if thou withdraw
Unheeded by the living and no friend
Take note of thy departure? All that breathe
Will share thy destiny. The gay will laugh
When thou art gone, the solemn brood of care
Plod on, and each one, as before, will chase
His favourite phantom; yet all these shall leave
Their mirth and their employments, and shall come
And make their bed with thee. As the long train
Of ages glide away, the sons of men,
The youth in life's green spring, and he who goes
In the full strength of years, matron, and maid,
And the sweet babe, and the grey-headed man,—
Shall one by one be gathered to thy side,
By those who, in their turn, shall follow them.

   So live, that, when thy summons comes to join
The innumerable caravan, that moves
To that mysterious realm, where each shall take
His chamber in the silent halls of death,
Thou go not, like the quarry-slave, at night,
Scourged to his dungeon, but, sustained and soothed
By an unfaltering trust, approach thy grave,
Like one that draws the drapery of his couch
About him, and lies down to pleasant dreams.

THOMAS HOOD

1799 - 1845

PAST AND PRESENT

I remember, I remember
   The house where I was born,
The little window where the sun
   Came peeping in at morn:
He never came a wink too soon
   Nor brought too long a day;
But now, I often wish the night
   Had borne my breath away.

I remember, I remember
   The roses, red and white,
The violets, and the lily-cups—
   Those flowers made of light!

The lilacs where the robin built,
  And where my brother set
The laburnum on his birth-day,—
  The tree is living yet!

I remember, I remember
  Where I was used to swing,
And thought the air must rush as fresh
  To swallows on the wing;
My spirit flew in feathers then
  That is so heavy now,
And summer pools could hardly cool
  The fever on my brow.

I remember, I remember
  The fir trees dark and high;
I used to think their slender tops
  Were close against the sky:
It was a childish ignorance,
  But now 'tis little joy
To know I'm farther off from Heaven
  Than when I was a boy.

RALPH WALDO EMERSON

(A) 1803 - 1882

THE POET

from " Merlin "

Thy trivial harp will never please
Or fill my craving ear;
Its chords should ring as blows the breeze,
Free, peremptory, clear.
No jingling serenader's art,
Nor tinkle of piano strings,
Can make the wild blood start
In its mystic springs.
The kingly bard
Must smite the chords rudely and hard,
As with hammer or with mace;
That they may render back
Artful thunder, which conveys
Secrets of the solar track,
Sparks of the supersolar blaze.

Merlin's blows are strokes of fate,
Chiming with the forest tone,
When boughs buffet boughs in the wood;
Chiming with the gasp and moan
Of the ice-imprisoned flood;
With the pulse of manly hearts;
With the voice of orators;
With the din of city arts;
With the cannonade of wars;
With the marches of the brave;
And prayers of might from martyrs' cave.

Great is the art,
Great be the manners, of the bard.
He shall not his brain encumber
With the coil of rhythm and number;
But, leaving rule and pale forethought,
He shall aye climb
For his rhyme.
" Pass in, pass in," the angels say,
" In to the upper doors,
Nor count compartments of the floors,
But mount to paradise
By the stairway of surprise."

THE RHODORA:

ON BEING ASKED, WHENCE IS THE FLOWER?

In May, when sea-winds pierced our solitudes,
I found the fresh Rhodora in the woods,
Spreading its leafless blooms in a damp nook,
To please the desert and the sluggish brook.
The purple petals, fallen in the pool,
Made the black water with their beauty gay;
Here might the red-bird come his plumes to cool,
And court the flower that cheapens his array.
Rhodora! if the sages ask thee why
This charm is wasted on the earth and sky,
Tell them, dear, that if eyes were made for seeing,
Then Beauty is its own excuse for being:
Why thou wert there, O rival of the rose!
I never thought to ask, I never knew:
But, in my simple ignorance, suppose
The self-same Power that brought me there brought you.

BRAHMA

If the red slayer think he slays,
  Or if the slain think he is slain,
They know not well the subtle ways
  I keep, and pass, and turn again.

Far or forgot to me is near;
  Shadow and sunlight are the same;
The vanished gods to me appear;
  And one to me are shame and fame.

They reckon ill who leave me out;
  When me they fly, I am the wings;
I am the doubter and the doubt,
  And I the hymn the Brahmin sings.

The strong gods pine for my abode,
  And pine in vain the sacred Seven;
But thou, meek lover of the good!
  Find me, and turn thy back on heaven.

THE SNOWSTORM

Announced by all the trumpets of the sky,
Arrives the snow, and, driving o'er the fields,
Seems nowhere to alight: the whited air
Hides hills and woods, the river, and the heaven,
And veils the farmhouse at the garden's end.
The sled and traveller stopped, the courier's feet
Delayed, all friends shut out, the housemates sit
Around the radiant fireplace, enclosed
In a tumultuous privacy of storm.

Come, see the north wind's masonry.
Out of an unseen quarry evermore
Furnished with tile, the fierce artificer
Curves his white bastions with projected roof
Round every windward stake or tree or door.
Speeding, the myriad-handed, his wild work
So fanciful, so savage, naught cares he
For number or proportion. Mockingly

On coop or kennel he hangs Parian wreaths;
A swan-like form invests the hidden thorn;
Fills up the farmer's lane from wall to wall,
Maugre the farmer's sighs; and at the gate
A tapering turret overtops the work.
And when his hours are numbered, and the world
Is all his own, retiring, as he were not,
Leaves, when the sun appears, astonished Art
To mimic in slow structures, stone by stone,
Built in an age, the mad wind's night-work,
The frolic architecture of the snow.

DAYS

Daughters of Time, the hypocritic Days,
Muffled and dumb like barefoot dervishes,
And marching single in an endless file,
Bring diadems and faggots in their hands.
To each they offer gifts after his will,
Bread, kingdoms, stars, and sky that holds them all.
I, in my pleached garden, watched the pomp.
Forgot my morning wishes, hastily
Took a few herbs and apples, and the Day
Turned and departed silent. I, too late,
Under her solemn fillet saw the scorn.

THOMAS LOVELL BEDDOES

1803 - 1849

DREAM-PEDLARY

If there were dreams to sell
    What would you buy?
Some cost a passing bell,
    Some a light sigh,
That shakes from life's fresh crown
Only a rose-leaf down.

If there were dreams to sell,
Merry and sad to tell,
And the crier rang the bell,
    What would you buy?

A cottage lone and still,
　　With bowers nigh,
Shadowy, my woes to still
　　Until I die.
Such pearl from life's fresh crown
Fain would I shake me down.
Were dreams to have at will,
This would best heal my ill,
　　This would I buy.

ELIZABETH BARRETT BROWNING

1806 - 1861

LOVE

from " Sonnets from the Portuguese "

If thou must love me, let it be for nought
Except for love's sake only. Do not say,
" I love her for her smile—her look—her way
Of speaking gently—for a trick of thought
That falls in well with mine, and certes brought
A sense of pleasant ease on such a day ".
For these things in themselves, Belovèd, may
Be changed, or change for thee—and love, so wrought,
May be unwrought so. Neither love me for
Thine own dear pity's wiping my cheeks dry—
A creature might forget to weep, who bore
Thy comfort long, and lose thy love thereby!
But love me for love's sake, that evermore
Thou may'st love on, through love's eternity.

　　•　　　•　　　•　　　•　　　•

How do I love thee? Let me count the ways.
I love thee to the depth and breadth and height
My soul can reach, when feeling out of sight
For the ends of Being and ideal Grace.
I love thee to the level of every day's
Most quiet need, by sun and candle-light.
I love thee freely, as men strive for right;
I love thee purely, as they turn from praise.

I love thee with the passion put to use
In my old griefs, and with my childhood's faith.
I love thee with a love I seemed to lose
With my lost saints—I love thee with the breath,
Smiles, tears, of all my life!—and, if God choose,
I shall but love thee better after death.

GRIEF

I tell you hopeless grief is passionless,
That only men incredulous of despair,
Half-taught in anguish, through the midnight air
Beat upward to God's throne in loud access
Of shrieking and reproach. Full desertness
In souls, as countries, lieth silent-bare
Under the blanching, vertical eye-glare
Of the absolute heavens. Deep-hearted man, express
Grief for thy dead in silence like to death—
Most like a monumental statue set
In everlasting watch and moveless woe
Till itself crumble to the dust beneath.
Touch it; the marble eyelids are not wet
If it could weep, it could arise and go.

HENRY WADSWORTH LONGFELLOW

(A) 1807 - 1882

CHAUCER

An old man in a lodge within a park;
    The chamber walls depicted all around
    With portraitures of huntsman, hawk, and hound,
    And the hurt deer. He listeneth to the lark,
Whose song comes with the sunshine through the dark
    Of painted glass in leaden lattice bound;
    He listeneth and he laugheth at the sound,
    Then writeth in a book like any clerk.
He is the poet of the dawn, who wrote
    The Canterbury Tales, and his old age
    Made beautiful with song; and as I read
I hear the crowing cock, I hear the note
    Of lark and linnet, and from every page
    Rise odours of ploughed field or flowery mead.

NATURE

As a fond mother, when the day is o'er,
  Leads by the hand her little child to bed,
  Half willing, half reluctant to be led,
  And leave his broken playthings on the floor,
Still gazing at them through the open door,
  Nor wholly reassured and comforted
  By promises of others in their stead,
  Which, though more splendid, may not please him more;
So Nature deals with us, and takes away
  Our playthings one by one, and by the hand
  Leads us to rest so gently, that we go
Scarce knowing if we wish to go or stay,
  Being too full of sleep to understand
  How far the unknown transcends the what we know.

MY LOST YOUTH

Often I think of the beautiful town
  That is seated by the sea;
Often in thought go up and down
The pleasant streets of that dear old town,
  And my youth comes back to me.
    And a verse of a Lapland song
    Is haunting my memory still:
    " A boy's will is the wind's will,
And the thoughts of youth are long, long thoughts."

I can see the shadowy lines of its trees,
  And catch, in sudden gleams,
The sheen of the far-surrounding seas,
And islands that were the Hesperides
  Of all my boyish dreams.
    And the burden of that old song,
    It murmurs and whispers still:
    " A boy's will is the wind's will,
And the thoughts of youth are long, long thoughts."

I remember the black wharves and the slips,
  And the sea-tides tossing free;
And Spanish sailors with bearded lips,
And the beauty and mystery of the ships,
  And the magic of the sea.

And the voice of that wayward song
  Is singing and saying still:
    " A boy's will is the wind's will,
And the thoughts of youth are long, long thoughts."

I remember the bulwarks by the shore,
  And the fort upon the hill;
The sunrise gun, with its hollow roar,
The drumbeat repeated o'er and o'er,
  And the bugle wild and shrill.
    And the music of that old song
    Throbs in my memory still:
    " A boy's will is the wind's will,
And the thoughts of youth are long, long thoughts."

I remember the sea-fight far away,
  How it thundered o'er the tide!
And the dead captains, as they lay
In their graves, o'erlooking the tranquil bay
  Where they in battle died.
    And the sound of that mournful song
    Goes through me with a thrill:
    " A boy's will is the wind's will,
And the thoughts of youth are long, long thoughts."

    .   .   .   .   .

Strange to me now are the forms I meet
  When I visit the dear old town;
But the native air is pure and sweet,
And the trees that o'er shadow each well-known street,
  As they balance up and down,
    Are singing the beautiful song,
    Are sighing and whispering still:
    " A boy's will is the wind's will,
And the thoughts of youth are long, long thoughts."

And Deering's Woods are fresh and fair,
  And with joy that is almost pain
My heart goes back to wander there,
And among the dreams of the days that were,
  I find my lost youth again.
    And the strange and beautiful song,
    The groves are repeating it still:
    " A boy's will is the wind's will,
And the thoughts of youth are long, long thoughts."

MILTON[1]

I pace the sounding sea-beach and behold
  How the voluminous billows roll and run,
  Upheaving and subsiding, while the sun
Shines through their sheeted emerald far unrolled
And the ninth wave, slow gathering fold by fold
  All its loose-flowing garments into one,
  Plunges upon the shore, and floods the dun
Pale reach of sands, and changes them to gold.
So in majestic cadence rise and fall
  The mighty undulations of thy song,
  O sightless bard, England's Mæonides!
And ever and anon, high over all
  Uplifted, a ninth wave superb and strong,
  Floods all the soul with its melodious seas.

THE DAY IS DONE

The day is done, and the darkness
    Falls from the wings of Night,
As a feather is wafted downward
    From an eagle in his flight.

I see the lights of the village
    Gleam through the rain and the mist,
And a feeling of sadness comes o'er me
    That my soul cannot resist:

A feeling of sadness and longing,
    That is not akin to pain,
And resembles sorrow only
    As the mist resembles the rain.

Come, read to me some poem,
    Some simple and heartfelt lay,
That shall soothe this restless feeling,
    And banish the thoughts of day.

Not from the grand old masters,
    Not from the bards sublime,
Whose distant footsteps echo
    Through the corridors of Time.

[1] Compare Wordsworth's sonnet on page 311.

For, like strains of martial music,
    Their mighty thoughts suggest
Life's endless toil and endeavour;
    And to-night I long for rest.

Read from some humbler poet,
    Whose songs gushed from his heart,
As showers from the clouds of summer,
    Or tears from the eyelids start:

Who, through long days of labour,
    And nights devoid of ease,
Still heard in his soul the music
    Of wonderful melodies.

Such songs have power to quiet
    The restless pulse of care,
And come like the benediction
    That follows after prayer.

Then read from the treasured volume
    The poem of thy choice,
And lend to the rhyme of the poet
    The beauty of thy voice.

And the night shall be filled with music,
    And the cares, that infest the day,
Shall fold their tents, like the Arabs,
    And as silently steal away.

JOHN GREENLEAF WHITTIER

(A) 1807 - 1892

THE WAITING

I wait and watch: before my eyes
    Methinks the night grows thin and gray;
I wait and watch the eastern skies
To see the golden spears uprise
    Beneath the oriflamme of day!

Like one whose limbs are bound in trance
I hear the day-sounds swell and grow,
  And see across the twilight glance,
Troop after troop, in swift advance,
  The shining ones with plumes of snow!

I know the errand of their feet,
  I know what mighty work is theirs;
I can but lift up hands unmeet
The threshing-floors of God to beat,
  And speed them with unworthy prayers.

I will not dream in vain despair
  The steps of progress wait for me:
The puny leverage of a hair
The planet's impulse well may spare,
  A drop of dew the tided sea.

The loss, if loss there be, is mine,
  And yet not mine if understood;
For one shall grasp and one resign,
One drink life's rue, and one its wine,
  And God shall make the balance good.

O power to do! O baffled will!
  O prayer and action! ye are one.
Who may not strive, may yet fulfil
The harder task of standing still,
  And good but wished with God is done!

OLIVER WENDELL HOLMES

(A) 1809 - 1894

THE LAST LEAF

I saw him once before,
As he passed by the door,
  And again
The pavement stones resound,
As he totters o'er the ground
  With his cane.

They say that in his prime,
Ere the pruning-knife of Time
  Cut him down,

Not a better man was found
By the Crier on his round
   Through the town.

But now he walks the streets,
And he looks at all he meets
   Sad and wan,
And he shakes his feeble head,
That it seems as if he said,
   " They are gone."

The mossy marbles rest
On the lips that he has prest
   In their bloom,
And the names he loved to hear
Have been carved for many a year
   On the tomb.

My grandmamma has said—
Poor old lady, she is dead
   Long ago—
That he had a Roman nose,
And his cheek was like a rose
   In the snow.

But now his nose is thin,
And it rests upon his chin
   Like a staff,
And a crook is in his back,
And a melancholy crack
   In his laugh.

I know it is a sin
For me to sit and grin
   At him here;
But the old three-cornered hat,
And the breeches, and all that,
   Are so queer!

And if I should live to be
The last leaf upon the tree
   In the spring,
Let them smile, as I do now,
At the old forsaken bough
   Where I cling.

EDGAR ALLAN POE

(A) 1809 - 1849

ISRAFEL

And the angel Israfel, whose heart-strings are a lute and who has the sweetest voice of all God's creatures.—KORAN.

In Heaven a spirit doth dwell
  " Whose heart-strings are a lute ;"
None sing so wildly well
As the angel Israfel,
And the giddy stars (so legends tell)
Ceasing their hymns, attend the spell
  Of his voice, all mute.

Tottering above
  In her highest noon,
  The enamoured moon
Blushes with love,
  While, to listen, the red levin
  (With the rapid Pleiads, even,
  Which were seven)
  Pauses in Heaven.

And they say (the starry choir
  And the other listening things)
That Israfeli's fire
Is owing to that lyre
  By which he sits and sings—
The trembling living wire
  Of those unusual strings.

But the skies that angel trod,
  Where deep thoughts are a duty,
Where Love's a grown-up God,
  Where the Houri glances are
Imbued with all the beauty
  Which we worship in a star.

Therefore, thou art not wrong,
  Israfeli, who despisest
An unimpassioned song;
To thee the laurels belong,
  Best bard, because the wisest!
Merrily live, and long!

The ecstasies above
  With thy burning measures suit—
Thy grief, thy joy, thy hate, thy love,
  With the fervour of thy lute—
  Well may the stars be mute!

Yes, Heaven is thine; but this
  Is a world of sweets and sours;
  Our flowers are merely—flowers,
And the shadow of thy perfect bliss
  Is the sunshine of ours.

If I could dwell
Where Israfel
  Hath dwelt, and he where I,
He might not sing so wildly well
  A mortal melody,
While a bolder note than this might swell
  From my lyre within the sky.

TO HELEN

Helen, thy beauty is to me
  Like those Nicèan barks of yore,
That gently, o'er a perfumed sea,
  The weary, way-worn wanderer bore
  To his own native shore.

On desperate seas long wont to roam,
  Thy hyacinth hair, thy classic face,
Thy Naiad airs have brought me home
  To the glory that was Greece,
  And the grandeur that was Rome.

Lo! in yon brilliant window-niche
  How statue-like I see thee stand,
The agate lamp within thy hand!
  Ah, Psyche, from the regions which
  Are Holy-Land!

THE CITY IN THE SEA

Lo! Death has reared himself a throne
In a strange city lying alone
Far down within the dim West,
Where the good and the bad and the worst and the best
Have gone to their eternal rest.
There shrines and palaces and towers
(Time-eaten towers that tremble not!)
Resemble nothing that is ours.
Around, by lifting winds forgot,
Resignedly beneath the sky
The melancholy waters lie.

No rays from the holy heaven come down
On the long night-time of that town;
But light from out the lurid sea
Streams up the turrets silently—
Gleams up the pinnacles far and free—
Up domes—up spires—up kingly halls—
Up fanes—up Babylon-like walls—
Up shadowy long-forgotten bowers
Of sculptured ivy and stone flowers—
Up many and many a marvellous shrine
Whose wreathèd friezes intertwine
The viol, the violet, and the vine.

Resignedly beneath the sky
The melancholy waters lie.
So blend the turrets and shadows there
That all seem pendulous in air,
While from a proud tower in the town
Death looks gigantically down.

There open fanes and gaping graves
Yawn level with the luminous waves;
But not the riches there that lie
In each idol's diamond eye—
Not the gaily-jewelled dead
Tempt the waters from their bed;
For no ripples curl, alas!
Along that wilderness of glass—

No swellings tell that winds may be
Upon some far-off happier sea—
No heavings hint that winds have been
On seas less hideously serene.

But lo, a stir is in the air!
The wave—there is a movement there!
As if the towers had thrust aside,
In slightly sinking, the dull tide—
As if their tops had feebly given
A void within the filmy Heaven.

The waves have now a redder glow—
The hours are breathing faint and low—
And when, amid no earthly moans,
Down, down that town shall settle hence,
Hell, rising from a thousand thrones,
Shall do it reverence.

TO ONE IN PARADISE

Thou wast all that to me, love,
    For which my soul did pine—
A green isle in the sea, love,
    A fountain and a shrine,
All wreathed with fairy fruits and flowers,
    And all the flowers were mine.

Ah, dream too bright to last!
    Ah, starry Hope! that didst arise
But to be overcast!
    A voice from out the Future cries,
" On! on! "—but o'er the Past
    (Dim gulf!) my spirit hovering lies
Mute, motionless, aghast!

For, alas! alas! with me
    The light of Life is o'er!
" No more—no more—no more—"
    (Such language holds the solemn sea
To the sands upon the shore)
    Shall bloom the thunder-blasted tree,
Or the stricken eagle soar!

And all my days are trances,
   And all my nightly dreams
Are where thy grey eye glances,
   And where thy footstep gleams—
In what ethereal dances,
   By what eternal streams.

A DREAM WITHIN A DREAM

Take this kiss upon the brow!
And, in parting from you now,
Thus much let me avow—
You are not wrong, who deem
That my days have been a dream;
Yet if Hope has flown away
In a night, or in a day,
In a vision, or in none,
Is it therefore the less *gone?*
All that we see or seem
Is but a dream within a dream.

I stand amid the roar
Of a surf-tormented shore,
And I hold within my hand
Grains of the golden sand—
How few! yet how they creep
Through my fingers to the deep,
While I weep—while I weep!
O God! can I not grasp
Them with a tighter clasp?
O God! can I not save
One from the pitiless wave?
Is *all* that we see or seem
But a dream within a dream?

ANNABEL LEE

It was many and many a year ago,
   In a kingdom by the sea,
That a maiden there lived whom you may know
   By the name of Annabel Lee;—
And this maiden she lived with no other thought
   Than to love and be loved by me.

She was a child and I was a child,
　　In this kingdom by the sea,
But we loved with a love that was more than love—
　　I and my Annabel Lee—
With a love that the wingèd seraphs of Heaven
　　Coveted her and me.

And this was the reason that, long ago,
　　In this kingdom by the sea,
A wind blew out of a cloud by night
　　Chilling my Annabel Lee;
So that her highborn kinsmen came
　　And bore her away from me,
To shut her up in a sepulchre
　　In this kingdom by the sea.

The angels, not half so happy in Heaven,
　　Went envying her and me:
Yes! that was the reason (as all men know,
　　In this kingdom by the sea)
That the wind came out of the cloud, chilling
　　And killing my Annabel Lee.

But our love it was stronger by far than the love
　　Of those who were older than we—
　　Of many far wiser than we—
And neither the angels in heaven above
　　Nor the demons down under the sea,
Can ever dissever my soul from the soul
　　Of the beautiful Annabel Lee:—

For the moon never beams without bringing me dreams
　　Of the beautiful Annabel Lee;
And the stars never rise but I see the bright eyes
　　Of the beautiful Annabel Lee;
And so, all the night-tide, I lie down by the side
Of my darling, my darling, my life and my bride,
　　In her sepulchre there by the sea—
　　In her tomb by the sounding sea.

ROMANCE

Romance, who loves to nod and sing,
With drowsy head and folded wing,
Among the green leaves as they shake
Far down within some shadowy lake,

To me a painted paroquet
Hath been—a most familiar bird—
Taught me my alphabet to say—
To lisp my very earliest word
While in the wild wood I did lie,
A child—with a most knowing eye.

Of late, eternal condor years
So shake the very Heaven on high
With tumult as they thunder by,
I have no time for idle cares
Through gazing on the unquiet sky.
And when an hour with calmer wings
Its down upon my spirit flings—
That little time with lyre and rhyme
To while away—forbidden things!
My heart would feel to be a crime
Unless it trembled with the strings.

ALFRED, LORD TENNYSON

1809 - 1892

MARIANA

" Mariana in the moated grange."—*Measure for Measure*

With blackest moss the flower-plots
   Were thickly crusted, one and all:
The rusted nails fell from the knots
   That held the peach to the garden-wall.
The broken sheds looked sad and strange:
   Unlifted was the clinking latch;
   Weeded and worn the ancient thatch
Upon the lonely moated grange.
      She only said, " My life is dreary,
        He cometh not," she said;
      She said, " I am aweary, aweary,
        I would that I were dead! "

Her tears fell with the dews at even;
    Her tears fell ere the dews were dried;
She could not look on the sweet heaven,
    Either at morn or eventide.
After the flitting of the bats,
    When thickest dark did trance the sky,
She drew her casement-curtain by,
And glanced athwart the glooming flats.
      She only said, " The night is dreary,
        He cometh not," she said;
      She said, " I am aweary, aweary,
        I would that I were dead! "

Upon the middle of the night,
    Waking she heard the night-fowl crow:
The cock sung out an hour ere light:
    From the dark fen the oxen's low
Came to her: without hope of change,
    In sleep she seemed to walk forlorn,
Till cold winds woke the grey-eyed morn
About the lonely moated grange.
      She only said, " The day is dreary,
        He cometh not," she said;
      She said, " I am aweary, aweary,
        I would that I were dead! "

About a stone-cast from the wall
    A sluice with blackened waters slept,
And o'er it many, round and small,
    The clustered marish-mosses crept.
Hard by a poplar shook alway,
    All silver-green with gnarlèd bark:
For leagues no other tree did mark
The level waste, the rounding gray.
      She only said, " My life is dreary,
        He cometh not," she said;
      She said, " I am aweary, aweary,
        I would that I were dead! "

And ever when the moon was low,
    And the shrill winds were up and away,
In the white curtain, to and fro,
    She saw the gusty shadow sway.

But when the moon was very low,
   And wild winds bound within their cell,
   The shadow of the poplar fell
Upon her bed, across her brow.
      She only said, " The night is dreary,
         He cometh not," she said;
      She said, " I am aweary, aweary,
         I would that I were dead! "

All day within the dreamy house,
   The doors upon their hinges creaked;
The blue fly sung in the pane: the mouse
   Behind the mouldering wainscot shrieked,
Or from the crevice peered about.
      Old faces glimmered thro' the doors,
      Old footsteps trod the upper floors,
Old voices called her from without.
      She only said, " My life is dreary,
         He cometh not," she said;
      She said, " I am aweary, aweary,
         I would that I were dead! "

THE MILLER'S DAUGHTER

It is the miller's daughter,
   And she is grown so dear, so dear,
   That I would be the jewel
   That trembles at her ear:
For hid in ringlets day and night,
I'd touch her neck so warm and white.

And I would be the girdle
   About her dainty, dainty waist,
And her heart would beat against me,
   In sorrow and in rest:
And I should know if it beat right,
I'd clasp it round so close and tight.

And I would be the necklace,
   And all day long to fall and rise
Upon her balmy bosom,
   With her laughter or her sighs:
And I would lie so light, so light,
I scarce should be unclasped at night.

ULYSSES

It little profits that an idle king,
By this still hearth, among these barren crags,
Matched with an aged wife, I mete and dole
Unequal laws unto a savage race,
That hoard, and sleep, and feed, and know not me.
I cannot rest from travel: I will drink
Life to the lees: all times I have enjoyed
Greatly, have suffered greatly, both with those
That loved me, and alone; on shore, and when
Thro' scudding drifts the rainy Hyades
Vext the dim sea. I am become a name;
For always roaming with a hungry heart
Much have I seen and known: cities of men
And manners, climates, councils, governments,
Myself not least, but honoured of them all;
And drunk delight of battle with my peers,
Far on the ringing plains of windy Troy.
I am a part of all that I have met;
Yet all experience is an arch wherethro'
Gleams that untravelled world, whose margin fades
For ever and for ever when I move.
How dull it is to pause, to make an end,
To rust unburnished, not to shine in use!
As tho' to breathe were life. Life piled on life
Were all too little, and of one to me
Little remains: but every hour is saved
From that eternal silence, something more,
A bringer of new things; and vile it were
For some three suns to store and hoard myself,
And this grey spirit yearning in desire
To follow knowledge, like a sinking star,
Beyond the utmost bound of human thought.
    This is my son, mine own Telemachus,
To whom I leave the sceptre and the isle—
Well-loved of me, discerning to fulfil
This labour, by slow prudence to make mild
A rugged people, and thro' soft degrees
Subdue them to the useful and the good.
Most blameless is he, centred in the sphere
Of common duties, decent not to fail
In offices of tenderness, and pay

Meet adoration to my household gods,
When I am gone. He works his work, I mine.
    There lies the port: the vessel puffs her sail:
There gloom the dark broad seas. My mariners,
Souls that have toiled, and wrought, and thought with me—
That ever with a frolic welcome took
The thunder and the sunshine, and opposed
Free hearts, free foreheads—you and I are old;
Old age hath yet his honour and his toil;
Death closes all: but something ere the end,
Some work of noble note, may yet be done,
Not unbecoming men that strove with Gods.
The lights begin to twinkle from the rocks:
The long day wanes: the slow moon climbs: the deep
Moans round with many voices. Come, my friends,
'Tis not too late to seek a newer world.
Push off, and sitting well in order smite
The sounding furrows; for my purpose holds
To sail beyond the sunset, and the paths
Of all the western stars, until I die.
It may be that the gulfs will wash us down:
It may be we shall touch the Happy Isles,
And see the great Achilles, whom we knew.
Tho' much is taken, much abides; and tho'
We are not now that strength which in old days
Moved earth and heaven; that which we are, we are;
One equal temper of heroic hearts,
Made weak by time and fate, but strong in will
To strive, to seek, to find, and not to yield.

BREAK, BREAK, BREAK

Break, break, break,
    On thy cold grey stones, O Sea!
And I would that my tongue could utter
    The thoughts that arise in me.

O well for the fisherman's boy,
    That he shouts with his sister at play!
O well for the sailor lad,
    That he sings in his boat on the bay!

And the stately ships go on
  To their haven under the hill;
But O for the touch of a vanished hand,
  And the sound of a voice that is still!

Break, break, break,
  At the foot of thy crags, O Sea!
But the tender grace of a day that is dead
  Will never come back to me.

THE EAGLE

He clasps the crag with hookèd hands:
Close to the sun in lonely lands,
Ringed with the azure world, he stands.

The wrinkled sea beneath him crawls;
He watches from his mountain walls,
And like a thunderbolt he falls.

BLOW, BUGLE, BLOW

Song from " The Princess "

The splendour falls on castle walls
  And snowy summits old in story:
The long light shakes across the lakes
  And the wild cataract leaps in glory.
Blow, bugle, blow, set the wild echoes flying,
Blow, bugle; answer, echoes, dying, dying, dying.

O hark, O hear! how thin and clear,
  And thinner, clearer, farther going!
O sweet and far from cliff and scar
  The horns of Elfland faintly blowing!
Blow, let us hear the purple glens replying:
Blow, bugle; answer, echoes, dying, dying, dying.

O love, they die in yon rich sky,
  They faint on hill or field or river;
Our echoes roll from soul to soul,
  And grow for ever and for ever.
Blow, bugle, blow, set the wild echoes flying,
And answer, echoes, answer, dying, dying, dying.

NORTHERN FARMER

NEW STYLE

Dosn't thou 'ear my 'erse's legs, as they canters awaäy?
Proputty, proputty, proputty—that's what I 'ears 'em saäy.
Proputty, proputty, proputty—Sam, thou's an ass for thy paäins:
Theer's moor sense i' one o' 'is legs nor in all thy braäins.
Woä—theer's a craw to pluck wi' tha, Sam: yon's parson's
    'ouse—
Doesn't thou knaw that a man mun be eäther a man or a mouse?
Time to think on it then; for thou'll be twenty this weeäk.
Proputty, proputty—woä then, woä—let ma 'ear mysèn speäk.

Me an' thy muther, Sammy, 'as beän a-talkin' o' thee;
Thou's beän talkin' to muther, an' she beän a-tellin' it me.
Thou'll not marry for munny—thou's sweet upo' parson's lass—
Noä—thou'll marry fur luvv—an' we boäth on us thinks tha an
    ass!
Seeä'd her to-daäy goä by—Saäint's daäy—they was ringing the
    bells.
She's a beauty, thou thinks—an' soä is scoors o' gells!
Them as 'as munny an' all—wot's a beauty?—the flower as blaws.
But proputty, proputty, sticks, an' proputty, proputty graws.

Do'ant be stunt:[1] taäke time: I knaws what maäkes tha sa mad.
Warn't I craäzed fur the lasses mysèn when I wur a lad?
But I knaw'd a Quaäker feller as often 'as towd ma this:
" Doänt thou marry for munny, but goä wheer munny is! "

An' I went wheer munny war: an' thy mother coom to 'and,
Wi' lots o' munny laäid by, an' a nicetish bit o' land.
Maäybe she warn't a beauty:—I niver giv it a thowt—
But warn't she as good to cuddle an' kiss as a lass as 'ant nowt?
Parson's lass 'ant nowt, an' she weänt 'a nowt when 'e's deäd,
Mun be a guvness, lad, or summut, and addle[2] her breäd:
Why? fur 'e's nobbut a curate, an' weänt nivir git naw 'igher;
An' 'e maäd the bed as 'e ligs on afoor 'e coom'd to the shire. . . .

Luvv? what's luvv? thou can luvv thy lass an' 'er munny too.
Maäkin' 'em goä togither as they've good right to do.
Couldn' I luvv thy muther by cause o' 'er munny laäid by?
Naäy—fur I luvv'd her a vast sight moor fur it: reäson why.

          [1] Obstinate.   [2] Earn.

Ay an' thy muther says thou wants to marry the lass,
Cooms of a gentleman burn: an' we boäth on us thinks tha an ass.
Woä then, proputty, wiltha?—an ass as near as mays nowt—[1]
Woä then, wiltha? dangtha!—the bees is as fell as owt.[2]

Breäk me a bit o' the esh for his 'eäd, lad, out o' the fence!
Gentleman burn! what's gentleman burn? is it shillins an'
     pence?
Proputty, proputty's ivrything 'ere, an', Sammy, I'm blest
If it isn't the saäme oop yonder, fur them as 'as it's the best.

Tis'n them as 'as munny as breäks into 'ouses an' steäls,
Them 'as coäts to their backs an' taäkes their regular meals.
Noä, but it's them as niver knaws wheer a meäl's to be 'ad.
Taäke my word for it, Sammy, the poor in a loomp is bad.

Looök thou theer wheer Wrigglesby beck comes out by the 'ill!
Feyther run oop to the farm, an' I runs oop to the mill;
An' I'll run oop to the brig[3], an' that thou'll live to see;
And if thou marries a good un I'll leäve the land to thee.
Thim's my noätions, Sammy, wheerby I means to stick;
But if thou marries a bad un, I'll leäve the land to Dick.—
Coom oop, proputty, proputty—that's what I 'ears 'im saäy—
Proputty, proputty, proputty—canter an' canter awaäy.

TEARS, IDLE TEARS

Tears, idle tears, I know not what they mean,
Tears from the depth of some divine despair
Rise in the heart, and gather to the eyes,
In looking on the happy Autumn-fields,
And thinking of the days that are no more.

Fresh as the first beam glittering on a sail,
That brings our friends up from the underworld,
Sad as the last which reddens over one
That sinks with all we love below the verge;
So sad, so fresh, the days that are no more.

[1] Makes nothing.   [2] The flies are as fierce as anything.   [3] Bridge.

Ah, sad and strange as in dark summer dawns
The earliest pipe of half-awakened birds
To dying ears, when unto dying eyes
The casement slowly grows a glimmering square;
So sad, so strange, the days that are no more.

Dear as remembered kisses after death,
And sweet as those by hopeless fancy feigned
On lips that are for others; deep as love,
Deep as first love, and wild with all regret;
O Death in Life, the days that are no more.

A VOICE

from "Maud"

A voice by the cedar tree,
In the meadow under the Hall!
She is singing an air that is known to me,
A passionate ballad gallant and gay,
A martial song like a trumpet's call!

Singing alone in the morning of life,
In the happy morning of life and of May,
Singing of men that in battle array,
Ready in heart and ready in hand,
March with banner and bugle and fife
To the death, for their native land.

Maud with her exquisite face,
And wild voice pealing up to the sunny sky,
And feet like sunny gems on an English green,
Maud in the light of her youth and her grace,
Singing of Death, and of Honour that cannot die,
Till I well could weep for a time so sordid and mean,
And myself so languid and base.

Silence, beautiful voice!
Be still, for you only trouble the mind
With a joy in which I cannot rejoice.
A glory I shall not find.
Still! I will hear you no more,
For your sweetness hardly leaves me a choice
But to move to the meadow and fall before
Her feet on the meadow grass, and adore,
Not her, who is neither courtly nor kind,
Not her, not her, but a voice.

CROSSING THE BAR

Sunset and evening star,
  And one clear call for me!
And may there be no moaning of the bar,
  When I put out to sea,

But such a tide as moving seems asleep,
  Too full for sound and foam,
When that which drew from out the boundless deep
  Turns again home.

Twilight and evening bell,
  And after that the dark!
And may there be no sadness of farewell,
  When I embark;

For though from out our bourne of Time and Place
  The flood may bear me far,
I hope to see my Pilot face to face
  When I have crossed the bar.

ROBERT BROWNING

1812 - 1889

"THE WILD JOYS OF LIVING"

David's Song from "Saul"

Oh, our manhood's prime vigour! No spirit feels waste,
Not a muscle is stopped in its playing, nor sinew unbraced.
Oh, the wild joys of living! the leaping from rock up to rock—
The strong rending of boughs from the fir-tree,—the cool silver
  shock
Of the plunge in a pool's living water,—the hunt of the bear,
And the sultriness showing the lion is couched in his lair.
And the meal—the rich dates—yellowed over with gold dust
  divine,
And the locust's-flesh steeped in the pitcher; the full draught of
  wine,
And the sleep in the dried river-channel where bulrushes tell
That the water was wont to go warbling so softly and well.

How good is man's life, the mere living! how fit to employ
All the heart and the soul and the senses, for ever in joy!
Hast thou loved the white locks of thy father, whose sword thou
    didst guard
When he trusted thee forth with the armies, for glorious reward?
Didst thou see the thin hands of thy mother, held up as men sung
The low song of the nearly-departed, and heard her faint tongue
Joining in while it could to the witness, " Let one more attest,
I have lived, seen God's hand thro' a lifetime, and all was for
    best . . ."
Then they sung thro' their tears in strong triumph, not much,—
    but the rest.
And thy brothers, the help and the contest, the working whence
    grew
Such result as from seething grape-bundles, the spirit strained
    true!
And the friends of thy boyhood—that boyhood of wonder and
    hope,
Present promise, and wealth of the future beyond the eye's scope,—
Till lo, thou art grown to a monarch; a people is thine;
And all gifts which the world offers singly, on one head combine!
On one head, all the beauty and strength, love and rage, like the
    throe
That, a-work in the rock, helps its labour, and lets the gold go:
High ambition and deeds which surpass it, fame crowning
    them—all
Brought to blaze on the head of one creature—King Saul!

IN A GONDOLA

The moth's kiss, first!
Kiss me as if you made believe
You were not sure, this eve,
How my face, your flower, had pursed
Its petals up; so, here and there
You brush it, till I grow aware
Who wants me, and wide open burst.

The bee's kiss, now!
Kiss me as if you entered gay
My heart at some noonday,
A bud that dares not disallow
The claim, so all is rendered up,
And passively its shattered cup
Over your head to sleep I bow.

SOLILOQUY OF THE SPANISH CLOISTER

Gr-r-r—there go, my heart's abhorrence!
  Water your damned flower-pots, do!
If hate killed men, Brother Lawrence,
  God's blood, would not mine kill you!
What? your myrtle-bush wants trimming?
  Oh, that rose has prior claims—
Needs its leaden vase filled brimming?
  Hell dry you up with its flames!

At the meal we sit together;
  Salve tibi! I must hear
Wise talk of the kind of weather,
  Sort of season, time of year:
Not a plenteous cork-crop: scarcely
  Dare we hope oak-galls, I doubt:
What's the Latin name for " parsley "?
  What's the Greek name for Swine's Snout?

Whew! We'll have our platter burnished,
  Laid with care on our own shelf!
With a fire-new spoon we're furnished,
  And a goblet for ourself,
Rinsed like something sacrificial
  Ere 'tis fit to touch our chaps—
Marked with L. for our initial!
  (He-he! There his lily snaps!)

Saint, forsooth! While brown Dolores
  Squats outside the Convent bank
With Sanchicha, telling stories,
  Steeping tresses in the tank,
Blue-black, lustrous, thick like horsehairs,
  —Can't I see his dead eye glow;
Bright as 'twere a Barbary corsair's?
  (That is, if he'd let it show!)

When he finishes refection,
  Knife and fork he never lays
Cross-wise, to my recollection,
  As do I, in Jesu's praise.

I, the Trinity illustrate,
  Drinking watered orange-pulp—
In three sips the Arian frustrate;
  While he drains his at one gulp!

Oh, those melons! If he's able
  We're to have a feast; so nice!
One goes to the Abbot's table,
  All of us get each a slice.
How go on your flowers? None double?
  Not one fruit-sort can you spy?
Strange!—And I, too, at such trouble,
  Keep them close-nipped on the sly!

There's a great text in Galatians,
  Once you trip on it, entails
Twenty-nine distinct damnations,
  One sure, if another fails;
If I trip him just a-dying,
  Sure of heaven as sure can be,
Spin him round and send him flying
  Off to hell, a Manichee?

Or, my scrofulous French novel
  On grey paper with blunt type!
Simply glance at it, you grovel
  Hand and foot in Belial's gripe;
If I double down its pages
  At the woeful sixteenth print,
When he gathers his greengages,
  Ope a sieve and slip it in't?

Or, there's Satan!—One might venture
  Pledge one's soul to him, yet leave
Such a flaw in the indenture
  As he'd miss, till, past retrieve,
Blasted lay that rose-acacia
  We're so proud of. *Hy, Zy, Hine* . . .
'st! There's Vespers! *Plena gratia
  Ave, Virgo.* Gr-r-r—you swine!

TWO IN THE CAMPAGNA

I wonder do you feel to-day
   As I have felt since, hand in hand,
We sat down on the grass, to stray
   In spirit better through the land,
This morn of Rome and May?

For me, I touched a thought, I know,
   Has tantalized me many times,
(Like turns of thread the spiders throw
   Mocking across our path) for rhymes
To catch at and let go.

Help me to hold it! First it left
   The yellowing fennel, run to seed
There, branching from the brickwork's cleft,
   Some old tomb's ruin; yonder weed
Took up the floating weft,

Where one small orange cup amassed
   Five beetles—blind and green they grope
Among the honey-meal; and last,
   Everywhere on the grassy slope
I traced it. Hold it fast!

The champaign with its endless fleece
   Of feathery grasses everywhere!
Silence and passion, joy and peace,
   An everlasting wash of air—
Rome's ghost since her decease.

Such life here, through such length of hours,
   Such miracles performed in play,
Such primal naked forms of flowers,
   Such letting Nature have her way
While Heaven looks from its towers!

How say you? Let us, O my dove,
   Let us be unashamed of soul,
As earth lies bare to heaven above!
   How is it under our control
To love or not to love?

I would that you were all to me,
  You that are just so much, no more,
Nor yours, nor mine, nor slave nor free!
  Where does the fault lie? What the core
Of the wound, since wound must be?

I would I could adopt your will,
  See with your eyes, and set my heart
Beating by yours, and drink my fill
  At your soul's springs—your part, my part
In life, for good and ill.

No. I yearn upward—touch you close,
  Then stand away. I kiss your cheek,
Catch your soul's warmth; I pluck the rose
  And love it more than tongue can speak—
Then the good minute goes.

Already how am I so far
  Out of that minute? Must I go
Still like the thistle-ball, no bar,
  Onward, whenever light winds blow,
Fixed by no friendly star?

Just when I seemed about to learn!
  Where is the thread now? Off again!
The old trick! Only I discern
  Infinite passion and the pain
Of finite hearts that yearn.

MY LAST DUCHESS

SCENE : FERRARA

That's my last Duchess painted on the wall,
Looking as if she were alive. I call
That piece a wonder, now: Fra Pandolf's hands
Worked busily a day, and there she stands.
Will't please you sit and look at her? I said
" Fra Pandolf " by design, for never read
Strangers like you that pictured countenance,
The depth and passion of its earnest glance,
But to myself they turned (since none puts by
The curtain I have drawn for you, but I)
And seemed as they would ask me, if they durst,
How such a glance came there; so, not the first

Are you to turn and ask thus. Sir, 'twas not
Her husband's presence only, called that spot
Of joy into the Duchess' cheek: perhaps
Fra Pandolf chanced to say " Her mantle laps
Over my Lady's wrist too much," or " Paint
Must never hope to reproduce the faint
Half-flush that dies along her throat "; such stuff
Was courtesy, she thought, and cause enough
For calling up that spot of joy. She had
A heart . . . how shall I say? . . . too soon made glad,
Too easily impressed; she liked whate'er
She looked on, and her looks went everywhere.
Sir, 'twas all one! My favour at her breast,
The drooping of the daylight in the West,
The bough of cherries some officious fool
Broke in the orchard for her, the white mule
She rode with round the terrace—all and each
Would draw from her alike the approving speech,
Or blush, at least. She thanked men,—good; but thanked
Somehow . . . I know not how . . . as if she ranked
My gift of a nine hundred years old name
With anybody's gift. Who'd stoop to blame
This sort of trifling? Even had you skill
In speech—(which I have not)—to make your will
Quite clear to such an one, and say " Just this
Or that in you disgusts me; here you miss,
Or there exceed the mark "—and if she let
Herself be lessoned so, nor plainly set
Her wits to yours, forsooth, and made excuse,
—E'en then would be some stooping, and I choose
Never to stoop. Oh, Sir, she smiled, no doubt,
Whene'er I passed her; but who passed without
Much the same smile? This grew; I gave commands;
Then all smiles stopped together. There she stands
As if alive. Will't please you rise? We'll meet
The company below, then. I repeat,
The Count your Master's known munificence
Is ample warrant that no just pretence
Of mine for dowry will be disallowed;
Though his fair daughter's self, as I avowed
At starting, is my object. Nay, we'll go
Together down, Sir! Notice Neptune, tho',
Taming a sea-horse, thought a rarity,
Which Claus of Innsbruck cast in bronze for me.

AMONG THE ROCKS

Oh, good gigantic smile o' the brown old earth,
   This autumn morning! How he sets his bones
To bask i' the sun, and thrusts out knees and feet
For the ripple to run over in its mirth;
   Listening the while, where on the heap of stones
The white breast of the sea-lark twitters sweet.

That is the doctrine, simple, ancient, true;
   Such is life's trial, as old earth smiles and knows.
If you loved only what were worth your love,
Love were clear gain, and wholly well for you:
   Make the low nature better by your throes!
Give earth yourself, go up for gain above.

A CAVALIER TUNE

King Charles, and who'll do him right now?
King Charles, and who's ripe for fight now?
Give a rouse: here's, in Hell's despite now,
King Charles!

Who gave me the goods that went since?
Who raised me the house that sank once?
Who helped me to gold I spent since?
Who found me in wine you drank once?

   (Cho.) *King Charles, and who'll do him right now?*
        King Charles, and who's ripe for fight now?
        Give a rouse: here's, in Hell's despite now,
        King Charles!

To whom used my boy George quaff else,
By the old fool's side that begot him?
For whom did he cheer and laugh else,
While Noll's damned troopers shot him?

   (Cho.) *King Charles, and who'll do him right now?*
        King Charles, and who's ripe for fight now?
        Give a rouse: here's, in Hell's despite now,
        King Charles!

HOME-THOUGHTS, FROM ABROAD

Oh, to be in England
Now that April's there,
And whoever wakes in England
Sees, some morning, unaware,
That the lowest boughs and the brush-wood sheaf
Round the elm-tree bole are in tiny leaf,
While the chaffinch sings on the orchard bough
In England—now!

And after April, when May follows,
And the whitethroat builds, and all the swallows—
Hark! where my blossomed pear-tree in the hedge
Leans to the field and scatters on the clover
Blossoms and dewdrops—at the bent-spray's edge—
That's the wise thrush; he sings each song twice over,
Lest you should think he never could recapture
The first fine careless rapture!
And though the fields look rough with hoary dew,
All will be gay when noontide wakes anew
The buttercups, the little children's dower,
—Far brighter than this gaudy melon-flower!

SONG

Nay, but you, who do not love her,
    Is she not pure gold, my mistress?
Holds earth aught—speak truth—above her?
    Aught like this tress, see, and this tress,
And this last fairest tress of all,
So fair, see, ere I let it fall!

Because, you spend your lives in praising;
    To praise, you search the wide world over;
So, why not witness, calmly gazing,
    If earth holds aught—speak truth—above her?
Above this tress, and this I touch
But cannot praise, I love so much!

THE LABORATORY

ANCIEN RÈGIME

Now that I, tying thy glass mask tightly,
May gaze thro' these faint smokes curling whitely,
As thou pliest thy trade in this devil's-smithy—
Which is the poison to poison her, prithee?

He is with her; and they know that I know
Where they are, what they do: they believe my tears flow
While they laugh, laugh at me, at me fled to the drear
Empty church, to pray God in, for them!—I am here.

Grind away, moisten and mash up thy paste,
Pound at thy powder,—I am not in haste!
Better sit thus, and observe thy strange things,
Than go where men wait me and dance at the King's.

That in the mortar—you call it a gum?
Ah, the brave tree whence such gold oozings come!
And yonder soft phial, the exquisite blue
Sure to taste sweetly,—is that poison too?

Had I but all of them, thee and thy treasures,
What a wild crowd of invisible pleasures!
To carry pure death in an earring, a casket,
A signet, a fan-mount, a filagree-basket!

Soon, at the King's, a mere lozenge to give
And Pauline should have just thirty minutes to live!
But to light a pastille, and Elise, with her head,
And her breast, and her arms, and her hands, should drop
    dead!

Quick—is it finished? The colour's too grim!
Why not soft like the phial's, enticing and dim?
Let it brighten her drink, let her turn it and stir,
And try it and taste, ere she fix and prefer!

What a drop! She's not little, no minion like me—
That's why she ensnared him: this never will free
The soul from those masculine eyes,—say, " no! "
To that pulse's magnificent come-and-go.

For only last night, as they whispered, I brought
My own eyes to bear on her so, that I thought
Could I keep them one half minute fixed, she would fall,
Shrivelled; she fell not; yet this does it all!

Not that I bid you spare her the pain!
Let death be felt and the proof remain;
Brand, burn up, bite into its grace—
He is sure to remember her dying face!

Is it done? Take my mask off! Nay, be not morose,
It kills her, and this prevents seeing it close:
The delicate droplet, my whole fortune's fee—
If it hurts her, beside, can it ever hurt me?

Now, take all my jewels, gorge gold to your fill,
You may kiss me, old man, on my mouth if you will!
But brush this dust off me, lest horror it brings
Ere I know it—next moment I dance at the King's!

MEETING AT NIGHT

The grey sea and the long black land;
And the yellow half-moon large and low;
And the startled little waves that leap
In fiery ringlets from their sleep,
As I gain the cove with pushing prow,
And quench its speed in the slushy sand.

Then a mile of warm sea-scented beach;
Three fields to cross till a farm appears;
A tap at the pane, the quick sharp scratch
And blue spurt of a lighted match,
And a voice less loud, thro' its joys and fears,
Than the two hearts beating each to each!

EVELYN HOPE

Beautiful Evelyn Hope is dead!
  Sit and watch by her side an hour.
That is her book-shelf, this her bed;
  She plucked that piece of geranium-flower,

Beginning to die, too, in the glass.
    Little has yet been changed, I think—
The shutters are shut, no light may pass
    Save two long rays thro' the hinge's chink.

Sixteen years old when she died!
    Perhaps she had scarcely heard my name—
It was not her time to love: beside,
    Her life had many a hope and aim,
Duties enough and little cares,
    And now was quiet, now astir—
Till God's hand beckoned unawares,
    And the sweet white brow is all of her.

Is it too late then, Evelyn Hope?
    What, your soul was pure and true,
The good stars met in your horoscope,
    Made you of spirit, fire and dew—
And just because I was thrice as old,
    And our paths in the world diverged so wide,
Each was nought to each, must I be told?
    We were fellow mortals, nought beside?

No, indeed! for God above
    Is great to grant, as mighty to make,
And creates the love to reward the love,—
    I claim you still, for my own love's sake!
Delayed it may be for more lives yet,
    Through worlds I shall traverse, not a few—
Much is to learn and much to forget
    Ere the time be come for taking you.

But the time will come,—at last it will
    When, Evelyn Hope, what meant, I shall say,
In the lower earth, in the years long still,
    That body and soul so pure and gay?
Why your hair was amber, I shall divine,
    And your mouth of your own geranium's red—
And what you would do with me, in fine,
    In the new life come in the old one's stead.

I have lived, I shall say, so much since then,
    Given up myself so many times,
Gained me the gains of various men,
    Ransacked the ages, spoiled the climes;

Yet one thing, one, in my soul's full scope,
    Either I missed or itself missed me—
And I want and find you, Evelyn Hope!
    What is the issue? let us see!

I loved you, Evelyn, all the while;
    My heart seemed full as it could hold—
There was place and to spare for the frank young smile
    And the red young mouth and the hair's young gold.
So, hush—I will give you this leaf to keep—
    See, I shut it inside the sweet cold hand.
There, that is our secret! go to sleep;
    You will wake, and remember, and understand.

AFTER

Take the cloak from his face, and at first
    Let the corpse do its worst.

How he lies in his rights of a man!
    Death has done all death can.
And absorbed in the new life he leads,
    He recks not, he heeds
Nor his wrong nor my vengeance—both strike
    On his senses alike,
And are lost in the solemn and strange
    Surprise of the change.

Ha, what avails death to erase
    His offence, my disgrace?
I would we were boys as of old
    In the field, by the fold—
His outrage, God's patience, man's scorn
    Were so easily borne.

I stand here now, he lies in his place—
    Cover the face.

PROSPICE

Fear death?—to feel the fog in my throat,
    The mist in my face,
When the snows begin, and the blasts denote
    I am nearing the place,

The power of the night, the press of the storm,
    The post of the foe;
Where he stands, the Arch Fear in a visible form,
    Yet the strong man must go:
For the journey is done and the summit attained,
    And the barriers fall,
Though a battle's to fight ere the guerdon be gained,
    The reward of it all.
I was ever a fighter, so—one fight more,
    The best and the last!
I would hate that death bandaged my eyes, and forbore,
    And bade me creep past,
No! let me taste the whole of it, fare like my peers
    The heroes of old,
Bear the brunt, in a minute pay glad life's arrears
    Of pain, darkness and cold.
For sudden the worst turns the best to the brave,
    The black minute's at end,
And the elements' rage, the fiend-voices that rave,
    Shall dwindle, shall blend,
Shall change, shall become first a peace out of pain,
    Then a light, then thy breast,
O thou soul of my soul! I shall clasp thee again,
    And with God be the rest!

EMILY BRONTË

1818 - 1848

THE OLD STOIC

Riches I hold in light esteem,
And love I laugh to scorn;
And lust of fame was but a dream,
That vanished with the morn:

And if I pray, the only prayer
That moves my lips for me
Is, " Leave the heart that now I bear,
And give me liberty! "

Yes, as my swift days near their goal,
'Tis all that I implore;
In life and death a chainless soul,
With courage to endure.

OH, FOR THE TIME WHEN I SHALL SLEEP

Oh, for the time when I shall sleep
Without identity,
And never care how rain may steep,
Or snow may cover me!
No promised heaven, these wild desires
Could all, or half fulfil;
No threatened hell, with quenchless fires,
Subdue this quenchless will!

So said I, and still say the same;
Still, to my death, will say—
Three gods, within this little frame,
Are warring night and day;
Heaven could not hold them all, and yet
They all are held in me;
And must be mine till I forget
My present entity!

Oh, for the time, when in my breast
Their struggles will be o'er!
Oh, for the day when I shall rest,
And never suffer more!

LAST LINES

No coward soul is mine,
No trembler in the world's storm-troubled sphere:
I see Heaven's glories shine,
And faith shines equal, arming me from fear.

O God within my breast,
Almighty, ever-present Deity!
Life—that in me hast rest,
As I—undying Life—have power in thee!

Vain are the thousand creeds
That move men's hearts: unalterably vain;
Worthless as withered weeds,
Or idlest froth amid the boundless main,

To waken doubt in one
Holding so fast by thine infinity;
So surely anchored on
The steadfast rock of immortality.

With wide-embracing love
Thy spirit animates eternal years,
Pervades and broods above;
Changes, sustains, dissolves, creates, and rears.

Though earth and man were gone,
And suns and universes ceased to be,
And Thou wert left alone,
Every existence would exist in Thee.

There is not room for Death,
Nor atom that his might could render void:
Thou—Thou art being and breath,
And what Thou art may never be destroyed.

JAMES RUSSELL LOWELL

(A) 1819 - 1891

PRELUDE

from " The Vision of Sir Launfal "

Not only around our infancy
Doth heaven with all its splendours lie;[1]
Daily, with souls that cringe and plot,
We Sinais climb and know it not.

Over our manhood bend the skies;
Against our fallen and traitor lives
The great winds utter prophecies;
With our faint hearts the mountain strives;
Its arms outstretched, the druid wood
Waits with its benedicite;
And to our age's drowsy blood
Still shouts the inspiring sea.

[1] Lowell here refers to a line in Wordsworth's Ode " Intimations of Immortality " on page 317.

Earth gets its price for what Earth gives us;
   The beggar is taxed for a corner to die in,
The priest hath his fee who comes and shrives us,
   We bargain for the graves we lie in;
At the devil's booth are all things sold,
Each ounce of dross costs its ounce of gold;
   For a cap and bells our lives we pay,
Bubbles we buy with a whole soul's tasking:
   'Tis heaven alone that is given away,
'Tis odly God may be had for the asking;
No price is set on the lavish summer;
June may be had by the poorest comer.

And what is so rare as a day in June?
   Then, if ever, come perfect days;
Then Heaven tries earth if it be in tune,
   And over it softly her warm ear lays:
Whether we look, or whether we listen,
We hear life murmur, or see it glisten;

Every clod feels a stir of might,
   An instinct within it that reaches and towers,
And, groping blindly above it for light,
   Climbs to a soul in grass and flowers;
The flush of life may well be seen
   Thrilling back over hills and valleys;
The cowslip startles in meadows green,
   The buttercup catches the sun in its chalice,
And there's never a leaf nor a blade too mean
   To be some happy creature's palace.

AUSPEX

My heart, I cannot still it,
Nest that had song-birds in it;
And when the last shall go,
The dreary days, to fill it,
Instead of lark or linnet,
Shall whirl dead leaves and snow.

Had they been swallows only,
Without the passion stronger
That skyward longs and sings,—
Woe's me, I shall be lonely
When I can feel no longer
The impatience of their wings!

A moment, sweet delusion,
Like birds the brown leaves hover;
But it will not be long
Before their wild confusion
Fall wavering down to cover
The poet and his song.

WALT WHITMAN

(A) 1819 - 1892

WHEN I HEARD THE LEARN'D ASTRONOMER

When I heard the learn'd astronomer,
When the proofs, the figures, were ranged in columns before me,
When I was shown the charts and diagrams, to add, divide, and
    measure them,
When I sitting heard the astronomer where he lectured with much
    applause in the lecture-room,
How soon unaccountable I became tired and sick,
Till rising and gliding out I wandered off by myself,
In the mystical moist night-air, and from time to time,
Looked up in perfect silence at the stars.

SONG OF MYSELF

(*Selections*)

A child said, *What is the grass?* fetching it to me with full hands;
How could I answer the child? I do not know what it is any
    more than he.

I guess it must be the flag of my disposition, out of hopeful green
    stuff woven.

Or I guess it is the handkerchief of the Lord,
A scented gift and remembrancer designedly dropt,
Bearing the owner's name someway in the corners, that we may
    see and remark, and say *Whose?*

Or I guess the grass is itself a child, the produced babe of the
    vegetation.

Or I guess it is a uniform hieroglyphic,
And it means, Sprouting alike in broad zones and narrow zones,

Growing among black folks as among white,
Kanuck, Tuckahoe, Congressman, Cuff, I give them the same,
    I receive them the same.

And now it seems to me the beautiful uncut hair of graves.

Tenderly will I use you curling grass,
It may be you transpire from the breasts of young men,
It may be if I had known them I would have loved them,
It may be you are from old people, or from offspring taken soon
    out of their mothers' laps,
And here you are the mothers' laps.

This grass is very dark to be from the white heads of old mothers,
Darker than the colourless beards of old men,
Dark to come from under the faint red roofs of mouths.
O I perceive after all so many uttering tongues,
And I perceive they do not come from the roofs of mouths for
    nothing.

I wish I could translate the hints about the dead young men and
    women,
And the hints about old men and mothers and the offspring taken
    soon out of their laps.

What do you think has become of the young and old men?
And what do you think has become of the women and children?

They are alive and well somewhere,
The smallest sprout shows there is really no death,
And if ever there was it led forward life, and does not wait at the
    end to arrest it,
And ceased the moment life appeared.

All goes onward and outward, nothing collapses,
And to die is different from what any one supposed, and luckier.

      •   •   •   •   •

With music strong I come, with my cornets and my drums,
I play not marches for accepted victors only, I play marches for
    conquered and slain persons.

Have you heard that it was good to gain the day?
I also say it is good to fall, battles are lost in the same spirit in
    which they are won.

I beat and pound for the dead,
I blow through my embouchures my loudest and gayest for them.

Vivas to those who have failed!
And to those whose war-vessels sank in the sea!
And to those themselves who sank in the sea!
And to all generals that lost engagements, and all overcome
heroes!
And the numberless unknown heroes equal to the greatest heroes
known!

. . . . .

I believe a leaf of grass is no less than the journey-work of the stars,
And the pismire is equally perfect, and a grain of sand, and the
egg of the wren,
And the tree-toad is a chef-d'œuvre for the highest,
And the running blackberry would adorn the parlours of heaven,
And the narrowest hinge in my hand puts to scorn all machinery,
And the cow crunching with depressed head surpasses any statue,
And a mouse is miracle enough to stagger sextillions of infidels.

. . . . .

Press close, bare-bosomed night—press close magnetic nourishing
night!
Night of south winds—night of the large few stars—
Still nodding night—mad naked summer night.
Smile, O voluptuous cool-breathed earth!
Earth of the slumbering and liquid trees!
Earth of departed sunset—earth of the mountains misty-topt!
Earth of the vitreous pour of the full moon just tinged with blue!
Earth of shine and dark mottling the tide of the river!
Earth of the limpid grey of clouds brighter and clearer for my
sake!

Far-swooping elbowed earth—rich apple-blossomed earth!
Smile, for your lover comes.

. . . . .

I think I could turn and live with animals, they are so placid and
self-contained,
I stand and look at them long and long.

They do not sweat and whine about their condition,
They do not lie awake in the dark and weep for their sins,
They do not make me sick discussing their duty to God,

Not one is dissatisfied, not one is demented with the mania of
  owning things,
Not one kneels to another, nor to his kind that lived thousands of
  years ago,
Not one is respectable or unhappy over the whole earth.

          o   o   o   •   •

I have said that the soul is not more than the body,
And I have said that the body is not more than the soul,
And nothing, not God, is greater to one than one's self is,
And whoever walks a furlong without sympathy walks to his own
  funeral drest in his shroud,
And I or you pocketless of a dime may purchase the pick of the
  earth.
And to glance with an eye or show a bean in its pod confounds
  the learning of all times,
And there is no trade or employment but the young man following
  it may become a hero,
And there is no object so soft but it makes a hub for the wheeled
  universe,
And I say to any man or woman, Let your soul stand cool and
  composed before a million universes.
And I say to mankind, Be not curious about God,
For I who am curious about each am not curious about God
(No array of terms can say how much I am at peace about God
and about death).

I hear and behold God in every object, yet understand God not
  in the least,
Nor do I understand who there can be more wonderful than
  myself.

Why should I wish to see God better than this day?
I see something of God each hour of the twenty-four, and each
  moment then,
In the faces of men and women I see God, and in my own face in
  the glass,
I find letters from God dropt in the street and every one is signed
  by God's name,
And I leave them where they are, for I know that wheresoe'er
  I go,
Others will punctually come for ever and ever.

ON THE BEACH AT NIGHT

On the beach at night,
Stands a child with her father,
Watching the east, the autumn sky.

Up through the darkness,
While ravening clouds, the burial clouds, in black masses spread-
    ing,
Lower sullen and fast athwart and down the sky,
Amid a transparent clear belt of ether yet left in the east,
Ascends large and calm the lord-star Jupiter,
And nigh at hand, only a very little above,
Swim the delicate sisters the Pleiades.
From the beach the child holding the hand of her father,
Those burial-clouds that lower victorious soon to devour all,
Watching, silently weeps.
Weep not, child,
Weep not, my darling,
With these kisses let me remove your tears,
The ravening clouds shall not long be victorious,
They shall not long possess the sky, they devour the stars only in
    apparition,
Jupiter shall emerge, be patient, watch again another night, the
    Pleiades shall emerge,
They are immortal, all those stars both silvery and golden shall
    shine out again,
The great stars and the little ones shall shine out again, they
    endure.
The vast immortal suns and the long-enduring pensive moons
    shall again shine.

Then, dearest child, mournest thou only for Jupiter?
Considerest thou alone the burial of the stars?

Something there is,
(With my lips soothing thee, adding I whisper,
I give thee the first suggestion, the problem and indirection),
Something there is more immortal even than the stars,
(Many the burials, many the days and nights passing away),
Something that shall endure longer even than lustrous Jupiter,
Longer than sun or any revolving satellite,
Or the radiant sisters the Pleiades.

DIRGE FOR TWO VETERANS

The last sunbeam
Lightly falls from the finished Sabbath,
On the pavement here, and there beyond it is looking
      Down a new-made double grave.

Lo, the moon ascending,
Up from the east the silvery round moon,
Beautiful over the house-tops ghastly, phantom moon
      Immense and silent moon.

I see a sad procession,
And I hear the sound of coming full-keyed bugles,
All the channels of the city streets they're flooding,
      As with voices and with tears.

I hear the great drums pounding,
And the small drums steady whirring,
And every blow of the great convulsive drums,
      Strikes me through and through.

For the son is brought with the father,
(In the foremost ranks of the fierce assault they fell,
Two veterans son and father dropt together,
      And the double grave awaits them.)

Now nearer blow the bugles,
And the drums strike more convulsive,
And the daylight o'er the pavement quite has faded,
      And the strong dead-march enwraps me.

In the eastern sky up-buoying,
The sorrowful vast phantom moves illumined,
('Tis some mother's large transparent face,
      In heaven brighter growing.)

O strong dead-march you please me!
O moon immense with your silvery face you soothe me!
O my soldiers twain! O my veterans passing to burial!
      What I have I also give you.

The moon gives you light,
And the bugles and the drums give you music,
And my heart, O my soldiers, my veterans,
    My heart gives you love.

GIVE ME THE SPLENDID SILENT SUN

Give me the splendid silent sun with all his beams full-dazzling,
Give me juicy autumnal fruit ripe and red from the orchard,
Give me a field where the unmowed grass grows,
Give me an arbour, give me the trellised grape,
Give me fresh corn and wheat, give me serene-moving animals
    teaching content,
Give me nights perfectly quiet as on high plateaus west of the
    Mississippi, and I looking up at the stars,
Give me odorous at sunrise a garden of beautiful flowers where I
    can walk undisturbed,
Give me for marriage a sweet-breathed woman of whom I should
    never tire,
Give me a perfect child, give me away aside from the noise of the
    world a rural domestic life,
Give me to warble spontaneous songs recluse by myself, for my
    own ears only,
Give me solitude, give me Nature, give me again, O Nature,
    your primal sanities!

DEATH CAROL

from " When Lilacs Last in the Dooryard Bloomed "

Come lovely and soothing death,
Undulate round the world, serenely arriving, arriving,
In the day, in the night, to all, to each,
Sooner or later delicate death.

Praised be the fathomless universe,
For life and joy, and for objects and knowledge curious,
And for love, sweet love—but praise! praise! praise!
For the sure-enwinding arms of cool-enfolding death.

Dark mother always gliding near with soft feet,
Have none chanted for thee a chant of fullest welcome?
Then I chant it for thee, I glorify thee above all,
I bring thee a song that when thou must indeed come, come
    unfalteringly.

Approach strong deliveress,
When it is so, when thou hast taken them I joyously sing the dead,
Lost in the loving floating ocean of thee,
Laved in the flood of thy bliss, O death.

From me to thee glad serenades,
Dances for thee I propose saluting thee, adornments and feastings
     for thee,
And the sights of the open landscape and the high-spread sky are
     fitting,
And life and the fields, and the huge and thoughtful night.

The night in silence under many a star,
The ocean shore and the husky whispering wave whose voice I
     know,
And the soul turning to thee, O vast and well-veiled death,
And the body gratefully nestling close to thee.

Over the tree-tops I float thee a song,
Over the rising and sinking waves, over the myriad fields and the
     prairies wide,
Over the dense-packed cities all and the teeming wharves
     and ways,
I float this carol with joy, with joy to thee, O death.

RECONCILIATION

Word over all, beautiful as the sky,
Beautiful that war and all its deeds of carnage must in time be
     utterly lost,
That the hands of the sisters Death and Night incessantly softly
     wash again, and ever again, this soiled world;
For my enemy is dead, a man divine as myself is dead,
I look where he lies white-faced and still in the coffin—I draw
     near,
Bend down and touch lightly with my lips the white face in the
     coffin.

THE LAST INVOCATION

At the last, tenderly,
From the walls of the powerful fortressed house,
From the clasp of the knitted locks, from the keep of the well-
     closed doors,
Let me be wafted.

Let me glide noiselessly forth;
With the key of softness unlock the locks—with a whisper,
Set ope the doors O soul.

Tenderly—be not impatient,
(Strong is your hold O mortal flesh.
Strong is your hold O love).

MATTHEW ARNOLD

1822 - 1888

PHILOMELA

Hark, ah, the nightingale—
The tawny-throated!
Hark, from that moonlit cedar what a burst!
What triumph! hark!—what pain!

O wanderer from a Grecian shore,
Still, after many years, in distant lands,
Still nourishing in thy bewildered brain
That wild, unquenched, deep-sunken old-world pain—
Say, will it never heal?
And can this fragrant lawn
With its cool trees, and night,
And the sweet, tranquil Thames,
And moonshine, and the dew,
To thy racked heart and brain
Afford no balm?

Dost thou to-night behold,
Here, through the moonlight on this English grass,
The unfriendly palace in the Thracian wild?
Dost thou again peruse
With hot cheeks and seared eyes
The too clear web, and thy dumb sister's shame?
Dost thou once more assay
Thy flight, and feel come over thee,
Poor fugitive, the feathery change
Once more, and once more seem to make resound
With love and hate, triumph and agony,
Lone Daulis, and the high Cephissian vale?
Listen, Eugenia—

How thick the bursts come crowding through the leaves!
Again—thou hearest?
Eternal passion!
Eternal pain!

REQUIESCAT

Strew on her roses, roses,
   And never a spray of yew!
In quiet she reposes;
   Ah, would that I did too!

Her mirth the world required;
   She bathed it in smiles of glee.
But her heart was tired, tired,
   And now they let her be.

Her life was turning, turning,
   In mazes of heat and sound.
But for peace her soul was yearning,
   And now peace laps her round.

Her cabined, ample spirit,
   It fluttered and failed for breath.
To-night it doth inherit
   The vasty hall of death.

DOVER BEACH

The sea is calm to-night.
The tide is full, the moon lies fair
Upon the Straits—on the French coast, the light
Gleams, and is gone; the cliffs of England stand,
Glimmering and vast, out in the tranquil bay.

Come to the window, sweet is the night air!
Only, from the long line of spray
Where the sea meets the moon-blanched sand,
Listen! you hear the grating roar
Of pebbles which the waves suck back, and fling,
At their return, up the high strand,
Begin, and cease, and then again begin,
With tremulous cadence slow, and bring
The eternal note of sadness in.

Sophocles long ago
Heard it on the Ægæan, and it brought
Into his mind the turbid ebb and flow,
Of human misery; we
Find also in the sound a thought,
Hearing it by this distant northern sea.

The sea of faith
Was once, too, at the full, and round earth's shore
Lay like the folds of a bright girdle furled;
But now I only hear
Its melancholy, long, withdrawing roar,
Retreating to the breath
Of the night-wind down the vast edges drear
And naked shingles of the world.

Ah, love, let us be true
To one another! for the world, which seems
To lie before us like a land of dreams,
So various, so beautiful, so new,
Hath really neither joy, nor love, nor light,
Nor certitude, nor peace, nor help for pain;
And we are here as on a darkling plain
Swept with confused alarms of struggle and flight,
Where ignorant armies clash by night.

SHAKESPEARE

Others abide our question. Thou art free.
We ask and ask. Thou smilest, and art still,
Out-topping knowledge. For the loftiest hill,
Who to the stars uncrowns his majesty,
Planting his steadfast footsteps in the sea,
Making the heaven of heavens his dwelling-place,
Spares but the cloudy border of his base
To the foiled searching of mortality;
And thou, who didst the stars and sunbeams know,
Self-schooled, self-scanned, self-honoured, self-secure,
Didst tread on earth unguessed at.—Better so!
All pains the immortal spirit must endure,
All weakness which impairs, all griefs which bow,
Find their sole speech in that victorious brow.

THE LAST WORD

Creep into thy narrow bed,
Creep, and let no more be said!
Vain thy onset! all stands fast.
Thou thyself must break at last.

Let the long contention cease!
Geese are swans, and swans are geese.
Let them have it how they will!
Thou art tired; best be still.

They out-talked thee, hissed thee, tore thee?
Better men fared thus before thee;
Fired their ringing shot and passed,
Hotly charged—and sank at last.

Charge once more, then, and be dumb!
Let the victors, when they come,
When the forts of folly fall,
Find thy body by the wall!

COVENTRY PATMORE

1823 - 1896

A FAREWELL

With all my will, but much against my heart,
We two now part.
My Very Dear,
Our solace is, the sad road lies so clear.
It needs no art,
With faint, averted feet
And many a tear,
In our opposèd paths to persevere.
Go thou to East, I West.
We will not say
There's any hope, it is so far away.
But, O my Best,
When the one darling of our widowhead,
The nursling Grief,
Is dead,

And no dews blur our eyes
To see the peach-bloom come in evening skies,
Perchance we may,
Where now this night is day,
And even through faith of still averted feet,
Making full circle of our banishment,
Amazèd meet;
The bitter journey to the bourne so sweet
Seasoning the termless feast of our content
With tears of recognition never dry.

THE TOYS

My little Son, who looked from thoughtful eyes
And moved and spoke in quiet grown-up wise,
Having my law the seventh time disobeyed,
I struck him, and dismissed
With hard words and unkissed,
—His Mother, who was patient, being dead.
Then, fearing lest his grief should hinder sleep,
I visited his bed,
But found him slumbering deep,
With darkened eyelids, and their lashes yet
From his late sobbing wet.
And I, with moan,
Kissing away his tears, left others of my own;
For, on a table drawn beside his head,
He had put, within his reach,
A box of counters and a red-veined stone,
A piece of glass abraded by the beach,
And six or seven shells,
A bottle with bluebells,
And two French copper coins, ranged there with careful art,
To comfort his sad heart.
So when that night I prayed
To God, I wept, and said:
" Ah, when at last we lie with trancèd breath,
Not vexing Thee in death,
And Thou rememberest of what toys
We made our joys,
How weakly understood
Thy great commanded good,

Then, fatherly not less
Than I whom Thou hast moulded from the clay,
Thou'lt leave Thy wrath, and say,
' I will be sorry for their childishness.' "

AN EVENING SCENE

The sheep-bell tolleth curfew-time;
   The gnats, a busy rout,
Fleck the warm air; the dismal owl
   Shouteth a sleepy shout;
The voiceless bat, more felt than seen,
   Is flitting round about.

The aspen leaflets scarcely stir;
   The river seems to think;
Athwart the dusk, broad primroses
   Look coldly from the brink,
Where, listening to the freshet's noise,
   The quiet cattle drink.

The bees boom past; the white moths rise
   Like spirits from the ground;
The gray flies hum their weary tune,
   A distant, dream-like sound;
And far, far off, to the slumb'rous eve,
   Bayeth an old guard-hound.

TRUTH

Here, in this little Bay,
Full of tumultuous life and great repose,
Where, twice a day,
The purposeless, glad ocean comes and goes,
Under high cliffs, and far from the huge town,
I sit me down.
For want of me the world's course will not fail;
When all its work is done, the lie shall rot;
The truth is great, and shall prevail,
When none cares whether it prevail or not.

GEORGE MEREDITH

1828 - 1909

LUCIFER IN STARLIGHT

On a starred night Prince Lucifer uprose.
Tired of his dark dominion swung the fiend
Above the rolling ball in cloud part screened,
Where sinners hugged their spectre of repose.
Poor prey to his hot fit of pride were those.
And now upon his western wing he leaned,
Now his huge bulk o'er Afric's sands careened,
Now the black planet shadowed Arctic snows.
Soaring through wider zones that pricked his scars
With memory of the old revolt from Awe,
He reached a middle height, and at the stars,
Which are the brain of heaven, he looked, and sank.
Around the ancient track marched, rank on rank,
The army of unalterable law.

WINTER HEAVENS

Sharp is the night, but stars with frost alive
Leap off the rim of earth across the dome.
It is a night to make the heavens our home
More than the nest whereto apace we strive.
Lengths down our road each fir-tree seems a hive,
Its swarms outrushing from the golden comb.
They waken waves of thoughts that burst to foam:
The living throb in me, the dead revive.
Yon mantle clothes us: there, past mortal breath,
Life glistens on the river of the death.
It folds us, flesh and dust; and have we knelt,
Or never knelt, or eyed as kine the springs
Of radiance, the radiance enrings:
And this is the soul's haven to have felt.

DIRGE IN WOODS

A wind sways the pines,
    And below
Not a breath of wild air;
Still as the mosses that glow
On the flooring and over the lines
Of the roots here and there.
The pine-tree drops its dead;
They are quiet, as under the sea.
Overhead, overhead
Rushes life in a race,
As the clouds the clouds chase;
    And we go,
And we drop like the fruits of the tree,
    Even we,
    Even so.

DANTE GABRIEL ROSSETTI

1828 - 1882

THE WOODSPURGE

The wind flapped loose, the wind was still,
Shaken out dead from tree and hill:
I had walked on at the wind's will,—
I sat now, for the wind was still.

Between my knees my forehead was,—
My lips, drawn in, said not Alas!
My hair was over in the grass,
My naked ears heard the day pass.

My eyes, wide open, had the run
Of some ten weeds to fix upon;
Among those few, out of the sun,
The woodspurge flowered, three cups in one.

From perfect grief there need not be
Wisdom or even memory:
One thing then learnt remains to me,—
The woodspurge has a cup of three.

LOVE SIGHT

When do I see thee most, belovèd one?
When in the light the spirits of mine eyes
Before thy face, their altar, solemnize
The worship of that Love through thee made known?
Or when, in the dusk hours (we two alone),
Close-kissed and eloquent of still replies
Thy twilight-hidden glimmering visage lies,
And my soul only sees thy soul its own?

O love, my love! if I no more should see
Thyself, nor on the earth the shadow of thee,
Nor image of thine eyes in any spring,—
How then should sound upon Life's darkening slope
The ground-whirl of the perished leaves of Hope,
The wind of Death's imperishable wing?

SILENT NOON

Your hands lie open in the long fresh grass,
The finger-points look through like rosy blooms;
Your eyes smile peace. The pasture gleams and glooms
'Neath billowing skies that scatter and amass.
All round our nest, far as the eye can pass,
Are golden kingcup-fields with silver edge
Where the cow-parsley skirts the hawthorn-hedge.
'Tis visible silence, still as the hour-glass.
Deep in the sun-searched growths the dragon-fly
Hangs like a blue thread loosened from the sky—
So this winged hour is dropt to us from above.
Oh! clasp we to our hearts, for deathless dower,
This close-companioned inarticulate hour
When twofold silence was the song of love.

THE BLESSÈD DAMOZEL

The blessèd damozel leaned out
    From the gold bar of Heaven;
Her eyes were deeper than the depth
    Of waters stilled at even;
She had three lilies in her hand,
    And the stars in her hair were seven.

Her robe, ungirt from clasp to hem,
　No wrought flowers did adorn,
But a white rose of Mary's gift,
　For service meetly worn;
Her hair that lay along her back
　Was yellow like ripe corn.

Herseemed she scarce had been a day
　One of God's choristers;
The wonder was not yet quite gone
　From that still look of hers;
Albeit, to them she left, her day
　Had counted as ten years.

(To one, it is ten years of years.
　. . . Yet now, and in this place,
Surely she leaned o'er me—her hair
　Fell all about my face. . . .
Nothing: the autumn fall of leaves.
　The whole year sets apace.)

It was the rampart of God's house
　That she was standing on;
By God built over the sheer depth
　The which is Space begun;
So high, that looking downward thence
　She scarce could see the sun.

It lies in Heaven, across the flood
　Of ether, as a bridge.
Beneath the tides of day and night
　With flame and darkness ridge
The void, as low as where this earth
　Spins like a fretful midge.

Around her, lovers, newly met
　'Mid deathless love's acclaims,
Spoke evermore among themselves
　Their heart-remembered names;
And the souls mounting up to God
　Went by her like thin flames.

And still she bowed herself and stooped
　Out of the circling charm;
Until her bosom must have made
　The bar she leaned on warm,

And the lilies lay as if asleep
 Along her bended arm.

From the fixed place of Heaven she saw
 Time like a pulse shake fierce
Through all the worlds. Her gaze still strove
 Within the gulf to pierce
Its path; and now she spoke as when
 The stars sang in their spheres.

The sun was gone now; the curled moon
 Was like a little feather
Fluttering far down the gulf; and now
 She spoke through the still weather.
Her voice was like the voice the stars
 Had when they sang together.

(Ah sweet! Even now, in that bird's song,
 Strove not her accents there,
Fain to be hearkened? When those bells
 Possessed the mid-day air,
Strove not her steps to reach my side
 Down all the echoing stair?)

" I wish that he were come to me,
 For he will come," she said.
" Have I not prayed to Heaven?—on earth,
 Lord, Lord, has he not prayed?
Are not two prayers a perfect strength?
 And shall I feel afraid?

" When round his head the aureole clings,
 And he is clothed in white,
I'll take his hand and go with him
 To the deep wells of light;
As unto a stream we will step down,
 And bathe there in God's sight.

" We two will stand beside that shrine,
 Occult, withheld, untrod,
Whose lamps are stirred continually
 With prayer sent up to God;
And see our old prayers, granted, melt
 Each like a little cloud.

" We two will lie i' the shadow of
    That living mystic tree
Within whose secret growth the Dove
    Is sometimes felt to be,
While every leaf that His plumes touch
    Saith His Name audibly.

" And I myself will teach to him,
    I myself, lying so,
The songs I sing here; which his voice
    Shall pause in, hushed and slow,
And find some knowledge at each pause,
    Or some new thing to know."

(Alas! We two, we two, thou say'st!
    Yea, one wast thou with me
That once of old. But shall God lift
    To endless unity
The soul whose likeness with thy soul
    Was but its love for thee?)

" We two," she said, " will seek the groves
    Where the lady Mary is,
With her five handmaidens, whose names
    Are five sweet symphonies,
Cecily, Gertrude, Magdalen,
    Margaret and Rosalys.

" Circlewise sit they, with bound locks
    And foreheads garlanded;
Into the fine cloth white like flame
    Weaving the golden thread,
To fashion the birth-robes for them
    Who are just born, being dead.

" He shall fear, haply, and be dumb:
    Then will I lay my cheek
To his, and tell about our love,
    Not once abashed or weak:
And the dear Mother will approve
    My pride, and let me speak.

" Herself shall bring us, hand in hand,
    To Him round whom all souls
Kneel, the clear-ranged unnumbered heads
    Bowed with their aureoles:
And angels meeting us shall sing
    To their citherns and citoles.

" There will I ask of Christ the Lord
    Thus much for him and me:—
Only to live as once on earth
    With Love, only to be,
As then awhile, for ever now
    Together, I and he."

She gazed and listened and then said,
    Less sad of speech than mild:—
" All this is when he comes." She ceased.
    Then light thrilled towards her, filled
With angels in strong level flight.
    Her eyes prayed, and she smiled.

(I saw her smile.) But soon their path
    Was vague in distant spheres:
And then she cast her arms along
    The golden barriers,
And laid her face between her hands,
    And wept. (I heard her tears.)

THOMAS EDWARD BROWN

1830 - 1897

VESPERS

O blackbird, what a boy you are!
How you do go it!
Blowing your bugle to that one sweet star—
How you do blow it!
And does she hear you, blackbird boy, so far?
Or is it wasted breath?
" Good Lord! she is so bright
To-night! "
The blackbird saith.

I BENDED UNTO ME

I bended unto me a bough of May,
That I might see and smell:
It bore it in a sort of way,
It bore it very well.
But when I let it backward sway,
Then it were hard to tell
With what a toss, with what a swing,
The dainty thing
Resumed its proper level,
And sent me to the devil.
I know it did—you doubt it?
I turned, and saw them whispering about it.

CHRISTINA GEORGINA ROSSETTI

1830 - 1894

A BIRTHDAY

My heart is like a singing bird
  Whose nest is in a watered shoot;
My heart is like an apple-tree
  Whose bough is bent with thick-set fruit;
My heart is like a rainbow shell
  That paddles in a halcyon sea;
My heart is gladder than all these
  Because my love is come to me.

Raise me a dais of silk and down;
  Hang it with vair and purple dyes;
Carve it in doves, and pomegranates,
  And peacocks with a hundred eyes;
Work it in gold and silver grapes,
  In leaves, and silver fleur-de-lys;
Because the birthday of my life
  Is come, my love is come to me.

REMEMBER

Remember me when I am gone away,
Gone far away into the silent land;
When you can no more hold me by the hand,
Nor I half turn to go, yet turning stay.
Remember me when no more, day by day,
You tell me of our future that you planned;
Only remember me; you understand
It will be late to counsel then or pray.
Yet if you should forget me for a while
And afterwards remember, do not grieve;
For if the darkness and corruption leave
A vestige of the thoughts that once I had,
Better by far you should forget and smile
Than that you should remember and be sad.

ALOOF

The irresponsive silence of the land,
The irresponsive sounding of the sea,
Speak both one message of one sense to me:—
" Aloof, aloof, we stand aloof; so stand
Thou too aloof bound with the flawless band
In inner solitude; we bind not thee.
But who from thy self-chain shall set thee free?
What heart shall touch thy heart? what hand thy hand ?"
And I am sometimes proud and sometimes meek,
And sometimes I remember days of old
When fellowship seemed not so far to seek
And all the world and I seemed much less cold,
And at the rainbow's foot lay surely gold,
And hope felt strong and life itself not weak.

WHEN I AM DEAD, MY DEAREST

When I am dead, my dearest,
Sing no sad songs for me;
Plant thou no roses at my head,
Nor shady cypress tree:

Be the green grass above me
With showers and dewdrops wet:
And if thou wilt, remember,
And if thou wilt, forget.

I shall not see the shadows,
I shall not feel the rain;
I shall not hear the nightingale
Sing on as if in pain:
And dreaming through the twilight
That doth not rise nor set,
Haply I may remember,
And haply may forget.

MIRAGE

The hope I dreamed of was a dream,
    Was but a dream; and now I wake,
Exceeding comfortless, and worn, and old,
    For a dream's sake.

I hang my harp upon a tree,
    A weeping willow in a lake;
I hang my silent harp there, wrung and snapt
    For a dream's sake.

Lie still, lie still, my breaking heart;
    My silent heart, lie still and break:
Life, and the world, and mine own self, are changed
    For a dream's sake.

THE BOURNE

Underneath the growing grass,
    Underneath the living flowers,
    Deeper than the sound of showers:
    There we shall not count the hours
By the shadows as they pass.

Youth and health will be but vain,
    Beauty reckoned of no worth:
    There a very little girth
    Can hold round what once the earth
Seemed too narrow to contain.

ECHO

Come to me in the silence of the night;
  Come in the speaking silence of a dream;
Come with soft rounded cheeks and eyes as bright
  As sunlight on a stream;
    Come back in tears,
O memory, hope and love of finished years.

O dream how sweet, too sweet, too bitter-sweet,
  Whose wakening should have been in Paradise,
Where souls brim-full of love abide and meet;
  Where thirsting longing eyes
    Watch the slow door
That opening, letting in, lets out no more.

Yet come to me in dreams, that I may live
  My very life again though cold in death;
Come back to me in dreams, that I may give
  Pulse for pulse, breath for breath:
    Speak low, lean low,
As long ago, my love, how long ago.

EMILY DICKINSON

(A) 1830 - 1886

THE ONLY NEWS I KNOW

The only news I know
Is bulletins all day
From Immortality.

The only shows I see,
To-morrow and To-day,
Perchance Eternity.

The only One I meet
Is God,—the only street,
Existence; this traversed

If other news there be,
Or admirabler show—
I'll tell it you.

SNAKE

A narrow fellow in the grass
Occasionally rides;
You may have met him,—did you not?
His notice sudden is.

The grass divides as with a comb,
A spotted shaft is seen;
And then it closes at your feet
And opens further on.

He likes a boggy acre,
A floor too cool for corn.
Yet when a child, and barefoot,
I more than once, at morn,

Have passed, I thought, a whip-lash
Unbraiding in the sun,—
When, stopping to secure it,
It wrinkled, and was gone.

Several of nature's people
I know, and they know me;
I feel for them a transport
Of cordiality;

But never met this fellow,
Attended or alone,
Without a tighter breathing,
And zero at the bone.

I'VE KNOWN A HEAVEN LIKE A TENT

I've known a Heaven like a tent
To wrap its shining yards,
Pluck up its stakes and disappear
Without the sound of boards
Or rip of nail, or carpenter,
But just the miles of stare
That signalize a show's retreat
In North America.

No trace, no figment of the thing
    That dazzled yesterday,
No ring, no marvel;
Men and feats
Dissolved as utterly
As birds' far navigation
Discloses just a hue;
A plash of oars—a gaiety,
Then swallowed up to view.

THERE'S BEEN A DEATH

There's been a death in the opposite house
    As lately as to-day.
I know it by the numb look
    Such houses have alway.

The neighbours rustle in and out,
    The doctor drives away.
A window opens like a pod,
    Abrupt, mechanically;

Somebody flings a mattress out,—
    The children hurry by;
They wonder if It died on that,—
    I used to when a boy.

The minister goes stiffly in
    As if the house were his,
And he owned all the mourners now,
    And little boys besides;

And then the milliner, and the man
    Of the appalling trade,
To take the measure of the house,
    There'll be that dark parade.

Of tassels and of coaches soon;
    It's easy as a sign,—
The intuition of the news
    In just a country town.

THERE IS NO TRUMPET LIKE THE TOMB

The Immortality she gave
We borrowed at her grave;
For just one plaudit banishing
The might of human love.

LOVE'S STRICKEN "WHY"

Love's stricken "why"
Is all that love can speak—
Built of but just a syllable
The hugest hearts that break.

GO NOT TOO NEAR A HOUSE OF ROSE

Go not too near a house of rose,
The depredation of a breeze
Or inundation of a dew
Alarm its walls away;

Nor try to tie the butterfly;
Nor climb the bars of ecstasy.
In insecurity to lie
Is joy's insuring quality.

MY LIFE CLOSED TWICE BEFORE ITS CLOSE

My life closed twice before its close;
It yet remains to see
If Immortality unveil
A third event to me,

So huge, so hopeless to conceive,
As these that twice befell.
Parting is all we know of heaven,
And all we need of hell.

LEWIS CARROLL

1832 - 1898

FATHER WILLIAM

" You are old, Father William," the young man said,
 " And your hair has become very white;
And yet you incessantly stand on your head—
 Do you think, at your age, it is right? "

" In my youth," Father William replied to his son,
 " I feared it might injure the brain;
But, now that I'm perfectly sure I have none,
 Why, I do it again and again."

" You are old," said the youth, " as I mentioned before,
 And have grown most uncommonly fat;
Yet you turned a back-somersault in at the door—
 Pray, what is the reason of that? "

" In my youth," said the sage, as he shook his gray locks,
 " I kept all my limbs very supple
By the use of this ointment—one shilling the box—
 Allow me to sell you a couple? "

" You are old," said the youth, " and your jaws are too weak
 For anything tougher than suet;
Yet you finished the goose, with the bones and the beak—
 Pray, how did you manage to do it? "

" In my youth," said his father, " I took to the law,
 And argued each case with my wife;
And the muscular strength which it gave to my jaw
 Has lasted the rest of my life."

" You are old," said the youth, " one would hardly suppose
 That your eye was as steady as ever;
Yet you balanced an eel on the end of your nose—
 What made you so awfully clever? "

" I have answered three questions, and that is enough,"
 Said his father. " Don't give yourself airs!
Do you think I can listen all day to such stuff?
 Be off, or I'll kick you down-stairs! "

JABBERWOCKY

'Twas brillig, and the slithy toves
  Did gyre and gimble in the wabe:
All mimsy were the borogoves,
  And the mome raths outgrabe.

" Beware the Jabberwock, my son!
  The jaws that bite, the claws that catch!
Beware the Jubjub bird, and shun
  The frumious Bandersnatch! "

He took his vorpal sword in hand;
  Long time the manxome foe he sought—
So rested he by the Tumtum tree,
  And stood awhile in thought.

And, as in uffish thought he stood,
  The Jabberwock, with eyes of flame,
Came whiffling through the tulgey wood,
  And burbled as it came!

One, two! One, two! And through and through
  The vorpal blade went snicker-snack!
He left it dead, and with its head
  He went galumphing back.

" And hast thou slain the Jabberwock?
  Come to my arms, my beamish boy!
O frabjous day! Callooh, Callay! "
  He chortled in his joy.

'Twas brillig, and the slithy toves
  Did gyre and gimble in the wabe:
All mimsy were the borogoves,
  And the mome raths outgrabe.

JAMES THOMSON

1834 - 1882

NIGHTMARE

from " The City of Dreadful Night "

As I came through the desert thus it was,
As I came through the desert: All was black,
In heaven no single star, on earth no track;
A brooding hush without a stir or note,
The air so thick it clotted in my throat;
And thus for hours; then some enormous things
Swooped past with savage cries and clanking wings:
        But I strode on austere;
        No hope could have no fear.

As I came through the desert, thus it was,
As I came through the desert: Eyes of fire
Glared at me throbbing with a starved desire;
The hoarse and heavy and carnivorous breath
Was hot upon me from deep jaws of death;
Sharp claws, swift talons, fleshless fingers cold
Plucked at me from the bushes, tried to hold:
        But I strode on austere;
        No hope could have no fear.

As I came through the desert thus it was,
As I came through the desert: Meteors ran
And crossed their javelins on the black sky-span;
The zenith opened to a gulf of flame,
The dreadful thunderbolts jarred earth's fixed frame:
The ground all heaved in waves of fire that surged
And weltered round me sole there unsubmerged:
        Yet I strode on austere;
        No hope could have no fear.

As I came through the desert thus it was,
As I came through the desert: Air once more,
And I was close upon a wild sea-shore;
Enormous cliffs arose on either hand,
The deep tide thundered up a league-broad strand;

White foam-belts seethed there, wan spray swept and flew:
The sky broke, moon and stars and clouds and blue:
        And I strode on austere:
        No hope could have no fear.

As I came through the desert thus it was,
As I came through the desert: From the right
A shape came slowly with a ruddy light;
A woman with a red lamp in her hand,
Bareheaded and barefooted on that strand;
O desolation moving with such grace!
O anguish with such beauty in thy face.
        I fell as on my bier,
        Hope travailed with such fear.

As I came through the desert thus it was,
As I came through the desert: I was twain,
Two selves distinct that cannot join again;
One stood apart and knew but could not stir,
And watched the other stark in swoon and her;
And she came on, and never turned aside,
Between such sun and moon and roaring tide:
        And as she came more near
        My soul grew mad with fear.

     ·   ·   ·   ·   ·

As I came through the desert thus it was,
As I came through the desert: When the tide
Swept up to her there kneeling by my side,
She clasped that corpse-like me, and they were borne
Away, and this vile me was left forlorn;
I know the whole sea cannot quench that heart,
Or cleanse that brow, or wash those two apart:
        They love; their doom is drear,
        Yet they nor hope nor fear;
        But I, what do I here?

WILLIAM MORRIS

1834 - 1896

TWO RED ROSES ACROSS THE MOON

There was a lady lived in a hall,
Large of eyes and slim and tall;
And ever she sang from noon to noon,
Two red roses across the moon.

There was a knight came riding by
In early spring, when the roads were dry;
And he heard that lady sing at the noon,
Two red roses across the moon.

Yet none the more he stopped at all,
But he rode a-gallop past the hall;
And left that lady singing at noon,
Two red roses across the moon.

Because, forsooth, the battle was set,
And the scarlet and gold had got to be met,
He rode on the spur till the next warm noon;
Two red roses across the moon.

But the battle was scattered from hill to hill,
From the windmill to the watermill;
And he said to himself, as it neared the noon,
Two red roses across the moon.

You scarce could see for the scarlet and blue,
A golden helm or a golden shoe;
So he cried, as the fight grew thick at the noon,
Two red roses across the moon.

Verily then the gold bore through
The huddled spears of the scarlet and blue;
And they cried, as they cut them down at the noon,
Two red roses across the moon.

I trow he stopped when he rode again
By the hall, though draggled sore with the rain;
And his lips were pinched to kiss at the noon
Two red roses across the moon.

Under the may she stooped to the crown,
All was gold, there was nothing of brown,
And the horns blew up in the hall at noon,
Two red roses across the moon.

LOVE IS ENOUGH

Love is enough: though the world be a-waning,
And the woods have no voice but the voice of complaining,
　Though the skies be too dark for dim eyes to discover
The gold-cups and daisies fair blooming thereunder,
Though the hills be held shadows, and the sea a dark wonder,
　And this day draw a veil over all deeds passed over,
Yet their hands shall not tremble, their feet shall not falter:
The void shall not weary, the fear shall not alter
　These lips and these eyes of the loved and the lover.

ALGERNON CHARLES SWINBURNE

1837 - 1909

MAN

from " Atalanta in Calydon "

Before the beginning of years,
　There came to the making of man
Time, with a gift of tears;
　Grief, with a glass that ran;
Pleasure, with pain for leaven;
　Summer, with flowers that fell;
Remembrance fallen from heaven,
　And madness risen from hell;
Strength without hands to smite;
　Love that endures for a breath;
Night, the shadow of light,
　And life, the shadow of death.
And the high gods took in hand
　Fire, and the falling of tears,
And a measure of sliding sand
　From under the feet of the years;
And froth and drift of the sea;
　And dust of the labouring earth;
And bodies of things to be
　In the houses of death and of birth;

And wrought with weeping and laughter,
　　And fashioned with loathing and love,
With life before and after
　　And death beneath and above,
For a day and a night and a morrow,
　　That his strength might endure for a span
With travail and heavy sorrow,
　　The holy spirit of man.
From the winds of the north and the south
　　They gathered as unto strife;
They breathed upon his mouth,
　　They filled his body with life;
Eyesight and speech they wrought
　　For the veils of the soul therein,
A time for labour and thought,
　　A time to serve and to sin;
They gave him light in his ways,
　　And love, and a space for delight,
And beauty and length of days,
　　And night, and sleep in the night.
His speech is burning fire;
　　With his lips he travaileth;
In his heart is a blind desire,
　　In his eyes foreknowledge of death;
He weaves, and is clothed with derision;
　　Sows, and he shall not reap;
His life is a watch or a vision
　　Between a sleep and a sleep.

"WHEN THE HOUNDS OF SPRING"

from "Atalanta in Calydon"

When the hounds of spring are on winter's traces,
　　The mother of months in meadow or plain
Fills the shadows and windy places
　　With lisp of leaves and ripple of rain;
And the brown bright nightingale amorous
Is half assuaged for Itylus,
For the Thracian ships and the foreign faces,
　　The tongueless vigil, and all the pain.

Come with bows bent and with emptying of quivers,
　　Maiden most perfect, lady of light,
With a noise of winds and many rivers,
　　With a clamour of waters, and with might;

Bind on thy sandals, O thou most fleet,
Over the splendour and speed of thy feet;
For the faint east quickens, the wan west shivers,
    Round the feet of the day and the feet of the night.

Where shall we find her, how shall we sing to her,
    Fold our hands round her knees, and cling?
O that man's heart were as fire and could spring to her,
    Fire, or the strength of the streams that spring!
For the stars and the winds are unto her
As raiment, as songs of the harp-player;
For the risen stars and the fallen cling to her,
    And the southwest-wind and the west-wind sing.

For winter's rains and ruins are over,
    And all the season of snows and sins;
The days dividing lover and lover,
    The light that loses, the night that wins;
And time remembered is grief forgotten,
And frosts are slain and flowers begotten,
And in green underwood and cover
    Blossom by blossom the spring begins.

The full streams feed on flower of rushes,
    Ripe grasses trammel a travelling foot,
The faint fresh flame of the young year flushes
    From leap to flower and flower to fruit;
And fruit and leaf are as gold and fire,
And the oat is heard above the lyre,
And the hoofèd heel of a satyr crushes
    The chestnut-husk at the chestnut-root.

And Pan by noon and Bacchus by night,
    Fleeter of foot than the fleet-foot kid,
Follows with dancing and fills with delight
    The Mænad and the Bassarid;
And soft as lips that laugh and hide
The laughing leaves of the trees divide,
And screen from seeing and leave in sight
    The god pursuing, the maiden hid.

The ivy falls with the Bacchanal's hair
    Over her eyebrows hiding her eyes;
The wild vine slipping down leaves bare
    Her bright breast shortening into sighs;

The wild vine slips with the weight of its leaves,
But the berried ivy catches and cleaves
To the limbs that glitter, the feet that scare
    The wolf that follows, the fawn that flies.

THE SEA

from "The Triumph of Time"

I will go back to the great sweet mother,
    Mother and lover of men, the sea.
I will go down to her, I and none other,
    Close with her, kiss her and mix with her;
Cling to her, strive with her, hold her fast;
O fair white mother, in days long past
Born without sister, born without brother,
    Set free my soul as thy soul is free.

O fair green-girdled mother of mine,
    Sea, that art clothed with the sun and the rain,
Thy sweet hard kisses are strong like wine,
    Thy large embraces are keen like pain.
Save me and hide me with all thy waves,
Find me one grave of thy thousand graves,
Those pure cold populous graves of thine,
    Wrought without hand in a world without stain.

I shall sleep, and move with the moving ships,
    Change as the winds change, veer in the tide;
My lips will feast on the foam of thy lips,
    I shall rise with thy rising, with thee subside;
Sleep, and not know if she be, if she were,
Filled full with life to the eyes and hair,
As a rose is fulfilled to the roseleaf tips
    With splendid summer and perfume and pride.

This woven raiment of nights and days,
    Were it once cast off and unwound from me,
Naked and glad would I walk in thy ways,
    Alive and aware of thy ways and thee;
Clear of the whole world, hidden at home,
Clothed with the green and crowned with the foam,
A pulse of the life of thy straits and bays,
    A vein in the heart of the streams of the sea.

SONG

Love laid his sleepless head
On a thorny rosy bed;
And his eyes with tears were red,
And pale his lips as the dead.

And fear and sorrow and scorn
Kept watch by his head forlorn,
Till the night was overworn,
And the world was merry with morn.

And Joy came up with the day,
And kissed Love's lips as he lay,
And the watchers ghostly and gray
Sped from his pillow away.

And his eyes as the dawn grew bright,
And his lips waxed ruddy as light:
Sorrow may reign for a night,
But day shall bring back delight.

THOMAS HARDY

1840 - 1928

THE DARKLING THRUSH

I leaned upon a coppice gate
    When Frost was spectre-gray,
And Winter's dregs made desolate
    The weakening eye of day.
The tangled bine-stems scored the sky
    Like strings from broken lyres,
And all mankind that haunted nigh
    Had sought their household fires.

The land's sharp features seemed to be
    The Century's corpse outleant;
His crypt the cloudy canopy,
    The wind his death-lament.

The ancient pulse of germ and birth
  Was shrunken hard and dry,
And every spirit upon the earth
  Seemed fervourless as I.

At once a voice burst forth among
  The bleak twigs overhead
In a full-hearted evensong
  Of joy unlimited;
An aged thrush, frail, gaunt and small,
  In blast-beruffled plume,
Had chosen thus to fling his soul
  Upon the growing gloom.

So little cause for carollings
  Of such ecstatic sound
Was written on terrestrial things
  Afar or nigh around,
That I could think there trembled through
  His happy good-night air
Some blessed hope, whereof he knew
  And I was unaware.

THE OXEN

Christmas Eve, and twelve of the clock,
  " Now they are all on their knees,"
An elder said as we sat in a flock
  By the embers in hearthside ease.

We pictured the meek mild creatures where
  They dwelt in their strawy pen,
Nor did it occur to one of us there
  To doubt they were kneeling then.

So fair a fancy few would weave
  In these years! Yet, I feel,
If some one said on Christmas Eve,
  " Come; see the oxen kneel

" In the lonely barton by yonder coomb[1]
  Our childhood used to know,"
I should go with him in the gloom,
  Hoping it might be so.
            [1] Farmyard in the hollow.

WEATHERS

This is the weather the cuckoo likes,
  And so do I;
When showers betumble the chestnut spikes,
  And nestlings fly;
And the little brown nightingale bills his best,
And they sit outside the " Traveller's Rest,"
And maids come forth sprig-muslin drest,
And citizens dream of the South and West.
  And so do I.

This is the weather the shepherd shuns,
  And so do I;
When beeches drip in browns and duns,
  And thresh, and ply;
And hill-hid tides throb, throe on throe,
And meadow rivulets overflow,
And drops on gate-bars hang in a row,
And rooks in families homeward go,
  And so do I.

HENRY AUSTIN DOBSON

1840 - 1921

IN AFTER DAYS

In after days when grasses high
O'ertop the stone where I shall lie,
 Though ill or well the world adjust
 My slender claim to honoured dust,
I shall not question or reply.

I shall not see the morning sky;
I shall not hear the night-wind's sigh;
 I shall be mute, as all men must
  In after days!

But yet, now living, fain were I
That some one then should testify,
 Saying—" He held his pen in trust
 To Art, not serving shame or lust."
Will none?—Then let my memory die
  In after days!

EDWARD ROWLAND SILL

(A) 1841 - 1887

OPPORTUNITY

This I beheld, or dreamed it in a dream:
There spread a cloud of dust along a plain:
And underneath the cloud, or in it, raged
A furious battle, and men yelled, and swords
Shocked upon swords and shields. A prince's banner
Wavered, then staggered backward, hemmed by foes.
A craven hung along the battle's edge,
And thought, " Had I a sword of keener steel—
That blue blade that the king's son bears,—but this
Blunt thing—! " he snapt and flung it from his hand,
And lowering crept away and left the field.
Then came the king's son, wounded, sore bestead,
And weaponless, and saw the broken sword,
Hilt-buried in the dry and trodden sand,
And ran and snatched it, and with battle-shout
Lifted afresh he hewed his enemy down,
And saved a great cause that heroic day.

ARTHUR O'SHAUGHNESSY

1844 - 1881

ODE

We are the music-makers,
     And we are the dreamers of dreams,
Wandering by lone sea-breakers,
     And sitting by desolate streams;
World-losers and world-forsakers,
     On whom the pale moon gleams:
Yet we are the movers and shakers
     Of the world for ever, it seems.

With wonderful deathless ditties
     We build up the world's great cities,
And out of a fabulous story
     We fashion an empire's glory:

One man with a dream, at pleasure,
   Shall go forth and conquer a crown;
And three with a new song's measure
   Can trample an empire down.

We, in the ages lying
   In the buried past of the earth,
Built Nineveh with our sighing,
   And Babel itself with our mirth;
And o'erthrew them prophesying
   To the old of the new world's worth;
For each age is a dream that is dying,
   Or one that is coming to birth.

ROBERT BRIDGES

1844 - 1930

NIGHTINGALES

Beautiful must be the mountains whence ye come,
And bright in the fruitful valleys the streams wherefrom
     Ye learn your song:
Where are those starry woods? O might I wander there,
  Among the flowers, which in that heavenly air
     Bloom the year long!

Nay, barren are those mountains and spent the streams:
Our song is the voice of desire, that haunts our dreams,
     A throe of the heart,
Whose pining visions dim, forbidden hopes profound,
  No dying cadence nor long sigh can sound,
     For all our art.

Alone, aloud in the raptured ear of men
We pour our dark nocturnal secret; and then,
     As night is withdrawn
From these sweet-springing meads and bursting boughs of
   May,
  Dream, while the innumerable choir of day
     Welcome the dawn.

A PASSER-BY

Whither, O splendid ship, thy white sails crowding,
　　Leaning across the bosom of the urgent West,
That fearest nor sea rising nor sky clouding,
　　Whither away, fair rover, and what thy quest?
　　Ah! soon, when Winter has all our vales opprest,
When skies are cold and misty, and hail is hurling,
　　Wilt thou glide on the blue Pacific, or rest
In a summer haven asleep, thy white sails furling.

I there before thee, in the country that well thou knowest,
　　Already arrived am inhaling the odorous air:
I watch thee enter unerringly where thou goest,
　　And anchor queen of the strange shipping there,
　　Thy sails for awnings spread, thy masts bare;
Nor is aught from the foaming reef to the snow-capped,
　　　grandest
　　Peak, that is over the feathery palms, more fair
Than thou, so upright, so stately, and still thou standest.

And yet, O splendid ship, unhailed and nameless,
　　I know not if, aiming a fancy, I rightly divine
That thou hast a purpose joyful, a courage blameless,
　　Thy port assured in a happier land than mine,
　　But for all I have given thee, beauty enough is thine,
As thou, aslant with trim tackle and shrouding,
　　From the proud nostril curve of a prow's line
In the offing scatterest foam, thy white sails crowding.

ALL BEAUTEOUS THINGS

　　　I love all beauteous things,
　　　　I seek and adore them;
　　　God hath no better praise,
　　　And man in his hasty days
　　　　Is honoured for them.

　　　I too will something make
　　　　And joy in the making;
　　　Although to-morrow it seem
　　　Like empty words of a dream
　　　　Remembered on waking.

GERARD MANLEY HOPKINS

1844 - 1889

HEAVEN-HAVEN

A NUN TAKES THE VEIL

I have desired to go
  Where springs not fail,
To fields where flies no sharp and sided hail,
  And a few lilies blow.

And I have asked to be
  Where no storms come,
Where the green swell is in the havens dumb
  And out of the swing of the sea.

THE HABIT OF PERFECTION

Elected Silence, sing to me
And beat upon my whorlèd ear,
Pipe me to pastures still, and be
The music that I care to hear.

Shape nothing, lips; be lovely-dumb;
It is the shut, the curfew sent
From there where all surrenders come
Which only makes you eloquent.

Be shellèd, eyes, with double dark
And find the uncreated light:
This ruck and reel which you remark
Coils, keeps, and teases simple sight.

Palate, the hatch of tasty lust,
Desire not to be rinsed with wine:
The can must be so sweet, the crust
So fresh that come in fasts divine!

Nostrils, your careless breath that spend
Upon the stir and keep of pride,
What relish shall the censers send
Along the sanctuary side!

O feel-of-primrose hands, O feet
That want the yield of plushy sward,
But you shall walk the golden street
And you unhouse and house the Lord.

And, Poverty, be thou the bride
And now the marriage feast begun,
And lily-coloured clothes provide
Your spouse not laboured-at nor spun.

PIED BEAUTY

Glory be to God for dappled things—
   For skies as couple-coloured as a brindled cow;
      For rose-moles all in stipple upon trout that swim;
Fresh-firecoal chestnut-falls; finches' wings;
   Landscapes plotted and pieced—fold, fallow and plough;
      And all trades, their gear and tackle and trim.
All things counter, original, spare, strange;
   Whatever is fickle, freckled (who knows how?)
      With swift, slow; sweet, sour; adazzle, dim;
He fathers-forth whose beauty is past change:
         Praise Him.

SPRING

Nothing is so beautiful as spring—
   When weeds, in wheels, shoot long and lovely and lush;
      Thrush's eggs look little low heavens, and thrush
Through the echoing timber does so rinse and wring
The ear, it strikes like lightnings to hear him sing;
   The glassy pear-tree leaves and blooms, they brush
   The descending blue; that blue is all in a rush
With richness; the racing lambs too have fair their fling.

What is all this juice and all this joy?
   A strain of the earth's sweet being in the beginning
In Eden garden.—Have, get, before it cloy,
   Before it cloud, Christ, lord, and sour with sinning,
Innocent mind and Mayday in girl and boy,
   Most, O Maid's child, thy choice and worthy the winning.

ALICE MEYNELL

1847 - 1922

RENOUNCEMENT

I must not think of thee; and, tired yet strong,
   I shun the thought that lurks in all delight—
     The thought of thee—and in the blue Heaven's height,
And in the sweetest passage of a song.
O just beyond the fairest thoughts that throng
   This breast, the thought of thee waits hidden yet bright;
     But it must never, never come in sight;
I must stop short of thee the whole day long.

But when sleep comes to close each difficult day,
   When night gives pause to the long watch I keep,
     And all my bonds I needs must loose apart,
Must doff my will as raiment laid away,
   With the first dream that comes with the first sleep
     I run, I run, I am gathered to thy heart.

CHIMES

Brief, on a flying night
   From the shaken tower,
A flock of bells take flight,
   And go with the hour.

Like birds from the cote to the gales,
   Abrupt—O hark!
A fleet of bells set sails,
   And go to the dark.

Sudden the cold airs swing,
   Alone, aloud,
A verse of bells takes wing
   And flies with the cloud.

WILLIAM ERNEST HENLEY

1849 - 1903

INVICTUS

Out of the night that covers me,
  Black as the Pit from pole to pole,
I thank whatever gods may be
  For my unconquerable soul.

In the fell clutch of circumstance
  I have not winced nor cried aloud.
Under the bludgeonings of chance
  My head is bloody, but unbowed.

Beyond this place of wrath and tears
  Looms but the horror of the shade,
And yet the menace of the years
  Finds, and shall find me, unafraid.

It matters not how strait the gate,
  How charged with punishments the scroll,
I am the master of my fate:
  I am the captain of my soul.

MARGARITAE SORORI

A late lark twitters from the quiet skies;
And from the west,
Where the sun, his day's work ended,
Lingers as in content,
There falls on the old, grey city
An influence luminous and serene,
A shining peace.

The smoke ascends
In a rosy-and-golden haze. The spires
Shine, and are changed. In the valley
Shadows rise. The lark sings on. The sun,
Closing his benediction,
Sinks, and the darkening air

Thrills with a sense of the triumphing night—
Night with her train of stars
And her great gift of sleep.

So be my passing!
My task accomplished and the long day done,
My wages taken, and in my heart
Some late lark singing,
Let me be gathered to the quiet west,
The sundown splendid and serene,
Death.

EDWIN MARKHAM

(A) 1852 - 1940

THE MAN WITH THE HOE

Written after seeing Millet's world-famous painting of a toiler in the abyss of labour.
   God made man in his own image: in the image of God made He him.—Genesis.

Bowed by the weight of centuries he leans
Upon his hoe and gazes on the ground,
The emptiness of ages in his face,
And on his back the burden of the world.
Who made him dead to rapture and despair,
A thing that grieves not and that never hopes,
Stolid and stunned, a brother to the ox?
Who loosened and let down this brutal jaw?
Whose was the hand that slanted back this brow?
Whose breath blew out the light within this brain?

Is this the Thing the Lord God made and gave
To have dominion over sea and land;
To trace the stars and search the heavens for power;
To feel the passion of Eternity?
Is this the dream He dreamed who shaped the suns
And markt their ways upon the ancient deep?
Down all the caverns of Hell to their last gulf
There is no shape more terrible than this—
More tongued with cries against the world's blind greed—
More filled with signs and portents for the soul—
More packt with danger to the universe.

What gulfs between him and the seraphim!
Slave of the wheel of labour, what to him
Are Plato and the swing of Pleiades?
What the long reaches of the peaks of song,
The rift of dawn, the reddening of the rose?
Through this dread shape the suffering ages look;
Time's tragedy is in that aching stoop;
Through this dread shape humanity betrayed,
Plundered, profaned and disinherited,
Cries protest to the Powers that made the world,
A protest that is also prophecy.

O masters, lords and rulers in all lands,
Is this the handiwork you give to God,
This monstrous thing distorted and soul-quencht?
How will you ever straighten up this shape;
Touch it again with immortality;
Give back the upward looking and the light;
Rebuild in it the music and the dream;
Make right the immemorial infamies,
Perfidious wrongs, immedicable woes?

O masters, lords and rulers in all lands,
How will the future reckon with this Man?
How answer his brute question in that hour
When whirlwinds of rebellion shake all shores?
How will it be with kingdoms and with kings—
With those who shaped him to the thing he is—
When the dumb Terror shall rise to judge the world,
After the silence of the centuries?

OUTWITTED

He drew a circle that shut me out—
Heretic, rebel, a thing to flout.
But Love and I had the wit to win:
We drew a circle that took him in!

OSCAR WILDE

1856 - 1900

REQUIESCAT

Tread lightly, she is near
    Under the snow,
Speak gently, she can hear
    The daisies grow.

All her bright golden hair
    Tarnished with rust,
She that was young and fair
    Fallen to dust.

Lily-like, white as snow,
    She hardly knew
She was a woman, so
    Sweetly she grew.

Coffin-board, heavy stone,
    Lie on her breast;
I vex my heart alone,
    She is at rest.

Peace, peace; she cannot hear
    Lyre or sonnet;
All my life's buried here.
    Heap earth upon it.

LIZETTE WOODWORTH REESE

(A) 1856 - 1935

TEARS

When I consider Life and its few years—
A wisp of fog betwixt us and the sun;
A call to battle, and the battle done
Ere the last echo dies within our ears;

A rose choked in the grass; an hour of fears;
The gusts that past a darkening shore do beat;
The burst of music down an unlistening street,—
I wonder at the idleness of tears.

Ye old, old dead, and ye of yesternight
Chieftains, and bards, and keepers of the sheep,
By every cup of sorrow that you had,
Loose me from tears, and make me see aright
How each hath back what once he stayed to weep:
Homer, his sight, David his little lad!

JOHN DAVIDSON

1857 - 1909

A BALLAD OF HELL

" A letter from my love to-day!
  Oh, unexpected, dear appeal! "
She struck a happy tear away,
  And broke the crimson seal.

" My love, there is no help on earth,
  No help in heaven; the dead-man's bell
Must toll our wedding; our first hearth
  Must be the well-paved floor of hell."

The colour died from out her face,
  Her eyes like ghostly candles shone;
She cast dread looks about the place,
  Then clenched her teeth and read right on.

" I may not pass the prison door;
  Here must I rot from day to day,
Unless I wed whom I abhor,
  My cousin, Blanche of Valencay.

" At midnight with my dagger keen,
  I'll take my life; it must be so.
Meet me in hell to-night, my queen,
  For weal and woe."

She laughed, although her face was wan,
  She girded on her golden belt,
She took her jewelled ivory fan,
  And at her glowing missal knelt.

Then rose, " And am I mad? " she said:
  She broke her fan, her belt untied;
With leather girt herself instead,
  And stuck a dagger at her side.

She waited, shuddering in her room,
  Till sleep had fallen on all the house.
She never flinched; she faced her doom:
  They two must sin to keep their vows.

Then out into the night she went,
  And, stooping, crept by hedge and tree;
Her rose-bush flung a snare of scent,
  And caught a happy memory.

She fell, and lay a minute's space;
  She tore the sward in her distress;
The dewy grass refreshed her face;
  She rose and ran with lifted dress.

She started like a morn-caught ghost
  Once when the moon came out and stood
To watch; the naked road she crossed,
  And dived into the murmuring wood.

The branches snatched her streaming cloak;
  A live thing shrieked; she made no stay!
She hurried to the trysting-oak—
  Right well she knew the way.

Without a pause she bared her breast,
  And drove her dagger home and fell,
And lay like one that takes her rest,
  And died and wakened up in hell.

She bathed her spirit in the flame,
  And near the centre took her post;
From all sides to her ears there came
  The dreary anguish of the lost.

The devil started at her side,
  Comely, and tall, and black as jet.
" I am young Malespina's bride;
  Has he come hither yet? "

" My poppet, welcome to your bed."
  " Is Malespina here? "
" Not he! To-morrow he must wed
  His cousin Blanche, my dear! "

" You lie, he died with me to-night."
  " Not he! it was a plot " . . . " You lie! "
" My dear, I never lie outright."
  " We died at midnight, he and I."

The devil went. Without a groan
  She, gathered up in one fierce prayer,
Took root in hell's midst all alone,
  And waited for him there.

She dared to make herself at home
  Amidst the wail, the uneasy stir.
The blood-stained flame that filled the dome,
  Scentless and silent, shrouded her.

How long she stayed I cannot tell;
  But when she felt his perfidy,
She marched across the floor of hell;
  And all the damned stood up to see.

The devil stopped her at the brink:
  She shook him off; she cried, " Away! "
" My dear, you have gone mad, I think."
  " I was betrayed: I will not stay."

Across the weltering deep she ran;
  A stranger thing was never seen:
The damned stood silent to a man;
  They saw the great gulf set between.

To her it seemed a meadow fair;
  And flowers sprang up about her feet.
She entered heaven; she climbed the stair
  And knelt down at the mercy-seat.

Seraphs and saints with one great voice
  Welcomed the soul that knew not fear.
Amazed to find it could rejoice,
  Hell raised a hoarse, half-human cheer.

WILLIAM WATSON

1858 - 1935

SONG

April, April,
Laugh thy girlish laughter;
Then, the moment after,
Weep thy girlish tears,
April, that mine ears
Like a lover greetest,
If I tell thee, sweetest,
All my hopes and fears.
April, April,
Laugh thy golden laughter,
But, the moment after,
Weep thy golden tears!

FRANCIS THOMPSON

1859 - 1907

THE HOUND OF HEAVEN

I fled Him, down the nights and down the days;
  I fled Him, down the arches of the years;
I fled Him, down the labyrinthine ways
  Of my own mind; and in the mist of tears
I hid from Him, and under running laughter.
          Up vistaed hopes I sped;
          And shot, precipitated,
Adown Titanic glooms of chasmed fears,

From those strong Feet that followed, followed after.
      But with unhurrying chase,
      And unperturbèd pace,
    Deliberate speed, majestic instancy,
      They beat—and a Voice beat
      More instant than the Feet—
" All things betray thee, who betrayest Me."

      I pleaded, outlaw-wise,
By many a hearted casement, curtained red,
  Trellised with intertwining charities
(For, though I knew His love Who followèd,
      Yet was I sore adread
Lest, having Him, I must have naught beside);
But, if one little casement parted wide,
  The gust of His approach would clash it to:
  Fear wist not to evade, as Love wist to pursue.
Across the margent of the world I fled,
  And troubled the gold gateways of the stars,
  Smiting for shelter on their clangèd bars;
      Fretted to dulcet jars
And silvern chatter the pale ports o' the moon.
I said to Dawn: Be sudden—to Eve: Be soon;
  With thy young skiey blossoms heap me over
      From this tremendous Lover—
Float thy vague veil about me, lest He see!
  I tempted all His servitors, but to find
My own betrayal in their constancy,
In faith to Him their fickleness to me,
  Their traitorous trueness, and their loyal deceit.
To all swift things for swiftness did I sue;
  Clung to the whistling mane of every wind.
      But whether they swept, smoothly fleet,
     The long savannahs of the blue;
      Or whether, Thunder-driven,
     They clanged his chariot 'thwart a heaven,
Plashy with flying lightnings round the spurn o' their feet:—
  Fear wist not to evade as Love wist to pursue.
      Still with unhurrying chase,
      And unperturbèd pace,
    Deliberate speed, majestic instancy,
      Came on the following Feet,
      And a Voice above their beat—
" Naught shelters thee, who wilt not shelter Me."

I sought no more that after which I strayed
       In face of man or maid;
But still within the little children's eyes
       Seems something, something that replies,
They at least are for me, surely for me!
I turned me to them very wistfully;
But just as their young eyes grew sudden fair
       With dawning answers there,
Their angel plucked them from me by the hair.
" Come then, ye other children, Nature's—share
With me " (said I) " your delicate fellowship;
       Let me greet you lip to lip,
       Let me twine with you caresses.
         Wantoning
       With our Lady-Mother's vagrant tresses,
         Banqueting
       With her in her wind-walled palace,
      Underneath her azured daïs,
      Quaffing, as your taintless way is,
       From a chalice
Lucent-weeping out of the dayspring."
       So it was done:
I in their delicate fellowship was one—
Drew the bolt of Nature's secrecies.
      I knew all the swift importings
      On the wilful face of skies;
      I knew how the clouds arise
      Spumèd of the wild sea-snortings;
       All that's born or dies
      Rose and drooped with; made them shapers
Of mine own moods, or wailful or divine;
      With them joyed and was bereaven.
      I was heavy with the even,
      When she lit her glimmering tapers
      Round the day's dead sanctities.
      I laughed in the morning's eyes.
I triumphed and I saddened with all weather,
      Heaven and I wept together,
And its sweet tears were salt with mortal mine.

Against the red throb of its sunset-heart
      I laid my own to beat,
      And share commingling heat;
But not by that, by that, was eased my human smart.

In vain my tears were wet on Heaven's grey cheek.
For ah! we know not what each other says,
      These things and I; in sound *I* speak—
Their sound is but their stir, they speak by silences.
Nature, poor stepdame, cannot slake my drouth;
      Let her, if she would owe me,
Drop yon blue bosom-veil of sky, and show me
      The breasts o' her tenderness:
Never did any milk of hers once bless
      My thirsting mouth.
      Nigh and nigh draws the chase,
      With unperturbèd pace,
      Deliberate speed, majestic instancy;
        And past those noisèd Feet
        A Voice comes yet more fleet—
    " Lo! naught contents thee, who content'st not Me."

Naked I wait Thy love's uplifted stroke!
My harness piece by piece Thou hast hewn from me,
      And smitten me to my knee;
      I am defenceless utterly.
      I slept, methinks, and woke,
And, slowly gazing, find me stripped in sleep.
In the rash lustihead of my young powers,
      I shook the pillaring hours
And pulled my life upon me; grimed with smears,
I stand amid the dust o' the mounded years—
My mangled youth lies dead beneath the heap.
My days have crackled and gone up in smoke,
Have puffed and burst as sun-starts on a stream.
      Yea, faileth now even dream
The dreamer, and the lute the lutanist;
Even the linked fantasies, in whose blossomy twist
I swung the earth a trinket at my wrist,
Are yielding; cords of all too weak account
For earth with heavy griefs so overplussed.
      Ah! is Thy love indeed
A weed, albeit an amaranthine weed,
Suffering no flowers except its own to mount?
      Ah! must—
      Designer infinite!—
Ah! must Thou char the wood ere Thou canst limn with it?
My freshness spent its wavering shower i' the dust;
And now my heart is as a broken fount,

Wherein tear-drippings stagnate, spilt down ever
    From the dank thoughts that shiver
Upon the sighful branches of my mind
    Such is; what is to be?
The pulp so bitter, how shall taste the rind?
I dimly guess what Time in mists confounds;
Yet ever and anon a trumpet sounds
From the hid battlements of Eternity;
Those shaken mists a space unsettle, then
Round the half-glimpsèd turrets slowly wash again.
    But not ere him who summoneth
    I first have seen, enwound
With glooming robes purpureal, cypress-crowned;
His name I know, and what his trumpet saith.
Whether man's heart or life it be which yields
    Thee harvest, must Thy harvest-fields
    Be dunged with rotten death?

    Now of that long pursuit
    Comes on at hand the bruit;
That Voice is round me like a bursting sea:
    " And is thy earth so marred,
    Shattered in shard on shard?
Lo, all things fly thee, for thou fliest Me!
    Strange, piteous, futile thing!
Wherefore should any set thee love apart?
Seeing none but I makes much of naught " (He said),
" And human love needs human meriting:
    How hast thou merited—
Of all man's clotted clay the dingiest clot?
    Alack, thou knowest not
How little worthy of any love thou art!
Whom wilt thou find to love ignoble thee
    Save Me, save only Me?
All which I took from thee I did but take,
    Not for thy harms,
But just that thou might'st seek it in My arms.
    All which thy child's mistake
Fancies as lost, I have stored for thee at home:
    Rise, clasp My hand, and come! "
    Halts by me that footfall:
    Is my gloom, after all,

Shade of His hand, outstretched caressingly?
 " Ah, fondest, blindest, weakest,
 I am He Whom thou seekest!
Thou dravest love from thee, who dravest Me."

THE HEART

O nothing, in this corporal earth of man,
That to the imminent heaven of his high soul
Responds with colour and with shadow, can
Lack correlated greatness. If the scroll
Where thoughts lie fast in spell of hieroglyph
Be mighty through its mighty habitants;
If God be in His Name; grave potence if
The sounds unbind of hieratic chants;
All's vast that vastness means. Nay, I affirm
Nature is whole in her least things exprest,
Nor know we with what scope God builds the worm.
Our towns are copied fragments from our breast;
 And all man's Babylons strive but to impart
 The grandeurs of his Babylonian heart.

TO A SNOWFLAKE

What heart could have thought you?—
Past our devisal
(O filigree petal!)
Fashioned so purely,
Fragilely, surely,
From what Paradisal
Imagineless metal,
Too costly for cost?
Who hammered you, wrought you,
From argentine vapour?—
" God was my shaper.
Passing surmisal,
He hammered, He wrought me,
From curled silver vapour,
To lust of his mind:—
Thou couldst not have thought me!

So purely, so palely,
Tinily, surely,
Mightily, frailly,
Insculped and embossed,
With His hammer of wind,
And His graver of frost."

" IN NO STRANGE LAND "

O world invisible, we view thee,
O world intangible, we touch thee,
O world unknowable, we know thee,
Inapprehensible, we clutch thee!

Does the fish soar to find the ocean,
The eagle plunge to find the air—
That we ask of the stars in motion
If they have rumour of thee there?

Not where the wheeling systems darken,
And our benumbed conceiving soars!—
The drift of pinions, would we hearken,
Beats at our own clay-shuttered doors.

The angels keep their ancient places;—
Turn but a stone, and start a wing!
'Tis ye, 'tis your estrangèd faces,
That miss the many-splendoured thing.

But, when so sad thou canst not sadder,
Cry—and upon thy so sore loss
Shall shine the traffic of Jacob's ladder
Pitched betwixt Heaven and Charing Cross.

Yea, in the night, my Soul, my daughter,
Cry—clinging Heaven by the hems . . .
And lo, Christ walking on the water
Not of Gennesareth, but Thames!

A. E. HOUSMAN

1859 - 1936

LOVELIEST OF TREES

Loveliest of trees, the cherry now
Is hung with bloom along the bough,
And stands about the woodland ride
Wearing white for Eastertide.

Now, of my threescore years and ten,
Twenty will not come again,
And take from seventy springs a score,
It only leaves me fifty more.

And since to look at things in bloom
Fifty springs are little room,
About the woodlands I will go
To see the cherry hung with snow.

IS MY TEAM PLOUGHING

" Is my team ploughing,
    That I was used to drive
And hear the harness jingle
    When I was man alive? "

Aye, the horses trample,
    The harness jingles now;
No change though you lie under
    The land you used to plough.

" Is football playing
    Along the river shore,
With lads to chase the leather,
    Now I stand up no more? "

Aye, the ball is flying,
    The lads play heart and soul;
The goal stands up, the keeper
    Stands up to keep the goal.

" Is my girl happy,
   That I thought hard to leave,
And has she tired of weeping
   As she lies down at eve? "

Aye, she lies down lightly,
   She lies not down to weep;
Your girl is well contented.
   Be still, my lad, and sleep.

" Is my friend hearty,
   Now I am thin and pine;
And has he found to sleep in
   A better bed than mine? "

Aye, lad, I lie easy,
   I lie as lads would choose;
I cheer a dead man's sweetheart.
   Never ask me whose.

WHEN I WAS ONE-AND-TWENTY

When I was one-and-twenty
   I heard a wise man say,
" Give crowns and pounds and guineas
   But not your heart away;
Give pearls away and rubies
   But keep your fancy free."
But I was one-and-twenty,
   No use to talk to me.

When I was one-and-twenty
   I heard him say again,
" The heart out of the bosom
   Was never given in vain;
'Tis paid with sighs a-plenty
   And sold for endless rue."
And I am two-and-twenty,
   And oh, 'tis true, 'tis true.

BREDON HILL

In summertime on Bredon
  The bells they sound so clear;
Round both the shires they ring them
  In steeples far and near,
  A happy noise to hear.

Here of a Sunday morning
  My love and I would lie,
And see the colored counties,
  And hear the larks so high
  About us in the sky.

The bells would ring to call her
  In valleys miles away:
" Come all to church, good people;
  Good people, come and pray."
  But here my love would stay.

And I would turn and answer
  Among the springing thyme,
" Oh, peal upon our wedding,
  And we will hear the chime,
  And come to church in time."

But when the snows at Christmas
  On Bredon top were strown,
My love rose up so early
  And stole out unbeknown
  And went to church alone.

They tolled the one bell only,
  Groom there was none to see,
The mourners followed after,
  And so to church went she,
  And would not wait for me.

The bells they sound on Bredon,
  And still the steeples hum.
" Come all to church, good people,—"
  Oh, noisy bells, be dumb;
  I hear you, I will come.

THE CHESTNUT CASTS HIS FLAMBEAUX

The chestnut casts his flambeaux, and the flowers
    Stream from the hawthorn on the wind away,
The doors clap to, the pane is blind with showers.
    Pass me the can, lad; there's an end of May.

There's one spoilt spring to scant our mortal lot,
    One season ruined of our little store.
May will be fine next year as like as not:
    Oh, aye, but then we shall be twenty-four.

We for a certainty are not the first
    Have sat in taverns while the tempest hurled
Their hopeful plans to emptiness, and cursed
    Whatever brute and blackguard made the world.

It is in truth iniquity on high
    To cheat our sentenced souls of aught they crave,
And mar the merriment as you and I
    Fare on our long fool's errand to the grave.

Iniquity it is; but pass the can.
    My lad, no pair of kings our mothers bore;
Our only portion is the estate of man:
    We want the moon, but we shall get no more.

If here today the cloud of thunder lours
    Tomorrow it will hie on far behests;
The flesh will grieve on other bones than ours
    Soon, and the soul will mourn in other breasts.

The troubles of our proud and angry dust
    Are from eternity, and shall not fail.
Bear them we can, and if we can we must.
    Shoulder the sky, my lad, and drink your ale.

ON WENLOCK EDGE

On Wenlock Edge the wood's in trouble;
    His forest fleece the Wrekin heaves;
The gale, it plies the saplings double,
    And thick on Severn snow the leaves.

'Twould blow like this through holt and hanger
    When Uricon the city stood:
'Tis the old wind in the old anger,
    But then it threshed another wood.

Then, 'twas before my time, the Roman
    At yonder heaving hill would stare:
The blood that warms an English yeoman,
    The thoughts that hurt him, they were there.

There, like the wind through woods in riot,
    Through him the gale of life blew high;
The tree of man was never quiet:
    Then 'twas the Roman, now 'tis I.

The gale, it plies the saplings double,
    It blows so hard, 'twill soon be gone:
To-day the Roman and his trouble
    Are ashes under Uricon.

KATHARINE TYNAN

1861 - 1931

SLOW SPRING

O year, grow slowly. Exquisite, holy,
    The days go on
With almonds showing the pink stars blowing,
    And birds in the dawn.

Grow slowly, year, like a child that is dear,
    Or a lamb that is mild,
By little steps, and by little skips,
    Like a lamb or a child.

RICHARD HOVEY

(A) 1864 - 1900

COMRADES

Comrades, pour the wine to-night,
　For the parting is with dawn.
Oh, the clink of cups together,
　With the daylight coming on!
　　Greet the morn
　　With a double horn,
When strong men drink together!

Comrades, gird your swords to-night,
　For the battle is with dawn.
Oh, the clash of shields together,
　With the triumph coming on!
　　Greet the foe
　　And lay him low,
When strong men fight together.

Comrades, watch the tides to-night,
　For the sailing is with dawn.
Oh, to face the spray together,
　With the tempest coming on!
　　Greet the sea
　　With a shout of glee,
When strong men roam together.

Comrades, give a cheer to-night,
　For the dying is with dawn.
Oh, to meet the stars together,
　With the silence coming on!
　　Greet the end
　　As a friend a friend,
When strong men die together.

ARTHUR SYMONS

1865 - 1945

IN THE WOOD OF FINVARA

I have grown tired of sorrow and human tears;
Life is a dream in the night, a fear among fears,
A naked runner lost in a storm of spears.

I have grown tired of rapture and love's desire;
Love is a flaming heart, and its flames aspire
Till they cloud the soul in the smoke of a windy fire.

I would wash the dust of the world in a soft green flood;
Here between sea and sea, in the fairy wood,
I have found a delicate, wave-green solitude.

Here, in the fairy wood, between sea and sea,
I have heard the song of a fairy bird in a tree,
And the peace that is not in the world has flown to me.

THE CRYING OF WATER

O water, voice of my heart, crying in the sand,
All night long crying with a mournful cry,
As I lie and listen, and cannot understand
The voice of my heart in my side or the voice of the sea.
O water crying for rest, is it I, is it I?
All night long the water is crying to me.

Unresting water, there shall never be rest
Till the last moon drop and the last tide fail,
And the fire of the end begin to burn in the west;
And the heart shall be weary and wonder and cry like the sea,
All life long crying without avail,
As the water all night long is crying to me.

THE TWENTIETH CENTURY

ROMANTIC REALISM

Two features distinguish the poetry of the first half of the twentieth century: the differences in technique, the differences in background. The first, though the less important, is the more obvious—so obvious that the beginning of the twentieth century threatens to become known as the era of experiment. In America the passion for new modes of expression was particularly strong; schools, movements, tendencies formed and split apart overnight. Sometimes the impulse was opposed to all familiar forms, but the fertility behind the departures roused the reader to fresh appraisals and an appreciation of the diversity of the art.

But the beginning of another poetic language was accomplished neither by innovations in technique nor originality of idea. Romantic realism was again in the ascendancy; " the glory of the commonplace " was no longer a rhetorical phrase. To the new poets " a leaf of grass was no less than the journey-work of the stars . . . and the running blackberry would adorn the parlours of heaven." The return to the material of casual life and the language of every day was swift and spontaneous. In England, Kipling gloried in the mechanical world, and glorified it. Masefield reanimated the rhymed narrative of swiftly moving events. Siegfried Sassoon, seconded by Wilfred Owen, recreated the pity and terror of the trenches. These proved Synge's contention that though the poetry of exaltation will always be the highest, " when men lose their poetic feeling for ordinary life, their exalted poetry is likely to lose its strength of exaltation in the way men cease to build beautiful churches when they have lost happiness in building shops."

National differences began to be more sharply accentuated, especially in America. Idioms that, at first, suggested a foreign origin, were localised so that such writers as Robert Frost, Edwin Arlington Robinson, Vachel Lindsay and Carl Sandburg are classed as definitely American rather than English poets. Robinson's dryly pointed stanzas became recognisably native, no longer sounding the overtones of Browning. Sandburg added his own mid-western metaphysics to the mysticism of " The Great Barbarian." Lindsay, letting in a torrent of sound from the vernacular, stressed not only the speed but the disrupted rhythms of his syncopated times. Frost, carrying the conversational tone to a new pitch of eloquence, widened his appeal with each new work, progressing from a narrator of New England dramas to a singer of universal lyrics.

It was in America that the experimental tendency was most varied. A tentative new tongue was shaped by the witty nuances of Wallace Stevens, the strangely dramatic juxtapositions of T. S. Eliot and Ezra Pound, the shifting modulations of Archibald MacLeish, the musical allusiveness of Hart Crane, the revivified classicism of John Crowe Ransom and Allen Tate, the arresting of light and movement accomplished by H. D. and Amy Lowell, to name only a representative few.

Nor, even in the midst of post-war depression, was the lyric note forgotten. Few quieter songs and few more confident have been fashioned than those of William Butler Yeats, Robert Graves, Ralph Hodgson, Walter de la Mare, W. H. Davies, and Charlotte Mew. In America a list of recent lyricists would barely begin with Conrad Aiken, Edna St. Vincent Millay, Sara Teasdale, Léonie Adams and Elinor Wylie.

The world of the first half of the twentieth century was shaken by two major and several minor wars, followed by the " cold war " which was anything but a substitute for peace. W. H. Auden characterised the epoch with a key poem, " The Age of Anxiety." Auden was perhaps the most eloquent spokesman as well as the most gifted technician of the harassed period, but Stephen Spender, C. Day Lewis, Louis MacNeice, George Barker, and Edith Sitwell were scarcely less articulate, while Dylan Thomas surpassed them all in wild and sometimes bewildering exuberance. On the other side of the Atlantic such " new " poets as Theodore Roethke, Elizabeth Bishop, Robert Lowell, and Richard Wilbur reflected, sometimes elliptically, the confusion of a generation that had lost its last illusion but was desperately in need of the sustaining vigour of belief, of discipline and dignity.

It remains to be seen how much of modern poetry is a true interpretation of the exacerbated temper of the times, a temporary expression of complex and often chaotic subject matter, and how much of it will attain the goal of the poet: the wonder, the intensity, and the enduring power of art.

RUDYARD KIPLING

1865 - 1936

MANDALAY

By the old Moulmein Pagoda, lookin' eastward to the sea,
There's a Burma girl a-settin', an' I know she thinks o' me;
For the wind is in the palm-trees, an' the temple-bells they say:
" Come you back, you British soldier; come you back to
Mandalay! "
Come you back to Mandalay,
Where the old Flotilla lay:
Can't you 'ear their paddles chunkin' from Rangoon to
Mandalay?
On the road to Mandalay,
Where the flyin'-fishes play,
An' the dawn comes up like thunder outer China 'crost
the Bay!

'Er petticut was yaller an' 'er little cap was green,
An' 'er name was Supi-yaw-let—jes' the same as Theebaw's
    Queen,
An' I seed her fust a-smokin' of a whackin' white cheroot,
An' a-wastin' Christian kisses on an 'eathen idol's foot:
        Bloomin' idol made o' mud—
        What they called the Great Gawd Budd—
        Plucky lot she cared for idols when I kissed 'er where she
           stud!
        On the road to Mandalay—

When the mist was on the rice-fields an' the sun was droppin'
    slow,
She'd git 'er little banjo an' she'd sing " *Kulla-lo-lo!* "
With 'er arm upon my shoulder an' her cheek agin my cheek
We useter watch the steamers an' the *hathis* pilin' teak.
        Elephints a-pilin' teak
        In the sludgy, squdgy creek,
        Where the silence 'ung that 'eavy you was 'arf afraid to
           speak!
        On the road to Mandalay—

But that's all shove be'ind me—long ago an' fur away,
An' there ain't no 'busses runnin' from the Bank to Mandalay;
An' I'm learnin' 'ere in London what the ten-year sodger tells:
" If you've 'eard the East a-callin', why, you won't 'eed nothin'
    else."
        No! you won't 'eed nothin' else
        But them spicy garlic smells
        An' the sunshine an' the palm-trees an' the tinkly temple
           bells!
        On the road to Mandalay—

I am sick o' wastin' leather on these gritty pavin'-stones,
An' the blasted Henglish drizzle wakes the fever in my bones;
Tho' I walks with fifty 'ousemaids outer Chelsea to the Strand,
An' they talks a lot o' lovin', but wot do they understand?
        Beefy face an' grubby 'and—
        Law! wot *do* they understand?
        I've a neater, sweeter maiden in a cleaner, greener land!
        On the road to Mandalay—

Ship me somewheres east of Suez where the best is like the worst,
Where there aren't no Ten Commandments, an' a man can raise
    a thirst;

For the temple-bells are callin' an' it's there that I would be—
By the old Moulmein Pagoda, lookin' lazy at the sea—
  On the road to Mandalay,
  Where the old Flotilla lay,
  With our sick beneath the awnings when we went to
   Mandalay!
  Oh, the road to Mandalay,
  Where the flyin' fishes play,
  An' the dawn comes up like thunder outer China 'crost
   the Bay!

THE LAST CHANTEY

" And there was no more sea "

Thus said the Lord in the Vault above the Cherubim,
 Calling to the Angels and the Souls in their degree:
  " Lo! Earth has passed away
  On the smoke of Judgment Day.
 That Our word may be established shall We gather up the
  sea? "

Loud sang the souls of the jolly, jolly mariners:
 " Plague upon the hurricane that made us furl and flee!
  But the war is done between us,
  In the deep the Lord hath seen us—
 Our bones we'll leave the barracout', and God may sink the
  sea! "

Then said the soul of Judas that betrayed Him:
 " Lord, hast Thou forgotten Thy covenant with me?
  How once a year I go
  To cool me on the floe?
 And Ye take my day of mercy if Ye take away the sea."

Then said the soul of the Angel of the Off-shore Wind:
 (He that bits the thunder when the bull-mouthed breakers
  flee):
  " I have watch and ward to keep
  O'er Thy wonders on the deep,
 And Ye take mine honour from me if Ye take away the sea! "

Loud sang the souls of the jolly, jolly mariners:
 " Nay, but we were angry, and a hasty folk are we.

If we worked the ship together
Till she foundered in foul weather,
Are we babes that we should clamour for a vengeance on the
    sea?"

Then said the souls of the slaves that men threw overboard:
  "Kennelled in the picaroon a weary band were we;
    But Thy arm was strong to save,
    And it touched us on the wave,
And we drowsed the long tides idle till Thy Trumpets tore the
    sea."

Then cried the soul of the stout Apostle Paul to God:
  "Once we frapped a ship, and she laboured woundily.
    There were fourteen score of these,
    And they blessed Thee on their knees,
When they learned Thy Grace and Glory under Malta by the
    sea!"

Loud sang the souls of the jolly, jolly mariners,
  Plucking at their harps, and they plucked unhandily:
    "Our thumbs are rough and tarred,
    And the tune is something hard—
May we lift a Deepsea Chantey such as seamen use at sea?"

Then said the souls of the gentlemen-adventurers—
  Fettered wrist to bar all for red iniquity:
    "Ho, we revel in our chains
    O'er the sorrow that was Spain's;
Heave or sink it, leave or drink it, we were masters of the sea!"

Up spake the soul of a grey Gothavn 'speckshioner—
  (He that led the flenching in the fleets of fair Fundee):
    "Oh, the ice-blink white and near,
    And the bowhead breaching clear!
Will Ye whelm them all for wantonness that wallow in the
    sea?"

Loud sang the souls of the jolly, jolly mariners,
  Crying: "Under Heaven, here is neither lead nor lea!
    Must we sing for evermore
    On the windless, glassy floor?
Take back your golden fiddles and we'll beat to open sea!"

Then stooped the Lord, and He called the good sea up to Him,
  And 'stablished its borders unto all eternity,
    That such as have no pleasure
    For to praise the Lord by measure,
They may enter into galleons and serve Him on the sea.

Sun, Wind, and Cloud shall fail not from the face of it,
  Stinging, ringing spindrift, nor the fulmar flying free;
    And the ships shall go abroad
    To the Glory of the Lord
Who heard the silly sailor-folk and gave them back their sea!

RECESSIONAL

God of our fathers, known of old,
  Lord of our far-flung battle-line,
Beneath whose awful hand we hold
  Dominion over palm and pine—
Lord God of Hosts, be with us yet,
Lest we forget—lest we forget!

The tumult and the shouting dies;
  The captains and the kings depart:
Still stands Thine ancient sacrifice,
  An humble and a contrite heart.
Lord God of Hosts, be with us yet,
Lest we forget—lest we forget!

Far-called, our navies melt away;
  On dune and headland sinks the fire:
Lo, all our pomp of yesterday
  Is one with Nineveh and Tyre!
Judge of the Nations, spare us yet,
Lest we forget—lest we forget!

If, drunk with sight of power, we loose
  Wild tongues that have not Thee in awe,
Such boastings as the Gentiles use,
  Or lesser breeds without the Law—
Lord God of Hosts, be with us yet,
Lest we forget—lest we forget!

For heathen heart that puts her trust
   In reeking tube and iron shard,
All valiant dust that builds on dust,
   And, guarding, calls not Thee to guard,
For frantic boast and foolish word—
Thy Mercy on Thy People, Lord!

WILLIAM BUTLER YEATS

1865 - 1939

THE SONG OF WANDERING AENGUS

I went out to the hazel wood,
Because a fire was in my head,
And cut and peeled a hazel wand,
And hooked a berry to a thread,
And when white moths were on the wing,
And moth-like stars were flickering out,
I dropped the berry in a stream
And caught a little silver trout.

When I had laid it on the floor
I went to blow the fire a-flame,
But something rustled on the floor,
And some one called me by my name:
It had become a glimmering girl
With apple blossoms in her hair
Who called me by my name and ran
And faded through the brightening air.

Though I am old with wandering
Through hollow lands and hilly lands,
I will find out where she has gone,
And kiss her lips and take her hands;
And walk among long dappled grass,
And pluck till time and times are done,
The silver apples of the moon,
The golden apples of the sun.

THE LAKE ISLE OF INNISFREE

I will arise and go now, and go to Innisfree,
And a small cabin build there, of clay and wattles made;
Nine bean rows will I have there, a hive for the honey bee,
     And live alone in the bee-loud glade.

And I shall have some peace there, for peace comes dropping
    slow,
Dropping from the veils of the morning to where the cricket
    sings;
There midnight's all a glimmer, and noon a purple glow,
     And evening full of the linnet's wings.

I will arise and go now, for always night and day
I hear lake water lapping with low sounds by the shore;
While I stand on the roadway, or on the pavements gray,
     I hear it in the deep heart's core.

AN OLD SONG RESUNG

Down by the salley gardens my love and I did meet;
She passed the salley gardens with little snow-white feet.
She bid me take love easy, as the leaves grow on the tree;
But I, being young and foolish, with her would not agree.

In a field by the river my love and I did stand,
And on my leaning shoulder she laid her snow-white hand.
She bid me take life easy, as the grass grows on the weirs;
But I was young and foolish, and now am full of tears.

WHEN YOU ARE OLD

When you are old and grey and full of sleep,
And nodding by the fire, take down this book,
And slowly read, and dream of the soft look
Your eyes had once, and of their shadows deep;

How many loved your moments of glad grace,
And loved your beauty with love false or true;
But one man loved the pilgrim soul in you,
And loved the sorrows of your changing face.

And bending down beside the glowing bars
Murmur, a little sadly, how love fled
And paced upon the mountains overhead
And hid his face amid a crowd of stars.

THE WILD SWANS AT COOLE

The trees are in their autumn beauty,
The woodland paths are dry,
Under the October twilight the water
Mirrors a still sky;
Upon the brimming water among the stones
Are nine and fifty swans.

The nineteenth Autumn has come upon me
Since I first made my count;
I saw, before I had well finished,
All suddenly mount
And scatter, wheeling, in great broken rings
Upon their clamorous wings.

I have looked upon those brilliant creatures,
And now my heart is sore.
All's changed since I, hearing at twilight,
The first time on this shore,
The bell-beat of their wings above my head,
Trod with a lighter tread.

Unwearied still, lover by lover,
They paddle in the cold,
Companionable streams or climb the air;
Their hearts have not grown old;
Passion or conquest, wander where they will,
Attend upon them still.

But now they drift on the still water
Mysterious, beautiful;
Among what rushes will they build,
By what lake's edge or pool
Delight men's eyes, when I awake some day
To find they have flown away?

RUNNING TO PARADISE

As I came over Windy Gap
They threw a halfpenny into my cap,
For I am running to Paradise;
And all that I need do is to wish
And somebody puts his hand in the dish
To throw me a bit of salted fish:
And there the king *is* but as the beggar.

My brother Mourteen is worn out
With skelping[1] his big brawling lout,
And I am running to Paradise;
A poor life do what he can,
And though he keep a dog and a gun,
A serving maid and a serving man:
And there the king *is* but as the beggar.

Poor men have grown to be rich men,
And rich men grown to be poor again,
And I am running to Paradise;
And many a darling wit's grown dull
That tossed a bare heel when at school,
Now it has filled an old sock full:
And there the king *is* but as the beggar.

The wind is old and still at play
While I must hurry upon my way,
For I am running to Paradise;
Yet never have I lit on a friend
To take my fancy like the wind
That nobody can buy or bind:
And there the king *is* but as the beggar.

[1] Hurrying.

LIONEL JOHNSON

1867 - 1902

THE DARK ANGEL

Dark Angel, with thine aching lust
To rid the world of penitence:
Malicious Angel, who still dost
My soul such subtile violence!

Because of thee, no thought, no thing,
Abides for me undesecrate:
Dark Angel, ever on the wing,
Who never reachest me too late!

When music sounds, then changest thou
Its silvery to a sultry fire:
Nor will thine envious heart allow
Delight untortured by desire.

Through thee, the gracious Muses turn
To Furies, O mine Enemy!
And all the things of beauty burn
With flames of evil ecstasy.

Because of thee, the land of dreams
Becomes a gathering place of fears:
Until tormented slumber seems
One vehemence of useless tears.

When sunlight glows upon the flowers,
Or ripples down the dancing sea:
Thou, with thy troop of passionate powers,
Beleaguerest, bewilderest me.

Within the breath of autumn woods,
Within the winter silences,
Thy venomous spirit stirs and broods,
O Master of impieties!

The ardour of red flame is thine,
And thine the steely soul of ice:
Thou poisonest the fair design
Of nature, with unfair device.

Apples of ashes, golden bright;
Waters of bitterness, how sweet!
O banquet of a foul delight,
Prepared by thee, dark Paraclete!

Thou art the whisper in the gloom,
The hinting tone, the haunting laugh:
Thou art the adorner of my tomb,
The minstrel of mine epitaph.

I fight thee, in the Holy Name!
Yet, what thou dost, is what God saith:
Tempter! should I escape thy flame,
Thou wilt have helped my soul from Death:

The second Death, that never dies,
That cannot die, when time is dead:
Live Death, wherein the lost soul cries,
Eternally uncomforted.

Dark Angel, with thine aching lust!
Of two defeats, of two despairs:
Less dread, a change to drifting dust,
Than thine eternity of cares.

Do what thou wilt, thou shalt not so,
Dark Angel! triumph over me:
Lonely, unto the Lone I go;
Divine, to the Divinity.

ERNEST DOWSON

1867 - 1900

CYNARA

Non Sum Qualis Eram Bonae Sub Regno Cynarae

Last night, ah, yesternight, betwixt her lips and mine
There fell thy shadow, Cynara! thy breath was shed
Upon my soul between the kisses and the wine;
And I was desolate and sick of an old passion,
    Yea, I was desolate and bowed my head:
I have been faithful to thee, Cynara! in my fashion.

All night upon mine heart I felt her warm heart beat,
Night-long within mine arms in love and sleep she lay;
Surely the kisses of her bought red mouth were sweet;
But I was desolate and sick of an old passion,
    When I awoke and found the dawn was grey:
I have been faithful to thee, Cynara! in my fashion.

I have forgot much, Cynara! gone with the wind,
Flung roses, roses riotously with the throng,
Dancing, to put thy pale, lost lilies out of mind;
But I was desolate and sick of an old passion,
    Yea, all the time, because the dance was long:
I have been faithful to thee, Cynara! in my fashion

I cried for madder music and for stronger wine,
But when the feast is finished and the lamps expire,
Then falls thy shadow, Cynara! the night is thine;
And I am desolate and sick of an old passion,
    Yea, hungry for the lips of my desire:
I have been faithful to thee, Cynara! in my fashion.

EDWIN ARLINGTON ROBINSON

(A) 1869 - 1935

FLAMMONDE

The man Flammonde, from God knows where,
With firm address and foreign air,
With news of nations in his talk
And something royal in his walk,
With glint of iron in his eyes,
But never doubt, nor yet surprise,
Appeared, and stayed, and held his head
As one by kings accredited.

Erect, with his alert repose
About him, and about his clothes,
He pictured all tradition hears
Of what we owe to fifty years.
His cleansing heritage of taste
Paraded neither want nor waste;
And what he needed for his fee
To live, he borrowed graciously.

He never told us what he was,
Or what mischance, or other cause,
Had banished him from better days
To play the Prince of Castaways.
Meanwhile he played surpassing well
A part, for most, unplayable;
In fine, one pauses, half afraid
To say for certain that he played.

For that, one may as well forgo
Conviction as to yes or no;
Nor can I say just how intense
Would then have been the difference
To several, who, having striven
In vain to get what he was given,
Would see the stranger taken on
By friends not easy to be won.

Moreover, many a malcontent
He soothed and found munificent;
His courtesy beguiled and foiled
Suspicion that his years were soiled;
His mien distinguished any crowd,
His credit strengthened when he bowed;
And women, young and old, were fond
Of looking at the man Flammonde.

There was a woman in our town
On whom the fashion was to frown;
But while our talk renewed the tinge
Of a long-faded scarlet fringe,
The man Flammonde saw none of that,
And what he saw we wondered at—
That none of us, in her distress,
Could hide or find our littleness.

There was a boy that all agreed
Had shut within him the rare seed
Of learning. We could understand,
But none of us could lift a hand.
The man Flammonde appraised the youth,
And told a few of us the truth;
And thereby, for a little gold,
A flowered future was unrolled.

There were two citizens who fought
For years and years, and over nought;
They made life awkward for their friends,
And shortened their own dividends.
The man Flammonde said what was wrong
Should be made right; nor was it long
Before they were again in line,
And had each other in to dine.

And these I mention are but four
Of many out of many more.
So much for them. But what of him—
So firm in every look and limb?
What small satanic sort of kink
Was in his brain? What broken link
Withheld him from the destinies
That came so near to being his?

What was he, when we came to sift
His meaning, and to note the drift
Of incommunicable ways
That make us ponder while we praise?
Why was it that his charm revealed
Somehow the surface of a shield?
What was it that we never caught?
What was he, and what was he not?

How much it was of him we met
We cannot ever know; nor yet
Shall all he gave us quite atone
For what was his, and his alone;
Nor need we now, since he knew best,
Nourish an ethical unrest:
Rarely at once will nature give
The power to be Flammonde and live.

We cannot know how much we learn
From those who never will return,
Until a flash of unforeseen
Remembrance falls of what has been.
We've each a darkening hill to climb;
And this is why, from time to time
In Tilbury Town, we look beyond
Horizons for the man Flammonde.

MR. FLOOD'S PARTY

Old Eben Flood, climbing alone one night
Over the hill between the town below
And the forsaken upland hermitage
That held as much as he should ever know
On earth again of home, paused warily.
The road was his with not a native near;
And Eben, having leisure, said aloud,
For no man else in Tilbury Town to hear:

" Well, Mr. Flood, we have the harvest moon
Again, and we may not have many more;
The bird is on the wing, the poet says,
And you and I have said it here before.
Drink to the bird." He raised up to the light
The jug that he had gone so far to fill,
And answered huskily: " Well, Mr. Flood,
Since you propose it, I believe I will."

Alone, as if enduring to the end
A valiant armour of scarred hopes outworn,
He stood there in the middle of the road
Like Roland's ghost winding a silent horn.
Below him, in the town among the trees,
Where friends of other days had honoured him,
A phantom salutation of the dead
Rang thinly till old Eben's eyes were dim.

Then, as a mother lays her sleeping child
Down tenderly, fearing it may awake,
He set the jug down slowly at his feet
With trembling care, knowing that most things break;
And only when assured that on firm earth
It stood, as the uncertain lives of men
Assurèdly did not, he paced away,
And with his hand extended paused again:

" Well, Mr. Flood, we have not met like this
In a long time; and many a change has come
To both of us, I fear, since last it was
We had a drop together. Welcome home! "

Convivially returning with himself,
Again he raised the jug up to the light;
And with an acquiescent quaver said:
" Well, Mr. Flood, if you insist, I might.

" Only a very little, Mr. Flood—
For auld lang syne. No more, sir; that will do."
So, for the time, apparently it did,
And Eben evidently thought so too;
For soon amid the silver loneliness
Of night he lifted up his voice, and sang,
Secure, with only two moons listening,
Until the whole harmonious landscape rang—

" For auld lang syne." The weary throat gave out,
The last word wavered; and the song being done,
He raised again the jug regretfully
And shook his head, and was again alone.
There was not much that was ahead of him,
And there was nothing in the town below—
Where strangers would have shut the many doors
That many friends had opened long ago.

VETERAN SIRENS

The ghost of Ninon would be sorry now
To laugh at them, were she to see them here,
So brave and so alert for learning how
To fence with reason for another year.

Age offers a far comelier diadem
Than theirs; but anguish has no eye for grace,
When time's malicious mercy cautions them
To think a while of number and of space.

The burning hope, the worn expectancy,
The martyred humour, and the maimed allure,
Cry out for time to end his levity,
And age to soften its investiture;

But they, though others fade and are still fair,
Defy their fairness and are unsubdued;
Although they suffer, they may not forswear
The patient ardour of the unpursued.

Poor flesh, to fight the calendar so long;
Poor vanity, so quaint and yet so brave;
Poor folly, so deceived and yet so strong,
So far from Ninon and so near the grave.

CHARLOTTE MEW

1870 - 1928

SEA LOVE

Tide be runnin' the great world over:
    'Twas only last June month I mind that we
Was thinkin' the toss and the call in the breast of the lover
    So everlastin' as the sea.

Here's the same little fishes that sputter and swim,
    Wi' the moon's old glim on the gray, wet sand;
An' him no more to me nor me to him
    Than the wind goin' over my hand.

I HAVE BEEN THROUGH THE GATES

His heart, to me, was a place of palaces and pinnacles and shining
    towers;
I saw it then as we see things in dreams—I do not remember how
    long I slept;
I remember the trees, and the high, white walls, and how the sun
    was always on the towers—
The walls are standing to-day, and the gates: I have been
    through the gates, I have groped, I have crept
Back, back. There is dust in the streets, and blood; they are
    empty; darkness is over them;
His heart is a place with the lights gone out, forsaken by great
    winds and the heavenly rain, unclean and unswept,
Like the heart of the holy city, old, blind, beautiful Jerusalem,
Over which Christ wept.

BESIDE THE BED

Some one has shut the shining eyes, straightened and folded
    The wandering hands quietly covering the unquiet breast:
So, smoothed and silenced you lie, like a child, not again to be
    questioned or scolded:
    But, for you, not one of us believes that this is rest.

Not so to close the windows down can cloud and deaden
    The blue beyond: or to screen the wavering flame subdue its
        breath:
Why, if I lay my cheek to your cheek, your grey lips, like dawn,
    would quiver and redden,
    Breaking into the old, odd smile at this fraud of death.

Because all night you have not turned to us or spoken
    It is time for you to wake; your dreams were never very deep:
I, for one, have seen the thin bright, twisted threads of them
    dimmed suddenly and broken.
    This is only a most piteous pretence of sleep!

WILLIAM HENRY DAVIES

1871 - 1940

LEISURE

What is this life if, full of care,
We have no time to stand and stare.

No time to stand beneath the boughs
And stare as long as sheep or cows.

No time to see, when woods we pass,
Where squirrels hide their nuts in grass.

No time to see, in broad daylight,
Streams full of stars, like skies at night.

No time to turn at Beauty's glance,
And watch her feet, how they can dance.

No time to wait till her mouth can
Enrich that smile her eyes began.

A poor life this if, full of care,
We have no time to stand and stare.

THE HERMIT

What moves that lonely man is not the boom
  Of waves that break against the cliff so strong;
Nor roar of thunder, when that travelling voice
  Is caught by rocks that carry far along.

'Tis not the groan of oak tree in its prime,
  When lightning strikes its solid heart to dust.
Nor frozen pond when, melted by the sun,
  It suddenly doth break its sparkling crust.

What moves that man is when the blind bat taps
  His window where he sits alone at night;
Or when the small bird sounds like some great beast
  Among the dead, dry leaves so frail and light;

Or when the moths on his night-pillow beat
  Such heavy blows he fears they'll break his bones;
Or when a mouse inside the papered walls,
  Comes like a tiger crunching through the stones.

A GREAT TIME

Sweet Chance, that led my steps abroad,
  Beyond the town, where wild flowers grow—
A rainbow and a cuckoo, Lord!
  How rich and great the times are now!
    Know, all ye sheep
    And cows that keep
On staring that I stand so long
  In grass that's wet from heavy rain—
A rainbow and a cuckoo's song
  May never come together again;
    May never come
    This side the tomb.

RALPH HODGSON

1872 - 1962

TIME, YOU OLD GYPSY MAN

Time, you old gypsy man,
  Will you not stay,
Put up your caravan
  Just for one day?

All things I'll give you
Will you be my guest,
Bells for your jennet
Of silver the best,
Goldsmiths shall beat you
A great golden ring,
Peacocks shall bow to you,
Little boys sing,
Oh, and sweet girls will
  Festoon you with may.
Time, you old gypsy,
Why hasten away?

Last week in Babylon,
Last night in Rome,
Morning, and in the crush
Under Paul's dome;
Under Paul's dial
You tighten your rein—
Only a moment,
And off once again;
Off to some city
Now blind in the womb,
Off to another
Ere that's in the tomb.

Time, you old gypsy man,
  Will you not stay,
Put up your caravan
  Just for one day?

EVE

Eve, with her basket, was
Deep in the bells and grass,
Wading in bells and grass
Up to her knees.
Picking a dish of sweet
Berries and plums to eat,
Down in the bells and grass
Under the trees.

Mute as a mouse in a
Corner the cobra lay,
Curled round a bough of the
Cinnamon tall. . . .
Now to get even and
Humble proud heaven and
Now was the moment or
Never at all.

" Eva ! " Each syllable
Light as a flower fell,
" Eva ! " he whispered the
Wondering maid,
Soft as a bubble sung
Out of a linnet's lung,
Soft and most silverly
" Eva ! " he said.

Picture that orchard sprite;
Eve, with her body white,
Supple and smooth to her
Slim finger-tips;
Wondering, listening,
Listening, wondering,
Eve with a berry
Half-way to her lips.

Oh, had our simple Eve
Seen through the make-believe!
Had she but known the
Pretender he was!

Out of the boughs he came,
Whispering still her name,
Tumbling in twenty rings
Into the grass.

Here was the strangest pair
In the world anywhere,
Eve in the bells and grass
Kneeling, and he
Telling his story low. . . .
Singing birds saw them go
Down the dark path to
The Blasphemous Tree.

Oh, what a clatter when
Titmouse and Jenny Wren
Saw him successful and
Taking his leave!
How the birds rated him,
How they all hated him!
How they all pitied
Poor motherless Eve!

Picture her crying
Outside in the lane,
Eve, with no dish of sweet
Berries and plums to eat,
Haunting the gate of the
Orchard in vain. . . .
Picture the lewd delight
Under the hill to-night—
" Eva! " the toast goes round,
" Eva! " again.

THE MYSTERY

He came and took me by the hand
    Up to a red rose tree,
He kept His meaning to Himself
    But gave a rose to me.

I did not pray Him to lay bare
    The mystery to me,
Enough the rose was Heaven to smell,
    And His own face to see.

WALTER DE LA MARE

1873 - 1956

THE LISTENERS

" Is there anybody there? " said the Traveller,
   Knocking on the moonlit door;
And his horse in the silence champed the grasses
   Of the forest's ferny floor.
And a bird flew up out of the turret,
   Above the Traveller's head:
And he smote upon the door again a second time;
   " Is there anybody there? " he said.
But no one descended to the Traveller;
   No head from the leaf-fringed sill
Leaned over and looked into his grey eyes,
   Where he stood perplexed and still.
But only a host of phantom listeners
   That dwelt in the lone house then
Stood listening in the quiet of the moonlight
   To that voice from the world of men:
Stood thronging the faint moonbeams on the dark stair
   That goes down to the empty hall,
Hearkening in an air stirred and shaken
   By the lonely Traveller's call.
And he felt in his heart their strangeness,
   Their stillness answering his cry,
While his horse moved, cropping the dark turf,
   'Neath the starred and leafy sky;
For he suddenly smote on the door, even
   Louder, and lifted his head:—
" Tell them I came, and no one answered,
   That I kept my word," he said.
Never the least stir made the listeners,
   Though every word he spake
Fell echoing through the shadowiness of the still house
   From the one man left awake:
Aye, they heard his foot upon the stirrup,
   And the sound of iron on stone,
And how the silence surged softly backward,
   When the plunging hoofs were gone.

NOD

Softly along the road of evening,
  In a twilight dim with rose,
Wrinkled with age, and drenched with dew
  Old Nod, the shepherd, goes.

His drowsy flock streams on before him,
  Their fleeces charged with gold,
To where the sun's last beam leans low
  On Nod the shepherd's fold.

The hedge is quick and green with brier,
  From their sand the conies creep;
And all the birds that fly in heaven
  Flock singing home to sleep.

His lambs outnumber a noon's roses,
  Yet, when night's shadows fall,
His blind old sheep-dog, Slumber-soon,
  Misses not one of all.

His are the quiet steeps of dreamland,
  The waters of no-more-pain;
His ram's bell rings 'neath an arch of stars,
  " Rest, rest, and rest again."

THE SONG OF SHADOWS

Sweep thy faint strings, Musician,
  With thy long lean hand;
Downward the starry tapers burn,
  Sinks soft the waning sand;
The old hound whimpers couched in sleep,
  The embers smoulder low;
Across the walls the shadows
  Come, and go.

Sweep softly thy strings, Musician,
  The minutes mount to hours;
Frost on the windless casement weaves
  A labyrinth of flowers;
Ghosts linger in the darkening air,
  Hearken at the open door;
Music hath called them, dreaming,
  Home once more.

AN EPITAPH

Here lies a most beautiful lady,
Light of step and heart was she;
I think she was the most beautiful lady
That ever was in the West Country.
But beauty vanishes; beauty passes;
However rare—rare it be;
And when I crumble, who will remember
This lady of the West Country?

G. K. CHESTERTON

1874 - 1936

THE PRAISE OF DUST

" What of vile dust? " the preacher said.
   Methought the whole world woke,
The dead stone lived beneath my foot,
   And my whole body spoke:

" You, that play tyrant to the dust,
   And stamp its wrinkled face,
This patient star that flings you not
   Far into homeless space,

" Come down out of your dusty shrine
   The living dust to see,
The flowers that at your sermon's end
   Stand blazing silently.

" Rich white and blood-red blossom; stones,
   Lichens like fire encrust;
A gleam of blue, a glare of gold,
   The vision of the dust.

" Pass them all by: till, as you come
   Where, at a city's edge,
Under a tree—I know it well—
   Under a lattice ledge,

" The sunshine falls on one brown head.
　　You, too; O cold of clay,
Eater of stones, may haply hear
　　The trumpets of that day

" When God to all his paladins
　　By his own splendour swore
To make a fairer face than heaven,
　　Of dust and nothing more."

THE DONKEY

When fishes flew and forests walked
　　And figs grew upon thorn,
Some moment when the moon was blood,
　　Then surely I was born;

With monstrous head and sickening cry
　　And ears like errant wings,
The devil's walking parody
　　On all four-footed things.

The tattered outlaw of the earth,
　　Of ancient crooked will;
Starve, scourge, deride me: I am dumb,
　　I keep my secret still.

Fools! For I also had my hour;
　　One far fierce hour and sweet:
There was a shout about my ears,
　　And palms before my feet!

AMY LOWELL

(A) 1874 - 1925

PATTERNS

I walk down the garden paths,
And all the daffodils
Are blowing, and the bright blue squills.
I walk down the patterned garden-paths
In my stiff, brocaded gown,

With my powdered hair and jewelled fan,
I too am a rare
Pattern. As I wander down
The garden paths.

My dress is richly figured,
And the train
Makes a pink and silver stain
On the gravel, and the thrift
Of the borders.
Just a plate of current fashion,
Tripping by in high-heeled, ribboned shoes.
Not a softness anywhere about me,
Only whalebone and brocade.
And I sink on a seat in the shade
Of a lime tree. For my passion
Wars against the stiff brocade.
The daffodils and squills
Flutter in the breeze
As they please.
And I weep;
For the lime tree is in blossom
And one small flower has dropped upon my bosom.

And the plashing of waterdrops
In the marble fountain
Comes down the garden paths.
The dripping never stops.
Underneath my stiffened gown
Is the softness of a woman bathing in a marble basin,
A basin in the midst of hedges grown
So thick, she cannot see her lover hiding,
But she guesses he is near,
And the sliding of the water
Seems the stroking of a dear
Hand upon her.
What is Summer in a fine brocaded gown!
I should like to see it lying in a heap upon the ground.
All the pink and silver crumpled up on the ground.

I would be the pink and silver as I ran along the paths,
And he would stumble after,
Bewildered by my laughter.
I should see the sun flashing from his sword-hilt and the buckles
    on his shoes.

I would choose
To lead him in a maze along the patterned paths,
A bright and laughing maze for my heavy-booted lover.
Till he caught me in the shade,
And the buttons of his waistcoat bruised my body as he clasped
    me,
Aching, melting, unafraid.
With the shadows of the leaves and the sundrops,
And the plopping of the waterdrops,
All about us in the open afternoon—
I am very like to swoon
With the weight of this brocade,
For the sun sifts through the shade.

Underneath the fallen blossom
In my bosom
Is a letter I have hid.
It was brought to me this morning by a rider from the Duke.
" Madam, we regret to inform you that Lord Hartwell
Died in action Thursday sennight."
As I read it in the white, morning sunlight,
The letters squirmed like snakes.
" Any answer, Madam? " said my footman.
" No," I told him.
" See that the messenger takes some refreshment.
No, no answer."
And I walked into the garden,
Up and down the patterned paths,
In my stiff, correct brocade.
The blue and yellow flowers stood up proudly in the sun
Each one.
I stood upright too,
Held rigid to the pattern
By the stiffness of my gown;
Up and down I walked,
Up and down.

In a month he would have been my husband.
In a month, here, underneath this lime,
We would have broke the pattern;
He for me, and I for him,
He as Colonel, I as Lady,
On this shady seat.
He had a whim
That sunlight carried blessing.

And I answered, " It shall be as you have said."
Now he is dead.

In Summer and in Winter I shall walk
Up and down
The patterned garden paths
In my stiff, brocaded gown.
The squills and daffodils
Will give place to pillared roses, and to asters, and to snow.
I shall go
Up and down
In my gown.
Gorgeously arrayed,
Boned and stayed.
And the softness of my body will be guarded from embrace
By each button, hook, and lace.
For the man who should loose me is dead,
Fighting with the Duke in Flanders,
In a pattern called a war.
Christ! What are patterns for?

APOLOGY

Be not angry with me that I bear
    Your colours everywhere,
    All through each crowded street,
        And meet
    The wonder-light in every eye,
        As I go by.

Each plodding wayfarer looks up to gaze,
    Blinded by rainbow haze,
    The snuff of happiness,
    No less,
    Which wraps me in its glad-hued folds
        Of peacock golds.

Before my feet the dusty, rough-paved way
    Flushes beneath its gray.
    My steps fall ringed with light,
        So bright,
It seems a myriad suns are strown
    About the town.

Around me is the sound of steepled bells,
　　And richly perfumed smells
　　Hang like a wind-forgotten cloud,
　　　　And shroud
　　Me from close contact with the world.
　　　　I dwell impearled.

You blazon me with jewelled insignia.
　　A flaming nebula
　　Rims in my life. And yet
　　　　You set
　　The word upon me, unconfessed
　　　　To go unguessed.

ROBERT FROST

(A) 1875 - 1963

MY NOVEMBER GUEST

My Sorrow, when she's here with me,
　　Thinks these dark days of autumn rain
Are beautiful as days can be;
She loves the bare, the withered tree;
　　She walks the sodden pasture lane.

Her pleasure will not let me stay.
　　She talks and I am fain to list:
She's glad the birds are gone away,
She's glad her simple worsted grey
　　Is silver now with clinging mist.

The desolate, deserted trees,
　　The faded earth, the heavy sky,
The beauties she so truly sees,
She thinks I have no eye for these,
　　And vexes me for reason why.

Not yesterday I learned to know
　　The love of bare November days
Before the coming of the snow,
But it were vain to tell her so,
　　And they are better for her praise.

AN OLD MAN'S WINTER NIGHT

All out of doors looked darkly in at him
Through the thin frost, almost in separate stars,
That gathers on the pane in empty rooms.
What kept his eyes from giving back the gaze
Was the lamp tilted near them in his hand.
What kept him from remembering the need
That brought him to that creaking room was age.
He stood with barrels round him—at a loss.
And having scared the cellar under him
In clomping there, he scared it once again
In clomping off; and scared the outer night,
Which has its sounds, familiar, like the roar
Of trees and crack of branches, common things,
But nothing so like beating on a box.
A light he was to no one but himself
Where now he sat, concerned with he knew what;
A quiet light, and then not even that.
He consigned to the moon, such as she was,
So late-arising, to the broken moon
As better than the sun in any case
For such a charge, his snow upon the roof,
His icicles along the wall to keep;
And slept. The log that shifted with a jolt
Once in the stove, disturbed him and he shifted,
And eased his heavy breathing, but still slept.
One aged man—one man—can't keep a house.
A farm, a countryside, or if he can,
It's thus he does it of a winter night.

HOME BURIAL

He saw her from the bottom of the stairs
Before she saw him. She was starting down.
Looking back over her shoulder at some fear.
She took a doubtful step and then undid it
To raise herself and look again. He spoke
Advancing toward her: " What is it you see
From up there always—for I want to know."
She turned and sank upon her skirts at that,
And her face changed from terrified to dull.

He said to gain time: " What is it you see,"
Mounting until she cowered under him.
" I will find out now—you must tell me, dear."
She, in her place, refused him any help
With the least stiffening of her neck and silence.
She let him look, sure that he wouldn't see,
Blind creature; and a while he didn't see.
But at last he murmured, " Oh," and again, " Oh."

" What is it—what? " she said.

       " Just that I see."

" You don't," she challenged. " Tell me what it is."

" The wonder is I didn't see at once.
I never noticed it from here before.
I must be wonted to it—that's the reason.
The little graveyard where my people are!
So small the window frames the whole of it.
Not so much larger than a bedroom, is it?
There are three stones of slate and one of marble,
Broad-shouldered little slabs there in the sunlight
On the sidehill. We haven't to mind *those*.
But I understand: it is not the stones,
But the child's mound——"

    " Don't, don't, don't, don't, she cried.

She withdrew shrinking from beneath his arm
That rested on the banister, and slid downstairs;
And turned on him with such a daunting look,
He said twice over before he knew himself:
" Can't a man speak of his own child he's lost? "
" Not you! Oh, where's my hat? Oh, I don't need it!
I must get out of here. I must get air.
I don't know rightly whether any man can."

" Amy! Don't go to some one else this time.
Listen to me. I won't come down the stairs."
He sat and fixed his chin between his fists.
" There's something I should like to ask you, dear."

" You don't know how to ask it."

       " Help me, then."

Her fingers moved the latch for all reply.

" My words are nearly always an offence.
I don't know how to speak of anything
So as to please you. But I might be taught,
I should suppose. I can't say I see how.
A man must partly give up being a man
With womenfolk. We could have some arrangement
By which I'd bind myself to keep hands off
Anything special you're a-mind to name.
Though I don't like such things 'twixt those that love.
Two that don't love can't live together without them.
But two that do can't live together with them."
She moved the latch a little. " Don't—don't go.
Don't carry it to some one else this time.
Tell me about it if it's something human.
Let me into your grief. I'm not so much
Unlike other folks as your standing there
Apart would make me out. Give me my chance.
I do think though, you overdo it a little.
What was it brought you up to think it the thing
To take your mother-loss of a first child
So inconsolably—in the face of love.
You'd think his memory might be satisfied—"

" There you go sneering now! "

                              " I'm not, I'm not!
You make me angry. I'll come down to you.
God, what a woman! And it's come to this,
A man can't speak of his own child that's dead."

" You can't because you don't know how to speak.
If you had any feelings, you that dug
With your own hand—how could you?—his little grave;
I saw you from that very window there,
Making the gravel leap and leap in air,
Leap up, like that, like that, and land so lightly
And roll back down the mound beside the hole.
I thought, Who is that man? I didn't know you.
And I crept down the stairs and up the stairs
To look again, and still your spade kept lifting.
Then you came in. I heard your rumbling voice
Out in the kitchen, and I don't know why,
But I went near to see with my own eyes.

You could sit there with the stains on your shoes
Of the fresh earth from your own baby's grave
And talk about your everyday concerns.
You had stood the spade up against the wall
Outside there in the entry, for I saw it."

" I shall laugh the worst laugh I ever laughed.
I'm cursed. God, if I don't believe I'm cursed."

" I can repeat the very words you were saying.
' Three foggy mornings and one rainy day
Will rot the best birch fence a man can build.'
Think of it, talk like that at such a time!
What had how long it takes a birch to rot
To do with what was in the darkened parlour.
You *couldn't* care! The nearest friends can go
With any one to death, comes so far short
They might as well not try to go at all.
No, from the time when one is sick to death,
One is alone, and he dies more alone.
Friends make pretence of following to the grave,
But before one is in it, their minds are turned
And making the best of their way back to life
And living people, and things they understand.
But the world's evil. I won't have grief so
If I can change it. Oh, I won't, I won't! "

" There, you have said it all and you feel better.
You won't go now, you're crying. Close the door.
The heart's gone out of it: why keep it up.
Amy! There's some one coming down the road! "

" You—oh, you think the talk is all. I must go—
Somewhere out of this house. How can I make you——"

" If—you—do! " She was opening the door wider.
" Where do you mean to go? First tell me that.
I'll follow and bring you back by force. I will!——"

TREE AT MY WINDOW

Tree at my window, window tree,
My sash is lowered when night comes on;
But let there never be curtain drawn
Between you and me.

Vague dream-head lifted out of the ground,
And thing next most diffuse to cloud,
Not all your light tongue talking aloud
Could be profound.

But, tree, I have seen you taken and tossed,
And if you have seen me when I slept,
You have seen me when I was taken and swept
And all but lost.

That day she put our heads together,
Fate had her imagination about her,
Your head so much concerned with outer,
Mine with inner, weather.

TO EARTHWARD

Love at the lips was touch
As sweet as I could bear;
And once that seemed too much;
I lived on air

That crossed me from sweet things,
The flow of—was it musk
From hidden grape-vine springs
Down hill at dusk?

I had the swirl and ache
From sprays of honeysuckle
That when they're gathered shake
Dew on the knuckle.

I craved strong sweets, but those
Seemed strong when I was young;
The petal of the rose
It was that stung

Now no joy but lacks salt
That is not dashed with pain
And weariness and fault;
I crave the stain

Of tears, the aftermark
Of almost too much love,
The sweet of bitter bark
And burning clove.

When stiff and sore and scarred
I take away my hand
From leaning on it hard
In grass and sand,

The hurt is not enough:
I long for weight and strength
To feel the earth as rough
To all my length.

STOPPING BY WOODS ON A SNOWY EVENING

Whose woods these are I think I know.
His house is in the village though;
He will not see me stopping here
To watch his woods fill up with snow.

My little horse must think it queer
To stop without a farmhouse near
Between the woods and frozen lake
The darkest evening of the year.

He gives his harness bells a shake
To ask if there is some mistake.
The only other sound's the sweep
Of easy wind and downy flake.

The woods are lovely, dark and deep.
But I have promises to keep,
And miles to go before I sleep.
And miles to go before I sleep.

JOHN MASEFIELD

1878–1966

THE PASSING STRANGE

Out of the earth of rest or range
Perpetual in perpetual change,
The unknown passing through the strange.

Water and saltness held together
To tread the dust and stand the weather,
And plough the field and stretch the tether,

To pass the wine-cup and be witty,
Water the sands and build the city,
Slaughter like devils and have pity,

Be red with rage and pale with lust,
Make beauty come, make peace, make trust,
Water and saltness mixed with dust;

Drive over earth, swim under sea,
Fly in the eagle's secrecy,
Guess where the hidden comets be;

Know all the deathly seeds that still
Queen Helen's beauty, Cæsar's will,
And slay them even as they kill;

Fashion an altar for a rood,
Defile a continent with blood,
And watch a brother starve for food:

Love like a madman, shaking, blind,
Till self is burnt into a kind
Possession of another mind;

Brood upon beauty, till the grace
Of beauty with the holy face
Brings peace into the bitter place;

Probe in the lifeless granites, scan
The stars for hope, for guide, for plan;
Live as a woman or a man;

Fasten to lover or to friend,
Until the heart break at the end
The break of death that cannot mend:

Then to lie useless, helpless, still,
Down in the earth, in dark, to fill
The roots of grass or daffodil.

Down in the earth, in dark, alone,
A mockery of the ghost in bone,
The strangeness, passing the unknown.

Time will go by, that outlasts clocks,
Dawn in the thorps will rouse the cocks,
Sunset be glory on the rocks:

But it, the thing, will never heed
Even the rootling from the seed
Thrusting to suck it for its need.

    .   .   .   .   .

Since moons decay and suns decline,
How else should end this life of mine?
Water and saltness are not wine.

But in the darkest hour of night,
When even the foxes peer for sight,
The byre-cock crows; he feels the light.

So, in this water mixed with dust,
The byre-cock spirit crows from trust
That death will change because it must.

For all things change: the darkness changes,
The wandering spirits change their ranges,
The corn is gathered to the granges.

The corn is sown again, it grows;
The stars burn out, the darkness goes;
The rhythms change, they do not close.

They change, and we, who pass like foam,
Like dust blown through the streets of Rome,
Change ever, too; we have no home.

Only a beauty, only a power,
Sad in the fruit, bright in the flower,
Endlessly erring for its hour,

But gathering as we stray, a sense
Of Life, so lovely and intense,
It lingers when we wander hence,

That those who follow feel behind
Their backs, when all before is blind,
Our joy, a rampart to the mind.

C. L. M.

In the dark womb where I began
My mother's life made me a man.
Through all the months of human birth
Her beauty fed my common earth.
I cannot see, nor breathe, nor stir,
But through the death of some of her.

Down in the darkness of the grave
She cannot see the life she gave.
For all her love, she cannot tell
Whether I use it ill or well,
Nor knock at dusty doors to find
Her beauty dusty in the mind.

If the grave's gates could be undone,
She would not know her little son,
I am so grown. If we should meet,
She would pass by me in the street,
Unless my soul's face let her see
My sense of what she did for me.

What have I done to keep in mind
My debt to her and womankind?
What woman's happier life repays
Her for those months of wretched days?
For all my mouthless body leeched
Ere Birth's releasing hell was reached?

What have I done, or tried, or said
In thanks to that dear woman dead?
Men triumph over women still,
Men trample women's rights at will,
And man's lust roves the world untamed.

.   o   o   o   o

O grave, keep shut lest I be shamed.

SEA-FEVER

I must go down to the seas again, to the lonely sea and the sky,
And all I ask is a tall ship and a star to steer her by,
And the wheel's kick and the wind's song and the white sails
    shaking,
And a grey mist on the sea's face and grey dawn breaking.

I must go down to the seas again, for the call of the running tide
Is a wild call and a clear call that may not be denied;
And all I ask is a windy day with the white clouds flying,
And the flung spray and the blown spume, and the sea-gulls
    crying.

I must go down to the seas again to the vagrant gypsy life.
To the gull's way and the whale's way where the wind's like a
    whetted knife;
And all I ask is a merry yarn from a laughing fellow-rover,
And quiet sleep and a sweet dream when the long trick's over.

EDWARD THOMAS

1878 - 1917

THE TRUMPET

Rise up, rise up,
And, as the trumpet blowing
Chases the dreams of men,
As the dawn glowing
The stars that left unlit
The land and water,
Rise up and scatter
The dew that covers
The print of last night's lovers—
Scatter it, scatter it!

While you are listening
To the clear horn,
Forget, men, everything
On this earth newborn,

Except that it is lovelier
Than any mysteries.
Open your eyes to the air
That has washed the eyes of the stars
Through all the dewy night:
Up with the light,
To the old wars;
Arise, arise!

IF I SHOULD EVER BY CHANCE

If I should ever by chance grow rich
I'll buy Codham, Cockridden, and Childerditch
Roses, Pyrgo, and Lapwater,
And let them all to my elder daughter.
The rent I shall ask of her will be only
Each year's first violets, white and lonely.
The first primroses and orchises—
She must find them before I do, that is.
But if she finds a blossom on furze
Without rent they shall all for ever be hers,
Codham, Cockridden, and Childerditch,
Roses, Pyrgo, and Lapwater—
I shall give them all to my elder daughter.

CARL SANDBURG

(A) 1878 - 1967

PLUNGER

Empty the last drop.
Pour out the final clinging heartbeat.
Great losers look on and smile.
Great winners look on and smile.

Plunger:
Take a long breath and let yourself go.

GRASS

Pile the bodies high at Austerlitz and Waterloo
Shovel them under and let me work—
        I am the grass; I cover all.
And pile them high at Gettysburg
And pile them high at Ypres and Verdun.
Shovel them under and let me work.
Two years, ten years, and passengers ask the conductor:
        What place is this?
        Where are we now?

        I am the grass,
        Let me work.

COOL TOMBS

When Abraham Lincoln was shovelled into the tombs, he forgot
the copperheads and the assassin . . . in the dust, in the cool
tombs.

And Ulysses Grant lost all thought of con men and Wall Street,
cash and collateral turned ashes . . . in the dust, in the cool
tombs.

Pocahontas' body, lovely as a poplar, sweet as a red haw in
November or a pawpaw in May, did she wonder? does she
remember? . . . in the dust, in the cool tombs?

Take any streetful of people buying clothes and groceries, cheer-
ing a hero or throwing confetti and blowing tin horns . . .
tell me if the lovers are losers . . . tell me if any get more
than the lovers . . . in the dust . . . in the cool tombs.

FOUR PRELUDES ON PLAYTHINGS
OF THE WIND

1

The woman named To-morrow
sits with a hairpin in her teeth
and takes her time
and does her hair the way she wants it
and fastens at last the last braid and coil
and puts the hairpin where it belongs
and turns and drawls: Well, what of it?
My grandmother, Yesterday, is gone.
What of it? Let the dead be dead.

2

The doors were cedar
and the panel strips of gold
and the girls were golden girls
and the panels read and the girls chanted:
     We are the greatest city,
      and the greatest nation:
      nothing like us ever was.
The doors are twisted on broken hinges.
Sheets of rain swish through on the wind
      where the golden girls ran and the panels
       read:
      We are the greatest city,
      the greatest nation,
      nothing like us ever was.

3

It has happened before.
Strong men put up a city and got
     a nation together,
And paid singers to sing and women
     to warble: We are the greatest city,
      the greatest nation,
      nothing like us ever was.

And while the singers sang
and the strong men listened
and paid the singers well,

there were rats and lizards who listened
... and the only listeners left now
... are ... the rats ... and the lizards.
And there are black crows
crying, " Caw, caw,"
bringing mud and sticks
building a nest
over the words carved
on the doors where the panels were cedar
and the strips on the panels were gold
and the golden girls came singing:
We are the greatest city,
the greatest nation:
nothing like us ever was.

The only singers now are the crows crying, " Caw caw."
And the sheets of rain whine in the wind and doorways.
And the only listeners now are ... the rats ... and the
    lizards.

4

The feet of the rats
scribble on the doorsills;
the hieroglyphs of the rat footprints
chatter the pedigrees of the rats
and babble of the blood
and gabble of the breed
of the grandfathers and the great-grandfathers
of the rats.
And the wind shifts
and the dust on a doorsill shifts
and even the writing of the rat footprints
tells us nothing, nothing at all
about the greatest city, the greatest nation
where the strong men listened
and the women warbled: Nothing like us ever was.

VACHEL LINDSAY

(A) 1879 - 1931

THE KALLYOPE YELL

1

Proud men
Eternally
Go about
Slander me,
Call me the " Calliope "
Sizz . . .
Fizz . . .

2

I am the Gutter Dream,
Tune-maker, born of steam,
Tooting joy, tooting hope.
I am the Kallyope,
Car called the Kallyope.
Willy willy willy wah HOO!
See the flags: snow-white tent,
See the bear and elephant,
See the monkey jump the rope,
Listen to the Kallyope, Kallyope, Kallyope!
Soul of the rhinoceros
And the hippopotamus
(Listen to the lion roar!)
Jaguar, cockatoot,
Loons, owls,
Hoot, hoot.
Listen to the lion roar,
Listen to the lion roar,
Listen to the lion R-O-A-R!
Hear the leopard cry for gore,
Willy willy willy wah HOO!
Hail the bloody Indian band,
Hail, all hail the popcorn stand,
Hail to Barnum's picture there,
People's idol everywhere,

Whoop whoop whoop WHOOP!
Music of the mob am I,
Circus day's tremendous cry:—
I am the Kallyope, Kallyope, Kallyope!
Hoot toot, hoot toot, hoot toot, hoot toot,
Willy willy willy wah HOO!
Sizz, fizz. . . .

3

Born of mobs, born of steam,
Listen to my golden dream,
Listen to my golden dream,
Listen to my G-O-L-D-E-N D-R-E-A-M!
Whoop whoop whoop whoop WHOOP!
I will blow the proud folk low,
Humanize the dour and slow,
I will shake the proud folk down,
(Listen to the lion roar!)
Popcorn crowds shall rule the town—
Willy willy willy wah HOO!
Steam shall work melodiously,
Brotherhood increase.
You'll see the world and all it holds
For fifty cents apiece.
Willy willy willy wah HOO!
Every day a circus day.

What?

Well, almost every day.
Nevermore the sweater's den,
Nevermore the prison pen.
Gone the war on land and sea
That aforetime troubled men.
Nations all in amity,
Happy in their plumes arrayed
In the long bright street parade.
Bands a-playing every day.

What?

Well, almost every day.
I am the Kallyope, Kallyope, Kallyope!
Willy willy willy wah HOO!
Hoot toot, hoot, toot,

Whoop whoop whoop whoop,
Willy willy willy wah HOO!
Sizz, fizz. . . .

4

Every soul
Resident
In the earth's one circus-tent!
Every man a trapeze king,
Then a pleased spectator there.
On the benches! In the ring!
While the neighbours gawk and stare
And the cheering rolls along.
Almost every day a race
When the merry starting gong
Rings, each chariot on the line,
Every driver fit and fine
With a steel-spring Roman grace.
Almost every day a dream.
Almost every day a dream.
Every girl,
Maid or wife,
Wild with music,
Eyes agleam
With that marvel called desire:
Actress, princess, fit for life,
Armed with honour like a knife,
Jumping thro' the hoops of fire.
(Listen to the lion roar!)
Making all the children shout.
Clowns shall tumble all about,
Painted high and full of song
While the cheering rolls along,
Tho' they scream,
Tho' they rage,
Every beast
In his cage,
Every beast
In his den
That aforetime troubled men.

5

I am the Kallyope, Kallyope, Kallyope,
Tooting hope, tooting hope, tooting hope, tooting hope;
Shaking window-pane and door
With a crashing cosmic tune,
With the war-cry of the spheres,
Rhythm of the roar of noon,
Rhythm of Niagara's roar,
Voicing planet, star and moon,
Shrieking of the better years.
Prophet-singers will arise,
Prophets coming after me,
Sing my song in softer guise
With more delicate surprise;
I am but the pioneer
Voice of Democracy;
I am the gutter dream,
I am the golden dream,
Singing science, singing steam,
I will blow the proud folk down,
(Listen to the lion roar!)
I am the Kallyope, Kallyope, Kallyope,
Tooting hope, tooting hope, tooting hope, tooting hope,
Willy willy willy wah HOO!
Hoot toot, hoot toot, hoot toot, hoot toot,
Whoop whoop, whoop whoop,
Whoop whoop, whoop whoop,
Willy willy willy wah HOO!
Sizz . . .
Fizz . . .

THE LEADEN-EYED

Let not young souls be smothered out before
They do quaint deeds and fully flaunt their pride.
It is the world's one crime its babes grow dull,
Its poor are ox-like, limp and leaden-eyed.

Not that they starve, but starve so dreamlessly;
Not that they sow, but that they seldom reap;
Not that they serve, but have no gods to serve
Not that they die, but that they die like sheep.

PADRAIC COLUM

1881 -

AN OLD WOMAN OF THE ROADS

O, to have a little house!
To own the hearth and stool and all!
The heaped-up sods upon the fire,
The pile of turf against the wall!

To have a clock with weights and chains
And pendulum swinging up and down!
A dresser filled with shining delph,
Speckled and white and blue and brown!

I could be busy all the day
Clearing and sweeping hearth and floor,
And fixing on their shelf again
My white and blue and speckled store!

I could be quiet there at night
Beside the fire and by myself,
Sure of a bed and loth to leave
The ticking clock and the shining delph!

Och! but I'm weary of mist and dark,
And roads where there's never a house nor bush
And tired I am of bog and road,
And the crying wind and the lonesome hush!

And I am praying to God on high,
And I am praying Him night and day,
For a little house—a house of my own—
Out of the wind's and the rain's way.

JAMES STEPHENS

1882 - 1950

THE SHELL

And then I pressed the shell
Close to my ear
And listened well,
And straightway like a bell
Came low and clear
The slow, sad murmur of the distant seas,
Whipped by an icy breeze
Upon a shore
Wind-swept and desolate.
It was a sunless strand that never bore
The footprint of a man,
Nor felt the weight
Since time began
Of any human quantity or stir
Save what the dreary winds and waves incur.
And in the hush of waters was the sound
Of pebbles rolling round,
For ever rolling with a hollow sound.
And bubbling sea-weeds as the waters go,
Swish to and fro
Their long, cold tentacles of slimy gray.
There was no day,
Nor ever came a night
Setting the stars alight
To wonder at the moon:
Was twilight only and the frightened croon,
Smitten to whimpers, of the dreary wind
And waves that journeyed blind—
And then I loosed my ear . . . O, it was sweet
To hear a cart go jolting down the street.

TO THE FOUR COURTS, PLEASE

The driver rubbed at his nettly chin
With a huge, loose forefinger, crooked and black,
And his wobbly, violet lips sucked in,
And puffed out again and hung down slack;

One fang shone through his lop-sided smile,
In his little pouched eye flickered years of guile.

And the horse, poor beast, it was ribbed and forked,
And its ears hung down, and its eyes were old,
And its knees were knuckly, and as we talked
It swung the stiff neck that could scarcely hold
Its big, skinny head up—then I stepped in,
And the driver climbed to his seat with a grin.

God help the horse and the driver too,
And the people and beasts who have never a friend,
For the driver easily might have been you,
And the horse be me by a different end.
And nobody knows how their days will cease,
And the poor, when they're old, have little of peace.

WALLACE STEVENS

(A) 1882 - 1955

PETER QUINCE AT THE CLAVIER

I

Just as my fingers on these keys
Make music, so the self-same sounds
On my spirit make a music, too.

Music is feeling, then, not sound;
And thus it is that what I feel,
Here in this room, desiring you,

Thinking of your blue-shadowed silk,
Is music. It is like the strain
Waked in the elders by Susanna:

Of a green evening, clear and warm,
She bathed in her still garden, while
The red-eyed elders, watching, felt

The basses of their beings throb
In witching chords, and their thin blood
Pulse pizzicati of Hosanna.

2

In the green water, clear and warm
Susanna lay,
She searched
The touch of springs,
And found
Concealed imaginings.
She sighed,
For so much melody.

Upon the bank, she stood
In the cool
Of spent emotions.
She felt, among the leaves,
The dew
Of old devotions.

She walked upon the grass,
Still quavering.
The winds were like her maids
On timid feet,
Fetching her woven scarves,
Yet wavering.

A breath upon her hand
Muted the night.
She turned—
A cymbal crashed,
And roaring horns.

3

Soon, with a noise like tambourines,
Came her attendant Byzantines.

They wondered why Susanna cried
Against the elders by her side:

And as they whispered, the refrain
Was like a willow swept by rain.

Anon, their lamps' uplifted flame
Revealed Susanna and her shame.

And then, the simpering Byzantines
Fled, with a noise like tambourines.

4

Beauty is momentary in the mind—
The fitful tracing of a portal;
But in the flesh it is immortal.

The body dies; the body's beauty lives.
So evenings die, in their green going,
A wave, interminably flowing.
So gardens die, their meek breath scenting
The cowl of Winter, done repenting.
So maidens die, to the auroral
Celebration of a maiden's choral.

Susanna's music touched the bawdy strings
Of those white elders; but, escaping,
Left only Death's ironic scraping.
Now, in its immortality, it plays
On the clear viol of her memory,
And makes a constant sacrament of praise.

TO THE ONE OF FICTIVE MUSIC

Sister and mother and diviner love,
And of the sisterhood of the living dead
Most near, most clear, and of the clearest bloom,
And of the fragrant mothers the most dear
And queen, and of diviner love the day
And flame and summer and sweet fire, no thread
Of cloudy silver sprinkles in your gown
Its venom of renown, and on your head
No crown is simpler than the simple hair.

Now, of the music summoned by the birth
That separates us from the wind and sea,
Yet leaves us in them, until earth becomes,
By being so much of the things we are,
Gross effigy and simulacrum, none
Gives motion to perfection more serene
Than yours, out of our imperfections wrought,
Most rare or ever of more kindred air
In the laborious weaving that you wear.

For so retentive of themselves are men
That music is intensest which proclaims
The near, the clear, and vaunts the dearest bloom,
And of all vigils musing the obscure,
That apprehends the most which sees and names,
As in your name, an image that is sure,
Among the arrant spices of the sun,
O bough and bush and scented vine, in whom
We give ourselves our likest issuance.

Yet not too like, yet not so like to be
Too near, too clear, saving a little to endow
Our feigning with the strange unlike, whence springs
The difference that heavenly pity brings.
For this, musician, in your girdle fixed
Bear other perfumes. On your pale head wear
A band entwining, set with fatal stones.
Unreal, give back to us what once you gave:
The imagination that we spurned and crave.

ANNA WICKHAM

1883 -

SELF-ANALYSIS

The tumult of my fretted mind
Gives me expression of a kind;
But it is faulty, harsh, not plain—
My work has the incompetence of pain.

I am consumed with a slow fire,
For righteousness is my desire;
Towards that good goal I cannot whip my will,
I am a tired horse that jibs upon a hill.

I desire Virtue, though I love her not—
I have no faith in her when she is got:
I fear that she will bind and make me slave
And send me songless to the sullen grave.

I am like a man who fears to take a wife,
And frets his soul with wantons all his life.
With rich, unholy foods I stuff my maw;
When I am sick, then I believe in law.

I fear the whiteness of straight ways—
I think there is no colour in unsullied days.
My silly sins I take for my heart's ease,
And know my beauty in the end disease.

Of old there were great heroes, strong in fight,
Who, tense and sinless, kept a fire alight:
God of our hope, in their great name,
Give me the straight and ordered flame!

SONG

I was so chill, and overworn, and sad,
To be a lady was the only joy I had.
I walked the street as silent as a mouse,
Buying fine clothes, and fittings for the house.

But since I saw my love
I wear a simple dress,
And happily I move
Forgetting weariness.

DOMESTIC ECONOMY

I will have few cooking-pots,
They shall be bright;
They shall reflect to blinding
God's straight light.
I will have four garments,
They shall be clean;
My service shall be good,
Though my diet be mean.
Then I shall have excess to give to the poor,
And right to counsel beggars at my door.

ENVOI

God, thou great symmetry,
Who put a biting lust in me
From whence my sorrows spring,
For all the frittered days
That I have spent in shapeless ways,
Give me one perfect thing.

JAMES ELROY FLECKER

1884 - 1915

STILLNESS

When the words rustle no more,
   And the last work's done,
When the bolt lies deep in the door,
   And Fire, our Sun,
Falls on the dark-laned meadows of the floor;

When from the clock's last chime to the next chime
   Silence beats his drum,
And Space with gaunt grey eyes and her brother Time
   Wheeling and whispering come,
She with the mould of form and he with the loom of rhyme:

Then twittering out in the night my thought-birds flee,
   I am emptied of all my dreams:
I only hear Earth turning, only see
   Ether's long bankless streams,
And only know I should drown if you
   Laid not your hand on me.

SARA TEASDALE

(A) 1884 - 1933

ARCTURUS IN AUTUMN

When, in the gold October dusk, I saw you near to setting,
   Arcturus, bringer of spring,
Lord of the summer nights, leaving us now in autumn,
   Having no pity on our withering;

Oh, then I knew at last that my own autumn was upon me.
   I felt it in my blood,
Restless as dwindling streams that still remember
   The music of their flood.

There in the thickening dark a wind-bent tree above me
   Loosed its last leaves in flight—
I saw you sink and vanish, pitiless Arcturus:
   You will not stay to share our lengthening night.

"LET IT BE FORGOTTEN"

Let it be forgotten, as a flower is forgotten,
   Forgotten as a fire that once was singing gold,
Let it be forgotten for ever and ever,
   Time is a kind friend, he will make us old.

If any one asks, say it was forgotten
   Long and long ago,
As a flower, as a fire, as a hushed footfall
   In a long-forgotten snow.

EZRA POUND

(A) 1885 -

BALLAD OF THE GOODLY FERE[1]

Simon Zelotes speaketh it somewhile after the Crucifixion

Ha' we lost the goodliest fere o' all
For the priests and the gallows-tree?
Aye, lover he was of brawny men,
O' ships and the open sea.

When they came wi' a host to take Our Man
His smile was good to see,
" First let these go! " quo' our Goodly Fere,
" Or I'll see ye damned," says he.

Aye, he sent us out through the crossed high spears,
And the scorn of his laugh rang free,
" Why took ye not me when I walked about
Alone in the town? " says he.

Oh, we drank his " Hale " in the good red wine
When we last made company,
No capon priest was the Goodly Fere
But a man o' men was he.

[1] Fere=Mate, companion.

I ha' seen him drive a hundred men
Wi' a bundle o' cords swung free,
When they took the high and holy house
For their pawn and treasury.

They'll no get him a' in a book I think
Though they write it cunningly;
No mouse of the scrolls was the Goodly Fere
But aye loved the open sea.

If they think they ha' snared our Goodly Fere
They are fools to the last degree.
" I'll go to the feast," quo' our Goodly Fere,
" Though I go to the gallows-tree."

" Ye ha' seen me heal the lame and the blind,
And wake the dead," says he,
" Ye shall see one thing to master all:
'Tis how a brave man dies on the tree."

A son of God was the Goodly Fere
That bade us his brothers be.
I ha' seen him cow a thousand men.
I ha' seen him upon the tree.

He cried no cry when they drave the nails
And the blood gushed hot and free,
The hounds of the crimson sky gave tongue
But never a cry cried he.

I ha' seen him cow a thousand men
On the hills o' Galilee,
They whined as he walked out calm between,
Wi' his eyes like the grey o' the sea.

Like the sea that brooks no voyaging
With the winds unleashed and free,
Like the sea that he cowed at Gennesaret
Wi' twey words spoke' suddenly.

A master of men was the Goodly Fere,
A mate of the wind and sea,
If they think they ha' slain our Goodly Fere
They are fools eternally.

I ha' seen him eat o' the honeycomb
Sin' they nailed him to the tree.

HUMBERT WOLFE

1885 - 1940

THE GREY SQUIRREL

Like a small grey
coffee-pot,
sits the squirrel.
He is not

all he should be,
kills by dozens
trees, and eats
his red-brown cousins.

The keeper on the
other hand,
who shot him, is
a Christian, and

loves his enemies,
which shows
the squirrel was not
one of those.

TULIP

Clean as a lady,
cool as glass,
fresh without fragrance
the tulip was.

The craftsman, who carved her
of metal, prayed:
" Live, oh thou lovely! "
Half metal she stayed.

ILIAD

False dreams, all false,
mad heart, were yours.
The word, and nought else,
in time endures,
Not you long after,
perished and mute,
will last, but the defter
viol and lute.
Sweetly they'll trouble
the listeners
with the cold dropped pebble
of painless verse.
Not you will be offered,
but the poet's false pain.
You have loved and suffered,
mad heart, in vain.
What love doth Helen
or Paris have
where they lie still in
a nameless grave?
Her beauty's a wraith,
and the boy Paris
muffles in death
his mouth's cold cherries.
Yes! these are less,
that were love's summer,
than one gold phrase
of old blind Homer.
Not Helen's wonder
nor Paris stirs,
but the bright, untender
hexameters.
And thus, all passion
is nothing made,
but a star to flash in
an Iliad.
Mad heart, you were wrong!
No love of yours,
but only what's sung,
when love's over, endures.

D. H. LAWRENCE

1885 - 1930

LIGHTNING

I felt the lurch and halt of her heart
  Next my breast, where my own heart was beating;
And I laughed to feel it plunge and bound,
And strange in my blood-swept ears was the sound
  Of the words I kept repeating,
Repeating with tightened arms, and the hot blood's blind-fold art.

Her breath flew warm against my neck,
  Warm as a flame in the close night air;
And the sense of her clinging flesh was sweet
Where her arms and my neck's blood-surge could meet.
  Holding her thus, did I care
That the black night hid her from me, blotted out every speck?

I leaned me forward to find her lips,
  And claim her utterly in a kiss,
When the lightning flew across her face,
And I saw her for the flaring space
  Of a second, afraid of the clips
Of my arms, inert with dread, wilted in fear of my kiss.

A moment, like a wavering spark,
  Her face lay there before my breast,
Pale love lost in a snow of fear,
And guarded by a glittering tear,
  And lips apart with dumb cries;
A moment, and she was taken again in the merciful dark.

I heard the thunder, and felt the rain,
  And my arms fell loose, and I was dumb.
Almost I hated her, she was so good,
Hated myself, and the place, and my blood,
  Which burned with rage, as I bade her come
Home, away home, ere the lightning floated forth again.

SIEGFRIED SASSOON

1886–1967

THE REAR-GUARD

Groping along the tunnel, step by step,
He winked his prying torch with patching glare
From side to side, and sniffed the unwholesome air.

Tins, boxes, bottles, shapes too vague to know,
A mirror smashed, the mattress from a bed:
And he, exploring fifty feet below
The rosy gloom of battle overhead.
Tripping, he grabbed the wall; saw someone lie
Humped at his feet, half-hidden by a rug,
And stooped to give the sleeper's arm a tug.
" I'm looking for headquarters." No reply.
" God blast your neck! " (For days he'd had no sleep.)
" Get up and guide me through this stinking place."
Savage, he kicked a soft, unanswering heap,
And flashed his beam across the livid face
Terribly glaring up, whose eyes yet wore
Agony dying hard ten days before;
And fists of fingers clutched a blackening wound.
Alone he staggered on until he found
Dawn's ghost that filtered down a shafted stair
To the dazed, muttering creatures underground
Who hear the boom of shells in muffled sound.
At last, with sweat of horror in his hair,
He climbed through darkness to the twilight air,
Unloading hell behind him step by step.

EVERY ONE SANG

Every one suddenly burst out singing;
And I was filled with such delight
As prisoned birds must find in freedom
Winging wildly across the white
Orchards and dark green fields; on; on;
        and out of sight.

Every one's voice was suddenly lifted,
And beauty came like the setting sun.
My heart was shaken with tears, and horror
Drifted away. . . . O, but every one
Was a bird; and the song was wordless; the
    singing will never be done.

EVERYMAN

The weariness of life that has no will
To climb the steepening hill:
The sickness of the soul for sleep, and to be still.

And then once more the impassioned pygmy fist
Clenched cloudward and defiant;
The pride that would prevail, the doomed protagonist.
Grappling the ghostly giant.

Victim and venturer, turn by turn; and then
Set free to be again
Companion in repose with those who once were men.

ALONE

" *When I'm alone* "—the words tripped off his tongue
As though to be alone were nothing strange.
" *When I was young,*" he said; " *when I was young. . . .*"

I thought of age, and loneliness, and change.
I thought how strange we grow when we're alone,
And how unlike the selves that meet and talk,
And blow the candles out, and say good night.
Alone. . . . The word is life endured and known
It is the stillness where our spirits walk
And all but inmost faith is overthrown.

"H. D." (Hilda Doolittle)

(A) 1886 - 1961

OREAD

Whirl up, sea—
Whirl your pointed pines.
Splash your great pines
On our rocks.
Hurl your green over us—
Cover us with your pools of fir.

HEAT

O wind, rend open the heat,
cut apart the heat,
rend it to tatters.

Fruit cannot drop
through this thick air—
fruit cannot fall into heat
that presses up and blunts
the points of pears
and rounds the grapes.

Cut through the heat—
plough through it,
turning it on either side
of your path.

LETHE

Nor skin nor hide nor fleece
        Shall cover you,
Nor curtain of crimson nor fine
Shelter of cedar-wood be over you,
        Nor the fir-tree
        Nor the pine.

Nor sight of whin nor gorse
    Nor river-yew,
Nor fragrance of flowering bush,
Nor wailing of reed-bird to waken you.
    Nor of linnet
Nor of thrush.

Nor word nor touch nor sight
    Of lover, you
Shall long through the night but for this:
The roll of the full tide to cover you
    Without question,
    Without kiss.

JOHN HALL WHEELOCK

(A) 1886 -

THE FISH-HAWK

On the large highway of the awful air that flows
    Unbounded between sea and heaven, while twilight screened
The sorrowful distances, he moved and had repose;
    On the huge wind of the Immensity he leaned
His steady body in long lapse of flight—and rose

Gradual, through broad gyres of ever-climbing rest,
    Up the clear stair of the eternal sky, and stood
Throned on the summit! Slowly, with his widening breast,
    Widened around him the enormous Solitude,
From the grey rim of ocean to the glowing west.

Headlands and capes forlorn of the far coast, the land
    Rolling her barrens toward the south, he, from his throne
Upon the gigantic wind, beheld: he hung—he fanned
    The abyss for mighty joy, to feel beneath him strown
Pale pastures of the sea, with heaven on either hand—

The world with all her winds and waters, earth and air,
    Fields, folds, and moving clouds. The awful and adored
Arches and endless aisles of vacancy, the fair
    Void of sheer heights and hollows hailed him as her lord
And lover in the highest, to whom all heaven lay bare!

Till from that tower of ecstasy, that baffled height,
  Stooping he sank; and slowly on the world's wide way
Walked, with great wing on wing, the merciless, proud Might,
  Hunting the huddled and lone reaches for his prey
Down the dim shore—and faded in the crumbling light.

Slowly the dusk covered the land. Like a great hymn
  The sound of moving winds and waters was; the sea
Whispered a benediction, and the west grew dim.
  Where evening lifted her clear candles quietly . . .
Heaven, crowded with stars, trembled from rim to rim.

WILLIAM ROSE BENÉT

(A) 1886 - 1950

PEARL DIVER

I had an image of the bright, bare Day
Like a tall diver poised above the surge
Of blackest night, where its vast fluctuant verge
Lapped against heaven's ramparts, broad and gray.
Flickering with ghostly fires, beneath him lay
That gulf where light must drown that light emerge.
His nimbused radiance stooped to dare its gurge,
Plunged, and flashed deep through showers of starry spray.

Swift his transfigured contours clove the dark,
Suffusing fathom on fathom of night aswirl
With tints of rose, all tremoring into one,
Till from cloud floors he plucked a filmy pearl
And held it high for earth and heaven to mark
The cold globe of the winter-shrunken sun.

ELINOR WYLIE

(A) 1887 - 1928

THE EAGLE AND THE MOLE

Avoid the reeking herd,
Shun the polluted flock,
Live like that stoic bird,
The eagle of the rock.

The huddled warmth of crowds
Begets and fosters hate;
He keeps, above the clouds,
His cliff inviolate.

When flocks are folded warm,
And herds to shelter run,
He sails above the storm,
He stares into the sun.

If in the eagle's track
Your sinews cannot leap,
Avoid the lathered pack,
Turn from the steaming sheep.

If you would keep your soul
From spotted sight or sound,
Live like the velvet mole;
Go burrow underground.

And there hold intercourse
With roots of trees and stones,
With rivers at their source,
And disembodied bones.

HYMN TO EARTH

Farewell, incomparable element,
Whence man arose, where he shall not return;
And hail, imperfect urn
Of his last ashes, and his firstborn fruit;
Farewell, the long pursuit,
And all the adventures of his discontent;
The voyages which sent
His heart averse from home:
Metal of clay, permit him that he come
To thy slow-burning fire as to a hearth;
Accept him as a particle of earth.

Fire, being divided from the other three,
It lives removed, or secret at the core;
Most subtle of the four,
When air flies not, nor water flows,
It disembodied goes,

Being light, elixir of the first decree,
More volatile than he;
With strength and power to pass
Through space, where never his least atom was:
He has no part in it, save as his eyes
Have drawn its emanation from the skies.
A wingless creature heavier than air,
He is rejected of its quintessence;
Coming and going hence,
In the twin minutes of his birth and death,
He may inhale as breath,
As breath relinquish heaven's atmosphere,
Yet in it have no share,
Nor can survive therein
Where its outer edge is filtered pure and thin:
It doth but lend its crystal to his lungs
For his early crying, and his final songs.

The element of water has denied
Its child; it is no more his element;
It never will relent;
Its silver harvests are more sparsely given
Than the rewards of heaven,
And he shall drink cold comfort at its side:
The water is too wide:
The seamew and the gull
Feather a nest made soft and pitiful
Upon its foam; he has not any part
In the long swell of sorrow at its heart.

Hail and farewell, belovèd element,
Whence he departed, and his parent once;
See where thy spirit runs
Which for so long hath had the moon to wife;
Shall this support his life
Until the arches of the waves be bent
And grow shallow and spent?
Wisely it cast him forth
With his dead weight of burdens nothing worth
Leaving him, for the universal years,
A little sea-water to make his tears.

Hail, element of earth, receive thy own,
And cherish, at thy charitable breast,
This man, this mongrel beast:

He ploughs the sand, and, at his hardest need,
He sows himself for seed;
He ploughs the furrow, and in this lies down
Before the corn is grown;
Between the apple bloom
And the ripe apple is sufficient room
In time, and matter, to consume his love
And make him parcel of a cypress grove.

Receive him as thy lover for an hour
Who will not weary, by a longer stay,
The kind embrace of clay;
Even within thine arms he is dispersed
To nothing, as at first;
The air flings downward from its four-quartered tower
Him whom the flames devour;
At the full tide, at the flood,
The sea is mingled with his salty blood:
The traveller dust, although the dust be vile,
Sleeps as thy lover for a little while.

BIRTHDAY SONNET

Take home Thy prodigal child, O Lord of Hosts!
Protect the sacred from the secular danger;
Advise her, that Thou never needst avenge her;
Marry her mind neither to man's nor ghost's
Nor holier domination's, if the costs
Of such commingling should transport or change her;
Defend her from familiar and stranger,
And earth's and air's contagions and rusts.

Instruct her strictly to preserve Thy gift
And alter not its grain in atom sort;
Angels may wed her to their ultimate hurt
And men embrace a spectre in a shift,
So that no drop of the pure spirit fall
Into the dust; defend Thy prodigal.

EDITH SITWELL

1887 - 1964

SIR BEELZEBUB

WHEN
Sir
Beelzebub called for his syllabub in the hotel in Hell
    Where Proserpine first fell,
Blue as the gendarmerie were the waves of the sea,

    (Rocking and shocking the bar-maid.)

Nobody comes to give him his rum but the
Rim of the sky hippopotamus-glum
Enhances the chances to bless with a benison
Alfred Lord Tennyson crossing the bar laid
With cold vegetation from pale deputations
Of temperance workers (all signed In Memoriam)
Hoping with glory to trip up the Laureate's feet,

    (Moving in classical meters). . . .

Like Balaclava, the lava came down from the
Roof, and the sea's blue wooden gendarmerie
Took them in charge while Beelzebub roared for his rum.

. . . None of them come!

STILL FALLS THE RAIN

THE RAIDS, 1940. NIGHT AND DAWN

Still falls the Rain—
Dark as the world of man, black as our loss—
Blind as the nineteen hundred and forty nails
Upon the Cross.

Still falls the Rain
With a sound like the pulse of the heart that is changed to the
    hammer-beat
In the Potter's Field, and the sound of the impious feet

On the Tomb:

Still falls the Rain
In the Field of Blood where the small hopes breed and the human
    brain
Nurtures its greed, that worm with the brow of Cain.

Still falls the Rain
At the feet of the Starved Man hung upon the Cross.
Christ that each day, each night, nails there, have mercy on us—
On Dives and on Lazarus:
Under the rain the sore and the gold are as one.

Still falls the Rain—
Still falls the blood from the Starved Man's wounded Side:
He bears in His Heart all wounds,—those of the light that died,
The last faint spark
In the self-murdered heart, the wounds of the sad uncompre-
    hending dark,

The wounds of the baited bear,—
The blind and weeping bear whom the keepers beat
On his helpless flesh . . . the tears of the hunted hare.

Still falls the Rain—
Then—O Ile leape up to my God: who pulles me doune—
See, see where Christ's blood streames in the firmament:
It flows from the Brow we nailed upon the tree
Deep to the dying, to the thirsting heart
That holds the fires of the world,—dark-smirched with pain
As Caesar's laurel crown.

Then sounds the voice of One who like the heart of man
Was once a child who among beasts has lain—
" Still do I love, still shed my innocent light, my Blood, for thee."

MARIANNE MOORE

1887 -

POETRY

I, too, dislike it: there are things that are important beyond all
    this fiddle.
  Reading it, however, with a perfect contempt for it, one dis-
    covers in

it, after all, a place for the genuine.
  Hands that can grasp, eyes
  that can dilate, hair that can rise
    if it must, these things are important not because a

high-sounding interpretation can be put upon them but because
          they are
  useful. When they become so derivative as to become unin-
          telligible,
  the same thing may be said for all of us, that we
    do not admire what
    we cannot understand: the bat
      holding on upside down or in quest of something to

eat, elephants pushing, a wild horse taking a roll, a tireless wolf
          under
  a tree, the immovable critic twitching his skin like a horse that
          feels a flea, the base-
  ball fan, the statistician—
    nor is it valid
      to discriminate against " business documents and

school-books; " all these phenomena are important. One must
          make a distinction
  however: when dragged into prominence by half poets, the
          result is not poetry,
  nor till the poets among us can be
    " literalists of
    the imagination "—above
      insolence and triviality and can present

for inspection, imaginary gardens with real toads in them, shall
          we have
  it. In the meantime, if you demand on the one hand,
  the raw material of poetry in
    all its rawness and
    that which is on the other hand
      genuine, then you are interested in poetry.

SILENCE

My father used to say,
' Superior people never make long visits,
have to be shown Longfellow's grave
or the glass flowers at Harvard.
Self-reliant like the cat
that takes its prey to privacy—
the mouse's limp tail hanging like a shoelace from its mouth—
they sometimes enjoy solitude,
and can be robbed of speech
by speech which has delighted them.
The deepest feeling always shows itself in silence;
not in silence, but restraint.'
Nor was he insincere in saying, ' Make my home your inn.'
Inns are not residences.

RUPERT BROOKE

1887 - 1915

THE SOLDIER

If I should die, think only this of me;
    That there's some corner of a foreign field
That is for ever England. There shall be
    In that rich earth a richer dust concealed;
A dust whom England bore, shaped, made aware,
    Gave, once, her flowers to love, her ways to roam,
A body of England's breathing English air,
    Washed by the rivers, blest by suns of home.

And think, this heart, all evil shed away,
    A pulse in the eternal mind, no less
        Gives somewhere back the thoughts by England given;
Her sights and sounds; dreams happy as her day;
    And laughter, learnt of friends; and gentleness,
        In hearts at peace, under an English heaven.

THE GREAT LOVER

I have been so great a lover: filled my days
So proudly with the splendour of Love's praise,
The pain, the calm, and the astonishment,
Desire illimitable, and still content,
And all dear names men use, to cheat despair,
For the perplexed and viewless streams that bear
Our hearts at random down the dark of life.
Now, ere the unthinking silence on that strife
Steals down, I would cheat drowsy Death so far,
My night shall be remembered for a star
That outshone all the suns of all men's days.
Shall I not crown them with immortal praise
Whom I have loved, who have given me, dared with me
High secrets, and in darkness knelt to see
The inenarrable godhead of delight?
Love is a flame:—we have beaconed the world's night.
A city:—and we have built it, these and I.
An emperor:—we have taught the world to die.
So, for their sakes I loved, ere I go hence,
And the high cause of Love's magnificence,
And to keep loyalties young, I'll write those names
Golden for ever, eagles, crying flames,
And set them as a banner, that men may know,
To dare the generations, burn, and blow
Out on the wind of Time, shining and streaming. . . .

These I have loved:
                    White plates and cups, clean-gleaming,
Ringed with blue lines; and feathery, faery dust;
Wet roofs, beneath the lamp-light; the strong crust
Of friendly bread; and many-tasting food;
Rainbows; and the blue bitter smoke of wood;
And radiant raindrops couching in cool flowers;
And flowers themselves, that sway through sunny hours,
Dreaming of moths that drink them under the moon;
Then, the cool kindliness of sheets, that soon
Smooth away trouble; and the rough male kiss
Of blankets; grainy wood; live hair that is
Shining and free; blue-massing clouds; the keen
Unpassioned beauty of a great machine;

The benison of hot water; furs to touch;
The good smell of old clothes; and other such—
The comfortable smell of friendly fingers,
Hair's fragrance, and the musty reek that lingers
About dead leaves and last year's ferns. . . .

        Dear names,
And thousand others throng to me! Royal flames;
Sweet water's dimpling laugh from tap or spring;
Holes in the ground; and voices that do sing:
Voices in laughter, too; and body's pain,
Soon turned to peace; and the deep-panting train;
Firm sands; the little dulling edge of foam
That browns and dwindles as the wave goes home;
And washen stones, gay for an hour; the cold
Graveness of iron; moist black earthen mould;
Sleep; and high places; footprints in the dew;
And oaks; and brown horse-chestnuts, glossy-new;
And new-peeled sticks; and shining pools on grass;—
All these have been my loves. And these shall pass,
Whatever passes not, in the great hour,
Nor all my passion, all my prayers, have power
To hold them with me through the gate of Death.
They'll play deserter, turn with traitor breath,
Break the high bond we made, and sell Love's trust
And sacramented covenant to the dust.
—Oh, never a doubt but, somewhere, I shall wake,
And give what's left of love again, and make
New friends now strangers. . . .

       But the best I've known
Stays here, and changes, breaks, grows old, is blown
About the winds of the world, and fades from brains
Of living men, and dies.

      Nothing remains.
O dear my loves, O faithless, once again
This one last gift I give: that after men
Shall know, and later lovers, far-removed
Praise you, " All these were lovely "; say, " He loved."

ROBINSON JEFFERS

(A) 1887 - 1962

HURT HAWKS

The broken pillar of the wing jags from the clotted shoulder,
The wing trails like a banner in defeat,
No more to use the sky forever but live with famine
And pain a few days: cat nor coyote
Will shorten the week of waiting for death, there is game without
      talons.

He stands under the oak-bush and waits
The lame feet of salvation; at night he remembers freedom
And flies in a dream, the dawns ruin it.
He is strong and pain is worse to the strong, incapacity is worse.
The curs of the day come and torment him
At distance, no one but death the redeemer will humble that head,
The intrepid readiness, the terrible eyes.
The wild God of the world is sometimes merciful to those
That ask mercy, not often to the arrogant.
You do not know him, you communal people, or you have for-
      gotten him;
Intemperate and savage, the hawk remembers him;
Beautiful and wild, the hawks, and men that are dying remember
      him.

　　　　　·　　　·　　　·　　　·　　　·

I'd sooner, except the penalties, kill a man than a hawk: but the
      great redtail
Had nothing left but unable misery
From the bone too shattered for mending, the wing that trailed
      under his talons when he moved.
We had fed him six weeks, I gave him freedom,
He wandered over the foreland hill and returned in the evening,
      asking for death,
Not like a beggar, still eyed with the old
Implacable arrogance. I gave him the lead gift in the twilight.
　　　　　　　　　　　　　　What fell was relaxed,
Owl-downy, soft feminine feathers; but what
Soared: the fierce rush: the night-herons by the flooded river
      cried fear at its rising
Before it was quite unsheathed from reality.

AGE IN PROSPECT

Praise youth's hot blood, if you will, I think that happiness
Rather consists in having lived clear through
Youth and hot blood, on to the wintrier hemisphere
Where one has time to wait and to remember.

Youth and hot blood are beautiful, so is peacefulness.
Youth had some islands in it, but age is indeed
An island and a peak; age has infirmities,
Not few, but youth is all one fever

To look around and to love in his appearances,
Though a little calmly, the universal God's
Beauty is better I think than to lip eagerly
The mother's breast or another woman's.

And there is no possession more sure than memory's;
But if I reach that grey island, that peak,
My hope is still to possess with eyes the homeliness
Of ancient loves, ocean and mountains,

And meditate the sea-mouth of mortality
And the fountain six feet down with a quieter thirst
Than now I feel for old age; a creature progressively
Thirsty for life will be for death too.

PROMISE OF PEACE

The heads of strong old age are beautiful
Beyond all grace of youth. They have strange quiet,
Integrity, health, soundness, to the full
They've dealt with life and been attempered by it.
A young man must not sleep; his years are war
Civil and foreign but the former's worse;
But the old can breathe in safety now that they are
Forgetting what youth meant, the being perverse,
Running the fool's gauntlet and being cut
By the whips of the five senses. As for me,
If I should wish to live long it were but
To trade those fevers for tranquillity,
Thinking though that's entire and sweet in the grave
How shall the dead taste the deep treasure they have?

JOHN CROWE RANSOM

(A) ~ 1888 - 1965

PARTING, WITHOUT A SEQUEL

She has finished and sealed the letter
At last, which he so richly has deserved,
With characters venomous and hatefully curved,
And nothing could be better.

But even as she gave it,
Saying to the blue-capped functioner of doom,
" Into his hands," she hoped the leering groom
Might somewhere lose and leave it.

Then all the blood
Forsook the face. She was too pale for tears,
Observing the ruin of her younger years.
She went and stood

Under her father's vaunting oak
Who kept his peace in wind and sun, and glistened
Stoical in the rain; to whom she listened
If he spoke.

And now the agitation of the rain
Rasped his sere leaves, and he talked low and gentle,
Reproaching the wan daughter by the lintel;
Ceasing, and beginning again.

Away went the messenger's bicycle,
His serpent's track went up the hill forever.
And all the time she stood there hot as fever
And cold as any icicle.

PIAZZA PIECE

—I am a gentleman in a dustcoat trying
To make you hear. Your ears are soft and small
And listen to an old man not at all;
They want the young men's whispering and sighing.

But see the roses on your trellis dying
And hear the spectral singing of the moon—
For I must have my lovely lady soon.
I am a gentleman in a dustcoat trying.

—I am a lady young in beauty waiting
Until my true love comes, and then we kiss.
But what grey man among the vines is this
Whose words are dry and faint as in a dream?
Back from my trellis, sir, before I scream!
I am a lady young in beauty waiting.

T. S. ELIOT

(A) 1888 - 1965

LA FIGLIA CHE PIANGE

O quam te memorem virgo . . .

Stand on the highest pavement of the stair—
Lean on a garden urn—
Weave, weave the sunlight in your hair—
Clasp your flowers to you with a pained surprise—
Fling them to the ground and turn
With a fugitive resentment in your eyes:
But weave, weave the sunlight in your hair.

So I would have had him leave,
So I would have had her stand and grieve,
So he would have left
As the soul leaves the body torn and bruised,
As the mind deserts the body it has used.

I should find
Some way incomparably light and deft,
Some way we both should understand,
Simple and faithless as a smile and shake of the hand.

She turned away, but with the autumn weather
Compelled my imagination many days,
Many days and many hours:
Her hair over her arms and her arms full of flowers,
And I wonder how they should have been together!
I should have lost a gesture and a pose.
Sometimes these cogitations still amaze
The troubled midnight and the noon's repose.

SWEENEY AMONG THE NIGHTINGALES

Apeneck Sweeney spreads his knees
Letting his arms hang down to laugh,
The zebra stripes along his jaw
Swelling to maculate giraffe.

The circles of the stormy moon
Slide westward toward the River Plate,
Death and the Raven drift above
And Sweeney guards the hornèd gate.

Gloomy Orion and The Dog
Are veiled; and hushed the shrunken seas;
The person in the Spanish cape
Tries to sit on Sweeney's knees;

Slips and pulls the table cloth,
Overturns a coffee-cup,
Reorganized upon the floor
She yawns and draws a stocking up;

The silent man in mocha brown
Sprawls at the window-sill and gapes;
The waiter brings in oranges
Bananas figs and hothouse grapes;

The silent vertebrate in brown
Contracts and concentrates, withdraws;
Rachel *née* Rabinovitch
Tears at the grapes with murderous paws;

She and the lady in the cape
Are suspect, thought to be in league;
Therefore the man with heavy eyes
Declines the gambit, shows fatigue,

Leaves the room and reappears
Outside the window, leaning in,
Branches of wistaria
Circumscribe a golden grin;

The host with some one indistinct
Converses at the door apart,
The nightingales are singing near
The Convent of the Sacred Heart,

And sang within the bloody wood
When Agamemnon cried aloud,
And let their liquid droppings fall
To stain the stiff dishonoured shroud.

A SONG FOR SIMEON

Lord, the Roman hyacinths are blooming in bowls and
The winter sun creeps by the snow hills;
The stubborn season has made stand.
My life is light, waiting for the death wind,
Like a feather on the back of my hand.
Dust in sunlight and memory in corners
Wait for the wind that chills towards the dead land.

Grant us thy peace.
I have walked many years in this city,
Kept faith and fast, provided for the poor,
Have given and taken honour and ease.
There went never any rejected from my door.
Who shall remember my house, where shall live my children's
    children
When the time of sorrow is come?
They will take to the goat's path, and the fox's home,
Fleeing from the foreign faces and the foreign swords.

Before the time of cords and scourges and lamentation
Grant us thy peace.
Before the stations of the mountain of desolation,
Before the certain hour of maternal sorrow,
Now at this birth season of decease,
Let the Infant, the still unspeaking and unspoken Word,
Grant Israel's consolation
To one who has eighty years and no to-morrow.

According to thy word.
They shall praise Thee and suffer in every generation
With glory and derision,
Light upon light, mounting the saint's stair.
Not for me the martyrdom, the ecstasy of thought and prayer,
Not for me the ultimate vision.

Grant me thy peace.
(And a sword shall pierce thy heart,
Thine also.)
I am tired with my own life and the lives of those after me,
I am dying in my own death and the deaths of those after me.
Let thy servant depart,
Having seen thy salvation.

THE HOLLOW MEN

Mistah Kurtz—he dead.
A penny for the Old Guy.

I

We are the hollow men
We are the stuffed men
Leaning together
Headpiece filled with straw   Alas!
Our dried voices, when
We whisper together
Are quiet and meaningless
As wind in dry grass
Or rats' feet over broken glass
In our dry cellar

Shape without form, shade without colour,
Paralyzed force, gesture without motion;

Those who have crossed
With direct eyes, to death's other Kingdom
Remember us—if at all—not as lost
Violent souls, but only
As the hollow men
The stuffed men.

2

Eyes I dare not meet in dreams
In death's dream kingdom
These do not appear:
There, the eyes are
Sunlight on a broken column

There is a tree swinging
And voices are
In the wind's singing
More distant and more solemn
Than a fading star.

Let me be no nearer
In death's dream kingdom
Let me also wear
Such deliberate disguises
Rat's coat, crowskin, crossed staves
In a field
Behaving as the wind behaves
No nearer—
Not that final meeting
In the twilight kingdom

3

This is the dead land
This is cactus land
Here the stone images
Are raised, here they receive
The supplication of a dead man's hand
Under the twinkle of a fading star.

Is it like this
In death's other kingdom
Waking alone
At the hour when we are
Trembling with tenderness
Lips that would kiss
Form prayers to broken stone.

4

The eyes are not here
There are no eyes here
In this valley of dying stars
In this hollow valley
This broken jaw of our lost kingdoms

In this last of meeting places
We grope together
And avoid speech
Gathered on this beach of the tumid river

Sightless, unless
The eyes reappear
As the perpetual star
Multifoliate rose
Of death's twilight kingdom
The hope only
Of empty men.

5

Here we go round the prickly pear
Prickly pear, prickly pear
Here we go round the prickly pear
At five o'clock in the morning.

Between the idea
And the reality
Between the motion
And the act
Falls the shadow
    For Thine is the Kingdom.

Between the conception
And the creation
Between the emotion
And the response
Falls the Shadow
    Life is very long.

Between the desire
And the spasm
Between the potency
And the existence
Between the essence
And the descent
Falls the Shadow.
    For Thine is the Kingdom.

For Thine is
Life is
For Thine is the

This is the way the world ends
This is the way the world ends
This is the way the world ends
Not with a bang but a whimper.

CONRAD AIKEN

(A) 1889 -

ANNIHILATION

While the blue moon above us arches
And the poplar sheds disconsolate leaves,
Tell me again why love bewitches
And what love gives.

Is it the trembling finger that traces
The eyebrow's curve, the curve of the cheek?
The mouth that quivers, while the hand caresses,
But cannot speak?

No, not these, not in these is hidden
The secret, more than in other things:
Not only the touch of a hand can gladden
Till the blood sings.

It is the leaf that falls between us,
The bell that murmurs, the shadows that move,
The autumnal sunlight that fades upon us,
These things are love.

It is the " No, let us sit here longer,"
The " Wait till to-morrow," the " Once I knew "—
These trifles, said as you touch my finger
And the clock strikes two.

The world is intricate, and we are nothing.
It is the complex world of grass,
The twig on the path, a look of loathing,
Feelings that pass—

These are the secret; and I could hate you
When, as I lean for another kiss,
I see in your eyes that I do not meet you,
And that love is this.

Rock meeting rock can know love better
Than eyes that stare or lips that touch.
All that we know in love is bitter,
And it is not much.

THE ONE-EYED CALENDAR

Stood, at the closed door, and remembered—
Hand on the doorpost faltered, and remembered—
The long ago, the far away, the near
With its absurdities—the calendar,
The one-eyed calendar upon the wall,
And time dispersed, and in a thousand ways,
Calendars torn, appointments made and kept,
Or made and broken, and the shoes worn out
Going and coming, street and stair and street,
Lamplight and starlight, fog and north-east wind,
St. Mary's ringing the angelus at six—

And it was there, at eight o'clock I saw
Vivien and the infinite, together,
And it was here I signed my name in pencil
Against the doorpost, and later saw the snow
Left by the messenger, and here were voices—
Come back later, do come back later, if you can,
And tell us what it was, tell us what you saw,
Put your heart on the table with your hand
And tell us all those secrets that are known
In the profound interstices of time—
The glee, the wickedness, the smirk, the sudden
Divine delight—do come back and tell us,
The clock has stopped, sunset is on the snow,
Midnight is far away, and morning farther—

And then the trains that cried at night, the ships
That mourned in fog, the days whose gift was rain,
June's daisy, and she loved me not, the skull
Brought from the tomb—and I was there, and saw
The bright spade break the bone, the trumpet-vine
Bugled with bees, and on my knees I picked
One small white clover in the cactus shade,
Put it in water and took it to that room
Where blinds were drawn and all was still—

                    Neighbours, I have come
From a vast everything whose sum is nothing,
From a complexity whose speech is simple;
Here are my hands and heart, and I have brought
Nothing you do not know, and do not fear.

Here is the evening paper at your door—
Here are your letters, I have brought the tickets,
The hour is early, and the speech is late.
Come, we are gods,—let us discourse as gods;
And weigh the grain of sand with Socrates;
Before we fall to kissing, and to bed.

EDNA ST. VINCENT MILLAY

(A) 1892 - 1950

SAY WHAT YOU WILL

Say what you will, and scratch my heart to find
The roots of last year's roses in my breast;
I am as surely riper in my mind
As if the fruit stood in the stalls confessed.
Laugh at the unshed leaf, say what you will,
Call me in all things what I was before,
A flutterer in the wind, a woman still;
I tell you I am what I was and more.
My branches weigh me down, frost cleans the air,
My sky is black with small birds bearing south:
Say what you will, confuse me with fine care,
Put by my word as but an April truth—
Autumn is no less on me that a rose
Hugs the brown bough and sighs before it goes.

WHAT'S THIS OF DEATH—

What's this of death, from you who never will die?
Think you the wrist that fashioned you in clay,
The thumb that set the hollow just that way
In your full throat and lidded the long eye
So roundly from the forehead, will let lie
Broken, forgotten, under foot some day
Your unimpeachable body, and so slay
The work he most had been remembered by?
I tell you this: whatever of dust to dust
Goes down, whatever of ashes may return
To its essential self in its own season,
Loveliness such as yours will not be lost,
But, cast in bronze upon his very urn,
Make known him Master, and for what good reason.

THOU ART NOT LOVELIER THAN LILACS

Thou art not lovelier than lilacs,—no,
Nor honeysuckle; thou art not more fair
Than small white single poppies,—I can bear
Thy beauty; though I bend before thee, though
From left to right, not knowing where to go,
I turn my troubled eyes, nor here nor there
Find any refuge from thee, yet I swear
So has it been with mist,—with moonlight so.
Like him who day by day unto his draught
Of delicate poison adds him one drop more
Till he may drink unharmed the death of ten,
Even so, inured to beauty, who have quaffed
Each hour more deeply than the hour before,
I drink—and live—what has destroyed some men.

DIRGE WITHOUT MUSIC

I am not resigned to the shutting away of loving hearts in the
    hard ground.
So it is, and so it will be, for so it has been, time out of mind:
Into the darkness they go, the wise and the lovely. Crowned
With lilies and with laurel they go; but I am not resigned.

Lovers and thinkers, into the earth with you.
Be one with the dull, the indiscriminate dust.
A fragment of what you felt, of what you knew,
A formula, a phrase remains,—but the best is lost.

The answers quick and keen, the honest look, the laughter, the
    love,—
They are gone. They have gone to feed the roses. Elegant and
    curled
Is the blossom. Fragrant is the blossom. I know. But I do not
    approve.
More precious was the light in your eyes than all the roses in the
    world.

Down, down, down into the darkness of the grave
Gently they go, the beautiful, the tender, the kind;
Quietly they go, the intelligent, the witty, the brave.
I know. But I do not approve. And I am not resigned.

ARCHIBALD MacLEISH

(A) 1892 -

YOU, ANDREW MARVELL

And here face down beneath the sun,
And here upon earth's noonward height,
To feel the always coming on,
The always rising of the night.

To feel creep up the curving east
The earthly chill of dusk and slow
Upon those under lands the vast
And ever-climbing shadow grow,

And strange at Ecbatan the trees
Take leaf by leaf the evening, strange,
The flooding dark about their knees,
The mountains over Persia change,

And now at Kermanshah the gate,
Dark, empty, and the withered grass,
And through the twilight now the late
Few travellers in the westward pass,

And Baghdad darken and the bridge
Across the silent river gone,
And through Arabia the edge
Of evening widen and steal on,

And deepen on Palmyra's street
The wheel rut in the ruined stone,
And Lebanon fade out and Crete
High through the clouds and overblown,

And over Sicily the air
Still flashing with the landward gulls,
And loom and slowly disappear
The sails above the shadowy hulls,

And Spain go under and the shore
Of Africa, the gilded sand,
And evening vanish and no more
The low pale light across that land,

Nor now the long light on the sea—

And here face downward in the sun
To feel how swift, how secretly,
The shadow of the night comes on. . . .

MEMORIAL RAIN

Ambassador Puser the ambassador
Reminds himself in French, felicitous tongue,
What these (young men no longer) lie here for
In rows that once, and somewhere else, were young—
All night in Brussels the wind had tugged at my door:
I had heard the wind at my door and the trees strung
Taut, and to me who had never been before
In that country it was a strange wind blowing
Steadily, stiffening the walls, the floor,
The roof of my room. I had not slept for knowing
He too, dead, was a stranger in that land
And felt beneath the earth in the wind's flowing
A tightening of roots and would not understand,
Remembering lake winds in Illinois,
That strange wind. I had felt his bones in the sand
Listening.

      —Reflects that these enjoy
Their country's gratitude, that deep repose,
That peace no pain can break, no hurt destroy,
That rest, that sleep—

      At Ghent the wind rose.
There was a smell of rain and a heavy drag
Of wind in the hedges but not as the wind blows
Over fresh water when the waves lag
Foaming and the willows huddle and it will rain:
I felt him waiting.

      —Indicates the flag
Which (may he say) enisles in Flanders' plain
This little field these happy, happy dead
Have made America—

In the ripe grain
The wind coiled glistening, darted, fled,
Dragging its heavy body: at Waereghem
The wind coiled in the grass above his head:
Waiting—listening—

—Dedicates to them
This earth their bones have hallowed, this last gift
A grateful country—

Under the dry grass stem
The words are blurred, are thickened, the words sift
Confused by the rasp of the wind, by the thin grating
Of ants under the grass, the minute shift
And tumble of dusty sand separating
From dusty sand. The roots of the grass strain,
Tighten, the earth is rigid, waits—he is waiting—

And suddenly, and all at once, the rain!

The people scatter, they run into houses, the wind
Is trampled under the rain, shakes free, is again
Trampled. The rain gathers, running in thinned
Spurts of water that ravel in the dry sand
Seeping into the sand under the grass roots, seeping
Between cracked boards to the bones of a clenched hand:
The earth relaxes, loosens; he is sleeping,
He rests, he is quiet, he sleeps in a strange land.

WILFRED OWEN

1893 - 1918

ANTHEM FOR DOOMED YOUTH

What passing-bells for these who die as cattle?
Only the monstrous anger of the guns.
Only the stuttering rifles' rapid rattle
Can patter out their hasty orisons.
No mockeries for them; no prayers nor bells,
Nor any voice of mourning save the choirs,—
The shrill, demented choirs of wailing shells;
And bugles calling for them from sad shires.

What candles may be held to speed them all?
Not in the hands of boys, but in their eyes
Shall shine the holy glimmers of good-byes.
The pallor of girls' brows shall be their pall;
Their flowers the tenderness of patient minds,
And each slow dusk a drawing-down of blinds.

THE YOUNG SOLDIER

It is not death
   Without hereafter
To one in dearth
   Of life and its laughter,

Nor the sweet murder
   Dealt slow and even
Unto the martyr
   Smiling at heaven:

It is the smile
   Faint as a myth,
Faint, and exceeding small
   On a boy's murdered mouth.

GREATER LOVE

Red lips are not so red
   As the stained stones kissed by the English dead.
Kindness of wooed and wooer
Seems shame to their love pure.
O Love, your eyes lose lure
   When I behold eyes blinded in my stead!

Your slender attitude
   Trembles not exquisite like limbs knife-skewed,
Rolling and rolling there
Where God seems not to care;
Till the fierce love they bear
   Cramps them in death's extreme decrepitude.

Your voice sings not so soft,—
    Though even as wind murmuring through raftered loft,—
Your dear voice is not dear,
Gentle, and evening clear,
As theirs whom none now hear
    Now earth has stopped their piteous mouths that coughed.

Heart, you were never hot,
    Nor large, nor full like hearts made great with shot;
And though your hand be pale,
Paler are all which trail
Your cross through flame and hail:
    Weep, you may weep, for you may touch them not.

SYLVIA TOWNSEND WARNER

1893 -

THE IMAGE

" Why do you look so pale, my son William?
    Where have you been so long? "
" I've been to my sweetheart, Mother,
    As it says in the song."[1]

" Though you be pledged and cried to the parish
    'Tis not fitting or right
To visit a young maiden
    At this hour of night."

" I went not for her sweet company,
    I meant not any sin,
But only to walk round her house
    And think she was within.

" Unbeknown I looked in at the window;
    And there I saw my bride
Sitting lonesome in the chimney-nook,
    With the cat alongside.

" Slowly she drew out from under her apron
    An image made of wax,
Shaped like a man, and all stuck over
    With pins and with tacks.

[1] The reference is to the ballad " Lord Randal " (see page 40).

" Hair it had, hanging down to its shoulders,
    Straight as any tow—
Just such a lock she begged of me
    But three days ago.

" She set it down to stand in the embers—
    The wax began to run,
Mother! Mother! That waxen image,
    I think it was your son! "

" 'Twas but a piece of maiden's foolishness,
    Never think more of it.
I warrant that when she's a wife
    She'll have a better wit."

" Maybe, maybe, Mother.
    I pray you, mend the fire.
For I am cold to the knees
    With walking through the mire.

" The snow is melting under the rain,
    The ways are full of mud;
The cold has crept into my bones,
    And glides along my blood.

" Take out, take out my winding sheet
    From the press where it lies,
And borrow two pennies from my money-box
    To put upon my eyes;

" For now the cold creeps up to my heart,
    My ears go Ding, go Dong:
I shall be dead long before day,
    For winter nights are long."

" Cursèd, cursèd be that Devil's vixen
    To rob you of your life!
And cursèd be the day you left me
    To go after a wife! "

" Why do you speak so loud, Mother?
    I was almost asleep.
I thought the churchbells were ringing
    And the snow lay deep.

" Over the white fields we trod to our wedding,
   She leant upon my arm—
What have I done to her that she
   Should do me this harm? "

EPITAPHS

After long thirty years re-met
I, William Clarke, and I, Jeanette
His wife, lie side by side once more;
But quieter than we lay before.

· · · ·

John Bird, a labourer, lies here,
Who served the earth for sixty year
With spade and mattock, drill and plough;
But never found it kind till now.

· · · · ·

Her grieving parents cradled here
Ann Monk, a gracious child and dear.
Lord, let this epitaph suffice:
Early to Bed and Early to Rise.

THE RIVAL

The farmer's wife looked out of the dairy:
She saw her husband in the yard;
She said: " A woman's life is hard,
The chimney smokes, the churn's contrary."
   She said:
" I of all women am the most ill-starred.

" Five sons I've borne and seven daughters,
And the last of them is on my knee.
Finer children you could not see.
Twelve times I've put my neck in the halter:
   You'd think
So much might knit my husband's love to me.

" But no! Though I should serve him double
He keeps another love outdoors,
Who thieves his strength, who drains his stores,
Who haunts his mind with fret and trouble;
   I pray
God's curse may light on such expensive whores.

" I am grown old before my season,
Weather and care have worn me down;
Each year delves deeper in my frown,
I've lost my shape and for good reason:
   But she
Yearly puts on young looks like an Easter gown.

" And year by year she has betrayed him
With blight and mildew, rain and drought,
Smut, scab, and murrain, all the rout;
But he forgets the tricks she's played him
   When first
The fields give a good smell and the leaves put out.

" Aye, come the Spring, and the gulls keening,
Over her strumpet lap he'll ride,
Watching those wasteful fields and wide,
Where the darkened tilth will soon be greening,`
   With looks
Fond and severe, as looks the groom on bride."

E. E. CUMMINGS

(A) 1894 - 1962

THIS IS THE GARDEN

this is the garden: colours come and go,
frail azures fluttering from night's outer wing
strong silent greens serenely lingering,
absolute lights like baths of golden snow.
This is the garden: pursèd lips do blow
upon cool flutes within wide glooms, and sing
(of harps celestial to the quivering string)
invisible faces hauntingly and slow.

This is the garden. Time shall surely reap,
and on Death's blade lie many a flower curled,
in other lands where other songs be sung;
yet stand they here enraptured, as among
the slow deep trees perpetual of sleep
some silver-fingered fountain steals the world.

CHARLES HAMILTON SORLEY

1895 - 1915

" SUCH IS DEATH "

1

Saints have adored the lofty soul of you.
Poets have whitened at your high renown.
We stand among the many millions who
Do hourly wait to pass your pathway down.
You, so familiar, once were strange: we tried
To live as of your presence unaware.
But now in every road on every side
We see your straight and steadfast signpost there.

I think it like that signpost in my land
Hoary and tall, which pointed me to go
Upward, into the hills, on the right hand,
Where the mists swim and the winds shriek and blow,
A homeless land and friendless, but a land
I did not know and that I wished to know.

2

Such, such is Death: no triumph: no defeat:
Only an empty pail, a slate rubbed clean,
A merciful putting away of what has been.
And this we know: Death is not Life effete,
Life crushed, the broken pail. We who have seen
So marvellous things know well the end not yet.

Victor and vanquished are a-one in death:
Coward and brave: friend, foe. Ghosts do not say,
" Come, what was your record when you drew breath? "
But a big blot has hid each yesterday
So poor, so manifestly incomplete.
And your bright Promise, withered long and sped,
Is touched; stirs, rises, opens and grows sweet
And blossoms and is you, when you are dead.

ROBERT GRAVES

1895 -

THE CORNER-KNOT

I was a child and overwhelmed: Mozart
Had snatched me up fainting and wild at heart
To a green land of wonder, where estranged
I dipped my feet in shallow brooks, I ranged
Rough mountains and fields yellow with small vetch:
Of which, though long I tried, I could not fetch
One single flower away, nor from the ground
Pocket one pebble of the scores I found
Twinkling enchanted there. So for relief
" I'll corner-knot," said I, " this handkerchief,
Faithful familiar that I hold or shake
In these cold airs for proof that I'm awake."
I tied the knot, the aspens all around
Shook, and the river-reeds were filled with sound;
Which failing presently, the insistent loud
Clapping of hands returned me to the crowd.
I felt and fumbling took away with me
The knotted witness of my ecstasy.
But flowers and streams were vanished past recall,
The aspens, the sad singing reeds and all.

Vanished: but that was twenty years ago.
Now again, listening to Mozart, I know
What then I never guessed, that he Mozart
Himself had been snatched up by curious art
To my green land: estranged and wild at heart
He too had crossed the brooks, essayed to pick
That yellow vetch with which the plains are thick,
And being put to it as I had been
To smuggle back some witness of the scene
Had knotted up his broad silk handkerchief
In common music, rippling flat and brief:
And home again, had sighed above the score,
" Yes, a remembrancer, but nothing more."
Oh, most mistaken, for that faithful knot
Once charged to witness how and where and what,

Though in itself a dull and idle thing,
Will yet by art again contrive to bring
Convoys of novices to that green land;
They gasp and stare and quite dumfounded stand.

STEPHEN VINCENT BENÉT

(A) 1898 - 1943

THE BALLAD OF WILLIAM SYCAMORE

(*1790-1871*)

My father, he was a mountaineer,
His fist was a knotty hammer;
He was quick on his feet as a running deer,
And he spoke with a Yankee stammer.

My mother, she was merry and brave,
And so she came to her labour,
With a tall green fir for her doctor grave
And a stream for her comforting neighbour.

And some are wrapped in the linen fine,
And some like a godling's scion;
But I was cradled on twigs of pine
In the skin of a mountain lion.

And some remember a white, starched lap
And a ewer with silver handles;
But I remember a coonskin cap
And the smell of bayberry candles.

The cabin logs, with the bark still rough,
And my mother who laughed at trifles,
And the tall, lank visitors, brown as snuff,
With their long, straight squirrel-rifles.

I can hear them dance, like a foggy song,
Through the deepest one of my slumbers,
The fiddle squeaking the boots along
And my father calling the numbers.

The quick feet shaking the puncheon-floor,
The fiddle squeaking and squealing,
Till the dried herbs rattled above the door
And the dust went up to the ceiling.

There are children lucky from dawn till dusk,
But never a child so lucky!
For I cut my teeth on " Money Musk "
In the Bloody Ground of Kentucky!

When I grew tall as the Indian corn,
My father had little to lend me,
But he gave me his great, old powder-horn
And his woodsman's skill to befriend me.

With a leather shirt to cover my back,
And a redskin nose to unravel
Each forest sign, I carried my pack
As far as a scout could travel.

Till I lost my boyhood and found my wife,
A girl like a Salem clipper!
A woman straight as a hunting-knife
With eyes as bright as the Dipper!

We cleared our camp where the buffalo feed,
Unheard-of streams were our flagons;
And I sowed my sons like apple-seed
On the trail of the Western wagons.

They were right, tight boys, never sulky or slow,
A fruitful, a goodly muster.
The eldest died at the Alamo.
The youngest fell with Custer.

The letter that told it burned my hand.
Yet we smiled and said, " So be it! "
But I could not live when they fenced the land.
For it broke my heart to see it.

I saddled a red, unbroken colt
And rode him into the day there;
And he threw me down like a thunderbolt
And rolled on me as I lay there.

The hunter's whistle hummed in my ear
As the city-men tried to move me,
And I died in my boots like a pioneer
With the whole wide sky above me.

Now I lie in the heart of the fat, black soil,
Like the seed of a prairie-thistle:
It has washed my bones with honey and oil
And picked them clean as a whistle.

And my youth returns, like the rains of Spring,
And my sons, like the wild geese flying;
And I lie and hear the meadow-lark sing
And have much content in my dying.

Go play with the towns you have built of blocks,
The towns where you would have bound me!
I sleep in my earth like a tired fox,
And my buffalo have found me.

HART CRANE

(A) 1899 - 1932

from " VOYAGES "

—And yet this great wink of eternity,
Of rimless floods, unfettered leewardings,
Samite sheeted and processioned where
Her undinal vast belly moonward bends,
Laughing the wrapt inflections of our love;

Take this Sea, whose diapason knells
On scrolls of silver snowy sentences,
The sceptred terror of whose sessions rends
As her demeanours motion well or ill,
All but the pieties of lovers' hands.

And onward, as bells off San Salvador
Salute the crocus lustres of the stars,
In these poinsettia meadows of her tides,—
Adagios of islands, O my Prodigal,
Complete the dark confessions her veins spell.

Mark how her turning shoulders wind the hours,
And hasten while her penniless rich palms
Pass superscription of bent foam and wave,—
Hasten, while they are true,—sleep, death, desire,
Close round one instant in one floating flower.

Bind us in time, O seasons clear, and awe.
O minstrel galleons of Carib fire,
Bequeath us to no earthly shore until
Is answered in the vortex of our grave
The seal's wide spindrift gaze toward paradise.

ALLEN TATE

(A) 1899 -

ODE TO FEAR

VARIATION ON A THEME BY COLLINS

Let the day glare: O Memory, your tread
Beats to the pulse of suffocating night—
Night peering from his dark but fire-lit head
Burns on the day his tense and secret light.

Now they dare not to hunt your savage dream
O Beast of the heart, those saints who cursed your name,
You are the current of the frozen stream,
Shadow invisible, ambushed and vigilant flame!

My eldest companion present in solitude
Watch-dog of Thebes when the blind hero strove,
'Twas your omniscience at the cross-road stood
When Laius the slain dotard drenched the grove.

Now to the fading harried eyes immune
Of prophecy you stalk us in the street
From the recesses of the August noon
World over, crouched on the air's feet.

You are the surety to immortal life
God's hatred of the universal stain,
The heritage, O fear, of ancient strife
Compounded with the tissue of the vein,

And I when all is said have seen your form
Most agile, and most treacherous to the world
When on a child's long day a dry storm
Burst on the cedars by the sunlight hurled.

LÉONIE ADAMS

(A) 1899 -

COUNTRY SUMMER

Now the rich cherry whose sleek wood
And top with silver petals traced,
Like a strict box its gems encased,
Has spilt from out that cunning lid,
All in an innocent green round,
Those melting rubies which it hid;
With moss ripe-strawberry-encrusted,
So birds gets half, and minds lapse merry
To taste that deep-red lark's-bite berry,
And blackcap-bloom is yellow-dusted

The wren that thieved it in the eaves
A trailer of the rose could catch
To her poor droopy sloven thatch,
And side by side with the wren's brood,—
O lovely time of beggars' luck—
Opens the quaint and hairy bud.
And full and golden is the yield
Of cows that never have to house,
But all night nibble under boughs,
Or cool their sides in the moist field.

Into the rooms flow meadow airs,
The warm farm-baking smell blows round;
Inside and out and sky and ground
Are much the same; the wishing star,
Hesperus, kind and early-born,
Is risen only finger-far.
All stars stand close in summer air,
And tremble, and look mild as amber;
When wicks are lighted in the chamber
You might say stars were settling there.

Now straightening from the flowery hay,
Down the still light the mowers look;
Or turn, because their dreaming shook,
And they waked half to other days,
When left alone in yellow stubble,
The rusty-coated mare would graze.

Yet thick the lazy dreams are born;
Another thought can come to mind,
But like the shivering of the wind,
Morning and evening in the corn.

LULLABY

Hush, lullay,
Your treasures all
     Encrust with rust.
Your trinket pleasures
     Fall
To dust.
Beneath the sapphire arch
Upon the grassy floor
Is nothing more
     To hold,
And play is over old.
Your eyes
     In sleepy fever gleam,
Your lids droop
     To their dream.
You wander late alone,
The flesh frets on the bone,
Your love fails
     In your breast.
Here is the pillow.
     Rest.

ROY CAMPBELL

1901 - 1957

THE ZULU GIRL

When in the sun the hot red acres smoulder,
Down where the sweating gang its labour plies,
A girl flings down her hoe, and from her shoulder
Unslings her child tormented by the flies.

She takes him to a ring of shadow pooled
By thorn-trees: purpled with the blood of ticks,
While her sharp nails, in slow caresses ruled,
Prowl through his hair with sharp electric clicks,

His sleepy mouth plugged by the heavy nipple,
Tugs like a puppy, grunting as he feeds:
Through his frail nerves her own deep languors ripple
Like a broad river sighing through its reeds.

Yet in that drowsy stream his flesh imbibes
An old unquenched unsmotherable heat—
The curbed ferocity of beaten tribes,
The sullen dignity of their defeat.

Her body looms above him like a hill
Within whose shade a village lies at rest,
Or the first cloud so terrible and still
That bears the coming harvest in its breast.

C. DAY LEWIS

1904 -

NEARING AGAIN THE LEGENDARY ISLE

Nearing again the legendary isle
Where sirens sang and mariners were skinned,
We wonder now what was there to beguile
That such stout fellows left their bones behind.

Those chorus-girls are surely past their prime,
Voices grow shrill and paint is wearing thin,
Lips that sealed up the sense from gnawing time
Now beg the favour with a graveyard grin.

We have no flesh to spare and they can't bite,
Hunger and sweat have stripped us to the bone;
A skeleton crew we toil upon the tide
And mock the theme-song meant to lure us on:

No need to stop the ears, avert the eyes
From purple rhetoric of evening skies.

THE CONFLICT

I sang as one
Who on a tilting deck sings
To keep their courage up, though the wave hangs
That shall cut off their sun.

As storm-cocks sing,
Flinging their natural answer in the wind's teeth,
And care not if it is waste of breath
Or birth-carol of spring.

As ocean-flyer clings
To height, to the last drop of spirit driving on
While yet ahead is land to be won
And work for wings.

Singing I was at peace,
Above the clouds, outside the ring:
For sorrow finds a swift release in song
And pride its poise.

Yet living here,
As one between two massing powers I live
Whom neutrality cannot save
Nor occupation cheer.

None such shall be left alive:
The innocent wing is soon shot down,
And private stars fade in the blood-red dawn
Where two worlds strive.

The red advance of life
Contracts pride, calls out the common blood,
Beats song into a single blade,
Makes a depth-charge of grief.

Move then with new desires,
For where we used to build and love
Is no man's land, and only ghosts can live
Between two fires.

WILLIAM EMPSON

1906 -

MISSING DATES

Slowly the poison the whole blood stream fills.
It is not the effort nor the failure tires.
The waste remains, the waste remains and kills.

It is not your system or clear sight that mills
Down small to the consequence a life requires;
Slowly the poison the whole blood stream fills.

They bled an old dog dry yet the exchange rills
Of young dog blood gave but a month's desires;
The waste remains, the waste remains and kills.

It is the Chinese tombs and the slag hills
Usurp the soil, and not the soil retires.
Slowly the poison the whole blood stream fills.

Not to have fire is to be a skin that shrills.
The complete fire is death. From partial fires
The waste remains, the waste remains and kills.

It is the poems you have lost, the ills
From missing dates, at which the heart expires.
Slowly the poison the whole blood stream fills.
The waste remains, the waste remains and kills.

JOHN BETJEMAN

1906 -

THE ARREST OF OSCAR WILDE AT THE CADOGAN HOTEL

He sipped at a weak hock and seltzer
  As he gazed at the London skies
Through the Nottingham lace of the curtains
  Or was it his bees-winged eyes?

To the right and before him Pont Street
  Did tower in her new built red,
As hard as the morning gaslight
  That shone on his unmade bed.

" I want some more hock in my seltzer,
  And Robbie, please give me your hand—
Is this the end or beginning?
  How can I understand?

" So you've brought me the latest *Yellow Book*:
  And Buchan has got in it now:
Approval of what is approved of
  Is as false as a well-kept vow.

" More hock, Robbie—where is the seltzer?
  Dear boy, pull again at the bell!
They are all little better than *cretins*,
  Though this *is* the Cadogan Hotel.

" One astrakhan coat is at Willis's—
  Another one's at the Savoy:
Do fetch my morocco portmanteau,
  And bring them on later, dear boy."

A thump, and a murmur of voices—
  (" Oh why must they make such a din? ")
As the door of the bedroom swung open
  And Two Plain Clothes POLICEMEN came in:

" Mr. Woilde, we 'ave come for tew take yew
  Where felons and criminals dwell:
We must ask yew tew leave with us quoietly
  For this *is* the Cadogan Hotel."

He rose, and he put down *The Yellow Book*.
  He staggered—and, terrible-eyed,
He brushed past the palms on the staircase
  And was helped to a hansom outside.

LOUIS MacNEICE

1907 - 1963

SUNDAY MORNING

Down the road someone is practising scales,
The notes like little fishes vanish with a wink of tails,
Man's heart expands to tinker with his car
For this is Sunday morning, Fate's great bazaar,
Regard these means as ends, concentrate on this Now,
And you may grow to music or drive beyond Hindhead anyhow,
Take corners on two wheels until you go so fast
That you can clutch a fringe or two of the windy past,

That you can abstract this day and make it to the week of time
A small eternity, a sonnet self-contained in rhyme.

But listen, up the road, something gulps, the church spire
Opens its eight bells out, skulls' mouths which will not tire
To tell how there is no music or movement which secures
Escape from the weekday time. Which deadens and endures.

WYSTAN HUGH AUDEN

1907 - 1973

WHO'S WHO

A shilling life will give you all the facts:
How Father beat him, how he ran away,
What were the struggles of his youth, what acts
Made him the greatest figure of his day:
Of how he fought, fished, hunted, worked all night;
Though giddy, climbed new mountains; named a sea:
Some of the last researchers even write
Love made him weep his pints like you and me.

With all his honours on, he sighed for one
Who, say astonished critics, lived at home;
Did little jobs about the house with skill
And nothing else; could whistle; would sit still
Or potter round the garden; answered some
Of his long marvellous letters, but kept none.

LAY YOUR SLEEPING HEAD, MY LOVE

Lay your sleeping head, my love,
Human on my faithless arm;
Time and fevers burn away
Individual beauty from
Thoughtful children, and the grave
Proves the child ephemeral:
But in my arms till break of day
Let living creature lie,
Mortal, guilty, but to me
The entirely beautiful.

Soul and body have no bounds:
To lovers as they lie upon
Her tolerant enchanted slope
In their ordinary swoon,
Grave the vision Venus sends
Of supernatural sympathy,
Universal love and hope;
While an abstract insight wakes
Among the glaciers and the rocks
The hermit's sensual ecstasy.

Certainty, fidelity
On the stroke of midnight pass
Like vibrations of a bell,
And fashionable madmen raise
Their pedantic boring cry:
Every farthing of the cost,
All the dreaded cards foretell,
Shall be paid, but from this night
Not a whisper, not a thought,
Not a kiss nor look be lost.

Beauty, midnight, vision dies:
Let the winds of dawn that blow
Softly round your dreaming head
Such a day of sweetness show
Eye and knocking heart may bless,
Find the mortal world enough;
Noons of dryness see you fed
By the involuntary powers,
Nights of insult let you pass
Watched by every human love.

IN MEMORY OF W. B. YEATS

I

He disappeared in the dead of winter:
The brooks were frozen, the airports almost deserted,
And snow disfigured the public statues;
The mercury sank in the mouth of the dying day.
O all the instruments agree
The day of his death was a dark cold day.

Far from his illness
The wolves ran on through the evergreen forests,
The peasant river was untempted by the fashionable quays;
By mourning tongues
The death of the poet was kept from his poems.

But for him it was his last afternoon as himself,
An afternoon of nurses and rumours;
The provinces of his body revolted,
The squares of his mind were empty,
Silence invaded the suburbs,
The current of his feeling failed: he became his admirers.

Now he is scattered among a hundred cities
And wholly given over to unfamiliar affections;
To find his happiness in another kind of wood
And be punished under a foreign code of conscience.
The words of a dead man
Are modified in the guts of the living.

But in the importance and noise of tomorrow
When the brokers are roaring like beasts on the floor of the Bourse,
And the poor have the sufferings to which they are fairly accus-
     tomed,
And each in the cell of himself is almost convinced of his freedom;
A few thousand will think of this day
As one thinks of a day when one did something slightly unusual.

O all the instruments agree
The day of his death was a dark cold day.

2

You were silly like us: your gift survived it all;
The parish of rich women, physical decay,
Yourself; mad Ireland hurt you into poetry.
Now Ireland has her madness and her weather still,
For poetry makes nothing happen: it survives
In the valley of its saying where executives
Would never want to tamper; it flows south
From ranches of isolation and the busy griefs,
Raw towns that we believe and die in; it survives,
A way of happening, a mouth.

3

Earth, receive an honoured guest;
William Yeats is laid to rest:
Let the Irish vessel lie
Emptied of its poetry.

Time that is intolerant
Of the brave and innocent,
And indifferent in a week
To a beautiful physique,

Worships language and forgives
Everyone by whom it lives;
Pardons cowardice, conceit,
Lays its honours at their feet.

Time that with this strange excuse
Pardoned Kipling and his views,
And will pardon Paul Claudel,
Pardons him for writing well.

In the nightmare of the dark
All the dogs of Europe bark,
And the living nations wait,
Each sequestered in its hate;

Intellectual disgrace
Stares from every human face,
And the seas of pity lie
Locked and frozen in each eye.

Follow, poet, follow right
To the bottom of the night,
With your unconstraining voice
Still persuade us to rejoice;

With the farming of a verse
Make a vineyard of the curse,
Sing of human unsuccess
In a rapture of distress;

In the deserts of the heart
Let the healing fountain start,
In the prison of his days
Teach the free man how to praise.

THEODORE ROETHKE

(A) 1908 -

ELEGY FOR JANE

(My student, thrown by a horse)

I remember the neckcurls, limp and damp as tendrils,
And her quick look, a sidelong pickerel smile;
And how, once startled into talk, the light syllables leaped for her,
And she balanced in the delight of her thought,
A wren, happy, tail into the wind,
Her song trembling the twigs and small branches.
The shade sang with her;
The leaves, their whispers turned to kissing;
And the mould sang in the bleached valleys under the rose.

Oh, when she was sad, she cast herself down into such a pure
    depth,
Even a father could not find her:
Scraping her cheek against straw;
Stirring the clearest water.

My sparrow, you are not here,
Waiting like a fern, making a spiney shadow.
The sides of wet stones cannot console me,
Nor the moss, wound with the last light.

If only I could nudge you from this sleep,
My maimed darling, my skittery pigeon.
Over this damp grave I speak the words of my love:
I, with no rights in this matter,
Neither father nor lover.

STEPHEN SPENDER

1909 -

AN ELEMENTARY SCHOOL CLASSROOM
IN A SLUM

Far far from gusty waves, these children's faces.
Like rootless weeds, the torn hair round their pallor.
The tall girl with her weighed-down head. The paper-
seeming boy with rat's eyes. The stunted unlucky heir
Of twisted bones, reciting a father's gnarled disease,
His lesson from his desk. At back of the dim class
One unnoted, mild and young: his eyes live in a dream
Of squirrels' game, in tree room, other than this.

On sour cream walls, donations. Shakespeare's head
Cloudless at dawn, civilized dome riding all cities.
Belled, flowery, Tyrolese valley. Open-handed map
Awarding the world its world. And yet, for these
Children, these windows, not this world, are world,
Where all their future's painted with a fog,
A narrow street sealed in with a lead sky,
Far far from rivers, capes, and stars of words.

Surely Shakespeare is wicked, the map a bad example
With ships and sun and love tempting them to steal—
For lives that slyly turn in their cramped holes
From fog to endless night? On their slag heap, these children
Wear skins peeped through by bones, and spectacles of steel
With mended glass, like bottle bits on stones.
Tyrol is wicked; map's promising a fable:
All of their time and space are foggy slum,
So blot their maps with slums as big as doom.

Unless, governor, teacher, inspector, visitor,
This map becomes their window and these windows
That open on their lives like catacombs,
Break, O break open, till they break the town
And show the children to green fields, and make their world
Run azure on gold sands, and let their tongues
Run naked into books, the white and green leaves open
The history theirs whose language is the sun.

I THINK CONTINUALLY OF THOSE

I think continually of those who were truly great.
Who, from the womb, remembered the soul's history
Through corridors of light where the hours are suns,
Endless and singing. Whose lovely ambition
Was that their lips, still touched with fire,
Should tell of the spirit clothed from head to foot in song.
And who hoarded from the spring branches
The desires falling across their bodies like blossoms.

What is precious is never to forget
The essential delight of the blood drawn from ageless springs
Breaking through rocks in worlds before our earth;
Never to deny its pleasure in the morning simple light,
Nor its grave evening demand for love;
Never to allow gradually the traffic to smother
With noise and fog, the flowering of the spirit.

Near the snow, near the sun, in the highest fields
See how these names are fêted by the waving grass,
And by the streamers of white cloud,
And whispers of wind in the listening sky.
The names of those who in their lives fought for life,
Who wore at their hearts the fire's centre.
Born of the sun, they travelled a short while towards the sun,
And left the vivid air signed with their honour.

W. R. RODGERS

1909 -

NEITHER HERE NOR THERE

In that land all Is and nothing's Ought;
No owners or notices, only birds;
No walls anywhere, only lean wire of words
Worming brokenly out from eaten thought;
No oats growing, only ankle-lace grass
Easing and not resenting the feet that pass;
No enormous beasts, only names of them;
No bones made, bans laid, or boons expected,
No contracts, entails, hereditaments,
Anything at all that might tie or hem.

In that land all's lackadaisical;
No lakes of coddled spawn, and no locked ponds
Of settled purpose, no netted fishes;
But only inkling streams and running fronds,
Fritillaried with dreams, weedy with wishes;
Nor arrogant talk is heard, haggling phrase,
But undertones, and hesitance, and haze;
On clear days mountains of meaning are seen
Humped high on the horizon; no one goes
To con their meaning, no one cares or knows.

In that land all's flat, indifferent; there
Is neither springing house nor hanging tent,
No aims are entertained, and nothing is meant,
For there are no ends and no trends, no roads,
Only follow your nose to anywhere.
No one is born there, no one stays or dies,
For it is a timeless land, it lies
Between the act and the attrition, it
Marks off bound from rebound, make from break, tit
From tat, also to-day from to-morrow.

No Cause there comes to term, but each departs
Elsewhere to whelp its deeds, expel its darts;
There are no homecomings, of course, no good-byes
In that land, neither yearning nor scorning,
Though at night there is the smell of morning.

ELIZABETH BISHOP

(A) 1911 -

THE FISH

I caught a tremendous fish
and held him beside the boat
half out of water, with my hook
fast in a corner of his mouth.
He didn't fight.
He hadn't fought at all.
He hung a grunting weight,
battered and venerable
and homely. Here and there
his brown skin hung in strips

like ancient wall-paper,
and its pattern of darker brown
was like wall-paper:
shapes like full-blown roses
stained and lost through age.
He was speckled with barnacles,
fine rosettes of lime,
and infested
with tiny white sea-lice,
and underneath two or three
rags of green weed hung down.
While his gills were breathing in
the terrible oxygen
—the frightening gills
fresh and crisp with blood,
that can cut so badly—
I thought of the coarse white flesh
packed in like feathers,
the big bones and the little bones,
the dramatic reds and blacks
of his shiny entrails,
and the pink swim-bladder
like a big peony.
I looked into his eyes
which were far larger than mine
but shallower, and yellowed,
the irises backed and packed
with tarnished tinfoil
seen through the lenses
of old scratched isinglass.
They shifted a little, but not
to return my stare.
—It was more like the tipping
of an object toward the light.
I admired his sullen face,
the mechanism of his jaw,
and then I saw
that from his lower lip
—if you could call it a lip—
grim, wet, and weapon-like,
hung five old pieces of fish-line,
or four and a wire leader
with the swivel still attached,
with all their five big hooks
grown firmly in his mouth.

A green line, frayed at the end
where he broke it, two heavier lines,
and a fine black thread
still crimped from the strain and snap
when it broke and he got away.
Like medals with their ribbons
frayed and wavering,
a five-haired beard of wisdom
trailing from his aching jaw
I stared and stared
and victory filled up
the little rented boat,
from the pool of bilge
where oil had spread a rainbow
around the rusted engine
to the bailer rusted orange,
the sun-cracked thwarts,
the oarlocks on their strings,
the gunnels—until everything
was rainbow, rainbow, rainbow!
And I let the fish go.

LAWRENCE DURRELL

1912 -

SWANS

Fraudulent perhaps in that they gave
No sense of muscle but a swollen languor
Though moved by webs: yet idly, idly
As soap-bubbles drift from a clay-pipe
They mowed the lake in tapestry,

Passing in regal exhaustion by us,
King, queen and cygnets, one by one,
Did one dare to remember other swans
In anecdotes of Gauguin or of Rabelais?
Some became bolsters for the Greeks,
Some rubber Lohengrins provided comedy.

The flapping of the wings excited Leda.
The procession is over and what is now
Alarming is more the mirror split

From end to end by the harsh clap
Of the wooden beaks, than the empty space
Which follows them about,
Stained by their whiteness when they pass.

We sit like drunkards and inhale the swans.

GEORGE BARKER

1913 -

O TENDER UNDER HER RIGHT BREAST

(Second Cycle of Love Poems: II)

O tender under her right breast
    Sleep at the waterfall
My daughter, my daughter, and be at rest
    As I at her left shall.

At night the pigeon in the eaves
    Leaves open its bright eye;
Nor will the Seven Sisters cease
    To watch you where you lie.

The pine like a father over your bed
    Will bend down from above
To lay in duty at your head
    The candles of its love.

And in their mothering embrace,
    Sleep on the Rockies' bosom;
The Okanogan Valley shall grace
    Canada round your cradle.

The silver spoon and the one-eyed man,
    The rabbit's foot and the clover,
Be at your bed from morning till
    As now, the day is over.

SONNET TO MY MOTHER

Most near, most dear, most loved and most far,
Under the window where I often found her
Sitting as huge as Asia, seismic with laughter,
Gin and chicken helpless in her Irish hand,
Irresistible as Rabelais but most tender for
The lame dogs and hurt birds that surround her,—
She is a procession no one can follow after
But be like a little dog following a brass band.
She will not glance up at the bomber or condescend
To drop her gin and scuttle to a cellar,
But lean on the mahogany table like a mountain
Whom only faith can move, and so I send
O all my faith and all my love to tell her
That she will move from mourning into morning.

DYLAN THOMAS

1914 - 1953

WHEN ALL MY FIVE AND COUNTRY SENSES SEE

When all my five and country senses see,
The fingers will forget green thumbs and mark
How, through the halfmoon's vegetable eye,
Husk of young stars and handful zodiac,
Love in the frost is pared and wintered by,
The whispering ears will watch love drummed away
Down breeze and shell to a discordant beach,
And, lashed to syllables, the lynx tongue cry
That her fond wounds are mended bitterly.
My nostrils see her breath burn like a bush.

My one and noble heart has witnesses
In all love's countries, that will grope awake;
And when blind sleep drops on the spying senses,
The heart is sensual, though five eyes break.

ESPECIALLY WHEN THE OCTOBER WIND

Especially when the October wind
With frosty fingers punishes my hair,
Caught by the crabbing sun I walk on fire
And cast a shadow crab upon the land,
By the sea's side, hearing the noise of birds,
Hearing the raven cough in winter sticks,
My busy heart who shudders as she talks
Sheds the syllabic blood and drains her words.

Shut, too, in a tower of words, I mark
On the horizon walking like the trees
The wordy shapes of women, and the rows
Of the star-gestured children in the park.
Some let me make you of the vowelled beeches,
Some of the oaken voices, from the roots
Of many a thorny shire tell you notes,
Some let me make you of the water's speeches.

Behind a pot of ferns the wagging clock
Tells me the hour's word, the neural meaning
Flies on the shafted disc, declaims the morning
And tells the windy weather in the cock.
Some let me make you of the meadow's signs;
The signal grass that tells me all I know
Breaks with the wormy winter through the eye.
Some let me tell you of the raven's sins.

Especially when the October wind
(Some let me make you of autumnal spells,
The spider tongued, and the loud hill of Wales)
With fist of turnips punishes the land,
Some let me make you of the heartless words.
The heart is drained that, spelling in the scurry
Of chemic blood, warned of the coming fury.
By the sea's side hear the dark-vowelled birds.

AFTER THE FUNERAL

In Memory of Ann Jones

After the funeral, mule praises, brays,
Windshake of sailshaped ears, muffle-toed tap
Tap happily of one peg in the thick
Grave's foot, blinds down the lids, the teeth in black,
The spittled eyes, the salt ponds in the sleeves,
Morning smack of the spade that wakes up sleep,
Shakes a desolate boy who slits his throat
In the dark of the coffin and sheds dry leaves,
That breaks one bone to light with a judgment clout,
After the feast of tear-stuffed time and thistles
In a room with a stuffed fox and a stale fern,
I stand, for this memorial's sake, alone
In the snivelling hours with dead, humped Ann
Whose hooded, fountain heart once fell in puddles
Round the parched worlds of Wales and drowned each sun
(Though this for her is a monstrous image blindly
Magnified out of praise; her death was a still drop;
She would not have me sinking in the holy
Flood of her heart's fame; she would lie dumb and deep
And need no druid of her broken body).
But I, Ann's bard on a raised hearth, call all
The seas to service that her wood-tongued virtue
Babble like a bellbuoy over the hymning heads,
Bow down the walls of the ferned and foxy woods
That her love sing and swing through a brown chapel,
Bless her bent spirit with four, crossing birds.
Her flesh was meek as milk, but this skyward statue
With the wild breast and blessed and giant skull
Is carved from her in a room with a wet window
In a fiercely mourning house in a crooked year.
I know her scrubbed and sour humble hands
Lie with religion in their cramp, her threadbare
Whisper in a damp word, her wits drilled hollow,
Her fist of a face died clenched on a round pain;
And sculptured Ann is seventy years of stone.
These cloud-sopped, marble hands, this monumental
Argument of the hewn voice, gesture and psalm
Storm me forever over her grave until
The stuffed lung of the fox twitch and cry Love
And the strutting fern lay seeds on the black sill.

DO NOT GO GENTLE INTO THAT GOOD NIGHT

Do not go gentle into that good night,
Old age should burn and rave at close of day;
Rage, rage against the dying of the light.

Though wise men at their end know dark is right,
Because their words had forked no lightning they
Do not go gentle into that good night.

Good men, the last wave by, crying how bright
Their frail deeds might have danced in a green bay,
Rage, rage against the dying of the light.

Wild men who caught and sang the sun in flight,
And learn, too late, they grieved it on its way,
Do not go gentle into that good night.

Grave men, near death, who see with blinding sight
Blind eyes could blaze like meteors and be gay,
Rage, rage against the dying of the light.

And you, my father, there on the sad height,
Curse, bless, me now with your fierce tears, I pray.
Do not go gentle into that good night.
Rage, rage against the dying of the light.

ROBERT LOWELL

(A) 1917 -

COLLOQUY IN BLACK ROCK

Here the jack-hammer jabs into the ocean;
My heart, you race and stagger and demand
More blood-gangs for your nigger-brass percussions,
Till I, the stunned machine of your devotion,
Clanging upon this cymbal of a hand,
Am rattled screw and footloose. All discussions
End in the mud-flat detritus of death.

My heart, beat faster, faster. In Black Mud
Hungarian workmen give their blood
For the martyre Stephen, who was stoned to death.
Black Mud, a name to conjure with: O mud
For watermelons gutted to the crust,
Mud for the mole-tide harbour, mud for mouse,
Mud for the armoured Diesel fishing tubs that thud
A year and a day to wind and tide; the dust
Is on this skipping heart that shakes my house,

House of our Saviour who was hanged till death.
My heart, beat faster, faster. In Black Mud
Stephen the martyre was broken down to blood:
Our ransom is the rubble of his death.

Christ walks on the black water. In Black Mud
Darts the kingfisher. On Corpus Christi, heart,
Over the drum-beat of St. Stephen's choir
I hear him, *Stupor Mundi*, and the mud
Flies from his hunching wings and beak—my heart,
The blue kingfisher dives on you in fire.

RICHARD WILBUR

(A) 1922 -

AFTER THE LAST BULLETINS

After the last bulletins the windows darken
And the whole city founders easily and deep,
Sliding on all its pillows
To the thronged Atlantis of personal sleep,

And the wind rises. The wind rises and bowls
The day's litter of news in the alleys. Trash
Tears itself on the railings,
Soars and falls with a soft crash,

Tumbles and soars again. In empty lots
Our journals spiral in a fierce noyade
Of all we thought to think,
Or caught in corners cramp and wad

And twist our words. And some from gutters flail
Their tatters at the tired patrolman's feet
Like all that fisted snow
That cried beside his long retreat

Damn you! damn you! to the emperor's horses' heels.
Oh none too soon through the air white and dry
Will the clear announcer's voice
Beat like a dove, and you and I

From the heart's anarch and responsible town
Rise by the subway-mouth to life again,
Bearing the morning papers,
And cross the park where saintlike men,

White and absorbed, with stick and bag remove
The litter of the night, and footsteps rouse
With confident morning sound
The songbirds in the public boughs.

PHILIP LARKIN

1922 -

NEXT, PLEASE

Always too eager for the future, we
Pick up bad habits of expectancy.
Something is always approaching; every day
Till then we say,

Watching from a bluff the tiny, clear
Sparkling armada of promises draw near.
How slow they are! And how much time they waste,
Refusing to make haste!

Yet still they leave us holding wretched stalks
Of disappointment, for, though nothing balks
Each big approach, leaning with brasswork prinked,
Each rope distinct,

Flagged, and the figurehead with golden tits
Arching our way, it never anchors; it's
No sooner present than it turns to past.
Right to the last

We think each one will heave to and unload
All good into our lives, all we are owed
For waiting so devoutly and so long.
But we are wrong:

Only one ship is seeking us, a black-
Sailed unfamiliar, towing at her back
A huge and birdless silence. In her wake
No waters breed or break.

SIDNEY KEYES

1922 - 1943

EARLY SPRING

Now that the young buds are tipped with a falling sun—
Each twig a candle, a martyr, St. Julian's branched stag—
And the shadows are walking the cobbled square like soldiers
With their long legs creaking and their pointed hands
Reaching the railings and fingering the stones
Of what expended, unprojected graves:
The soil's a flirt, the lion Time is tamed,
And pain like a cat will come home to share your room.

NEUTRALITY

Here not the flags, the rhythmic
Feet of returning legions; nor at household shrines
The small tears' offering, the postcards
Treasured for years, nor the names cut in brass.
Here not the lowered voices.
Not the drum.

Only at suppertime, rain slanting
Among our orchards, printing its coded
But peaceful messages across our pavements.
Only the cryptic swift performing
His ordered evolutions through our sky.
Only the growing.

And in the night, the secret voices
Of summer, the progression

Of hours without suspense, without surprise.
Only the moon beholds us, even the hunting owl
May watch us without malice.
Without envy.

We are no cowards, we are pictures
Of ordinary people, as you once were.
Blame not nor pity us; we are the people
Who laugh in dreams before the ramping boar
Appears, before the loved one's death.
We are your hope.

LONGER POEMS

The following important longer poems are not included in this volume because of the lack of space. They are, however, easily accessible and the list should be considered as a supplement.

Geoffrey Chaucer: The Parlement of Foules; The Canterbury Pilgrims; Troilus and Criseyde

Edmund Spenser: Prothalamion; Epithalamion; Astrophel (an Elegy); The Faerie Queene

Philip Sidney: Astrophel and Stella

Christopher Marlowe: Hero and Leander

William Shakespeare: Venus and Adonis; Lucrece

John Donne: The Second Anniversary; An Epithalamion

John Milton: Paradise Lost; On the Morning of Christ's Nativity; Comus

John Dryden: Absalom and Achitophel

Alexander Pope: An Essay on Criticism; An Essay on Man; Moral Essays; Epistle to Dr. Arbuthnot

John Dyer: Grongar Hill

James Thomson: The Seasons

Samuel Johnson: London; The Vanity of Human Wishes

Oliver Goldsmith: The Deserted Village

Thomas Gray: The Bard; The Progress of Poesy

Thomas Chatterton: The Bristowe Tragedie

William Blake: The Book of Thel; Milton; The Everlasting Gospel

Robert Burns: The Cotter's Saturday Night

George Gordon, Lord Byron: Don Juan; Childe Harold's Pilgrimage

William Wordsworth: The Prelude; The Excursion

Samuel Taylor Coleridge: Christabel

Walter Scott: The Battle of Flodden Field (from " Marmion ")

Percy Bysshe Shelley: Queen Mab; Adonais; Alastor or the Spirit of Solitude; Epipsychidion; Prometheus Unbound

John Keats: Hyperion; Endymion; Lamia; Isabella, or the Pot of Basil

Robert Browning: Sordello; Fra Lippo Lippi; Christmas Eve; The Flight of the Duchess; The Ring and the Book; In a Balcony

Elizabeth Barrett Browning: Sonnets from the Portuguese

Alfred, Lord Tennyson: Maud; In Memoriam; The Lady of Shalott

Matthew Arnold: Sohrab and Rustum; The Scholar-Gipsy

John Greenleaf Whittier: Snowbound

A. C. Swinburne: Anactoria; Hymn to Proserpine; Hertha; Tristam of Lyonesse

Coventry Patmore: The Angel in the House

Henry Wadsworth Longfellow: The Golden Legend

INDEX OF FORMS AND TYPES

This Index is suggestive rather than exhaustive. No attempt has been made to divide the book arbitrarily into classes and subjects, nor has it seemed necessary to define the ballad, the lyric, the ode, the sonnet, et cetera. It is taken for granted that the reader is familiar with these forms, or that, if he is not, he will refer to one of the many volumes which analyse the structure of verse and its technique. Here the editor has merely arranged most of the poems for the convenience of readers interested in classification and for those who wish to compare examples of the various forms.

THE BALLAD

BLANK VERSE

DESCRIPTIVE VERSE

DIDACTIC OR RELIGIOUS VERSE

THE ELEGY

Many of the following poems, being in the nature of songs, might be classified as lyrics. Their subject as well as their measured rhythm suggests a separate division.

THE EPIGRAM

THE EPITAPH

FREE (OR CADENCED) VERSE

THE LULLABY

THE LYRIC

See, also the listed poems under " The Pastoral " and " Lullabies "

MYSTICAL AND METAPHYSICAL VERSE

THE NARRATIVE

This category includes all the tales listed under " The Ballad " on page 635 as well as the following stories in verse.

ODD FORMS, STRANGE DEVICES

THE ODE

THE PASTORAL

The following poems might, with equal justice, be grouped under " The Lyric " on page 637. But the Elizabethans and their successors have made so definite a place for bucolic verse—the true variety as well as the artificial pastoral—that it has been thought advisable to list it separately.

THE SONNET

THE SPENSERIAN STANZA

TERZA RIMA

A form rarely encountered in English except in strict translations of
Dante's *Divina Commedia*.

VILLANELLE

POETIC FORMS AND PATTERNS

Although condensed and limited, this addendum presents the
chief poetic designs and devices. It is not a complete outline, but
rather a brief explanation of the principal forms of poetry and the
common properties of versification. The definitions are general,
not inclusive, popular (in the sense that they do not list exceptions
to the rules) rather than pedagogic. However, most of the
traditional forms have been included and only the rare or archaic
terms have been omitted.

The poems which illustrate the various forms do not appear in
the body of the book, but are in addition to those referred to by
page number.

The problems of rhythm and accent, of duration and pause, have been variously interpreted. The very nature of accent has given rise to controversy, some scholars maintaining it is due to a change in pitch of the voice, others to an increase of volume of tone. It is, however, generally accepted as *stress*, and in the following paragraphs it will be so regarded.

In English verse the rhythm is based upon this stress or accent, "the measured undulation of accented and unaccented syllables being its essential feature without which it becomes prose" (Brewer). The measures of Latin and Greek poetry, however, are not governed by accent, but are based upon quantity (the time consumed in pronouncing a syllable, a long syllable being considered equal to two short syllables), the laws governing quantity being far more strict than the rules determining English verse. Although classical prosody lists about thirty combinations of stressed and unstressed syllables (divided into accented and unaccented "feet"), the fundamental ones in English verse are five.

1. *The Iambic foot* is an unaccented syllable followed by an accented one. It is commonly expressed thus: ˘ ´; such words as *ŏppóse, dĕlíght, ămúse* being, in themselves, iambic feet. English verse is founded on the iambic beat; it might be said that our very speech tends to fall into iambics. An illustrative couplet:

> Ă bóok ŏf vérsĕs úndĕrnéath thĕ boúgh,
>
> Ă júg ŏf wíne, ă lóaf ŏf bréad—ănd thóu.

2. *The Trochaic foot* is an accented syllable followed by an unaccented one. It is commonly expressed thus: ´ ˘; such words as *gáthĕr, héartlĕss, féelĭng* being, in themselves, trochaic feet. It is second in importance to the iambic measure. An illustrative example:

> Sòft ănd éasў ís thў crádlĕ
>
> Cóarse ănd hárd thў Sáviour lay.

It should be noted that the majority of trochaic lines in English show a deficient last foot; that is to say, the last syllable is often omitted as in the second line of the example quoted.

3. *The Dactylic foot* is an accented syllable followed by two

unaccented ones. It is commonly expressed thus: ´ ˘˘ ; such words as *háppĭnĕss, séntĭmĕnt, mérrĭlȳ* being, in themselves, dactylic feet. Grace and a lilting movement are achieved by its use. An illustrative example:

> Lóve ăgaĭn, sóng ăgaĭn, nést ăgaĭn, yóung ăgaĭn.

4. *The Anapæstic foot* consists of two unaccented syllables followed by an accented syllable. It is commonly expressed thus: ˘˘´ ; such words as *ĭntĕrrúpt, sŭpĕrséde, dĭsăppéar* being, in themselves, anapæstic feet. It is a speedy and propulsive rhythm. An illustrative example:

> Wĭth thĕ shéep ĭn thĕ fóld aňd the cóws ĭn theĭr stálls.

Both the dactyllic and anapæstic measures tend to become monotonous and, therefore, most poets who employ them vary the measures by introducing two-syllable (iambic or trochaic) feet. It might be added that the poem which adheres absolutely to one foot or accent is rare, most poems of any length revealing a variety of accents. See Pope's " The Craft of Verse" (262).

5. *The Spondee* consists of two strongly accented syllables, expressed thus: ´´; compound words like *heártbréak, chíldhóod, wíneglás̀s* being perfect spondees. It is mostly found in classic poetry and is used chiefly for occasional, grave emphasis. An illustrative example:

> Slów Spóndée stálks; stróng fóot.

The Metre or measure of a verse is determined by the number of feet in the line. The terms explain themselves: *monometer*—one foot; *dimeter*—two feet; *trimeter*—three feet; *tetrameter*—four feet; *pentameter*—five feet; *hexameter*—six feet; *heptameter*—seven feet; *octameter*—eight feet. Thus the following line:

> Tŏ héar | thĕ lárk | bĕgín | hĭs flíght

is a line of four feet; since it is a compound of four iambic feet it would be classified as *iambic tetrameter*.

STANZA FORMS

In the same way that feet are combined into the structure of a line, lines are combined into the pattern of a poem. These patterns, or stanzas, have certain distinct characteristics and are usually classified as follows:

The Couplet (formerly called the "distich") consists of two lines of matched verse in immediate succession. It has always been popular, especially for sharp or epigrammatic effect. The form has been a favourite since the time of Chaucer's "Canterbury Tales," Dryden having brought it to a kind of perfection which Pope tightened into a "thought couplet," each couplet being a unit in itself.

> A little learning is a dangerous thing;
> Drink deep, or taste not the Pierian spring.
>
> *Pope*

The Tercet (sometimes known as the "triplet") is a stanza of three lines rhyming together. Examples of this pattern may be found in Crashaw's "Wishes for the Supposed Mistress" (222), Herrick's "Upon Julia's Clothes" (183), Herbert's "Paradise" (187), Symons' "In the Wood of Finvara" (505). A further illustration is Browning's:

> Boot, saddle, to horse, and away!
> Rescue my castle before the hot day
> Brightens to blue from its silvery grey.

The Quatrain, the commonest stanza form, consists of four lines rhymed in a variety of ways. Perhaps the most familiar arrangement is the ballad metre, in which the second and fourth lines are rhymed while the first and third are unrhymed. See "Childe Maurice" (26), "The Douglas Tragedy" (29), "Sir Patrick Spens" (35). Almost as well known is the quatrain in which the rhymes are *a-b-a-b*, as, for example, Emerson's:

> By the rude bridge that arched the flood,   a
> Their flag to April's breeze unfurled,   b
> Here once the embattled farmers stood   a
> And fired the shot heard round the world.   b

A form of quatrain somewhat less familiar is one in which the lines rhyme *a-b-b-a*, as, for example, Tennyson's:

> Our little systems have their day;   a
> They have their day and cease to be: b
> They are but broken lights of Thee,   b
> And thou, O Lord, art more than they.   a

The variations are great and range from the clipped stanzas of Herbert's "Discipline" (186) to the long measure of Charlotte Mew's "Beside the Bed" (523). The quatrain itself, in its various shapes, appears throughout this volume too numerously to be listed.

The Quintet is a five-line stanza variously rhymed, although the favourite formula seems to be *a-b-a-b-b*; Swinburne's "Hertha" is written in this form, a particularly fluent example, with its long-rolling last line:

> I the grain and the furrow,   a
> The plough-cloven clod   b
> And the ploughshare drawn thorough,   a
> The germ and the sod,   b
> The deed and the doer, the seed and the sower, the dust which
>   is God.   b

Shelley's "To a Skylark" (353), Waller's "Go, Lovely Rose" (195) and Christina Rossetti's "The Bourne" (462) are among the more famous poems built on the quintet.

The Sestet is a six-line stanza in which the possibilities of line and rhyme arrangement are almost endless. It may be composed of interlacing couplets as in Shakespeare's "O Mistress Mine" (141), or a mingling of rhymed and unrhymed lines as in D. G. Rossetti's "The Blessèd Damozel" (455), or the quaint arrangement which Robert Burns made his own in "To a Mouse" (295) and "The Hermit":

> In this lone cave, in garments lowly,   a
> Alike a foe to noisy folly,   a
> And brow-bent gloomy melancholy,   a
> I wear away   b
> My life, and in my office holy,   a
> Consume the day.   b

The term "sestet" is also used to designate the last six lines of the sonnet.

The Septet, a rather uncommon but flexible seven-line form, is chiefly esteemed in the variation known as *rime royal*, so called because it was supposedly first employed by King James I of Scotland. Chaucer was fond of using it (*vide* his "Tale of the Man of Law" and "Troilus and Criseyde" and "Parlement of Foules"); Masefield erected his "The Widow in the Bye Street," "Dauber" and others on this design.

> On every bough the briddes herde I singe,   a
> With boys of aungel in hir armonye,   b
> Som besyed hem hir briddes forth to bringe;   a
> The litel conyes to hir pley gunne hye,   b
> And further al aboute I gan espye   b
> The dreadful roo, the buk, the hert and hinde, c
> Squerels, and bestes smale of gentil kinde.   c

The Octave, a stanza of eight lines, presents infinite possibilities for the poet. It may be composed of the linking of two quatrains (*a-b-a-b-c-d-c-d*) or two triplets with an intervening pair of rhyming lines (*a-a-a-b-c-c-c-b*), as in the first example quoted below, or a quatrain, a triplet and an extra, final rhyme (*a-b-a-b-c-c-c-b*), as in the second example. Robert Bridges' "A Passer-by" (481) presents still another arrangement (*a-b-a-b-b-c-b-c*).

Upon Saint Crispin's Day	a
Fought was this noble fray,	a
Which fame did not delay	a
To England to carry.	b
O when shall English men	c
With such acts fill a pen?	c
Or England breed again	c
Such a King Harry?	b

Agincourt   *Michael Drayton*

From too much love of living,	a
From hope and fear set free,	b
We thank with brief thanksgiving	a
Whatever gods may be	b
That no life lives for ever;	c
That dead men rise up never;	c
That even the weariest river	c
Winds somewhere safe to sea.	b

The Garden of Proserpine   *A. C. Swinburne*

A particular form of the eight-line stanza is known as *ottava rima* since it was adapted from the Italian. The arrangement is *a-b-a-b-a-b-c-c*, and examples of it are found in Byron's "Don Juan" (349).

The term "octave" is also used to designate the first eight lines of the sonnet.

The Spenserian Stanza is a solemn, nine-line stanza, invented by Spenser. Its rhyme-scheme is intricate (*a-b-a-b-b-c-b-c-c*) and the ninth line (called the Alexandrine) is one foot longer than the others, rounding out the stanza with an impressive sonority. Among the poems built on Spenserian stanza are Byron's "Childe Harold" (349), Byron's "Ocean" (351), Keats' "The Eve of St. Agnes" (379), Shelley's "Adonais" and Spenser's "The Faerie Queene," one stanza of which follows:

For take thy balance, if thou be so wise,	a
And weigh the wind that under heaven doth blow;	b
Or weigh the light that in the east doth rise;	a
Or weigh the thought that from man's mind doth flow:	b
But if the weight of these thou canst not show,	b

> Weigh but one word which from thy lips doth fall:　　c
> For how canst thou these greater secrets know　　b
> That does not know the least thing of them all?　　c
> Ill can he rule the great that cannot reach the small.　　c

The ten-, eleven-, and twelve-line stanzas are combinations of smaller units and are rather uncommon. The fourteen-line stanza (the sonnet) has developed into one of the richest patterns in English poetry and must be considered separately.

THE SONNET

The sonnets in this volume are listed on pages 639-640. Although they show a variety of rhyme-schemes, their basic structure is identical. All sonnets are built on fourteen lines, the lines themselves (with few exceptions) being composed of ten syllables—iambic pentameter. These fourteen lines are usually divided into the first eight (the octave) and the second six (the sestet). The three main types are the Petrarchan (or Italian), the Shakespearian, and the Miltonic sonnet.

The Petrarchan Sonnet is the strictest, permitting only two rhymes in the octave and not more than three (often two) in the sestet. The octave is rhymed *a-b-b-a-a-b-b-a*. The sestet allows a variation in the line arrangement, the favourite pattern being either *c-d-e-c-d-e* or *c-d-c-d-c-d*. An example of the Petrarchan sonnet follows:

> O Earth, lie heavily upon her eyes;　　a
> Seal her sweet eyes weary of watching, Earth;　　b
> Lie close around her;　leave no room for mirth　　b
> With its harsh laughter, nor for sound of sighs.　　a
> She hath no questions, she hath no replies,　　a
> Hushed in and curtained with a blessèd dearth　　b
> Of all that irked her from the hour of birth;　　b
> With stillness that is almost Paradise.　　a
>
> Darkness more clear than noonday holdeth her,　　c
> Silence more musical than any song;　　d
> Even her very heart has ceased to stir:　　c
> Until the morning of Eternity　　e
> Her rest shall not begin nor end, but be;　　e
> And when she wakes she will not think it long.　　d

Rest　　　　　　　　　　　　　　　　　　　　*Christina Rossetti*

The Shakespearean Sonnet, perfected but not invented by Shakespeare, completely departs from the finely interlaced Italian model. It is actually nothing more than a set of three quatrains concluded and cemented by a couplet. An example:

No longer mourn for me when I am dead   a
Than you shall hear the surly sullen bell   b
Give warning to the world that I am fled   a
From this vile world with vilest worms to dwell;   b
Nay, if you read this line, remember not   c
The hand that writ it, for I love you so   d
That I in your sweet thoughts would be forgot   c
If thinking on me then should make you woe.   d
O if, I say, you look upon this verse   e
When I perhaps compounded am with clay,   f
Do not so much as my poor name rehearse,   e
But let your love even with my life decay,   f
    Lest the wise world should look into your moan   g
    And mock you with me after I am gone.   g

From " Sonnets "   *William Shakespeare*

The Miltonic Sonnet is an adaptation of the Petrarchan with a
striking difference. The Italian model separated the octave and
sestet by a break in thought; the octave usually presented a
general idea while the sestet pointed it and made it particular.
Instead of dividing his sonnets in two parts, Milton unrolled his
thought and his rich music without interruption through the
fourteen lines. An example:

Avenge, O Lord, thy slaughtered Saints, whose bones   a
    Lie scattered on the Alpine mountains cold;   b
    Even them who kept thy truth so pure of old,   b
When all our fathers worshipped stocks and stones,   a
Forget not: in thy book record their groans   a
    Who were thy sheep, and in their ancient fold   b
    Slain by the bloody Piedmontese, that rolled   b
Mother with infant down the rocks. Their moans   a
The vale redoubled to the hills, and they   c
    To Heaven. Their martyred blood and ashes sow   d
O'er all th' Italian fields, where still doth sway   c
    The triple Tyrant; that from these may grow   d
A hundredfold, who, having learnt thy way,   c
    Early may fly the Babylonian woe.   d

" On the Late Massacre in Piedmont "   *John Milton*

THE BALLADE AND RONDEAU

The Ballade is the most popular as well as the most important
of the strict forms brought over from France. Villon immortalised
the form and Chaucer used it in England as early as the fourteenth
century—*vide* "Ballade of Good Counsel" (106-107). It is com-
posed of three stanzas of eight lines and a half-stanza (the Envoy)

of four lines. The rhymes of the first stanza are arranged in the order *a-b-a-b-b-c-b-c*, and this arrangement is repeated in all the other stanzas—the envoy being *b-c-b-c*. No rhyme-word or rhyming sound may be repeated throughout the entire ballade.

The outstanding feature of the ballade is its *refrain*. The refrain is the line which ends all the stanzas and the envoy; it is repeated in its entirety and gives a unity to the poem.

I hid my heart in a nest of roses,	a
Out of the sun's way, hidden apart;	b
In a softer bed than the soft white snow's is,	b
Under the roses I hid my heart.	a
Why would it sleep not? Why should it start,	b
When never a leaf of the rose-tree stirred?	c
What made sleep flutter his wings and part?	b
Only the song of a secret bird.	c
Lie still, I said, for the wind's wing closes,	a
And mild leaves muffle the keen sun's dart;	b
Lie still, for the wind on the warm seas dozes,	a
And the wind is unquieter yet than thou art.	b
Does a thought in thee still as a thorn's wound smart?	b
Does the fang still fret thee of hope deferred?	c
What birds the lips of thy sleep dispart?	b
Only the song of a secret bird.	c
The green land's name that a charm encloses,	a
It never was writ in the traveller's chart,	b
And sweet on its trees as the fruit that grows is;	a
It never was sold in the merchant's mart.	b
The swallows of dreams through its dim fields dart,	b
And sleep's are the tunes in its tree-tops heard;	c
No hound's note wakens the wildwood hart,	b
Only the song of a secret bird.	c

ENVOY

In the world of dreams I have chosen my part,	b
To sleep for a season and hear no word	c
Of true love's truth or of light love's art,	b
Only the song of a secret bird.	c

A Ballade of Dreamland   *A. C. Swinburne*

The Rondeau is a nimbler form usually employed for sprightly themes although it can be used gravely as in Dobson's "In After Days" (478). It is composed of thirteen lines built on only two rhymes, the refrain being a repetition of the first part of the first line. Using *x* to represent the refrain, the rhyme-scheme would be *a-a-b-b-a, a-a-b-x, a-a-b-b-a-x*. An example:

What is to come we know not. But we know   a
That what has been was good—was good to show,   a
   Better to hide, and best of all to bear.   b
  We are the masters of the days that were: b
We have lived, we have loved, we have suffered—even so.   a

Shall we not take the ebb who had the flow?   a
Life was our friend. Now, if it be our foe—   a
   Dear, though it break and spoil us!—need we care   b
    What is to come?   x

Let the great winds their worst and wildest blow,   a
Or the gold weather round us mellow slow: a
   We have fulfilled ourselves, and we can dare   b
   And we can conquer, though we may not share   b
In the rich quiet of the afterglow.   a
    What is to come?   x

What Is To Come   *W. E. Henley*

Leigh Hunt's "Jenny Kissed Me" (346) is often referred to as
a rondeau; actually it bears no resemblance to the form of the
rondeau except the repetition of the first phrase as a sort of refrain.

THE VILLANELLE

Originally used for pastoral subjects, the *Villanelle* has become
so stylised that its simplicity is quite artificial. It is composed of
five three-line stanzas and a concluding stanza of four lines, each
stanza ending with an alternating line of the first verse. In the
last stanza both of these lines appear together as a concluding
couplet. Only two rhymes are permitted throughout the verses.
Henley has described the very essence of this form as follows:

A dainty thing's the Villanelle.   a 1
   Sly, musical, a jewel in rhyme,   b
It serves its purpose passing well.   a 2
A double-clappered silver bell   a
   That must be made to clink in chime,   b
A dainty thing's the Villanelle;   a 1
And if you wish to flute a spell,   a
   Or ask a meeting 'neath the lime,   b
It serves its purpose passing well.   a 2
You must not ask of it the swell   a
   Of organs grandiose and sublime—   b
A dainty thing's the Villanelle;   a 1
And, filled with sweetness, as a shell   a
   Is filled with sound, and launched in time,   b
It serves its purpose passing well.   a 2

Still fair to see and good to smell	a
As in the quaintness of its prime,	b
A dainty thing's the Villanelle;	a 1
It serves its purpose passing well.	a 2

THE ODE

Derived from a Greek word meaning "song," the Ode, according to the lexicographers, became "a form of stately and elaborate verse." Originally chanted, the ode was built on a set of themes and responses and sung by divided choirs, half the singers intoning the strophe, the other half replying with the antistrophe, and both uniting with the epode. Most of the odes in English verse depart from the Greek model, although Swinburne's "Athens" and some of his political odes preserve the antique mode, while Dryden's "Alexander's Feast" (236) blends the responsive voices in the antique manner. Cowley invented a variation on the form which he called the Pindaric ode—an irregular, passionate declamation in which the form is swept aside on a wave of emotion—Cowley failing to comprehend that Pindar varied the verse-arrangement of his odes but that each was consistently and strictly patterned.

Since Cowley, the shape of the ode has grown more and more uncertain. The odes of Coleridge, Wordsworth and Tennyson, though eloquent, are irregular. The magnificent odes of Keats and Shelley are, in reality, extended and sustained lyrics. The term itself has been broadened; strophe and antistrophe have disappeared; the length and stanza-pattern are unpredictable. To-day the ode may be recognised not by its form at all, but rather by its tone: an intense, richly elaborated and often profound apostrophe.

BLANK VERSE

Blank verse may be defined as (1) any unrhymed regular measure or (2) unrhymed verse in iambic pentameter. Most scholars favour the second interpretation, although the unrhymed dactylic hexameter of Longfellow's "Evangeline" and the unrhymed trochaic tetrameter of his "Hiawatha" are obviously a variety of blank verse. But the term "blank verse" seems inevitably attached to the iambic five-accented line first employed in English by Henry Howard, Earl of Surrey, and glorified by Shakespeare's dramas, Milton's epics and Wordsworth's meditations. Along with its sonority, its great strength lies in its flexibility. It can deviate from strict metrical regularity without injuring the rolling line—in fact the departures, the endless variety of effects, reveal its never-exhausted power. Every master of blank verse has given the measure new modulations and stamped it with his characteristic idiom. (Examples of blank verse contained in this volume are listed on page 636.)

VARIOUS DEVICES

Besides the patterns already defined the poet has recourse to various devices. Some of the most easily recognisable are *Alliteration, Rhyme, Assonance, Onomatopœia, Metonymy, Synecdoche, Simile* and *Metaphor*.

Devices of Sound

Alliteration is the repetition of the same consonant sound in words or syllables succeeding each other at close intervals. Usually it refers to the repetition of a sound or letter at the beginning of words, like:

Fields ever fresh and groves ever green.

But, besides the repetition of f and g in this line, there is alliteration of the v sounds, half buried in the midst of the words. It is the most recognisable of devices, often overused—Swinburne having carried it to the point of parody—but extremely effective as an enrichment of rhyme, even a substitute for it, as in Anglo-Saxon poetry. A famous example is Tennyson's:

The moan of doves in immemorial elms,
And murmuring of innumerable bees.

Rhyme, sometimes spelled *rime*, has been variously defined. However, the principle laid down by Thomas Hood still holds: "A rhyme must commence on an accented syllable. From the accented vowel of that syllable to the end, the words intended to rhyme must be *identical* in sound, but the letter or letters preceding the accented vowel must be *unlike* in sound." "Night" and "fight," for example, are true rhymes, but "night" and "knight" do not rhyme, there being nothing unlike in the sound preceding the vowel. Neither can "night" and "ride" be said to rhyme, for though the sound preceding the vowel is different, the sound *following* the vowel is not identical, as it should be to constitute a true rhyme. "Night" and "ride" is an instance of assonance.

Assonance is the matching of the vowel-sound alone, irrespective of the consonant (or sound) which follows it. Thus "base" and "face" would be true rhyme, whereas "base" and "fade" would be assonance. The old ballads and folk-poetry are full of assonance, sometimes purposeful, sometimes accidental, as in "Sir Patrick Spens" (35):

> The anchor broke, the topmast *split*,
>   'Twas such a deadly *storm*.
> The waves came over the broken *ship*
>   Till all her sides were *torn*.

Onomatopœia is the formation of the words by the imitation of sounds, the words thus formed vividly suggesting the object or action producing the sound. Such words are found in the cradle of the individual as well as in the infancy of the race: *bow-wow, ding-dong, hum, buzz*, etc. Though not confined to verse, words like *whiz, crash, crunch, crackle, jangle* have become properties of the poet.

Devices of Sense

Metonymy and *Synecdoche* are figures of speech in which a word or phrase is used to suggest another word or thought, or in which a part is used for the whole or a whole for a part. They might be called "figures of association" and though they are recognisable, they are not easily distinguishable. Thus in Shirley's "The Levelling Dust" (192) "sceptre and crown" and "scythe and spade" are used to symbolise the kings and peasants which the phrases suggest. When Kipling in "Recessional" (511) speaks of England holding dominion over "palm and pine" he suggests, by selecting typically northern and southern trees, the extent of the British Empire. We say "the kettle is boiling" when we mean the water in the kettle is boiling, or "We enjoy Keats" when we mean that we enjoy the writings of Keats.

Simile and *Metaphor* are poetry's most constant properties. The power of each lies in fixing the attention on one object by comparing it to another. When the comparison is direct and introduced by *like* or *as* it is a simile; when the comparison is indirect or implied, without the use of *like* or *as*, it is a metaphor. Burns, "O my Luve is like a red, red rose" (305) and Wordsworth's "I wandered lonely as a cloud" (306) are among the most familiar similes; Campion's "There is a garden in her face" (150) and Brown's "O blackbird, what a boy you are!" (459) are vivid examples of metaphor. Poetry might be said to be founded on the vigour and range of the metaphorical mind. Its element is surprise. To relate the hitherto unrelated, to make the strange seem familiar and the familiar seem strange is the aim of metaphor. Through this heightened awareness, poetry, though variously defined, is invariably pronounced and unmistakably perceived.

L. U.

INDEX

653